AF607966

RECONSIDERING C.B. MACPHERSON

From Possessive Individualism to Democratic Theory and Beyond

Reconsidering C.B. Macpherson

From Possessive Individualism to Democratic Theory and Beyond

PHILLIP HANSEN

UNIVERSITY OF TORONTO PRESS
Toronto Buffalo London

Toronto Buffalo London
www.utppublishing.com

ISBN 978-1-4426-3059-8

Library and Archives Canada Cataloguing in Publication

Hansen, Phillip Birger, 1949–, author
Reconsidering C.B. Macpherson : from possessive individualism to democratic theory and beyond / Phillip Hansen.

Includes bibliographical references and index.
ISBN 978-1-4426-3059-8 (cloth)

1. Macpherson, C.B. (Crawford Brough), 1911–1987 – Criticism and interpretation. 2. Democracy. 3. Individualism. 4. Liberalism. I. Title.

JC253.M35H35 2015 320.5 C2015-905452-4

This book has been published with the help of a grant from the Federation for the Humanities and Social Sciences, through the Awards to Scholarly Publications Program, using funds provided by the Social Sciences and Humanities Research Council of Canada.

University of Toronto Press acknowledges the financial assistance to its publishing program of the Canada Council for the Arts and the Ontario Arts Council, an agency of the Government of Ontario.

Canada Council for the Arts
Conseil des Arts du Canada

Funded by the Government of Canada
Financé par le gouvernement du Canada

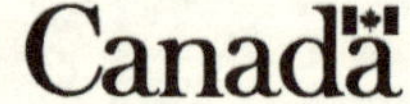

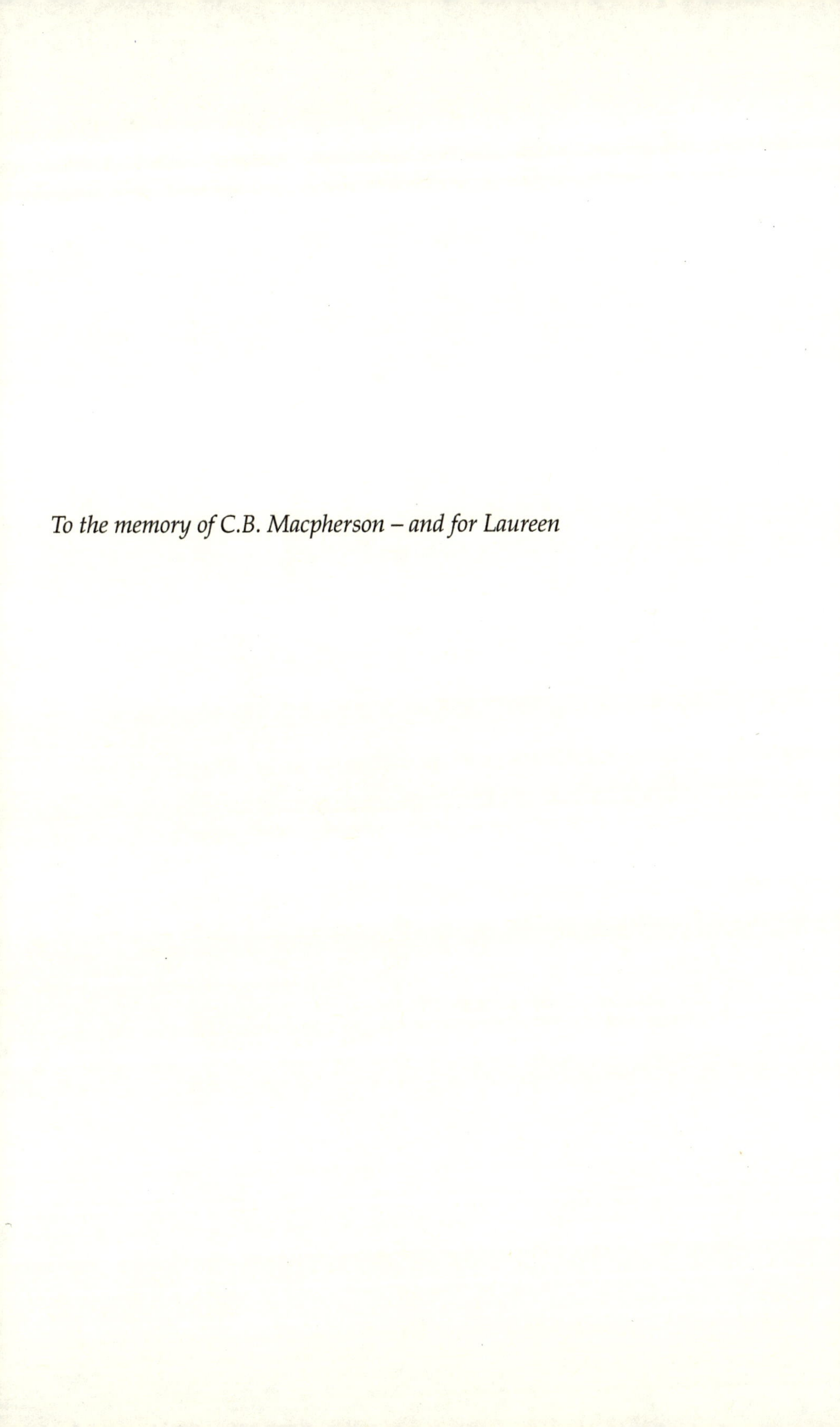

To the memory of C.B. Macpherson – and for Laureen

Contents

Acknowledgments

In the fall of 1971 I was a wide-eyed young graduate student at the University of Toronto, drawn there by the prospect of studying with C.B. Macpherson. I was not to be disappointed. From his graduate seminar in political theory (where we considered the essays that later formed the core of his *Democratic Theory: Essays in Retrieval*) to his key role as a member of my PhD thesis committee, to his generous support as a referee on behalf of my efforts to obtain an academic appointment, C.B. Macpherson played a huge part in my development as a scholar and teacher. I early on made a commitment to myself that one day I would write about his work, both to acknowledge, in a way that I hoped would resonate with others, the impact he had on my own thinking and the debt I owed to him, and to make as strong a case as I was able for the significance of his ideas for political theory and philosophy. This book is the result.

I have been sustained over the years by the friendship, kindness, and support of many people, too numerous to mention individually. But they know who they are. I am deeply grateful to each of them.

However, in relation to this work there are three individuals I do wish to single out. I met and first studied with Alkis Kontos in that fall of 1971. Initially as teacher and mentor, then as a friend, and always as a supporter, Alkis has been a constant source of insight, personal and professional, generous in spirit, and delightful company to boot. I will always remember the sessions he and I enjoyed in the basement pub at the University of Toronto faculty club, where we were privileged to serve as a sounding board for Macpherson as he prepared the essays eventually published in his final work, *The Rise and Fall of Economic Justice*. I relish the passion we both share for political theory and for Macpherson. Thank you, Alkis.

Both from our work together and from his own writings, I have learned much from Brian Caterino. He has a staggeringly broad grasp of critical theory and has profoundly shaped my own understanding of that tradition. He read with care an earlier version of this book and in the pages that follow will recognize his influence and the debt I owe him. Thank you, Brian.

Daniel Quinlan, my editor at the University of Toronto Press, provided constant support and encouragement while expertly shepherding the manuscript through the editorial process. I very much respect and admire his combination of editorial skill and personal empathy. Thank you, Daniel.

I must thank as well the readers for the Press for their comments, suggestions, and criticisms. And I would be remiss if I did not also thank Frank Cunningham, who carefully read the manuscript, offered valuable criticisms and suggestions, and has been most encouraging throughout.

The bulk of the manuscript that formed the basis of this book was written during a pre-retirement leave provided by the University of Regina. I am grateful to the university, and in particular the Faculty of Arts and its dean, Richard Kleer, for its support. I am grateful as well for the support of my home Department of Philosophy and Classics over the course of the decade I spent there.

Once again the members of the Bushwakker Brewpub seminar group – Joe Roberts, Sheila Roberts, Lorne Brown, and Fay Hutchinson – have been there for me, as close friends, patient listeners, and sources of encouragement for my efforts. As colleagues for many years at the University of Regina, Joe, Lorne, and I strongly believed that C.B. Macpherson and his legacy were important for progressive scholarship and politics. I hope this work successfully conveys our shared commitment to both.

My son, Michael Joel-Hansen, has grown into a fine young man. He has in his own way developed a strong interest in and enthusiasm for politics and public affairs, ideas, and spirited conversation. Any credit does not belong to me, alone. Much of it must go to his mother, Jan Joel, herself deeply committed to the same values and concerns – and also a student in C.B. Macpherson's final graduate seminar at the University of Toronto.

Finally, to my wonderful wife, Laureen Gatin (and her son, Brian, daughter-in-law, Meghan, daughter, Sarah, and grandchildren, Emilie, Xavier, and Shay): There are no words enough.

Phillip Hansen
Regina, Saskatchewan
April 2015

RECONSIDERING C.B. MACPHERSON

From Possessive Individualism to Democratic Theory and Beyond

Introduction

C.B. Macpherson occupies an ambiguous place in contemporary political thought. He is certainly not obscure; indeed there is a significant body of critical analysis of his work. But at the same time, his ideas command little attention in most accounts. The concept for which he is best known – possessive individualism – is widely cited in many different contexts and even recurs from time to time as a topic of debate. Yet it is also marginal to current liberal and democratic theory. It is viewed almost as an artefact of an earlier period, its value and significance, about which in any case there was always serious disagreement, apparently surpassed by other more recent and innovative ideas.

Yet in an era in which neoliberalism is triumphant, where the market rules and where liberal democratic theory and practice have made their peace with market values – and are considered respectable only to the degree that they have done so – Macpherson's exploration of what he called the "possessive market society," and the project for a renewed and revitalized liberal democracy more attuned to the best of human possibilities that emerges from this, offers a uniquely powerful and insightful way of assessing what the triumph of the market means for individuals and their ability to live fully human lives. It offers important elements of a critical engagement with the social challenges and pathologies of the present and suggestions about how we might see our way forward in the face of them.

In this book I reconsider Macpherson's work in order to demonstrate its continuing vitality. But I first wish to offer a backdrop to how I view the task of reconsidering his ideas and concerns, his claims and his concepts.

In 1975 the Annual Meeting of the Canadian Political Science Association at the University of Alberta in Edmonton included in its program a panel honouring C.B. Macpherson. As is customary for such events, academics of different persuasions with an interest in and knowledge of the scholar's work presented papers to which the distinguished honouree was invited to respond. At sixty-three, Macpherson, two years removed from the publication of his *Democratic Theory: Essays in Retrieval* and almost a decade and a half after the appearance of his most influential work, *The Political Theory of Possessive Individualism*, was arguably at the peak of his creativity, academic visibility, and influence. The papers selected for subsequent publication in the CPSA journal, the *Canadian Journal of Political Science*, reflected his stature. Macpherson sought to synthesize liberalism and socialism, Mill and Marx, and confronted challenges from both camps. Hence the *CJPS* published essays by Kenneth Minogue, an English political thinker staunchly committed to classical liberalism and its individualist assumptions, and Victor Svacek, a Marxist graduate student of Macpherson's.

It is doubtful if many recall an obscure exchange triggered by papers that may be dimly remembered only by the authors themselves; certainly the positions they represented have been advanced by better-known and more widely read scholars. Nonetheless the arguments presented by each writer were telling and provide a cogent example of how Macpherson's work was appraised by liberals and Marxists. While both acknowledged value in Macpherson's ideas (more so in the case of Svacek), each found those ideas wanting in their ultimate capacity to represent and advance the core values of their distinctive perspectives.

Understandably Macpherson responded by defending his views against both critics, while acknowledging his broadly Marxian outlook and consequently his closer proximity to (and empathy with) Svacek's analysis; indeed he claimed that Svacek had more successfully grasped his key ideas than had most of his critics. In this light he succinctly summarized his project: on the basis of what he took to be core elements of Marx's outlook, he sought to revise liberal democratic theory in a way that emphasized its humanist, egalitarian dimensions while downplaying, if not jettisoning altogether, its possessive individualist, market-driven, and competitive legacy, which he believed had regrettably come to dominate not only theory but also actual political practices and institutions. He put it this way: "What I have been trying to do all along (and am still trying to do) [is] to work out a revision of liberal democratic theory, a revision which clearly owes a good deal to Marx, in the hope of making that theory more democratic while rescuing that valuable part of the liberal tradition which is submerged when liberalism is identified with capitalist market relations."[1]

This claim, stated with Macpherson's typical lucidity, could hardly be accounted a surprise – likely most readers of Macpherson would readily accept this as his overall purpose. Of course they could well disagree about how desirable or plausible this project might be; certainly Minogue does. And indeed it accurately conveys Macpherson's central concerns. From the point of view of current conventional political theory and philosophy, it establishes his place at the nexus of normative and historical political theory. It is from this vantage point that his contribution has been most often appraised.[2] Broadly speaking, the consensus on his work is that while it is provocative and suggestive, and not without specific and thoughtful insights into the traditions of liberalism and democracy, it ultimately falls short of its intended aim to provide a more secure and defensible basis for a renewed democratic theory and practice. This is because, quite apart from his allegedly dubious Marxist assumptions (Marxism and liberal democracy being apparently fundamentally opposed), his position stands at odds with the realities of actually existing liberal democratic societies. On the one hand, the theory of possessive individualism itself, which argues that the dominant strain in classical liberalism emphasizes individual self-ownership and thus views society as a congeries of market-like contractual relations, is at best one-sided and misleading, because it fails to appreciate the richer moral dimensions of the tradition stemming from Hobbes and Locke. For his liberal critics, Macpherson wrongly presents Hobbes and Locke, Bentham and Mill as apologists for capitalism rather than as architects of a powerful and compelling account of freedom and reason.

On the other hand, Macpherson is judged guilty of holding an inadequate set of assumptions about human nature that in turn undergirds an excessively harmonistic account of the human capacity for cooperation. This account wrongly assumes that the problem of liberal democracy is that it is subordinated to a set of capitalist property relations that stand at odds with the allegedly "real" qualities of human beings, or rather the qualities they would develop and display, were they not held in thrall to bourgeois political, social, and economic institutions. One form of this criticism reproaches Macpherson for an ostensibly reductionist picture of individuals as driven overwhelmingly by economic imperatives, in the process slighting non-economic motives for action (this tends to be the view of *political* or democratic liberals). Another somewhat contrary position holds that Macpherson fails to see or acknowledge that in fact capitalist private property is a key guarantor of freedom precisely because it conforms to the dominant elements, the competitive character, that define human beings (a position typically staked out by *economic* or free market liberals). But for political and economic liberals alike, Macpherson ultimately gets it wrong – on the plane both of facts and of values.

Kenneth Minogue combines both sets of criticisms. Perhaps this is why, aside from a summary of his core theoretical concern, Macpherson did something perhaps a bit unusual: he took issue not only with Minogue's explicit position but also with what he interpreted as his unstated assumptions. It is easy to miss this, because he slips in his rejoinder almost unnoticed at the end of his commentary. Macpherson's remarks are intended to respond to Minogue's criticism – one shared by many of his liberal or conservative critics in particular – that his analysis is too abstract and fails to reflect reality adequately, "that the level of argument is virtually without exemplification."[3] As Macpherson sees it, Minogue

> wants to stay closer to the observable world of affairs than he believes I have done. He complains ... that I never give down-to-earth examples to support my general propositions ... The trouble is that down-to-earth examples are likely to illustrate not real underlying relations between people, or between things, or between people and things, but only apparent relations. This is so in the nature of the case: if the example is down-to-earth enough it is bound to deal with appearances, not realities. It is indeed evident that the sun sets in the west; this is the level of appearance beyond which down-to-earth examples generally do not get.[4]

This argument is striking. To be sure it undoubtedly reflects Macpherson's adoption of the Marxian conception of ideology and commodity fetishism, whereby the real relations of capitalism thrust up misleading appearances that disguise their power-laden, exploitive character. Possessive individualism, Macpherson's key category and the basis of his impact on political theory and philosophy, might be thought the ultimate reference point in this respect, the wedge that allows him to contrast the claims of liberal economic individualism to maximize liberty and equality with the realities of capitalist society.[5]

Yet at the same time I believe that Macpherson's response does more than this. To my mind it raises meta-methodological, even metaphysical, issues he was not normally seen as addressing, or even remotely interested in considering. Nonetheless – and this forms the core of what I wish to explore in this study – I think that both examining the specific claims and arguments that have come to define Macpherson's legacy and pursuing the implications of the admittedly brief but suggestive comments he offered in response to Kenneth Minogue provide a fuller picture of Macpherson's work and its contemporary significance than has been available.

But why go to such lengths to illuminate Macpherson's contributions when in his own words, from which he never dissented, he so clearly laid out the commitment informing his project: to revise the received understanding of liberal democracy in a more radical and humanistic direction? Why examine more admittedly implicit, if not arcane and even obscure, questions raised by his work, questions in which he himself betrayed little interest and indeed likely viewed as distractions from the "real" challenges that needed to be addressed?[6] (From personal experience I can attest that he was bemused by any suggestion that his writings harboured such issues or that it was even worthwhile to spend time and effort considering if they did.) Would I be in effect scratching where there is no itch, perhaps even, to use the title of one of Macpherson's most incisive and important essays, engaging in the deceptive task of political theory?[7] In any case it might plausibly be claimed that the basis for such an interpretive strategy is pretty thin – some scattered remarks concluding a response to the criticisms of another writer.[8]

I acknowledge the challenge here. However, I zero in on Macpherson's remarks not simply in order to say something "new" about his work that no one has said before, thereby implicitly casting doubt on the value of other interpretations or perspectives. In fact my intention is quite the opposite: to enrich our understanding of Macpherson that other analysts have insightfully provided by hopefully showing that his work has an interpretive and analytic depth, even beyond what most analysts have identified, that testifies to his ongoing relevance for contemporary debates about capitalism, democracy, and indeed human social possibilities and prospects more generally, for Macpherson's response to Minogue does not simply stand alone. It rather points to a dimension of his work that both demonstrates the robustness of his key concepts and ideas and, perhaps even more significantly, offers additional and, I believe, less fully appreciated resources for a progressive critical theory of contemporary society.

I want to argue that the value of Macpherson's work lies not only in his specific arguments on behalf of a democratic society that involves more than, to use his own terms, a "mechanism for choosing and authorizing governments." It also involves what might be called the (non-deceptive) task of political theory, the mode of thought out of which and in terms of which specific concepts emerge, illuminate, and make rationally accessible the phenomena with which they are concerned.

This mode of thought entails concepts that are not only identifying markers but also emergent and dynamic articulations that weave together the empirical and the normative and open up the range of circumstances and possibilities that people always and already enmeshed in historically formed social relations confront as agents of a certain sort. A concept such as "possessive individualism," not only suggests a key theme in the tradition of classical liberalism that can be appraised according to the extent to which the theorists to whom it is applied explicitly or implicitly identify with it. It also and more importantly provides a point of contact with social practices and institutions as these have developed out of, shape, and are in turn shaped by the wants, needs, and purposes of associated individuals. It serves, in other words, as a diagnostic tool crafted from within the bounds and constraints of lived experience in society. And as with any diagnostic tool, its value lies in its capacity to provide an orienting focal point that offers the prospect of successfully identifying problems and challenges – in Macpherson's case, the problems and prospects of present society in light of hopes for, and requirements for, a more democratic society in the future. In the end, Macpherson's conceptual universe is a normatively charged attempt to identify and critically appraise existing and prospective possibilities for human fulfilment where such fulfilment has roots in values that people might be said to always and already hold and would ideally wish to see more fully realized in their everyday lives and relationships.

Thus I argue that there is in Macpherson's work what I would call *a suppressed philosophical dimension*: a more or less systematic, if only implicit, meta-conceptual basis of and framework for his specific conceptual universe that gives his ideas richness and meaning. My hope in proceeding in this fashion is to pursue a form of critical reflection that has parallels to what Erica Sherover-Marcuse called the disengaging of a theory from a body of thought, where "the aim of such a venture is to focus attention on a body of thought in such a way that new contours of this thought structure emerge as a result of the process of critical examination." To interrogate a body of thought in this fashion is to undertake a conceptual reconstruction that "consists of making explicit what in the texts is only implicit, articulating the theoretical constructs which a thinker uses to analyze or explicate those issues which engage her or his reflective interests."[9]

If I am right about this, then Macpherson's work is linked with a tradition that includes, as examples, the notion of "objective spirit" (Hegel), "form of life" (Wittgenstein), and "hermeneutic circle" (Gadamer), as well as the ideas of Marx and Mill. Moreover, if political *theory* (a more or less coherent network of propositions about political reality) can be distinguished from political *philosophy* (meta-assumptions and commitments that render specific concepts and propositions rational and coherent),[10] then Macpherson can be accounted as both a theorist and a philosopher, and it is the combination of both dimensions that gives his work a continuing vitality. This claim forms the core of my approach in this work.[11]

In what follows I attempt to explore what I understand to be the key dimensions of Macpherson's body of work and, where necessary, link them to the kinds of theoretical and philosophical concerns I have noted here. In the process of doing so, I also attempt to relate his ideas to thinkers with whom, in my view, he should be linked because they share a broadly comparable critical perspective. Most notably here are members of the Frankfurt School of critical theory, especially Max Horkheimer and Herbert Marcuse, but also including more recent contributors to this body of thought: Jürgen Habermas and Axel Honneth. Occasionally, as in the work of William Leiss, Macpherson's affinities with these thinkers have been noted;[12] I intend here to further explore and hopefully more completely illuminate the connection and its value for contemporary political and social thought.

Both Macpherson and members of the Frankfurt School viewed (and in key respects still view) capitalism and liberal democracy as dynamic, historically evolving, and fundamentally contradiction-laden socio-economic and political forms whose development has brought domination, misery, and unfreedom, but also the potential for freedom, equality, and human fulfilment on a scale never before seen. As critical analysts of capitalism, both saw social and political theory as critique, rooted in a self-conscious awareness that thought was historically conditioned by and responded to the development of capitalist relations and values.[13]

This attempt to trace ties between Macpherson and other thinkers is intended not only to locate him more fully in the history of political thought. It is also designed to reinforce the importance of a way of thinking, to which Macpherson made a significant and still largely unappreciated contribution, that views the task of political theory and philosophy as inherently practical and thus historical. The practical and historical come together in the assumption that thought "proves" itself in its capacity to clarify for its audience – potential or actual – the situation in which individual agents, who are understood to have certain interests and capabilities, find themselves. Such thought addresses relations among individuals involving who they are, how they live now, and who they would ideally like to become. Therefore the "truths" it seeks to illuminate are not timeless but situated and inherently tentative.

But far from being a weakness, this is a strength. Only if thought links up with embedded values and commitments of agents who always and already are "living" out the aspirations identified by the theory can its claims be validated in practice. At the same time, the theory itself is not necessarily invalidated if the agents at whom it is directed fail to act in accordance with its claims. By its nature, theory hovers between the actual and the possible (or, in Hegelian terms, the existent and the genuinely actual, which is only thus insofar as it is adequate to the demands and requirements of reason) and draws its meaning and strength from its occupying precisely this vantage point. To say that theory is practical, then, does not mean that it possesses direct instrumental efficacy; indeed to think this way is to reinforce the elements of "traditional" as opposed to "critical" theory – very likely the direct application of theory to practice would reinforce existing social and political values, relations, and institutions rather than challenge them.[14] It rather relates to the unavoidably interpretive and thus normative condition in which individuals, who are also at the same time necessarily social beings capable of speech and action, find themselves.[15] The fear that the forces of domination would prove too powerful – coupled nonetheless with the hope that as long as there are humans in whom the capacity for something better remains alive social transformation cannot be completely ruled out – shapes the sense of what is practically possible and necessary.

Macpherson himself appeared to hold a comparable view of theory as expressing the demands of practical reason in the sense suggested above. In his paper, Svacek criticized Macpherson on Marxist grounds for failing to provide a theory or account of the transition to socialism, i.e., offer an answer to Lenin's question "What is to be done?" In response Macpherson indicated that he was "not persuaded that forcible revolution is the only way to a new society, or that Marx always thought it was." But his position was more than simply tactical or pragmatic. He went on to say that, with respect more generally to a theory of transition, "I do not regard that as my *métier*. There is still much to be done in improving the theoretical understanding of those forces (including the force of ideas), at least at a level of some abstraction. And by the principle of comparative advantage in any social division of labour I have thought myself better occupied with seeking to improve the theoretical understanding."[16]

I have entitled this study *Reconsidering C.B. Macpherson: From Possessive Individualism to Democratic Theory and Beyond*. But it could well have been called "Retrieving" C.B. Macpherson. This of course suggests Macpherson's own *Democratic Theory: Essays in Retrieval*. Macpherson believed that democratic theory needed to be reinvigorated by incorporating forgotten, ignored, or insufficiently understood conceptions of democratic life and the theorists who advanced them. I hope to do something similar with Macpherson's ideas and his place in the ranks of contemporary political theorists.

Perhaps the most appropriate metaphor for such a project is that of a constellation: bringing into juxtaposition ideas that give shape to an overall conception of a phenomenon but without claiming this establishes a definitive, final, and fixed account of this phenomenon.[17] The idea of a constellation stresses mutual determination without causality, where concepts inhabit a force field such that the boundaries delimiting them are permeable and not rigid. Concepts related in a constellation can mutually illuminate and inform each other without requiring that one concept is assimilated to another, or that differences characterizing them are transcended in a new, definitive, and absolute synthesis. I think that "retrieving" Macpherson's ideas in this way opens them up by demonstrating their capacity not only to describe but to provoke and prod, to represent not endpoints of analysis but starting points for further reflection. I hope in what follows to remain always faithful to this charge.

There is one additional aspect to my approach in this study. While at various points I allude to the extensive debates that Macpherson's work has generated, I do not systematically engage them. In any event I think that Jules Townshend has offered a lucid summary and appraisal of these debates in his fine study, *C.B. Macpherson and the Problem of Liberal Democracy*. My intention in what follows is to offer from a distinctive perspective a detailed exploration and account of Macpherson's body of work, a reconstruction from the "inside," as it were. In the process I believe that his ideas will turn out to express fresh and exciting possibilities that would not be so evident on the basis of earlier, familiar, and entrenched points of view.

I begin the study in chapter 1 with an exploration of the concept of possessive individualism. As I've suggested, this idea should be viewed not simply as a description of the commitments of thinkers in the classical liberal tradition, but also and more adequately as a critical tool of analysis that is derived immanently from the ideas of those thinkers themselves. In this respect it stands at the intersection of, and reflects the tension between, the human condition or situation in the context of a certain set of social relations and human possibilities both realized and denied – between history and ontology. So understood, the concept is best appreciated as a core and indispensable element of a critical account of the dilemmas, challenges, and pathologies of a specific socio-historical situation, an account accessible, at least in principle, to those living with and through the demands of that situation.

Chapter 2 expands upon the analysis in chapter 1 by exploring in greater detail Macpherson's ontology: his account of human nature and its relation to democratic possibilities. This is an issue that Macpherson addressed in greater and more explicit detail as he developed in the wake of his analysis of possessive individualism the core elements of his theory of radical democracy. At the heart of this discussion is Macpherson's conception of what he calls the net transfer of powers. And this dimension of his account also takes us into the realm of his suppressed philosophical dimension and in turn connects him with contemporary currents of political theory, even where he did not explicitly draw the connection. In developing over a series of writings the concept of the net transfer of powers, and the treatment of human nature intertwined with it, the trajectory of his thought in important respects parallels the development of the critical theory of the Frankfurt School. From Max Horkheimer's accounts of morality and what he called the anthropology of the bourgeois era to the more recent work of Jürgen Habermas and Axel Honneth that attempts to provide normative justification for a critical theory of the present, critical theory has sought to illuminate contemporary social pathologies and prospects for change. More than just offering a parallel to this work, Macpherson's approach can, I believe, stand on its own as a distinctive contribution to precisely the task that critical theory has set for itself.

Chapter 3 explores Macpherson's relation to Marx and how this shapes his account of the main elements of and tensions within the theory and practice of liberal democracy. This is the point at which for Macpherson political theory intersects with political economy, and it includes his attempts to demonstrate what he called the economic penetration of political theory.[18] But it also includes what I believe to be a richer and more accurate reading of Marx that is more sensitive to the ontological dimensions of Marx's own project beyond the attempt to develop a critique of political economy (i.e., capitalism). When played off against each other, both Macpherson and Marx show the continuing vitality of their critical theoretical and philosophical approaches. Here, too, the work of the Frankfurt School figures significantly.

In chapters 4 and 5, I zero in specifically on Macpherson's accounts of democracy and democratic theory, and explore the broad range of concerns and issues in the history and theory of liberalism and democracy that this work took on board. Interestingly, while Macpherson may well be often recognized as a democratic theorist, and there has been in contemporary democratic theory some reference to Macpherson's work, I do not believe that the import of this work has been fully understood or appreciated. What I attempt to do in these two chapters is to retrieve the retrieved. I believe this is necessary, because in my view there has been a failure by most analysts to see that the critique of possessive individualism and the theory of democracy are not separate but connected: Macpherson's democratic theory (really, as I hope to show, a critique of democratic theory) emerged immanently from his account of liberalism. As I argue in chapter 1, possessive individualism is not so much a descriptor as a category of articulation that allows us to appreciate the dilemmas and social pathologies that emerge from the entrenchment of possessive (capitalist) market relations. The requirements of democracy can come into view only via the critical appraisal that possessive individualism was intended to establish. In other words, there is, I think, yet again a definite link between Macpherson and the Frankfurt School. Macpherson wrote like a traditional theorist but was really a critical theorist. His approach may have been Anglo-analytic but his substance was, so to speak, Continental. [19]

I conclude my discussion in chapter 5 with an attempt to more specifically relate Macpherson's account to what I take to be key themes in contemporary democratic theory. The literature on democracy is enormous and it is impossible in the context of this study to do justice to more that some key issues, the choice of which I acknowledge is contestable. Nonetheless, I do believe it is possible to identify a certain "tilt" in much democratic theorizing, especially among many thinkers who have come to figure prominently in current debates.[20]

Chapter 6 concludes the study. In light of the previous chapters, it attempts to offer a more explicit methodological (and meta-methodological) interpretation of Macpherson's work for the purpose of developing what I have called his suppressed philosophical dimension. In this respect it summarizes what I hope had already become visible in previous chapters, in which my intention was to read Macpherson from the perspective of this dimension. At the same time I hope it will also open up the possibility for further reflection about the significance of Macpherson's work. This is, for me, the most challenging chapter in the book and the one for which I would especially request the indulgence of the reader.

The challenging quality of this chapter is not simply a reflection of my own position on the significance of Macpherson's work and my ongoing efforts to explore its dimensions. It also reflects my desire to demonstrate again that Macpherson situated his account between past and future, that there is an open-ended quality to it in the face of the theoretical and historical challenges he confronted. The context for my approach here is the current era, which may be summarized as the return of Social Darwinism. In a little-acknowledged essay from the 1960s, when prospects for a more humane society and a more radical democracy seemed considerably brighter than they do today, Macpherson wrote of a race between technology and ontology.[21] In the face of both the optimism of the time and his own largely optimistic outlook, he warned of the consequences for the human condition of allowing the development of species powers of production, and of the social relations within which they are embedded and which they in turn shape, to proceed without democratic control, that is, under the auspices of an unregulated commitment to capitalist values and practices – in short, a reinvigorated and triumphant possessive individualism. Developments between then and now have proven him sagacious indeed. So Macpherson leaves us not with a fixed doctrine but rather with an ongoing challenge: to retrieve what is valuable in our cultural legacy and reimagine what it would be like to build a democratic society in which all would be equally entitled to use and develop their distinctively human capacities.

Chapter One

Possessive Individualism as Critique: History, Ontology, and the Roots of Liberalism

The political theory of possessive individualism is a signal accomplishment and the centrepiece of C.B. Macpherson's work. Indeed it is no accident that his later, more explicitly extensive work on alternative conceptions of democracy and the possibility and necessity of recasting liberal democratic theory took shape in the period after he had completed his path-breaking account of the tensions and contradictions of liberal individualism: the critical theory of bourgeois values, institutions, and practices that possessive individualism entailed provided the immanent foundation of Macpherson's democratic theory. That is, the resolution of the contradictions in thought and experience that the theory of possessive individualism is intended to illuminate gives rise to the conditions under which that resolution would occur. Such a resolution must achieve a certain articulation, coherence, and plausibility that make sense, at least potentially, for members of a liberal or liberal democratic society. It does so by bringing to the surface claims generated by dominant social values that are denied or distorted by the historically emergent social relations in which these values are rooted. The key here is that these claims and values point beyond themselves. That is, by sheer virtue of their normative content they can be read as demanding social relations beyond the here and now. Powerful liberal ideas and ideals of freedom, equality, democracy – indeed, individualism itself – may be thought of in this way. And the historical pattern of development of liberal societies can be interpreted as involving the ever more complete (without being completed) realization of this normative content.[1]

Possessive individualism represents C.B. Macpherson's reading of the tensions in liberal theory and practice. He called it "the unifying assumption" underlying English liberalism from the seventeenth to the nineteenth century, while arguing that "central difficulties of liberal democratic thought from John Stuart Mill to the present might be better understood if they were seen to have been set by the persistence and deep-rootedness of that assumption."[2] This is how most of Macpherson's readers, and certainly his (liberal) critics, have understood him and have responded accordingly. They seek to show either that Macpherson is textually "right" or "wrong" about the presence of this assumption in the writings of liberal theorists, starting with Hobbes.

But I want to argue that in calling possessive individualism a unifying assumption, Macpherson is not, or not merely, calling attention to the failure to appreciate or acknowledge the presence of this assumption in the tradition of English liberalism, a failure that can at least in part be attributed to ideological distortion. To be sure this is an element of the picture. But beyond this, as a unifying if unstated assumption, "possessive individualism" represents a reading of the normative and practical significance of liberal values and institutions that Macpherson believed provided us with a novel and superior insight into our political condition. It involves a claim about liberalism and liberal democracy that ideally resonates with our sense of the lived tensions and dilemmas we encounter in our experience of life in capitalist market societies. In other words, it is a cornerstone of a critical theory of the present that is possible only on the basis of an exploration of the past that lives on and powerfully shapes the present: namely, the legacy of liberalism from its seventeenth-century origins down to our own time.

And indeed I think it does attain this status, that it puts into focus in a powerful and distinctive way the tensions, contradictions, and possibilities of liberalism and existing and possible forms of liberal democracy. But this is emphatically not to claim that the concept is non-contestable or non-contentious (nor, needless to say, does it imply that all social phenomena can be explained ultimately in terms of it). Rather, possessive individualism provides a basis for engagement with core political and social questions, and its very contestable character is a measure of its contribution to an understanding of these questions. I think a case can be made that the issues it raises and the phenomena it adumbrates are inescapable: that a failure or unwillingness to address it impairs significantly a confrontation with the challenges of liberalism and democracy, indeed of what constitutes individual agency itself.

In this chapter I seek to explore in detail Macpherson's account of possessive individualism and relate it to other accounts of the political and socio-economic character of bourgeois or capitalist society that in my view build upon and reflect the issues possessive individualism raises. As Frank Cunningham puts it, Macpherson's work very much addresses the political, economic, and cultural dimensions of modern capitalist society. When, for example, two current members of the Frankfurt Institute for Social Research, Axel Honneth and Martin Hartmann, write of the contemporary power of neoliberal values as simultaneously resting upon and reinforcing what they call "a normatively charged economization of social contexts,"[3] they are following a path that Macpherson played a major role in clearing.

Possessive Individualism: Liberalism, Capitalism, and Marx

At the heart of Macpherson's account of possessive individualism is the work of Thomas Hobbes. So in an important sense the status of his theory is very much tied up with that of Hobbes, a figure of considerable and lingering controversy in the history of political thought. Hobbes is justly renowned as the philosopher of the overwhelming power of the authoritarian state – his (in)famous Leviathan – that is required in the face of the threat posed by human passions for gain and glory that always threaten to trigger a war of all against all. Yet he is also the ultimate individualist in that the cornerstone of his philosophy is his atomistic account of human nature, the essential core of which is freedom understood as the maximization of motion on the part of independent monads. The purpose of political and social arrangements is to provide the conditions that would facilitate the achievement by self-contained individuals of their goals and purposes. Analysts of Hobbes and the tensions in his work have had to negotiate the challenges posed by his combination of authoritarianism and individualism, of compulsion and freedom. Macpherson believed he had found a way to deal with these challenges that was more faithful to Hobbes's intentions and his accomplishments and as a result better able to articulate the gaps and contradictions in his work. In so doing he laid the basis for what he saw as the core dilemmas confronting liberal democratic theory and practice.

In a way still not fully appreciated by his critics, Macpherson had enormous respect for Hobbes and his accomplishments. The contradictions in Hobbes's writings were those of a great thinker who remained faithful to the reality he sought to capture through his concepts and ideas. For Macpherson, the dilemmas and challenges posed by any careful consideration of Hobbes's account were – and are – those of a possessive market society. In confronting them, Hobbes set a standard of rigour unmatched by his successors in the tradition of English liberalism. For those successors, Hobbes proved irresistible, his work an unavoidable backdrop to their own. Their ideas necessarily reflected their encounter with Hobbes, whether this encounter was explicit or not. It may not be going too far to claim that the key measure of the value of subsequent liberal thought resided in how faithfully thinkers responded to the challenge Hobbes laid out for them.

Indeed, for Macpherson, Hobbes's greatness lay not in putting forth timeless truths about human nature and political society, but precisely in his unsurpassable ability to represent the reality of the emerging capitalist market order in England. In other words, Hobbes is not diminished by being situated historically. He is enhanced. This is a main point of contention between Macpherson and his liberal and conservative critics. But it is utterly central to Macpherson's position. It speaks to a wide gamut of issues in political theory and philosophy that I hope to address throughout this study.[4]

In particular it highlights the complex relation that Macpherson's account bears to both liberalism and Marxism, especially the latter. The critique he offers of Hobbes and his successors owes – as I believe Macpherson himself intended – a considerable debt to the epistemological and methodological assumptions Marx lays out at the beginning of *Capital* as the basis for his critique of political economy.[5] And just as Marx has most frequently been read, by friends and foes alike, in a way that underplays the significance of these assumptions for Marx's judgments about social, economic and political questions, so, too, I would argue, has Macpherson.

Thus Macpherson titles the first section of his chapter on Hobbes "Philosophy and Political Theory." Before getting down to laying out what Hobbes says, Macpherson opens up the question of how to read Hobbes and his arguments. As Macpherson presents it and as I believe he saw it (although his discussion here is unfortunately a bit too abbreviated), the question of how to read Hobbes opened up the larger issue of what it means to do philosophy or political theory in the current period; and the very fact this was so, itself testified to Hobbes's greatness and enduring significance. While Hobbes has been questioned on a variety of grounds, the key issue for Macpherson concerned the status of Hobbes's attempt to deduce "political obligation from the supposed or observed facts of man's nature,"[6] and thus the relation of logical to historical inquiry. Specifically, in challenging the assumption present then (and as Frank Cunningham notes, still present today) among mainstream philosophers that the logical validity of a theory is necessarily separate from questions of its historical genesis or significance, and therefore it is illicit to derive moral or value claims from matters of fact, Macpherson wanted to signal to us that Hobbes's theory – and indeed anyone else's – had to be appraised ultimately on the basis of its historical and logical adequacy, with both necessarily intertwined.[7] In response to the idea that history is ephemeral while logic is timeless, and therefore the content of a theory and its adequacy must be considered separately from and prior to its historical origins, Macpherson suggests that this begs the question and that it "may equally well be that one cannot establish what a theory is without making historical as well as logical conjectures about Hobbes's unclear as well as unstated assumptions. In any case, it seems worth trying whether an inquiry at once logical and historical can throw a different light on Hobbes's theory, and can bring out essentials of it that have been left in the shadows by the prevailing sorts of logical analysis."[8]

In making this claim I think Macpherson had in mind a specific understanding of historical inquiry. I do not believe he was interested here in historical events so much as in what might be called the historical constitution of a certain social structure, which came to completion only after Hobbes had written but of whose key elements he had a remarkable prescience, because to the careful observer like Hobbes they were already making themselves evident in his own time.[9] This will turn out to be what Macpherson calls a possessive market society, which as a social form achieved its fullest development only in the nineteenth and twentieth centuries.

In taking this tack Macpherson subjects Hobbes and English liberalism to the kind of critique that Marx brought to bear in *Capital* on the tradition of political economy. Marx had claimed that it was essential to grasp the completed structure of a phenomenon from the perspective of its finished form as it had emerged historically – hence the famous claim that the anatomy of "man" is the key to that of the ape. In the same vein Macpherson appraises the dilemmas of Hobbes and his successors from the point of view of what we know now about the nature of liberalism and liberal democracy and their relation to the social and political forms of which they strive to make sense and to which they contribute the tools of both everyday and scholarly conceptual understanding. It is how we can best grasp why Hobbes continues to speak to us such that his limitations cast light upon the limitations of our own society. And although this might appear arbitrary or capricious, for both Macpherson and Marx the starting point of analysis is given by the nature of the material with which they are working, the question that drives the inquiry. For Macpherson this involves "the difficulty of finding a firm theoretical basis for the liberal democratic state" in a context in which "fundamental political principles of the seventeenth century" upon which we continue to rely for this basis seem no longer adequate.[10] Yet at the same time these principles cannot simply be thrust aside, because they continue to shape individual behaviour and social structures. This was also true of Marx in his critique of political economy: the contradictions that characterized the capitalist mode of production could be brought to light fully and faithfully only by working through the categories in terms of which the most advanced understanding of the system manifested itself. For him value-constituting abstract labour that existed only in the very process of exchange provided the key in a system in which no external criteria outside that system could any longer govern productive activity.

Similarly, for Macpherson the problem of establishing a firm theoretical foundation for liberal democracy turned at least initially on the question of generating a binding theory of political obligation in a context in which there no longer were external criteria – divine will or natural law in the traditional sense – in terms of which such a theory could be cast.[11] As for Marx, so for Macpherson: the solution had to be immanent, firmly embedded in the historically structured form of life within which individuals found themselves. In Hobbes's case, physiological-cum-psychological properties of human "matter in motion" – sense, imagination, memory, reason, appetites, and aversions, as he spells these out in the opening chapters of *Leviathan* – are roughly equivalent to Marx's concrete labour that at the same time generates abstract value-constituting labour only when and as objects are brought into exchange and thus into relation with one another. As Macpherson reads him, the propositions about human motivation that Hobbes advances are designed to lay the basis for a binding theory of political obligation that is internal to the system of relations among individuals. These individuals are driven by the interplay of appetites and aversions, with no need for, and even more importantly no possibility of, going outside those relations for the necessary moral requirements for what Hobbes calls peace and commodious living. The phenomenon of apparently isolated individual producers undertaking concrete labours, who come into relation with each other via the mechanism of abstract, value-constituting labour in exchange, are paralleled in Hobbes by the phenomenon of apparently isolated individual bearers of certain physiological properties who similarly come into relation with each other by what turns out to be an exchange of powers. In other words, apparently pure properties of sense, etc., are transformed into abstract, value-constituting mechanisms for the generation of power in a system of market exchanges. Physiological properties – concrete labour for Marx, the material forces of human motivation for Hobbes – do not directly determine the structure of human social relations but do so only via the process of real abstraction: the actions of human beings who in their interactions generate objective connections with each other without intending or even being consciously aware of doing so.[12]

For both Marx and Macpherson, to get to this connection requires therefore an exercise in theoretical abstraction that of necessity cannot simply posit as its starting point specific empirical relations, be they those of a capitalist economy or a liberal (democratic) political system. A fully concrete picture of either is possible only when this process of real abstraction is brought to light and clarified. Hence Marx begins his critique of classical political economy not with the economic facts or categories – including capital, itself – of a capitalist society, but with the apparently remote and obscure concept of the commodity. Macpherson likewise does not begin his critique of Hobbes and classical liberalism with the overt political values or institutions of a liberal society, but rather with the apparently obscure issue of whether one could derive moral obligation from purported facts of human nature. (The reason why the beginnings are obscure is that we tend to take both commodities and moral obligations for granted.)

Yet for both Marx and Macpherson these starting points are not transcendent, a priori. Rather they emerge from an in-depth immersion in the relevant material: political economy and political theory always and already drenched with social and historic content as the condition and possibility of being understood by those who "live" this content and can and do make sense of it by means of those ideas and values that political economy and political theory address. Thus Marx's claim in defence of his method from the 1872 postface to the second edition of *Capital*: "Of course the method of presentation must differ in form from that of inquiry. The latter has to appropriate the material in detail, to analyse its different forms of development and to track down their inner connection. Only after this work has been done can the real movement be appropriately presented. If this is done successfully, if the life of the subject matter is now reflected back in the ideas, then it may appear as if we have before us an *a priori* construction."[13]

Marx begins with the commodity, the economic cell-form of a society given over to ever more extensive and pervasive commodity production, in order to demonstrate that the commodity form assumed by objects produced to satisfy human needs is in fact a social form of human production: an object assumes the form of a commodity only in a society in which individual producers confront each other as exchangers of the products of private concrete labours. The commodity character of an object appears as an inherent material property of it. But the objectivity of the commodity emerges only in exchange – in a social relation between producers that does not appear as such. In other words, the commodity form, an apparently material objective property of stand-alone things, is in reality shot through with social content. To give this a hermeneutic, linguistic-interpretive twist, to use the term *commodity* is always and already to confront and potentially open up a set of historically evolved social relations and accompanying behavioural patterns on the part of those who are formed by and in turn shape these relations.[14]

I think Macpherson does something comparable in exploring the ultimate social meaning of Hobbes's basic physiological postulates about human "motion." To be sure he writes that Hobbes argues "from the physiological to the social motion of man," as if the two forms of motion could be kept completely separate. His point is that Hobbes cannot move directly from the one to the other without incorporating social assumptions; this is what makes it possible for Hobbes to present both the necessary behaviour of individuals in society and his stark account of life in the state of nature. And these assumptions make sense only in the context of a certain form of society, just as for Marx the central role of the commodity form is consistent only with a certain form of society. For both Macpherson and Marx this is a capitalist market society. From Macpherson's point of view there is a question of exactly "how far back in [Hobbes's] argument from the physiological to the social motion of man he put the necessary assumptions," although ultimately this is less important than the question of "with what kind of society is the social motion at which he arrives consistent?"[15]

But I think that in terms of his argument Macpherson might well have claimed – and more accurately claimed – that the basic physiological-cum-psychological claims Hobbes makes are themselves already socially drenched, that even such apparently purely natural and non-social qualities such as sense, imagination, etc., are interpretive and tied to a social form of life. I think this is why Macpherson starts with the matter of deriving obligation from fact, and why he claims that "the rule that obligation cannot be deduced from fact is itself historically questionable."[16] If the basic "facts" of human motion (or nature) are always and already socially mediated, then the derivation of obligation from those facts becomes not only possible but even necessary: the facts themselves are not neutral. In other words, Macpherson is right that the question of at what point in his argument Hobbes introduces his social assumptions is less pressing than what those assumptions are: they have been there all along.[17] For Marx the commodity proves to be a mysterious thing until its social content is made manifest. And although they seem to be more straightforward, Hobbes's basic assumptions about human motion are also in a way mysterious – until *their* social content is brought into view.

I think that for Macpherson, the point of political theory is not to identify fixed properties of isolable objects. Rather, it is to capture and address the dynamism of a particular social order and present the reader with dilemmas, predicaments, challenges, and opportunities. Its task is not to establish universal and eternal truths or certainties but to provide encounters with the demands of social life and their impact on individual life situations – to open up possibilities of self-clarification. I think that, as an analytic category, possessive individualism should be seen in this way. It poses for us the challenge of identifying how we behave, how we are required to behave by the demands of social life, and whether and how we might behave otherwise.

This means that whatever specific form Macpherson's account assumes, his is ultimately and unavoidably an exercise in persuasion. The question is not so much whether one can "prove" possessive individualism but rather whether it holds up as a better way of capturing something important about the sorts of agents we are, given what we know about society, Hobbes, and liberalism and liberal democracy. I think it does, but those seeking certainty about this, one way or another, will likely be disappointed.

The core of the argument Macpherson makes about possessive individualism and Hobbes's impact is in its essentials well known. As noted above, Macpherson starts with the proposition that there is a serious flaw in liberal democratic theory that limits its capacity to provide appropriately secure foundations for democratic practice in a society that purportedly upholds democratic values but in reality restricts democratic possibilities for a significant portion of its population. He sees this as the result of a deeply rooted commitment embedded within liberal theory, not to individualism as such but rather to what he viewed as its core seventeenth-century characteristic: its possessive character. The most cogent and perhaps best-known statement of the argument is worth quoting in full:

> Its possessive quality is found in its conception of the individual as essentially the proprietor of his own person or capacities, owing nothing to society for them. The individual was seen neither as a moral whole, nor as part of a larger social whole, but as an owner of himself. The relation of ownership, having become for more and more men the critically important relation determining their actual freedom and actual prospect of realizing their full potentialities, was read back into the nature of the individual. The individual, it was thought, is free inasmuch as he is proprietor of his person and capacities. The human essence is freedom from dependence on the wills of others, and freedom is a function of possession. Society becomes a lot of free individuals related to each other as proprietors of their own capacities and of what they have acquired by their exercise. Society consists of relations of exchange between proprietors. Political society becomes a calculated device for the protection of this property and for the maintenance of an orderly relation of exchange.

Macpherson goes on to note,

> Possessive assumptions are present not only in the two main systematic theories of political obligation (Hobbes's and Locke's) but also, where they might be least expected, in the theories of the radical Levellers and the gentry-minded Harrington ... [These] assumptions, which do correspond substantially to the actual relations of a market society, were what gave liberal theory its strength in the seventeenth century, but ... became the source of its weakness in the nineteenth, when the development of the market society destroyed certain prerequisites for deriving a liberal theory from possessive assumptions, while yet the society conformed so closely to those assumptions that they could not be abandoned. They have not been abandoned yet, nor can they be while market relations prevail.[18]

There are some significant points about this account that are I think worth considering. Primary among these is the intimate connection between freedom and possession, where this freedom is identified with the ability to avoid dependence on the wills of others. Because of this, individuals cannot be in their essence social beings – the individual is considered neither a moral whole (in more contemporary terms, an ethical whole, since the implication is that moral wholeness is a socially mediated characteristic and, in line with much current thinking, this suggests ethical rather than individual moral considerations) nor an indelible part of a larger social whole. Yet at the same time, even as freedom, a central liberal individualist value, is so understood, the reality of an individual's life as an agent seeking to maximize appetites and minimize aversions is precisely such dependence: society is a set of exchange relations, which involves more than trading things. The need for orderly relations of exchange follows from the basic dynamic of interaction involved. Agents find themselves in the predicament of being simultaneously and unavoidably dependent – their capacity to own or possess requires the existence of political society and its ability to protect the ownership rights of individuals, including their self-ownership – and yet at the same time compelled to resist any dependence. Finally, possessive individualist assumptions are not simply an ideological cover that could be ripped away, a form of false consciousness tout court, but essential and unavoidable "while market relations prevail."

Thomas Hobbes: The Struggle for Power, the Morality of the Market, and the Paradox of Individualism

These issues are central for an appreciation of what Macpherson sees as the complex character of Hobbes's ideas and his place in the history of modern English liberalism. For Macpherson, as indeed for most analysts, the core element at the heart of Hobbes's work is power. Exploring Hobbes's conception of power, first of the individual and then of the great artificial figure of the sovereign – his Leviathan – turns out to be a very challenging task. The problem, as already noted, revolves around the need to demonstrate how the basic account of humans as physical bodies in motion continuously seeking to maximize this motion gives rise to the haunting picture of a condition of "meer Nature." In this condition, individuals universally contend with one another for gain, safety, and glory, and, where not restrained by political authority, ultimately and unavoidably find themselves in a war of all against all that threatens to make life "solitary, poore, nasty, brutish and short." The attempt by self-moving, appetitive machines to maximize their motion, i.e., maximally fulfil their desires, is not on the surface tied to mutual and destructive contention. As Macpherson sees it, Hobbes makes two key moves that lay the groundwork for his stark account of the state of nature, moves that brought about the "main transition from man the machine by itself, to man the machine as a unit in a series of social relationships."[19] First, in his discussion of the intellectual virtues in chapter 8 of *Leviathan* he claims that "Vertue generally, in all sorts of subjects, is somewhat that is valued for eminence; and consisteth in comparison. *For if all things were equally in all men, nothing would be prized.*"[20] At the basis of this eminence stand differences in wit or intelligence, themselves the product of different degrees of passion for power, riches, knowledge, and honours. These, in turn, are the products of both inheritance and social customs and education.

This conception of virtue is then carried forward into Hobbes's accounts in chapters 10 and 11 of, respectively, power and manners – those qualities that permit individuals to live in peace and unity. For Macpherson what matters here is that Hobbes not only establishes that people necessarily contend for eminence in a struggle for power in society but also lays out this account of their behaviour prior to introducing the device of a state of nature. Starting in chapter 10 with the apparently neutral definition of power as any present means to some future apparent good, Hobbes ends up in the next chapter with the claim that all are driven by a relentless desire to acquire power after power that ends only with death, and that this is power over others. Immediately following his original definition of power, Hobbes claims that there are two kinds of power, natural and instrumental, and that natural power consists of the eminence of an individual's endowed faculties and capacities. In turn, natural power becomes the basis for acquiring instrumental powers – riches, reputation, friends, and good luck. And this process is continuous and cumulative. The acquisition of instrumental powers facilitates the further acquisition of such powers in a never-ending process. According to Hobbes in his *Elements of Law Natural and Politic*, this process is rooted in the reality that because the power of each individual hinders and resists the power of another, power is nothing more or less than the excess of the power of one in relation to another.

This universal and ongoing dynamic of power not only characterizes relations between individuals but also defines in a fundamental way the normative core of individual agency as such: it constitutes identities. Thus Hobbes argues in chapter 10 of *Leviathan* that the "*Value*, or WORTH of a man, is as of all other things, his Price; that is to say, so much as would be given for the use of his Power: and therefore is not absolute; but a thing dependant on the need and judgement of another ... For let a man (as most men do,) rate themselves as the highest Value they can; yet their true Value is no more than it is esteemed by others." And further: "To Value a man at a high rate, is to *Honour* him; at a low rate, is to *Dishonour* him. But high, and low, in this case, is to be understood by comparison to the rate that each man setteth on himselfe."[21] Individuals are driven to exact the highest value they can command, while resisting like efforts of others. Since value, price, and power are all interconnected in defining who one is, everyone is ultimately drawn into a struggle for power, at one and the same time both seeking power over others and resisting the power-seeking of those others.

Thus, in society, individuals necessarily behave invasively, certainly to acquire power over others on the part of those who wish greater power and thus an increased ability to realize their (limitless) desires, but also and perhaps even more often to resist the loss of whatever power they may already possess. As Hobbes sees it, where power and desire are so intimately linked – indeed the desire for power might be thought the ultimate general desire, since the capacity to satisfy all other specific desires depends upon it – and given the reality that, as Hobbes puts it in chapter 11 of *Leviathan* – happiness or felicity "consisteth not in the repose of a mind satisfied" but rather in a "continuall progresse, from one object to another; the attaining of the former, being still but the way to the later" – individuals strive for power after power that ends only in death. And the quest is universal, because even the individual content with the power he currently possesses must continue to seek additional power if only to protect what he already has: "He cannot ensure the power and means to live well, which he hath present, without the acquisition of more."[22]

What is decisive for Macpherson's account here is that, under these circumstances, the powers of individuals that Hobbes describes – primarily instrumental or acquired powers in the form of riches, liberality, and reputation, indeed, any quality that makes someone loved or feared by many – "consist in offensive and defensive strength against others ... Hobbes has in effect defined acquired power as ability to command the services of other men."[23] And this is how individuals relate *in society*, where there is a sovereign political authority, as opposed to the state of nature where such authority is absent. Hence the struggle for power and the acquisition of power over others does not proceed primarily by means of open force, which would be incompatible with a working, civilized social order with effective government, but instead by means of a market in power where "power is treated as a commodity, regular dealings in which establish market prices."[24]

It is for this reason that for Macpherson the question of what model of society conforms most fully to Hobbes's position becomes fundamental. This would have to be a society that permits widespread invasive behaviour and allows room for individuals to more or less peacefully convert the powers of others to their benefit while resisting the efforts of others to convert theirs. And it is here that Macpherson lays the foundation for two core elements that will come to significantly define his overall body of work and especially his account of democracy. One is the concept of the net transfer of powers. The other is the idea that within liberalism there have developed two competing ontological perspectives or accounts of human nature: individuals as infinite consumers and appropriators, and individuals as active doers and exerters of their distinctively human capacities. The first, which Macpherson will refine and elaborate throughout virtually all of his subsequent writings, is explicit in his treatment of Hobbes and the social basis of his ideas. The second, which will also come to play an increasingly decisive role in his work, does not explicitly appear here. But it is implied by the idea that Hobbes's account, and indeed the tradition of English liberalism as a whole, can be seen to embody and express these competing ontologies once the social and historical context of liberal ideas is explored, and especially, beginning in the nineteenth century, once liberal thinkers themselves were compelled to respond to the social and historical forces and conditions liberalism helped constitute. (And we should recall again that the trigger for the analysis of possessive individualism was the need to account for the crisis of political obligation in liberal and liberal democratic theory that emerged in the nineteenth and twentieth centuries.) I will explore this more fully in chapter 2.

What Macpherson calls the net transfer of powers is intimately tied to his account of the model of society most compatible with Hobbes's analysis of the pervasive struggle for power that characterizes human behaviour and follows from the circumstances of their living together. Indeed, for Macpherson, Hobbes both saw, and saw the need for, such a transfer, mediated by a competitive market in power, in order for society to accommodate universal invasive behaviour. Of course Hobbes himself did not explicitly so label it. But as Macpherson reads him, he needs such a notion in order to make coherent his claims about the necessary behaviour of individuals in society, behaviour that threatens to turn utterly lethal in the state of nature, in which there is no sovereign power able to "overawe" the competitors for power. For Macpherson the question becomes: what kind of society has as its central organizing principle pervasive market competition as "a means by which men who want more may convert more of the powers of others to their use than others convert of theirs" and where "what is unique about the transfer ... is that it is maintained by continual competition between individuals at all levels"?[25] Only such a model of society would meet the requirements of Hobbes's argument, a society in which individuals "may, and do, continually seek to transfer to themselves some of the powers of others, in such a way as to compel everyone to compete for more power, and all this by peaceable and legal methods which do not destroy the society by open force."[26] This model is what Macpherson calls a possessive market society – essentially a modern capitalist market social order.

Macpherson's approach is once again reminiscent of that of Marx. Marx sought to spell out the historical specificity of the capitalist mode of production, which had come to be seen as natural and eternal, by developing a more complex account on the basis of a simpler model that highlights what might otherwise be obscure or insufficiently appreciated. In a comparable manner, Macpherson attempted to indicate the historical specificity of the model of society that best fit Hobbes's assumptions. He lays out three models for comparison: customary or status society, simple market society, and possessive market society. These are designed to establish the distinction between pre- or non-capitalist social orders, such as feudal societies, and fully established capitalist ones. What fundamentally distinguishes a customary or status society from either the simple market or possessive market society is that in a customary society there is an authoritative allocation of productive work and rewards. The picture is of a long-term and stable social order with more or less fixed ranks that comes with widely recognized and politically enforced obligations for all ranks. By contrast full-fledged market societies do away with such authoritative allocation; for this to work there must be individual and alienable property in land and other productive resources, with individuals seeking to maximize benefits or utilities through the use of their resources in a system of enforceable relations of contract.

Macpherson acknowledges that his model of a simple market society is not intended to be taken as a literal picture of any society that exists or is known to have existed. It is thus not an actual transitional model between a status (feudal) and possessive market (capitalist) social and economic system. What it does is to highlight some readily recognizable features of all market societies, including fully capitalist ones, which involve extensive and pervasive contractual relations between legally free and equal proprietors. Again the comparison with Marx is noteworthy. There are clear parallels with Marx's initial account in volume 1 of *Capital* of a society of simple commodity production and circulation. In his attempt to single out, examine, and clarify the commodity or value form as the social form of objects produced under the capitalist mode of production, Marx deliberately excludes capital as self-expanding or valorizing value. Only after laying out the structural features of the commodity does Marx turn his attention to capital as the necessary solution to the problem of how to resolve objective contradictions in the account of "pure" or simple commodity exchange. The examination of capital turns out to be an examination of a new and different kind of commodity: labour power. Marx will argue that for this commodity to emerge there must be a separation of labour from the means of labour – a class division that manifests itself as the generation and appropriation of surplus value, i.e., as capital itself.

However, there is another aspect to Marx's approach that I think we can detect in Macpherson's as well. The society of simple commodity production and circulation cannot stand on its own. But it does represent the necessary form of appearance of a capitalist social order that assumes the character of a mass of commodities whose social characteristics seem to be objective material properties of the commodities themselves. For individuals who act within and are formed by the objective requirements of a society characterized by ubiquitous commodity production, this is how it appears to them, namely as a society of equals who are equally related to each other by and through commodities. So for Marx this society is not simply a way station on the road to a more comprehensive understanding of capital and capitalism. It also and just as importantly represents how individuals actually understand themselves and their relations – it is simultaneously true and false. It is thus central to the very idea of a "critique" of political economy.

Macpherson's model of a simple market society plays a comparable role in his critique of political theory. It, too, highlights important features of modern capitalist market societies, absent two critical features: the alienability or commodification of labour and the desire of some individuals to increase their levels of satisfactions and hence power relative to others. The critical factor is the alienability of labour. It is this characteristic that allows for a peaceful and legal struggle for power that permits some to make over for their own use in achieving a higher level of utilities the powers of others, a struggle and transfer that becomes ever more pervasive and persistent as class divisions emerge and harden. Here the analyses of Marx and Macpherson meet and overlap: if for Marx what defines and makes possible the existence of capital is wage labour, the commodification of labour as labour power, for Macpherson the commodification of labour defines a possessive market society in which there is legally constrained invasive behaviour and ongoing, compulsive transfers of power. Both the appropriation of surplus value and the net transfer of powers become possible and come about for the same reason: the dynamics of a competitive market society gradually produce, if it were not already present, an enduring class division between those who own and control the means of life and labour, and are able to set the terms of access to them, and those with only their capacity to labour to sell, who must make over this capacity to those who control access. Whether for Marx or for Macpherson, there is a cost to those without property in the material means of life: the ceding of surplus value to the capitalist (Marx); the loss of command over the direction and use of one's capacities (Macpherson).[27]

And just as Marx's depiction of a society of simple commodity production and exchange was intended not just as an exercise in analytic clarification but also as a depiction of how the world appears to its agents, at least most of the time, so too is Macpherson's account of a simple market society. To be sure, Macpherson does not advance this claim. The analytic purpose is made explicit: "It is doubtful if a society closely approximating to this model has ever existed for very long. But the model is introduced in order to separate the features common to all market societies from those which are found only in full market societies."[28] However, this is where he leaves the matter.

I think his case would have been strengthened had he indicated that most people, including perhaps Hobbes, himself, in his time (although this is less certain) have viewed or view their society as if it indeed were a simple market social order. To everyday consciousness the net transfer of powers is as difficult to ascertain, even as invisible, as the appropriation of surplus value. From the point of view of Marx's critique of political economy and Macpherson's critique of political theory, this is how such a society necessarily presents itself – the appearance is not the product of delusion per se on the part of individual agents who are also social agents.

To understand the simple market society in this light is to do more than fill in the gaps in the analysis. *It is even more importantly to grasp more fully and accurately the concept of possessive individualism itself, and to enhance its normative meaning and weight*. Possessive individualism offers a way of identifying and making sense of the relation of a simple market society as the immediately visible form of social life to the possessive market society with its net transfer of powers that provides the structural constraints within which individuals act, even if these constraints fail to "appear." In *Democratic Theory: Essays in Retrieval*, Macpherson will both acknowledge once again Hobbes's insight into the struggle for power in a bourgeois social order and at the same time suggest his limitations: that he failed to see the net transfer because he mechanistically measured the powers of individuals after such a transfer had occurred. In other words he saw the *product* of the struggle for power while failing to fully grasp the *process*.

Put otherwise, in the implied but unstated significance of the simple market model of society there is more evidence of what I have called Macpherson's suppressed philosophical dimension. In the language of the Continental philosophy with which Macpherson was not fully comfortable but that nonetheless helps capture what he was trying to do, the notion of possessive individualism is won by mediation. Its key elements and significant consequences, manifested in the passage from the simple to the possessive market model, are brought forward in the movement from the one to the other – to what can appear only via passage from the immediate to what is mediated, from appearance to essence. Possessive individualism turns out to be about both what is seen and what is unseen from the point of view of individuals and political theorists alike.

Hobbes does not specifically say that his assumptions are possessive individualist, an omission that Macpherson's critics such as John Dunn and James Tully have noted. But it makes sense of Hobbes's position in a way that demonstrates his limitations (Macpherson will build on this in his future work on democratic theory) but more importantly his strengths. In a way, for Macpherson, Hobbes has not been fully appreciated, even by his defenders, to say nothing of his critics and detractors. This is no more evident than in his view of political obligation and what Macpherson sees as his deduction of obligation from the facts of human nature and society, of "ought" from "is." Specifically he sees Hobbes as justifying the necessity of a sovereign strictly on the basis of self-interest alone.

As I suggested above, from the outset Macpherson places the question of the deduction of obligation, political and moral, from fact at the core of his account. While it has been a theme in the assessment of Hobbes's thought, it is not immediately obvious why this issue should be so central for Macpherson. From the vantage point of a certain Marxist outlook, such a concern would seem idealist, an indication that Macpherson is insufficiently "materialist." From this perspective, morality is a form of bourgeois ideology, a tool in the hands of the capitalist class to keep subordinate classes in check by presenting capitalist social relations as right and eternal because mandated by some transcendent standard, such as God or Reason. Paying significant attention to it, much less making it central to the analysis, detracts from the "real" task at hand: providing a materialist critique of capitalism that can foster the development of proletarian revolutionary consciousness. For his part, Macpherson likely accepted something of this position, if certainly not the criticism of his own argument that some proponents of it might mount. And although he never specifically said so, Macpherson could well have had in mind here Marx's famous claim from the *Communist Manifesto* that under the rule of the bourgeoisie, "all fixed, fast-frozen relations, with their train of ancient and venerable prejudices and opinions are swept away, all new-formed ones become antiquated before they can ossify. All that is solid melts into air, all that is holy is profaned, and man is at last compelled to face with sober senses, his real conditions of life, and his relations with his kind."[29] The justification and even unavoidable necessity of deducing right from fact may be thought a reflection of the revolutionary impact of the emergence of the bourgeois social order.

But if the issue of deducing obligation from fact parallels Marx's critique of the commodity, then the question of morality and the hold that moral views and habits exert on individuals is about more than simply false consciousness. It also addresses how and why individuals genuinely live in a "space" of normative reasons that provide standards of judgments and motives for actions in the life situations they encounter. And as the critique of the commodity turns on the presence of equality in exchange that is both real and illusory, so, too, does the account of Hobbes's methodology in deducing right from fact. The assumption of equality is a core feature of Hobbes's account of political obligation.

According to Macpherson, there are two kinds of equality relevant for Hobbes's deduction of obligation from fact: equality of ability and equality of expectations. Both in turn draw from Hobbes's materialist and market assumptions, his physiological claims about humans as self-moving machines driven by their appetites and aversions, and his view of social relations as built on the opposition of individual powers and the consequent struggle for power in a market in which the value or worth of a "man" as the price for the use of his power is determined, and no other measure of worth is possible or needed. Equality of ability is ultimately the capacity of even the weakest person to kill the strongest. Equality of expectations is equality of the hope of individuals to attain their ends and thus satisfy their desires, ultimately the desire as self-moving machines for self-preservation. Both forms of equality generate equal individual rights to recognition *as* equals of others and thus to a moral obligation that will sustain and be sustained by political obligation to a sovereign. "The materialist assumption enabled him to say that individuals had equal need of continued motion, and to argue that, in the absence of reasons to the contrary, equal need could be taken as establishing equal moral right, and so providing the possibility of moral obligation. The market assumptions enabled him to say that men were equal in insecurity and so to infer the necessity of moral obligation."[30]

At one level, equality of insecurity provides a compelling basis for the generation of moral obligation without reference to some transcendent source. Under these circumstances, individuals acknowledge each other as equals such that no one can claim by nature superior right, i.e., the right to dominate. They can thus accept the kind of binding obligation Hobbes thought necessary for the creation and maintenance of a sovereign power able to overawe them. When individuals recognize themselves as equally insecure, they will be more apt to accept such equality of right. And while this might be thought an acknowledgment of prudential obligation, because based on factual self-interest, as opposed to moral obligation, as Macpherson sees it, once transcendent standards of moral judgment are jettisoned, the distinction between prudential and moral obligation disappears.

There is, however, a tension or ambiguity inherent in the claim to equality of insecurity. As the (capitalist) possessive market society develops and generates class divisions between owners and non-owners of productive resources, there emerges within the general and equal insecurity of all individuals open to invasion in the market a pronounced inequality of insecurity between classes. Those with only their labour power to sell find their position to be significantly more precarious than those who employ them. Hobbes did not quite see this, understandably from Macpherson's point of view because the reality of it, or at least its full impact, did not become completely visible until the nineteenth century. In any event, under the circumstances, recognition of equality of insecurity could not alone establish the conditions needed for the political obligation Hobbes sought to establish.

At the same time it is possible to detect in Hobbes another form of equality that could pass muster as universal and thus be capable of sustaining the deduction of right from fact. This was equality of subordination to the rules or laws of the market that determines with objective if not supernatural force the real, effective powers, and hence identities, of individuals. As Macpherson puts it,

> Hobbes saw, accurately, that in a possessive market society all values and entitlements are in fact established by the operation of the market, and all morality tends to be the morality of the market. The possessive market society *does* establish rights by facts: every man's entitlements are determined by the actual competitive relationship between the powers of individuals. If the determination of values and rights by the market is accepted as justice by all members of the society, there is a sufficient basis for rational obligation, binding on all men, to an authority which could maintain and enforce the market system … For if there is no alternative to the market society, or if the only alternative is anarchy, every man in it who sees his true position has no rational alternative but to support a political authority which can maintain that society as a regular orderly system."[31]

It may be noted here that the two forms of equality, equality of insecurity and equality as equal subordination to market rules, overlap. Equal subordination goes along with another key element that Macpherson associates with Hobbes's position, namely his recognition that social order no longer depended upon, and could no longer support, the maintenance of supposedly permanent hierarchical relations based on enduring, ontologically grounded differential needs, capacities, and entitlements and thus moral and political inequality. (Indeed Hobbes appears to have believed that the whole idea of natural hierarchy was in any case what we would now call ideological, as his sharp criticism of Aristotle suggested.) To be sure, at least in Hobbes's eyes, overturning the justification of hierarchy in theory, as it was being overturned in practice, should have paved the way for the triumph of his own universal and eternal account of human nature as opposed to the falsely eternal claims of earlier misguided attempts at "civil philosophy." To Macpherson, Hobbes claimed too much. He failed to see that his thought got to the heart not of all societies at all times but of the possessive market society as it was taking root in seventeenth-century England. On its own, this was a more than considerable accomplishment, even if it did not quite live up to Hobbes's own lofty expectations.

And this accomplishment may have been even greater than Macpherson acknowledges. Both dimensions of equality have played and continue to play critical roles in framing the question of political obligation or, to put it in more contemporary terms, political legitimacy.[32] No doubt the "mix" of the two positions can and does vary in different historical periods and under different social and political conditions. How people understand themselves as equally or unequally insecure – or to put it another way, whether and how they see the presence of classes and the impact class has on their individual life prospects – is strongly related to how fully they experience, accept, or at least fail to question subservience to market rules. Although this dimension of equality is not explicit in Hobbes – Macpherson reads it as immanent in his reasoning about the central place of market morality – it might be thought primary. Even where people see inequality of insecurity in class terms, they might not be inclined to reject market institutions or behaviour if subordination to market rules is seen as unavoidable and eternal, i.e., in full accordance with human possibilities (which is, of course, Hobbes's position). Where they do see insecurity in this way, there is a greater likelihood that they will call market society into question. This has happened to various extents at different times in different liberal democratic and non-liberal democratic possessive market social orders. One could indeed make the case that the political dynamics of modern and contemporary capitalist societies are shaped by the interplay of the two forms of equality – with the apparent inevitability and permanence of a society governed by market laws undergirding the contemporary neoliberal era.

However, I think Macpherson might have somewhat underestimated here the individualist dimension of insecurity so explicitly central to Hobbes: the sense that individuals are ultimately vulnerable not simply to class exploitation but also to physical invasion by others. Although Macpherson is right that reducing class inequalities would enhance the sense of security of all (a point Rousseau, among others, also tellingly made), it is doubtful that the feeling of individual vulnerability could ever be completely eliminated. I would not wish to claim that Macpherson completely avoids this issue. In fact his respect for liberal individualist, if not possessive individualist, values is evident in his argument on behalf of the need to secure for individuals what he will call counter-extractive liberty – his reformulation of the classical, Hobbesian negative liberty, freedom as the absence of impediments to the pursuit of one's aims. This suggests the constitutional protections against forcible invasion of individuals that is characteristic of liberalism and liberal democracy. However, at least in his treatment of Hobbes in *Possessive Individualism*, Macpherson seems to have presented the distinction between the two forms of equality a bit too sharply. This complicates his attempt to establish the nature of the problem of political obligation and his proposed means of addressing it.

This said, Macpherson's position here nonetheless illuminates the critical nature of his project. It raises the question of what we are to make of the human possibilities and qualities Hobbes identifies as permanent, qualities that Macpherson sees as real but not eternal. As a concept, possessive individualism is itself at the heart of this question. But Macpherson more explicitly addresses it in his treatment of ontology, of human nature: are human beings infinite appropriators or consumers, who, in any conceivable society, would be prone to invade others, by force if permitted, in a never-ending quest for power over them? Or are they at least potentially and, to a greater extent than we might know under current social conditions developers, doers and exerters of their distinctively human capacities in a more solidaristic and cooperative way?[33] Macpherson wanted us to ponder this because Hobbes did. Of course Hobbes did not deliberately hold such an aim, but nonetheless the power of his analysis and the normative commitments it unavoidably advances – commitments that make it essential to address the deduction of right from fact – bring it out.

Macpherson completes his account of Hobbes by noting what he sees as his key weakness: his argument on behalf of the absolute need for a self-perpetuating sovereign power. Whether a single individual or an assembly of representatives, Hobbes felt that the holders of sovereign authority needed to designate their own successors; otherwise responsibility would be thrown back onto the fragmented body of competitive and conflictual individuals who were incapable without the cohesion provided by the sovereign of settling on a choice. The result could only be a return to the natural condition of war that required the sovereign in the first place. According to Macpherson, Hobbes failed to see the possibility of the class of owners of the means of life and labour enjoying a sufficient common interest to hold their representatives accountable without the society lapsing into anarchy. It would be Locke who, building on Hobbes, provided a more agreeable justification of political authority that made it subordinate to a civil society dominated by men of property.

But this does not in the end diminish Hobbes's insight and significance. From the perspective of liberal and liberal democratic thought, perhaps his most significant accomplishment was that he captured the peculiar combination of freedom and compulsion that is at the core of a possessive market society and its moral standards: "The market makes men free; it requires for its effective operation that all men be free and rational; yet the independent rational decisions of each man produce at every moment a configuration of forces which confronts each man compulsively. All men's choices determine, and each man's choice is determined by, the market."[34]

What Macpherson calls the "paradox of Hobbes's individualism," which "starts with equal rational individuals and demonstrates that they must submit themselves wholly to a power outside themselves," is in fact the central paradox and defining feature of possessive individualism, itself, wherever and however it might be articulated.[35] And it now becomes even clearer why Macpherson devotes so much effort to the issue of deriving obligation from fact. No resort to transcendent standards of value, especially as such standards relate to human freedom and equality, can properly recognize, much less capture, the dialectic of freedom and compulsion that is peculiarly and powerfully central to a possessive market society. The "compulsions of the market society do somewhat demean the free rational individual who is usually put at the centre of ethical theory [traditionally understood in terms of transcendent values]. The morality of the market is not entirely acceptable to the humanist."[36] Only *within* the market can standards *of* the market become visible. A market society characterized by pervasive commodification is possible only when the historical development of human productive capacities and powers of social organization reduces if not eliminates altogether the need to call upon externally imposed standards of right.

Macpherson here advances a claim that will to a considerable extent shape the rest of his life's work: "A theory of obligation built on recognition and acceptance of the compulsions and morality of the market must seem perverse to the humanist who does not fully accept the values of the possessive market society as the highest, or a sufficient, morality."[37] The task then becomes how to come up with a better theory of obligation and a more fully humanist moral framework. Once we understand what is entailed by our immersion in the requirements of market morality – in the requirements of possessive individualism – the need to reconsider and reimagine the demands and possibilities of human nature and liberal democracy becomes an objectively compelling task in the face of our embedded commitments to freedom, reason, and equality. Democracy and possessive individualism do not stand apart or alone. They are intertwined at their roots. Macpherson's focus on the derivation of right from fact in Hobbes is not simply an external analytic exercise. It defines the shared conceptual space that Macpherson and Hobbes occupy.

In his treatment of Hobbes, Macpherson lays out everything essential to the theory of possessive individualism. His exploration of the tradition of English liberalism represents further refinements of this analysis. But it is Hobbes who stands as the ultimate standard bearer of bourgeois right, a genuinely scientific analyst of the requirements of a possessive market society. Writing from later historical vantage points, subsequent liberal thinkers built on Hobbes's foundations and often did so brilliantly. However, they never surpassed him in his incisive grasp of the demands and requirements of a market society. In his introduction to his edited version of *Leviathan*, Macpherson writes that bourgeois self-interest "has in fact sustained a sovereign state, Hobbesian in almost every respect except the self-perpetuating power of the sovereign body, in most bourgeois societies since Hobbes's time. Hobbes built better than he knew, and better than most of his modern critics know."[38] This is a judgment from which Macpherson never dissented.

John Locke: Property, Class, and Civil Society

However, build on these foundations subsequent thinkers did. And no one built more tellingly or with greater impact than John Locke, the other key figure in *The Political Theory of Possessive Individualism*. One could indeed claim that if Hobbes provided the core elements of possessive individualism, and its scientific foundations, it was Locke who most importantly carried forward Hobbes's accomplishments and gave the theory its most enduring social content. In Locke's hands, possessive individualism is associated with what are still today recognizable, indeed dominant, features of a capitalist, liberal democratic social order. Viewed from the perspective of the history of liberalism and liberal democracy as a whole, Locke's influence has been and remains enormous – his "success" outstrips even that of Hobbes. For Macpherson, the key to grasping Locke's importance lay in his account of, and justification of, private property, not merely in goods for consumption but also in the means of life and labour. The question of property will later become central to Macpherson's attempt to develop a more radical and humanistic account of a liberal democracy beyond possessive individualism.

But as is the case with his treatment of Hobbes, Macpherson's account of Locke goes further than what he clearly intends as his key claims. Specifically he identifies and addresses an important dynamic at work in liberal democratic societies caught up in the contradictions of liberalism. In doing so, he provides a critical standard for appraising such societies that has real potential for political analysis in the present. He again demonstrates that possessive individualism is not just a descriptive category but a form of conceptual articulation that brings to life phenomena that would not otherwise be fully grasped or understood.

In any event, there is a powerful case to be made that it is in fact Locke, and not Hobbes, who stands as the prototypical possessive individualist, for it is in his work that all of the core elements of possessive individualism most fully emerge. Hobbes, to be sure, laid the groundwork, especially in demonstrating the possibility of deducing right or obligation from the facts of human nature. But it was Locke who carried this through to the point at which possessive individualism "was the predominant assumption of English political thinking from Locke until, say, James Mill. This was the period of the solid establishment of capitalism, when the whole society was recast in market relations, a greatly enlarged working class was created in dependence on the sale of its labour, production was enormously expanded, and unlimited possibilities appeared." Indeed, for Macpherson, while Hobbes "went even further than Locke in making man a commodity with an exchange value … he saw too clearly that domination over things was domination over men, and vice versa, *which is perhaps why he is not to be counted entirely in the liberal tradition*."[39]

This observation is both lucid and striking. It suggests that Locke's liberalism is both more and less realistic, that it demonstrates both greater clarity and deeper obscurity, with both dimensions inherently interrelated. Put otherwise, possessive individualism becomes truer as its full meaning and implications become less visible. Its complexity as a category highlights core elements of an increasingly complex and tension-laden reality. It is, to repeat, a critical reading of a certain normatively charged, historically developing social form of life and not a specific descriptive attribute consciously adopted by theorists, where such adoption viewed abstractly would be arbitrary. It "pays off" in that it provides a way of grasping how an evolving liberal order founded on the claim to liberate individuals increasingly ensnares them in networks of deterministic social and political relations that are themselves the basis and outcome of the actions of the very individuals so liberated. Individual freedom comes to take on paradoxical or contradictory features, as Hobbes grasped, and it is Locke's theory that most fully expresses this.

However, if Hobbes is not entirely in the liberal tradition, he is also not entirely out of it either. And to the extent he is outside it, while being within it, his work provides an immanent critical vantage point not available to thinkers such as John Locke or James Mill. The dialectic of a liberalism that contradicts its highest claims in the very process of ostensibly realizing them provides the dominant theme in Macpherson's treatment of the liberal tradition and Locke's place within it. It is most clearly evident in Locke's account of property and so explains the central place Macpherson accords it. But I will also argue that it assumes a certain lucidity and even urgency in a claim that Macpherson makes about the necessary qualities of the Lockean or liberal state. This claim is offered as almost just a sidebar to his more extensive and better-known analysis of property, but in fact it captures something very important about the kind of political order that a possessive market society both requires and sustains.

Recall that in exploring the theoretical basis of market society and Hobbes's importance in establishing it, Macpherson discussed Hobbes's deduction of moral and political obligation from the equal subordination of all to the compulsive pressures of the market, and the universal insecurity it produced. Equal insecurity and the fragmentation it expressed required that the sovereign power, which enforced the rules of the market society, be self-perpetuating.

As it turned out, this was unacceptable when proposed and in any case unnecessary for the maintenance of a stable possessive market society. Hobbes saw the necessity for a self-perpetuating sovereign because "if the person or persons who hold sovereign power were not acknowledged to have the right to appoint their successors, then whenever any successors had to be chosen, the real power would be thrown back to the fragmented and opposed powers of all the separate members of the society, thus negating the whole purpose for which they had authorized sovereign power."[40] While his point is understandable, given his core assumptions about human motivation and behaviour, Hobbes failed to see the possibility of class cohesion: that the class of owners in a market society could establish a common interest strong enough to ensure that authority over the appointment or election of members to a sovereign body could safely reside with it. The sovereign body could be securely upheld by such a class and be accountable to it, power could be peacefully transferred, and the laws regulating relations among market actors could continue to be enforced.

If Hobbes missed this point, Locke most assuredly did not. Coupled with his reintroduction of the older precepts of natural law, Locke was able to produce a theory at once more appealing yet less revealing, more realistic yet less incisive than that of Hobbes.

As Macpherson sees it, property stands as the cornerstone of Locke's political thought. His defence of a natural right to property as private property has been hugely influential and constitutes the core achievement at the heart of a fully realized possessive individualism. This is because, in Locke's hands, individualism turns into its opposite: a class-divided civil society in which the ostensible freedom of all mandated by natural law becomes compulsion for the many, and a class-based state dedicated in the name of freedom to the preservation of unequal property. What Macpherson sees as the transformation of Locke's right to property by virtue of its own internal dynamic is the key to addressing and resolving fundamental challenges and contradictions that Locke's theory poses. Spelling out what this transformation involves is the task Macpherson sets for himself.

Earlier I noted that critics of Macpherson have often been apt to argue that he illicitly "read" possessive individualism into the English liberal tradition in order to support what is an ultimately unjustifiable socialist-inspired critique of the limits of liberalism, a reading of liberalism that explicitly ignores its commitment to human freedom and dignity. For Macpherson's part, however, the problem was rather the opposite: possessive individualism had been read *out* of the tradition by most of its defenders. Whatever the motivations of his critics (Macpherson tended to be rather silent on this), their approach either left or created interpretive difficulties that could be properly addressed only once the presence of possessive assumptions was acknowledged. While he noted this explicitly in Hobbes, it was no less present, and even more telling, in Locke. If there had been any illicit importation of unjustified and unjustifiable assumptions into liberalism, this most clearly applied to the tendency to read Locke as a liberal democrat, albeit one who understandably, given the time at which he wrote, could not have been expected to lay out the elements of fully realized liberal democratic political order.

For Macpherson this approach blocked a clear understanding of Locke's theory: "Neither its strength nor its weakness, nor even its meaning, are apt to be understood until we stop reading back into it the assumptions of a later age."[41] Macpherson's treatment of Locke's account of property is based on the view that once we stop reading him from the vantage point of "the modern tradition of humane liberalism ... his doctrine of property appears in a new light, or, rather, *is restored to the meaning it must have had for Locke and his contemporaries*."[42]

Of course Locke himself had made property central to his account of political obligation, particularly in his most famous and influential work, the *Second Treatise of Government*. Yet it was Macpherson's view that beyond this, property was vital to the development of a historically informed, critical account of liberalism and democracy because it was not exclusively about ownership of things but more importantly social relations between individuals. (This is why it becomes important for Macpherson to show that Locke's theory of property "is a justification of the natural right not only to unequal property but to unlimited individual appropriation."[43]) Macpherson did not fully develop his theory of property until he worked up more systematically his account of democracy, with property as a centrepiece. But key elements of what he believed an account of property was required to address were laid out in his treatment of Locke, for this spoke to the developing tensions at the heart of possessive individualism itself. These tensions will involve ambiguities around what it means to be independent of the wills of others.

As was the case in his treatment of Hobbes, Macpherson claims that Locke's account of property could be most fully understood in the context of unstated social assumptions that were taken for granted. As Macpherson sees it, Locke made central the importance of, and necessity for, the accumulation of capital as the dominant form of social wealth and its necessary correlate, the commodification of labour and thus the presence of the wage relation. It is Macpherson's view that these assumptions and their corresponding social relations, along with the appropriate normative values, were sufficiently widespread that, for the most part, Locke did not feel the need to spell them out explicitly.

Macpherson's analysis of Locke's theory of property is relatively well known. I'll try simply to summarize its key points here while, where possible, indicating aspects of this account that have not been as widely recognized and emphasized as they might be.

The core of Locke's account of property is in chapter 5 of his *Second Treatise*, arguably the most famous justification of private property in the English language; certainly its impact on free market libertarians such as Robert Nozick has been considerable.[44] Central to his account is the assertion and justification of a natural, individual right to property. Locke's equally celebrated limits on the power of civil government, immensely influential in the history of the liberal constitutional state, have their basis in the need to respect and guard this right.

In contrast to Hobbes, for whom there was not nor could there be a natural right to property, Locke tells us that in the state of nature all enjoy "a *state of perfect freedom* to order their actions, and dispose of their possessions and persons, as they think fit, within the bounds of the law of nature, without asking leave or depending upon the will of any other man." This law of nature, which is the law of reason, "teaches all mankind, who will but consult it, that being all *equal and independent*, no one ought to harm another in his life, health, liberty, or possessions."[45] Individuals enjoy equality by nature and thus no one possesses jurisdiction over anyone else, "there being nothing more evident, than that creatures of the same species and rank, promiscuously born to all the same advantages of nature, and the use of the same faculties, should also be equal one amongst another without subordination or subjection."[46]

It should be noted that Locke's "state of perfect freedom" combines the ability and right of individuals to "order their actions," that is, act autonomously, with the disposition of their possessions and persons. Whether these in fact are identical is very much at the core of the analysis Macpherson provides, and this point is decisive for a critical understanding of liberalism. Certainly Locke thought they were at least intimately intertwined, if not identical. In other words, the relation between autonomy and property goes to the core of the meaning of Locke's individualism, and Macpherson grasped this. In the end, Locke's individualism will turn out to have conflicting dimensions.

Macpherson traces out the relation of property to freedom, rationality, and political authority by exploring the core elements of Locke's account of the state of nature. There are two facets to this relation, and both turn on the complex character of natural law and natural right. One involves the right to property and the change Macpherson detects in this right directly as a consequence of the introduction of money. The other involves the willingness and ability of individuals to follow the law of nature and thus to demonstrate their capacity to live rational lives. Both are connected and both turn on Locke's bringing to his account of human nature and necessary relations between individuals assumptions derived from society. And this turns out to be a more fully developed bourgeois society than what Hobbes took as his model. Macpherson's ultimate claim was that "the result of Locke's work was to provide a moral basis for a class state from postulates of equal individual natural rights."[47] This was a contradiction that flowed out of the internal dynamic of Locke's theory, specifically a contradiction at the core of his postulate of equal natural rights, and manifested itself in "his attempt to state in universal (non-class) terms, rights and obligations which necessarily had a class content."[48]

Locke's account of the natural right to property starts with the claim that God gave the earth to humankind in common for their sustenance. However, for this common grant to be of any use it must be appropriated by individuals. Hence people come to have property "in several parts" without "any express compact of all the commoners."[49] Sustenance is secured by an exclusive taking in of the earth held in common, as opposed to collective access to a common store.

In other words, individualism and property have an almost primordial link (which is why Macpherson sees Locke as perhaps the real architect of possessive individualism, although he did not go the whole way of Hobbes and reduce all moral values to market values). So Locke bases individual appropriation on self-ownership. All have property in their own person, property to which no one else has a right: "The labour of his body and the work of his hands, we may say, are properly his." What one removes from what nature has provided in common and mixed with one's own labour becomes one's own. This includes "the grass my horse has bit; the turfs my servant has cut; and the ore I digged in any place ... The *labour* that was mine, removing them out of that common state they were in, hath *fixed* my *property* in them."[50]

However, the law of nature, the law of reason that dictates that individuals ought to respect the rights of others as independent equals to life, health, liberty, and possessions, imposes certain limits on how much any individual might acquire through the exercise of personal capacities. In the first place one is entitled to appropriate from the common stock provided by nature up to the point "where there is enough, and as good, left in common for others." Second, "As much as any one can make use of to any advantage of life before it spoils, so much he may by his labour fix a property in: whatever is beyond this, is more than his share, and belongs to others." Finally, and evidently a consequence of and necessitated by the first two limitations, individuals are restricted to what they may appropriate by means of their own labour, since mixing one's labour with what nature has provided fixes one's property in it.[51] Macpherson calls these limitations: respectively, the sufficiency limitation, the spoilage limitation, and the labour limitation.

All this might imply some absolute restrictions on what any individual might hold, and thus some conception of full equality in possessions. However, Locke's subsequent argument indicates that the limitations under natural law were not intended to guarantee equal possessions or condemn unequal ones. Property in goods for consumption ("the fruits of the earth") is one thing. But property in land is quite another, and this is where Locke's real interest lies: "*As much land* as a man tills, plants, improves, cultivates, and can use the product of, so much is his *property*." And although property in land can be established in accordance with the sufficiency limitation, in reality this opens up the prospect of some with, and some without, land; i.e., it implies inequality in property holdings. Thus although God gave the earth in common, "He gave it to the use of the industrious and rational (and *labour* was to be *his title* to it) not to the fancy or covetousness of the quarrelsome and contentious." Locke is referring here to those who might wish to "free ride" on the cultivating labour of others. Moreover – and this point is tied to a normative shift in the argument from individual natural rights to social utility – what is left in common remains uncultivated (for apparently no one has an incentive to work the land unless one can possess it exclusively) and is thus of no benefit to humankind. God commanded and human wants required that humans labour, so that subduing the earth and having dominion become one. The command to subdue meant the right to appropriate; thus the conditions of human life itself required private possessions.[52]

As Macpherson notes, Locke establishes the moral basis for unlimited and thus unequal accumulation within the bounds of natural law itself and therefore in a manner consistent with the limits on acquisition. But the limitations are there and follow from the claim that under natural right and law everyone necessarily has a right to property because no one has jurisdiction over another. In other words, freedom from falling under the jurisdiction of others is tied to the necessity for everyone to appropriate. And since appropriation is based on labour, which God has commanded that everyone must undertake, it would seem that even if unequal and unlimited appropriation were in principle allowable, it would have to give way to an equal right to appropriate that in turn reflected the universal necessity to labour.

Clearly in no society has it been possible for all equally to appropriate. This would seem at first glance to render any conceivable society illegitimate from the perspective of natural law and its limitations on acquisition. (This is roughly the conclusion that Rousseau would draw.) But Locke does not take this view; indeed his purpose is to justify unlimited accumulation and inequality as natural and just. He could do so because, while initially the sufficiency limitation restricted one's holdings, something else occurred in the state of nature that transformed the character of ownership: "the same *rule of propriety (viz.)* that every man should have as much as he could make use of, would hold still in the world, without straitening any body, since there is land enough in the world to suffice double the inhabitants, had not the *invention of money*, and the tacit agreement of men to put a value on it, introduced (by consent) larger possessions and a right to them."[53]

The introduction of money "by a tacit and voluntary consent," some little piece of yellow metal that would not waste or decay, made it possible and desirable to appropriate beyond both the sufficiency and spoilage limitations. The reason why the latter is overcome is obvious: precious metals such as gold or silver do not spoil, so one might accumulate unlimited amounts of them, "the *exceeding of the bounds of his just property* not lying in the largeness of his possession, but the perishing of anything uselessly in it." Clearly the spoilage limitation did not in principle rule out large possessions. What made significantly expanded holdings possible, and even desirable, was "*the use of money*, some lasting thing that men might keep without spoiling ... that by mutual consent men would take in exchange for the truly useful, but perishable supports of life."[54] This is surely one indication of Locke struggling with the problem of how to reconcile market values with traditional natural law, even given the relatively simple argument. Consenting to the use of money is consenting to relations of exchange. Both forms of consent are for Locke natural and must therefore be in conformity with natural law. They must be at least initially consistent with the claim that no one may exercise jurisdiction over another without consent, a picture of a world of autonomous, self-contained individuals equally free and entitled to enter into relations with others while remaining as free as before. These issues complicate the apparently straightforward overcoming of the spoilage limitation.

But however straightforward overcoming this limitation might be, transcending the other two, namely the sufficiency and labour limitations, poses more of a challenge. Macpherson notes that with regard to the sufficiency limitation, the idea that individuals may appropriate only to the point at which they leave enough and as good for others, Locke was less clear and his argument underwent change over time.[55] As I read Macpherson, this is because the sufficiency and labour limitations, and hence their overcoming, are connected: both ultimately assume the presence in the state of nature of developed markets, including a market in labour.

The sufficiency limitation, recall, emerged from the fact that property went beyond the fruits of the earth to the earth itself such that "*as much land* as a man tills, plants, improves, cultivates, and can use the product of, so much is his *property*." He immediately adds: "He by his labour does, as it were, inclose it from the common."[56] The picture is of an individual appropriator and proprietor cultivating as much land as would generate a product that could be used without being wasted; "whatever is beyond this, is more than his share, and belongs to others."[57] Everyone has the right to life, that is, a right to subsistence. Appropriating land and consequently what it can produce beyond what one can use would violate this right.

However, "it is plain, that men have agreed to a disproportionate and unequal *possession of the earth*, they having, by a tacit and voluntary consent, found out a way how a man may fairly possess more land than he can use the product of, by receiving in exchange for the overplus gold and silver, which may be hoarded up without injury to any one; these metals not spoiling or decaying in the hands of the possessor. This partage of things in an inequality of private possessions, men have made practicable out of the bounds of society, and without compact." Moreover, "as different degrees of industry were apt to give men possessions in different proportions, so this *invention of money* gave them the opportunity to continue and enlarge them."[58] The incentive to accumulate ever greater amounts of land now exists and eventually results in all the land being taken up by some, while others end up without any.

But why should this incentive emerge? Why, in other words, would anyone want more than one can make use of *now* when, before the introduction of money, one wanted only what one needed and in fact could use? It is not merely the wish to hoard that accounts for this desire. Locke was a mercantilist and wanted money to stimulate trade, in other words for use as capital. Money is a commodity – it has exchange value, it can enter into exchange with other commodities. But it does not merely facilitate exchange, that is, the enlargement of trade beyond the level of barter. The value of money as something more than a mere medium of exchange is the product of consent that is rooted in the reality of its unequal distribution. It is a mechanism for the transfer of surplus: money "by compact transfers that profit, that was the reward of one man's labour, into another man's pocket."[59]

It is still contrary to natural law to appropriate more than one can use the product of before it spoils. "But now that it is possible to exchange any amount of produce for an asset which never spoils, it is neither unjust nor foolish to accumulate any amount of land in order to make it produce a surplus which can be converted to money and used as capital."[60] This is the Marxian understanding of capital as self-expanding or self-valorizing value and demonstrates once again the importance of Marx's critical approach to Macpherson's analysis.

The impetus to accumulate and thus the necessity for extensive commercial relations is starkly laid out by Locke: absent something "fit to supply the place of *money*; what reason could any one have there to enlarge his possessions beyond the use of his family, and a plentiful supply to its *consumption*, either in what their own industry produced, or they could barter for like, perishable, useful commodities, with others? Where there is not some thing, both lasting and scarce, and so valuable to be hoarded up, there men will not be apt to enlarge their *possessions of land* ... [nor] draw *money* to him by the sale of the product."[61] And this matters because, according to Locke, only land deployed as capital and brought into cultivation yields the maximum possible product – one acre under cultivation produces the equivalent of ten acres left in common and uncultivated. Indeed for Locke, one who encloses and cultivates ten acres of land and therefore produces the equivalent of one hundred "left to nature" might be said to "give" ninety acres to humankind, that is, maximize social well-being or utility.[62]

For Macpherson, this is the key to transcending the sufficiency limitation. If there is now an incentive to accumulate land beyond what is needed for the immediate consumption of the landowner and family, then the result will be that eventually all the land will be appropriated and a significant body of individuals will be unable to appropriate for themselves. This would seem to violate the law of nature. However, with the dramatically expanded productivity of land appropriated privately as capital, it now becomes possible for everyone to gain at least a minimum subsistence. And this was always the basis of the natural right and necessity to appropriate. Thus,

> if there is not enough and as good *land* left for others, there is enough and as good (indeed a better) *living* left for others. And the right of all men to a

> living was the fundamental right from which Locke had in the first place deduced their right to appropriate land … So, when the results of appropriation beyond the initial limit are measured by the fundamental test (provision of the necessities of life for all others) rather than by the instrumental test (availability of enough land for others to get the necessities of life from), appropriation beyond the limit takes on a positive virtue.[63]

The provision of "the necessities of life for others" is anything but a matter of charity. It is an issue of right, where right is explicitly tied to the (compulsive) necessity to labour that God commanded (and our wants demanded). And this is where the overcoming of the labour limitation comes to the fore. It would seem that an individual is entitled to appropriate only what one has specifically mixed one's labour with. However, from the outset, Locke counted "the turfs my servant has cut" as part of this labour, strongly suggesting that he took for granted the right to own not only one's own labour but that of others.[64]

And indeed Macpherson argues that Locke, himself a considerable man of property, most assuredly did assume the ownership of the labour of others.[65] This was both a matter of right – all had property in their own person, which necessarily entailed a right to sell or alienate one's capacity to labour – and fact – that Locke saw and accepted the widespread existence in his own time of wage labour and indeed viewed it as essential and unavoidable for the requirements of an extensive commercial economy driven by the accumulation of capital and the production relations involved. In Macpherson's view, the empirical and the normative were linked via Locke's reading back into the state of nature the social relations of a developed commercial economy, with the market for labour included with other markets.[66] "Freely" selling or alienating one's capacity to labour in exchange for a money wage is thus tied to everyone's consent to the introduction of money in the state of nature and thus its consequences, namely, inequality in property holdings and the necessity, supposedly taken up freely as a matter of right, for those without access to the means of labour to sell their labour.

Hence the state of nature has two stages, one before and one after the introduction of money. And because, on Macpherson's account, money functions as capital for Locke from the outset, conceptions of the free individual, the starting and end points of his theory, likewise shift. Or perhaps more accurately, the always present dual meaning of individualism and the tensions shaping it come to the fore in the completed picture of the state of nature. For Macpherson, Locke held together two views of individualism and freedom. On the one hand, individuals are by nature free and equal, because they cannot be rightfully subjected to the jurisdiction of anyone else without their consent. On the other hand, individuals are free insofar as they are owners of their persons and capacities, while owing nothing to society for their exercise. This dualism, which is in the nature of both/and rather than either/or, arises out of and points to a number of ambiguities in Locke's position about the state of nature and civil society.

It is well known that, explicitly parting company with Hobbes, Locke distinguishes the state of nature from the state of war. The state of nature is peaceable and governed by natural law. Indeed, as we have seen, Locke's state of nature is so significantly social that it can sustain a morally recognized right to private property and a developed market economy. Indeed individuals who live according to the demands of reason without a common superior acknowledge the limits on their behaviour essential for this kind of social order, because "truth and keeping of faith belongs to men, as men, and not as members of society."[67] The state of war, a state of enmity and destruction, is as distant from the state of nature "as a state of peace, good will, mutual assistance and preservation, and a state of enmity, malice, violence and mutual destruction, are one from another."[68]

Yet the state of nature, where there is no common superior or political authority, tends to turn into the state of war. Locke appears to make two arguments here: one in his chapter on the state of nature and the other, significantly, in his later discussion of the ends for which government is instituted, i.e., the reasons why individuals would leave the state of nature. Each roughly parallels the two dimensions of individualism and freedom. The first argument builds on Locke's admission that, in spite of the universal human capacity to adhere to the law of nature, there are "offenders" against it. These individuals demonstrate a settled design on the lives, properties, and ultimately the freedom of others and by doing so attempt to exercise absolute power over them. They are properly in a state of war with those they attack and may be destroyed as "beasts of prey."[69] Even further, Locke also notes that where there is no common superior to decide controversies between individuals, "every the least difference" is apt to end in a state of war. So however peaceable in principle the state of nature might be, it is rational for individuals to leave it and enter society.[70]

The second argument builds on this latter point. In setting out the ends for which political society and government are established, the chief of which is the preservation of property, Locke argues that individuals are and should be willing to leave the state of nature, because although one is the "absolute lord of his own person and possessions, equal to the greatest, and subject to no body," enjoyment of this right is uncertain and vulnerable to invasion by others. While all are equal, the "greater part" of humankind is "no strict observers of equity and justice," so one's property is unsafe and insecure. For an individual, the conclusion Locke draws is the same as in the first case: "It is not without reason, that he seeks out, and is willing to join in society with others, who are already united, or have a mind to unite, for the mutual *preservation* of their lives, liberties and estates, which I call by the general name, *property*."[71]

So starting out with a position apparently completely at odds with that of Hobbes, Locke ends up with an account that shares much with that of his predecessor. As Macpherson sees it, Locke's position reflects what he identifies as a two-stage account of the state of nature: before and after the introduction of money. As we have seen, once money is introduced, there emerges a class division between owners and non-owners of productive wealth in an organized commercial market society. Where Locke has in mind the first or pre-monetary stage without class division, and thus his conception of the individual as by nature equal and free of the jurisdiction of others, he views society as composed of undifferentiated equals. By contrast, when he considers the relations in place after the introduction of money, he has in mind a society no longer of undifferentiated individuals but rather one divided into two classes whose members live such dissimilar lives that there are profound natural, moral differences between them. And the conception of individuals as self-owners and proprietors now becomes the decisive one.

This is why a central and distinctive theme in Macpherson's treatment of Locke, one that links his critical political economy approach inextricably with normative political theory, is the idea that Locke necessarily assumes by virtue of his analysis a differential class rationality and consequently a class differential in rights once civil society has been established. The key here is a change in the meaning of, and the relation between, appropriation and labour. Where before the introduction of money everyone who laboured had appropriated, once money entered the scene, and with it the right to unlimited appropriation and the consequent inequality of ownership of land that left some with no land of their own to work, appropriation and labour parted company.

Where rational behaviour initially consisted of both appropriation and labour under the limitations of natural law, once these limitations had been superseded, full rationality now consisted in (unlimited) appropriation of land as capital, "which involves appropriating the surplus product of other men's labour, i.e. of the labour of those who have no land of their own."[72] Since not everyone could now appropriate, not everyone could be considered fully rational. Members of the labouring class, unable to gain the means of labour necessary for them to live, had to subject themselves to those who possessed these means. In being subjected to the wills of others, they lost their ability to order their lives in accordance with the law of reason and hence lost that full proprietorship in their persons that was the basis for natural right. Moreover Locke assumed that those with property only in their ability to labour would live hand to mouth, struggling for a bare subsistence and consequently unable to think beyond the immediately pressing demands of sheer survival.[73] In other words, appropriating and labouring became separate, with the former and not the latter embodying full rationality.

So whether individualism was held to consist in the freedom to live one's life without falling under the authority of others without one's consent, or in the ownership of one's person and capacities and what could be acquired by their exercise, with no obligation to society, those compelled to sell their labour could not be accounted as fully capable of meeting the demands of freedom and reason. It is Macpherson's distinctive claim that the origins of Locke's position lay in recognizing the class relations of his society, formulating his conceptions of freedom, reason, and agency on that basis, and then reading these back into his state of nature – that is, making them essential elements of human nature as such, in all times and places.

Hence Locke's ambiguous picture of the state of nature. When viewed from the perspective of the full rationality of those who have successfully appropriated, the state of nature appears governed by the demands of reason without the need for a common superior. When viewed from the perspective of those who exhibit only limited rationality because they lack the means to acquire, the state of nature appears more threatening, indeed more like the state of war.

Hence, too, what Macpherson sees as Locke's ambiguous account of civil society. The key issue here is the question of membership: who is fully in civil society and thus a full member of the body politic to whom political authority is ultimately accountable? Here, according to

Macpherson, Locke's equivocation on the meaning of property is critical. Where Locke defines property as including life, liberty, and estates, everyone has an interest in leaving the state of nature and entering civil society because everyone has something to protect, even if only one's life. Where Locke defines property more narrowly as goods or estates, his theory clearly addresses the needs and interests of the owning class. Thus while everyone, owner and non-owner alike, was obligated to the society, only the owners, the fully rational accumulators who enjoyed estates along with life and liberty, could be full members and enjoy full political rights.[74]

But it is important to note that the fully bourgeois picture of the rational human being as an accumulator and appropriator does not displace the autonomist account of the free individual who was not entitled to exercise arbitrary power over others without consent, or have it exercised over oneself. Both accounts of the individual – as free and equal and as a proprietor of one's person and capacities – are needed and retained. And they are needed because they capture the realities of a market society and its normative foundations. The notion of the free and equal individual translates into the idea that all are equally capable of shifting for themselves and therefore responsible for their fate. "And only if men are assumed to be equally capable of shifting for themselves, can it be thought equitable to put them on their own, and leave them to confront each other in the market without the protections which the old natural law doctrine upheld. The assumption that men are equally rational in capacity for shifting for themselves thus makes it possible to reconcile the justice of the market with the traditional notions of commutative and distributive justice [both of which Hobbes famously rejected]."[75] This conception fits with Locke's view of the state of nature as an inherently peaceable condition characterized by universal rationality, the antithesis of the state of war.

On the other hand, the conception of self-proprietorship, so central to possessive individualism, powerfully links up with the idea that rationality is not universal but class specific and therefore differs between classes. "The seventeenth-century bourgeois observer could scarcely fail to see a deep-rooted difference between the rationality of the poor and the men of some property. The difference was in fact a difference in their ability or willingness to order their lives according to the bourgeois moral code. But … this appeared to be a difference in men's ability to order their lives by moral rules as such."[76] On this reading of human nature, the state of nature appears to be a much more uncertain and insecure place where "the industrious and rational" are potentially at risk in the face of "the covetousness of the quarrelsome and contentious." Indeed it is not difficult to see Locke's "beasts of prey," the few offenders against the law of nature with settled designs on the lives and properties of others, transformed into a large and potentially dangerous body of individuals, driven by the pressures of compulsive labour in the service of the struggle for survival, and with a demonstrated inability to live according to moral demands of reason. The only guarantee of protection is to quit the state of nature and give up the individual right to enforce the law of nature to a political community and its standing rules.

And there is an additional wrinkle that Macpherson does not specifically identify or address, but that strengthens his argument and further demonstrates its complexity. If one compelling reason why rational individuals (especially property owners) would and should contract to establish civil society and political authority is the threat posed by those who would invade through covetousness, another, as noted above, is the reality that the greater part of humankind is no great observer of equity and justice. Now, obviously this includes the subordinate labouring class already convicted of lacking full rationality. But I would argue that it also includes members of the propertied class itself who pay obeisance precisely to equity and justice – these are, after all, the core elements of the bourgeois moral code – but without political authority to enforce contracts find themselves at odds with each other in ways that likewise threaten to bring on the state of war, or at least undermine property and markets. It seems to me that this reading is all the more plausible in light of the claim that in the state of nature every least difference is apt to generate conflict up to and including the state of war itself. Hence a social contract is required both to protect those with property against those without and to protect members of the bourgeois class in their competitive struggle for accumulation from each other. In a manner of speaking, to the original claim of universal rationality (however ultimately compromised by Locke's class assumptions) there could be added the claim of universal self-interest (also, to be sure, with a class dimension) – which of course Locke also advanced. What Macpherson identifies as the twin conceptions of individualism in Locke cross over and intersect in a way that reflects the reality of bourgeois society.

Possessive Individualism and the Enduring Dilemmas of Bourgeois Society

This complex analysis paves the way for what I would argue is one of the more fascinating, underappreciated, and ultimately powerfully suggestive dimensions of Macpherson's account. It is one that tells us a good deal about that account, but much more besides.

In recent years, there has been considerable emphasis placed on the individualist, libertarian side of Locke's political thought. Much of it draws upon his hugely influential theory of property and has been perhaps most visibly expressed by Robert Nozick's account of the morally primary right to property that Locke provides. This right, which exists prior to government and which no government or other organized social force ought to impair, save to provide appropriate security for individuals in the free pursuit of their private interests, has been taken up by defenders of the free market, especially market libertarian anarchists hostile to the "statist" tradition said to characterize mainstream and radical political thought. Similarly, Locke's constitutional theory, which stresses the importance of holding government accountable to civil society and permits members of the society to resist and even replace any government that oversteps its proper bounds and behaves tyrannically, has likewise enjoyed something of a renaissance.

Both readings of Locke fit well with the general shift in the last three decades towards neoliberal free market values, especially in advanced capitalist countries such as the United States and United Kingdom. And certainly there is a considerable basis for it in Locke's political thought. This is especially the case when that view is read through the prism of his conception of individualism as the right to order one's life as one sees fit, without non-consensual interference from others. This not only provides a basis for the right to individual private property, it also serves as a cornerstone of Locke's conception of constitutionally limited government since, unlike Hobbes, Locke denied that any government could exercise unlimited arbitrary power over its citizens. This was a consequence of his position that individuals in the state of nature were forbidden from claiming and exercising arbitrary power over others, and so could not transfer such power to any political authority they may set up once they agreed by contract to leave the state of nature and establish civil and political society.

The liberal individualist reading of Locke has tended to obscure another account that in the past helped shape interpretations of his work. Based on the extensive power that civil society (if not government) exercised over its members once they had contracted to form it on the basis of majority consent, this view saw Locke not as a proponent of individualism but rather as a "collectivist." In effect civil society, moved by the will of the majority, exercised an absolute sovereignty virtually equivalent to that of Hobbes's Leviathan. Locke was thus no defender of individual natural rights, but of the sanctity of the majority. Reflecting an era that had seen the emergence of Nazism and Stalinism, this interpretation viewed Locke's political thought as aligned less with liberalism or liberal democracy, and more with the so-called totalitarian democratic theory allegedly defended by Rousseau and his successors.[77] Whether Locke was a "liberal" or "totalitarian" democrat, an "individualist" or a "collectivist" was an issue Macpherson felt compelled to address, since it represented what he saw as an "unsettled problem" posed by the conflicting dimensions of Locke's political theory.[78]

Macpherson acknowledged that under the social contract rational individuals agreed to hand over to civil society all the rights and powers necessary to achieve the expansive ends for which the society was formed, with the majority as the judge. However, this did not make Locke a "collectivist" opponent of individualism. Quite the opposite: it was Locke's very individualism that made the collective supremacy of civil society necessary, because only in this way could sufficient power be mustered to counteract the potentially destructive impact of unalloyed individual self-assertion.

The key here is precisely the complex and even contradictory meanings Macpherson found in Locke's account of the individualism. "Locke's individualism does not consist entirely in his maintaining that individuals are by nature free and equal and can only be subjected to the jurisdiction of others by their own consent … Fundamentally it consists in making the individual the natural proprietor of his own person and capacities, owing nothing to society for them."[79] Under the circumstances, individualism is fully realized in accumulating property, and so the social and political authority required for it must be sufficiently strong to maintain the required institution of property. As earlier discussed, this built upon and reinforced a fundamental class division that is "natural" and thus necessarily social as well. Class membership trumps atomic individualism, including for those in the owning class.

On the surface it thus appears that everyone sacrifices freedom to order. The Hobbesian problem and its distasteful solution returns. However, as Macpherson saw it, this misses the reality that the civil society and its government are constructed by and operate on behalf of the propertied. They and they alone are full members of civil society and enjoy full political rights, including the right to vote, especially on matters of taxation.[80] Given that this is the case, and as long as government remained under their control and accountable to them, men of property could reasonably entrust individualism to the collective supremacy of the society. Locke's constitutionalism turns out to be less about guarding the rights of the individual against the state and more about protecting expanding property and the collective interests of those who hold it.

Of course this still remains, and must be, in its essentials the Hobbesian solution after all: Locke's individualism "does not exclude but on the contrary demands the supremacy of the state over the individual. It is not a question of the more individualism, the less collectivism; rather, the more thorough-going the individualism, the more complete the collectivism."[81] This insight seems to me to be as significant today as it was when Macpherson offered it up.

But if this was the Hobbesian solution, it came with a difference. Instead of a lot of isolated, atomistic individuals for whom the overwhelmingly dominant source of social and political cohesion was a state in principle all powerful, Locke's civil society enjoyed an existing natural basis of cohesion in the powerful common interest of the class of those who owned property. Spared from the need to do all the heavy lifting, Locke's state could be less powerful and intrusive. The "private" everyday economic relations of civil society did much of the work of securing compliance with the demands of order. This made Locke's solution both more empirically plausible and normatively acceptable.

There is I think an important conclusion to be drawn from this, although not one drawn explicitly by Macpherson, himself, or by his critics (especially his liberal critics, who tend to view him, as we have seen, as a socialist collectivist). This conclusion owes something to Marx and the Frankfurt School, if not most forms of Marxism. Locke may not be Hobbes, or at least fully Hobbesian. But on Macpherson's reading, what Locke does accomplish is to demonstrate that collectivism is the best a fully realized capitalist society can achieve as a form of common life. In a sense, critics such as Willmoore Kendall are correct: individualism (as autonomy) is indeed sacrificed to the collective. But this is not the triumph or consequence of a radical majoritarian democracy. In fact Macpherson considered Locke's credentials as a democrat to be highly dubious. It is instead the consequence of an unalloyed liberalism, at least where property rights trump, or more accurately define, human rights – that is, where individualism is not that of agents who are "by nature free and equal and can only be rightfully subjected to the jurisdiction of others by their own consent," but rather of one who is "the natural proprietor of his own person and capacities, owing nothing to society for them."[82]

In essence, Macpherson presents the bourgeois social order as one of pervasive and all-encompassing alienation, for the propertied and non-propertied alike. Whether and how there can be a different form of communal solidarity that is at the same time the realization of individualism, and not its ultimate denial in a collectivist social order, will prove to be a decisive if largely underdeveloped and underappreciated dimension of Macpherson's democratic theory.[83]

There is another aspect to this as well. Macpherson raised this in his attempt to address another related "unsettled problem" in Locke, namely that of the relation between individual and majority consent. As Macpherson saw it, a key indication that Locke had in mind the defence of property as such, that is, as a collective institution, was that while he noted and acknowledged (and undoubtedly encountered in his personal life) the conflict of individual interests among those with property, he could assume that "the common interest that propertied men had in the security of property was more important, and could be seen by any rational self-interested man of property to be more important, than their divergent interests as owners of land, of money, or of mercantile stock." While individual differences would still exist, "every rational man will see that he must consent to whatever is acceptable to the majority, for without this there can be ... no adequate protection for the institution of property. His self-interested rational will is to submit to the will of the majority of rational property-owners; by ellipsis, his will *is* the will of the majority."[84]

In effect this is the formula for the general will. Kendall saw Locke linked to Rousseau, and so did Macpherson. To a considerable extent, this explains Macpherson's indifference and even hostility to Rousseau as a theorist of democracy. The key difference for Macpherson that separates Rousseau from Locke is that Rousseau wanted an institution of private property that at the same time was not capitalist – that is, given over to unlimited accumulation. In effect, Rousseau wanted to hold onto the autonomist dimension of Locke's individualism, while shedding the possessive component. As Macpherson saw it, this was a delusion, an attempt to realize a simple as opposed to a possessive market society. (He viewed the Levellers as having made the same mistake.) It reflected a petit bourgeois vision of a democracy of equal, small-property-owners doomed by the very logic of the market it otherwise accepted.[85] The only outcome would be an authoritarian collectivism, a reactionary populism that would almost inevitably become more desperate as the process of capitalist development ever more ruthlessly undermined its necessary presuppositions.[86]

Whether this should be the final word on Rousseau is doubtful; certainly he has more to bring to debates about democracy than this argument would allow. For one thing, Rousseau appeared as well to see the inherent authoritarianism of a possessive market society; indeed his notion of the will-of-all might be thought the equivalent of Macpherson's conception of collectivism. And Rousseau also offers an account of liberty as independence and self-determination that has important points of contact with that of Macpherson. Nonetheless it does say something not only about Macpherson's Marxism (Marxists have been understandably hostile to Rousseau) but just as importantly his liberalism. There is more to be said about this, too. But I would note here that in seeking to move democratic theory beyond both possessive individualism and general will communalism, Macpherson shares common ground with the later efforts of Jürgen Habermas to develop a theory of radical democracy that transcends both liberal and republican models.[87]

All of these complex dimensions highlight the implications of Locke's holding simultaneously two conceptions of individualism, and thus of right and freedom, that are both equally necessary in order to get the kind of political obligation he required and yet deeply at odds in fundamental respects. For Macpherson, the consequences were monumental: "The greatness of seventeenth-century liberalism was its assertion of the free rational individual as the criterion of the good society; its tragedy was that this very assertion was necessarily a denial of individualism to half the nation."[88] And if I am correct in my reading of Macpherson's position, he was here being too restrictive: there is a sense that the other half, too, lost the capacity for free rationality that ought to be available to all.

And this I hope helps establish my key claim: that the concept of possessive individualism is not a descriptive attribute applied to various theorists, but a conceptual achievement that comes from a careful reading of the theoretical tensions in English seventeenth-century liberalism, tensions that accurately represented what was historically occurring in English society. *Possessive individualism was not defined in abstract opposition to the notion of the free, rational, and thus autonomous individual. It represented instead what happens when the two conceptions of individualism simultaneously come together, collide, interpenetrate, and come apart. This is what makes it a critical tool of analysis rather than an arbitrary, reductionist, ideologically driven imposition. It thus opens up debate about the nature of democracy and liberalism, not shuts it down.* For Macpherson, at least as he presented his case here, the debate or discussion had to start with recognition of a dilemma: "Either we reject possessive individualist assumptions, in which case our theory is unrealistic, or we retain them, in which case we cannot get a valid theory of obligation."[89]

In her introduction to *Thinking*, volume 1 of the posthumously published *The Life of the Mind*, Hannah Arendt suggested that her reflections were inspired by a Kantian question that emerged from her account of the trial of the Nazi functionary Adolf Eichmann: "After having been struck by a fact that, willy-nilly, 'put me in possession of a concept' (the banality of evil), I could not help raising the *quaestio juris* and asking myself 'by what right I possessed and used it.'"[90] In a sense Macpherson implicitly posed the same question about his own accomplishment: having come up with a concept (possessive individualism), by what right did he possess and use it? I suggest that the other dimensions of his work, particularly in the years after the publication of *The Political Theory of Possessive Individualism*, represented his attempt to answer it.

So in the end perhaps "the critic who remarked that I never write about anything except possessive individualism" ironically got it right after all.

Chapter Two

Human Nature and Democratic Possibilities: Macpherson, Ontology, and the Fate of Liberal Democracy

Today it is claimed that the bourgeois ideals of Freedom, Equality, and Justice have proven themselves to be poor ones; however, it is not the ideals of the bourgeoisie, but conditions which do not correspond to them, which have shown their untenability ... These ideas and values are nothing but the isolated traits of the rational society, as they are anticipated in morality as a necessary goal ... The content of the ideas is not eternal, but is subject to historical change ... The unity of such concepts results less from the invariability of their elements than from the historical development of the circumstances under which their realization is necessary.

Max Horkheimer

Man is not a bundle of appetites seeking satisfaction, but a bundle of energies seeking to be exerted.

C.B. Macpherson

C.B. Macpherson's account of possessive individualism was keyed to a specific task, namely, to address the lack of a coherent and binding theory of political obligation in a liberal democratic capitalist social order, or what he called a possessive market society. He felt that the development of capitalism and liberal democracy had undermined the ability of liberal democratic thought to carry out this task. As noted in the previous chapter, to use more contemporary language, which he would later also adopt, Macpherson identified the serious possibility, if not the likelihood, of a potentially permanent, deep-seated crisis of legitimacy of the liberal democratic state.[1] Tracing this to the continuing presence of possessive individualist assumptions in liberal democratic theory, which were nevertheless required as long as capitalist market relations remained dominant, he argued the need for a viable theory to establish on a new basis what he saw as the core prerequisites of a valid form of political obligation of the sort Hobbes and Locke had been able to provide for classical liberalism. These prerequisites were, respectively, the need for everyone to see oneself as equal in some fundamental way that overrode otherwise significant inequalities; and the existence of sufficient cohesion of self-interests among those with the power to make and unmake governments that was capable of offsetting the centrifugal forces of market competition. Central to both was widespread acceptance of the rightness, or at least the unavoidable inevitability, of subordination to the rules or laws of the market and the consequent commitment to market relations as the only plausible form of orderly social relations. In Macpherson's view, the emergence in the nineteenth century of a politically conscious and articulate working class armed with a different vision of society undermined, if not destroyed, these prerequisites. The working class contested the inevitability of capitalist market relations, to say nothing of the idea of equal subordination to them, and in pressing for democratic political rights challenged the exclusive political power of the bourgeoisie that had sustained cohesion in defence of private property.

Macpherson's claim is clearly indebted to the Marxian account of the core political and social contradictions of capitalist society and their historical unfolding. Nonetheless it is interesting that his starting point is the distinctively liberal issue of political obligation. The question why rational individuals ought to quit their "natural," pre-political condition and agree to obey the state is typically at the heart a liberalism that posits autonomous individual rights and interests as the starting point of political analysis. The idea of an "unencumbered self" (Michael Sandel) with no natural or pre-existing social ties is anathema to Marxists, and was to Macpherson as well. So it is anything but obvious that political obligation should be the core issue.

The Cold War setting of the 1950s and 1960s was undoubtedly decisive here. Macpherson certainly wished to promote detente between the East and West, the United States and the Soviet Union. Indeed he suggested that a plausible replacement for equal insecurity in the face of the laws of the market could be equal insecurity in the face of the threat of potential worldwide nuclear destruction.[2] Acknowledgment of this reality could go some distance towards overcoming potentially lethal conflict between the Cold War powers (as indeed it did in the 1980s). In any case, espousing openly Marxist views was not without risk, given the climate of the times. And it should not be forgotten that Macpherson always sought to address liberals on their own grounds, which to a significant extent he shared. Demonstrating that liberalism's most compelling moral commitments should lead liberals to at least question their tradition's possessive individualist inheritance and thus the social and political institutions of a possessive market society was and remained a core purpose informing his political thought.

I would like, however, to suggest another reason why Macpherson emphasized political obligation. Viewed from the perspective of his completed body of work, political obligation might best be understood as a placeholder. The task of repairing liberal democratic theory, one imposed by the immanent logic of the analysis of possessive individualism, required more than a new and viable account of political obligation in the liberal or liberal democratic tradition. It required addressing the question posed by an older tradition of political thought: what is the good life? In other words, alongside Hobbes, Mill, and Marx there is Aristotle. To be sure, I would not wish to present Macpherson as an Aristotelian in any accepted sense of the term. But there is no doubt that for him liberalism had to be supplemented by a more comprehensive account of the human situation, one that stressed not just a form of government and polity but a way of life. Indeed he will later offer a view of democracy in precisely these terms.

One possible clue that political obligation was a placeholder, and what it was holding a place for, can perhaps be found in what Macpherson did *not* say in offering as his alternative basis for obligation equal insecurity in the face of potential nuclear destruction. He took for granted that the agent who could recognize and act appropriately on this new understanding was the individual as Hobbes and Locke had more or less understood: "the self-interested individual" about whom "we postulate no more than the degree of rational understanding which it has been always necessary to postulate for any moral theory of political obligation."[3] Yet the thrust of his argument in *The Political Theory of Possessive Individualism* stressed at least implicitly the need go beyond. Self-interest would not be enough. A new form of political obligation would not be enough. There needed to be a new conception of social and political life, and a new conception of the free and rational individual. Clearly there were those then who offered alternatives. Macpherson, however, had perhaps not quite reached the point in the development of his thinking where his own conception of the needed alternatives had fully matured.

In this chapter I want to explore how Macpherson indeed went beyond political obligation and a possessive individualist understanding of freedom, reason, and human possibilities. I attempt to examine Macpherson's account of human nature, or ontology, and with this the terms most appropriate for laying out political values and institutional requirements. At the heart of Macpherson's reflections is a concept he introduced in *The Political Theory of Possessive Individualism* but did not systematically develop there: the net transfer of powers. If Macpherson's ideas are best understood in terms of a constellation and thus exist in a force field in which they are dynamically shaped and in turn shape our orientation to complex socio-historical phenomena, then the net transfer of powers locates his assumptions about human nature in relation to the possibilities for free and rational individuals in a free and rational society. As with Max Horkheimer, so with Macpherson: the unity of his concepts "results less from the invariability of their elements than from the historical development of the circumstances under which their realization is necessary." These circumstances are those that for Macpherson give rise to the need to move beyond possessive individualism and what it would mean to do so.

The Net Transfer of Powers: From Possessive Individualism to Developmental Liberalism and the Road to Democracy

Macpherson introduced the concept of the net transfer of powers in his discussion of Hobbes, where he presented it as a key feature of Hobbes's account of the necessary behaviour of individuals in a society characterized by a market in power. But he subsequently devoted considerable effort to developing and clarifying the notion, as the role it played in his political theory became increasingly important. It is for this reason that I suggest its decisive significance for Macpherson's account of human nature and not just its place in offering a critical account of existing social institutions. Or rather, its place in existing institutions is precisely why it assumes such significance in Macpherson's reflections on ontology: human nature and social structure entail and imply each other. If possessive individualism and the tensions that define it are simultaneously normative and descriptive, the net transfer of powers captures both dimensions and focuses them on questions of human flourishing and human possibilities.

To recall, Macpherson took as his starting point Hobbes's striking notion that a person's powers, roughly one's capacities to achieve one's aims or ends, was the product of market competition where one's powers contended with those of everyone else. With power understood in this way so essential to one's very identity as an agent, Hobbes argued that the value of someone was the price others would give for the use of those powers. It is ultimately the contention and potential chaos of market competition under which individuals sought both to command the powers of others and to resist the efforts of others to command theirs, with their value as persons the result of these two conflicting forces, that made society such a dynamic and threatening place and thus required the strong hand of authority to hold this competition within reasonable bounds.

Hobbes's world is one populated by self-contained, equal, and atomistic competitors, where no one could claim or establish a "natural" advantage or right to rule. This depiction remains the core of a possessive market society, which emerged from and reflects the freeing of individuals from traditional norms and practices and puts them on their own in shifting equally for themselves.[4] However, with the development of unequal socio-economic classes characterized by ownership and non-ownership of the means of life and labour, the market for power is "socialized." The transfers that occur are systematic and institutionalized as unequal relations between classes. Hence, when "an increasing proportion of the population becomes dependent on selling its labour," those with capital and land "can therefore, by employing the labour of others, get a net transfer of some of the powers of others (or some of the product of those powers) to themselves."[5]

Moreover, if an individual, in order to be human in the basic sense of maintaining one's existence, must have access to the means of labour, then one's powers "must therefore by definition include access to the means of labour. A man's powers are therefore reduced when he has less than free access to the means of labour. If he can get no access, his powers are reduced to zero, and in a competitive society he ceases to exist. If he can get access, but not freely, his powers are reduced by the price he has to pay for access, and that price measures the amount of his power that is transferred to another."[6]

It is evident from this observation that Macpherson's conception of powers and their transfer has both empirical and normative components. He stressed here the measurable dimensions of this transfer, an approach consistent with the clearly quantitative dimension of

Hobbes's work and the objectifying and quantifying operations of the market mechanism. However, the reference to what is required for one to be fully human – and in particular the need for access to the means of labour – raises normative issues of appropriate forms of human existence and experience. Along with the quantitative measure of the net transfer of powers there was a qualitative aspect that needed to be recognized and theorized, if the full impact of possessive individualist assumptions and practices was to be captured, and the possibilities for transforming and moving beyond the requirements of a possessive market social order were to be identified.

Macpherson came to recognize the limits of his original position and the need to explore more fully and concretely the underdeveloped normative dimension. This is why, in my view, the net transfer of powers constitutes an important link between the analysis of possessive individualism and the development and elaboration of his theory of democracy, and why therefore it forms a core element of Macpherson's concern with ontology.

Macpherson began to more fully flesh out the net transfer of powers in his 1965 book, *The Real World of Democracy*, the published version of his Massey Lectures for the Canadian Broadcasting Corporation. Much in this brief study is dated or dubious, notably his distinguishing among three models of "real world" democracy: liberal, non-liberal communist, and non-liberal underdeveloped (i.e., populist or Third World). As was the case with *The Political Theory of Possessive Individualism*, his approach reflected his commitment to detente in the Cold War setting of the time, the need for rapprochement between East and West (and now with the non-capitalist, non-communist countries included). Macpherson now presented this need as a moral imperative for capitalist liberal democracies engaged, he argued, in a competition with non-liberal states with what he saw as influential alternative claims to the mantle of democracy. There was, he believed, a level of urgency to this competition for liberal democracies, which faced an increasingly serious normative deficit arising out of the continuing, and now outmoded, presence of possessive individualist assumptions and practices.

In light of subsequent historical developments, this claim is clearly an artefact of the era, with little significance for contemporary concerns or debates.[7] However, it did provide the scaffolding upon which Macpherson erected a more detailed and suggestive account of the meaning and content of human powers and the nature of the net transfer of powers. And this would subsequently inform further development of the idea.

Central to Macpherson's account of liberal democracy is the claim that, like all political orders, it is a double system of power: a set of enforceable rules under which individuals are prevented from physically interfering with others, and under which the state holds a monopoly on the legitimate use of force or constraint; and a set of mechanisms by which it maintains social relations of power between individuals and groups, that is, relations outside the state. These are primarily relations of property. In other words, a liberal democratic system enforces order both between contentious individuals and between at least potentially contentious social classes.

Macpherson's argument, which I suggest continues to be of considerable interest, is that while all political systems are double systems of power, with the rise of the liberal (later, liberal democratic) state, the second "face" of power underwent a significant change.[8] In the precapitalist era, social power was directly political power: "In any society where the whole work of the society is authoritatively allocated to people in different quantities, and where the whole product is authoritatively distributed between them in a way that does not correspond to the different contributions they have made, it is easy to see that there is a power relation between people, which is being enforced by the state. In such a society, some men are getting the benefit of some part of the powers of other men."[9] Significantly this transfer of benefit "is easily enough seen in societies where the ownership of the means of labour is legally restricted to certain ranks or classes."[10]

However, things changed once the triumph of liberalism did away with what Macpherson in *The Political Theory of Possessive Individualism* had called the authoritative allocation of work and reward, that is, once status or customary society gave way to the possessive market social order. Now the state, as before, sustains and enforces the rules required for the successful maintenance of a certain set of social relations. But because these relations are "free" relations among property owners entitled to enter their commodities into market exchange in pursuit of the best deal for themselves, they lack the visibly compulsive character of earlier social relations sustained by political authority. In other words they are no longer about power, or at least political power, which is the purview of the state. There is now, apparently, only one system of power, that of the coercive regulation of relations between individuals in order to maintain the security of persons and property. What was once seen as the task of exercising power qua the authoritative allocation of work and reward is now changed. "The job of the liberal state is simply to protect and enforce the mechanism of free contract, and to ensure each the right to such property as he can acquire by his labour and by his contracts." The relations involved "do not appear to be relations by which some people are enabled to transfer part of the powers of others to themselves."[11]

Here Macpherson drew upon his analysis in *Possessive Individualism* to make the point that, however hidden, there is in the capitalist market society a compulsive net transfer of powers between owners and non-owners of the means of labour. And, as before, he noted that if "a man's powers must include access to the means of labour, then his powers are diminished when he has less than free access to the means of labour." But he now added something else, namely, a more explicit statement of exactly why one's powers are diminished by lack of such access. He began to point in the direction of a critical theory of power and powers that will prove decisive for his treatment of ontology and his subsequent conception of a radically reformulated theory of democracy.

The obvious objection to Macpherson's claim of a net transfer of powers, even in a possessive market society without an explicitly political allocation of work and rewards, is that under the rule of free competition among legal equals everyone gets exactly the value of the individual's contribution to the productive effort of the society. Under market rules each is treated justly, at least where the market is functioning freely and properly. There can be, in the circumstances, no transfer of powers.

For Macpherson, this is indeed the case – but only if

> you take the powers of a man to be simply the strength and skill which he possesses ... But if you take the powers of man to be not just the strength and skill he possesses, but his ability to use that strength and skill to produce something, the case is altogether different. For then his powers must include not only his *capacity* to labour (that is, his strength and skill) but also his *ability* to labour, his ability to use his strength and skill ... [and] a human being, to be human, must be able to use his strength and skill for purposes he has consciously formed.[12]

This is why access to the means of labour is so decisive: it is not sufficient to simply possess strength and skills, or even to exercise them at the behest of someone else who provides such access on (market) terms they are able to set via "free" competition. Of course where one lacks property in the means of labour, one has, in order to live, little choice but to obtain access on terms set by the market, i.e., by those who own these means. And in the circumstances, this necessarily involves a transfer of powers, an indirect authoritative allocation of work and rewards, even without a central and visible authority, that is, an institution of formal political power.

As dependent as it is on the analysis in *Possessive Individualism*, the argument here represents a subtle but significant shift. Appropriately human powers are now powers that are not only owned and exercised, but exercised for one's own conscious purposes. This is a step in the direction of bringing Macpherson's conception of powers more fully and explicitly in conformity with the twin dimensions of individualism discussed in the previous chapter: individualism as self-possession and as self-direction (i.e., autonomy).

But it is only a step, because Macpherson here does not spell out as fully as needed what it is about formulating and carrying out conscious purposes that requires free access to the means of labour. It is obviously coherent and meaningful to speak of conscious purposes in the context of the sale of one's labour as a commodity (as Macpherson indeed will subsequently acknowledge in his account of one powerful strain of liberal democratic ontology). Nonetheless, Macpherson here gives us a sense of why and how there can be a net transfer of powers, even under ostensibly free market relations where there is no formal and explicit coercion. The sense he conveys is that powers exist fully only in their exercise and in this exercise manifest something of the essential character of what it means to be a free and rational being.

And although he does not pursue this line of analysis, Macpherson also implies that one's powers must be exercised cooperatively if they are to be sufficiently rich to meet the historically emerging possibilities for free and rational individual action. While strength, skills, and other capacities can be, and typically in a capitalist market society are, possessions to be deployed strategically in a competitive context, they are diminished when so understood and exercised. In other words, powers are not fixed entities unchanged by the mode through which they are exercised, be it competitively or cooperatively. They are rather more modalities of experience that involve possibilities for individual development. From Macpherson's perspective, relating to one's own powers and capacities strictly as an owner – that is, viewing oneself as a commodity and acting accordingly – limits one's possibilities, because commodification involves certain restrictive forms of interaction. This restriction lies precisely in the inability to deploy one's capacities according to one's conscious purposes that has an intrinsic value not captured by quantitative measures of market returns. This is obscured by the obvious fact that capitalism "has been enormously more productive than any previous system, and so has been able to afford a higher material standard for everybody than could any previous system." This greater productivity "can, and generally does, more than offset the transfer of part of their powers from the working force, at least for all except the lowest one-quarter or so who are at or below the poverty line."[13] And as it will turn out, this enhanced productivity, historically unprecedented, will come to be seen by Macpherson as shaping the acquisitiveness of those who manifest possessive individualist qualities most fully.

Yet the net transfer remains. It is quantitative – it can be measured – but more importantly, qualitative. It is and must be possible "to conceive of a system in which high productivity does not require the transfer of powers from non-owners."[14] However lucratively compensated, there is no possibility of fully offsetting the loss occasioned by the transfer of powers. This goes beyond the fact that, even in the most fully advanced welfare state, "if welfare transfers get so large as to eat up profits there would be no more incentive to capitalist enterprise, and so no more capitalist enterprise."[15] The compulsive nature of the transfer, which must continue if capitalist relations are to be maintained, necessarily raises the question of the meaning and reality of freedom and equality. This is so, even if participation in these relations is "voluntary," as compared to the explicitly visible authoritative allocation of work and rewards characteristic of customary or status society.

Clearly this line of argument once again owes much to Marx. But it also points to the dilemmas and challenges of individualism, a value Macpherson never wavered from defending. And it is still not clear exactly how individualism was to be conceived in light of the apparent necessity to transcend capitalist relations in order to eliminate the net transfer of powers. In short, it remained unclear, or at least insufficiently argued, why the loss of control over the use of one's powers not only undermined their exercise but altered their meaning in destructive ways. But the path to clarifying the meaning of human powers was beginning to come more fully into focus.

A clue to where Macpherson was going can be found in his discussion in *The Real World of Democracy* of what he called the "myth" of maximization: the claim that the capitalist market will, if permitted to function properly, maximize the production and distribution of material utilities. For Macpherson, this involved two claims: that the market maximizes aggregate utility, and that it does so equitably. Neither holds up. The first claim fails because of the inability to establish interpersonal comparisons of utility. The second, and its failure, gets to the heart of the mythical status of the claim, because it highlights the preconditions such maximization required: "First, the market can only be shown to maximize utilities when a certain income distribution is taken as given: the market can only maximize the satisfactions people can afford to buy. And secondly, the market cannot reward people in proportion to the energy and skill they expend, since it has to reward ownership as well. It has to look after the transfer of powers."[16]

But while he mentioned the transfer of powers here, his primary focus was elsewhere. What rendered maximization mythical was that it reflected the entrenchment under capitalism of a distinctive and morally dubious conception of the human essence as consisting in possession or acquisition, at the heart of which is the individual maximization of satisfactions. Such maximization was seen as the epitome of rational action. This, Macpherson argued, theoretically and historically displaced the "traditional idea, which goes back as far as Aristotle" that "the human essence is activity in pursuit of a conscious, rational purpose."[17] The mythical element here seemed to have, for Macpherson, two dimensions. One is the idea that the other, non-liberal conceptions of democracy then in his view extant – the communist and underdeveloped models – challenged the notion of market-based maximization as the essence of rational behaviour in a democratic society, and did so in the name of something like the traditional conception of the human essence. In clinging to the myth of maximization, existing liberal democracies, and the theory justifying them, were threatened in the face of worldwide moral and ideological competition from the other two alternatives.

The other dimension, though, might well hold more promise for a contemporary appraisal of Macpherson's position. In effect Macpherson claimed that the theory of market-based maximization presents the competitive maximization of utilities as universal, universally true, and timeless. However, this view flies in the face not only of the supposed reality of competition with other models, as well as the traditional notion of the human essence, but also of that element of liberalism indebted to the natural law tradition that stressed autonomous self-direction.

Although not fully, or fully enough, drawn together, the core elements of Macpherson's account of ontology – the net transfer of powers and two competing conceptions of the human essence – had been put into play. They needed further development and clarification. The net transfer of powers would provide the key.

Macpherson further refined his analysis in an essay entitled, appropriately enough, "The Maximization of Democracy."[18] To the earlier claim that the liberal democratic state and society maximize utility he now added an additional claim: that Western, liberal democracies in addition maximize individual powers. Both claims are joined in the theory justifying liberal democratic institutions and practices. While the former claim embodied the principles of classical (economic) liberalism, the latter represented a necessary addition to the theory once the liberal state had been democratized. Macpherson's point – still framed in this essay by the idea that there was a worldwide competition between alternative models of democracy – was that the two maximizing claims existed uneasily and in fact contradicted each other. But given the history and institutions of liberal democracy, where "liberalism" meant "capitalism," they were equally entrenched and equally unavoidable. This made the justifying theory of liberal democracy defective, indeed unstable.

Clearly this restates the argument from *Possessive Individualism* that liberal democratic theory and its conception of political obligation needed to be dramatically recast. Yet there was now a shift in the focus of the argument, away from a primary concern with political obligation and towards a more explicit and extensive account of human fulfilment and the social relations needed to accomplish it. Recall that in making his case in *Possessive Individualism* for a new, binding basis for obligation, Macpherson had argued that the individual to whom a proposal for this new basis would have to be put was the self-interested, instrumentally rational, essentially Hobbesian individual. But that would not do here. In broadening the focus in the way he did, Macpherson made his task both more extensive and more difficult. First of all, he had to broaden the understanding of self-interest in a context in which, because of the strength of possessive individualist commitments and practices, the utilitarian maximizing claim exerted a powerful impact. Second, he had to demonstrate that there were in fact two maximizing claims, that maximizing utilities was not the same as maximizing individual powers. Third, even if this were successful, Macpherson needed also to demonstrate that there is a significant cost to thwarting the maximization of individual powers, and that this cost could be overcome by institutional change that was realistic and historically plausible.

The argument thus had to be both theoretically compelling and normatively appealing. Macpherson sought to address these challenges by offering more complex, and, he clearly believed, more accurate, accounts of how human powers might be and should be understood. The point was to show that however wedded we might be to Hobbesian self-interest and utilitarian maximization, we are always and already committed – in ways that, to be sure, needed to be made clearer and more specific – to a different understanding of our powers and their exercise and development. In order to be persuasive, Macpherson drew out more specifically than before a distinction that I have suggested was implicit in his conception of powers all along: a distinction between an empirical or descriptive and a normative understanding of powers. In this essay Macpherson wrote of and contrasted a *descriptive* conception of powers and an *ethical* one. He linked this treatment of powers to the net transfer of powers and moved into a consideration of competing notions of the human essence.

By the descriptive conception of powers of an individual, Macpherson meant essentially what Hobbes meant:

> his present means, however acquired, to ensure future gratification of his appetites ... [This] includes his natural capacities *plus* whatever additional powers (means to ensure future gratifications) he has acquired by getting command over the energies and skill of other men, or *minus* whatever part of his energies and skill he has lost to some other men ... One man's powers, defined as his present means to get what he wants in the future, will include the command he has acquired over other men's energies and skills; another will include merely what is left of his energy and skill after some of it has been transferred to others.[19]

This concept of powers is descriptive in two senses: it identifies one's powers as a datum to be taken as given, and it offers no judgment as to the appropriateness of how these powers are acquired or distributed, or whether or not their acquisition and exercise conforms to some standard of moral rightness beyond their potential to ensure future gratifications.

Yet since one's powers include whatever energies and skills have been transferred from others (net of one's own energies and skills transferred in a like manner to others), it was evident for Macpherson that no descriptive conception of powers can ever truly be merely that. As understood here, the descriptive notion, in the words of Charles Taylor, "secretes a notion of the good, and a set of valuations, which cannot be done away with."[20] The descriptive conception of powers is explicitly and inextricably intertwined with the net transfer of powers, which Macpherson identified with the compulsive character of market competition in a possessive market society.

The suppressed normative dimension comes out clearly in Macpherson's other conception, the ethical. This continues the line of thought Macpherson had suggested in *The Real World of Democracy*, when he alluded to the idea of exercising one's capacities according to one's own conscious purposes and had identified it with pre-liberal, classical notions of the human essence. The ethical conception "is based on the proposition that the end or purpose of man is to use and develop his uniquely human attributes or capacities ... A man's powers, in this view, are his potential for realizing the essential human attributes said to have been implanted in him by Nature or God, not (as with Hobbes) his present means, however acquired, to ensure future gratification of his attributes." Macpherson went on to argue that this notion of powers, "being a concept of a potential for realizing some human end, necessarily includes in a man's powers not only his natural capacities (his energy and skill) but also his *ability* to exert them. It therefore includes *access* to whatever things outside himself are requisite to that exertion. It must therefore treat as a diminution of a man's powers whatever stands in the way of realizing his human end, including any limitation of that access."[21]

Thus both accounts of powers and their maximization are linked, indeed are defined in relation to each other. The question of access to what is necessary for the exercise of one's powers, and specifically access to the means of labour, cements this tie. It is important to see how, in my view, this plays into Macpherson's analysis, for there are elements here that are not so easily seen and that, to be sure, Macpherson did not fully spell out at this point in the argument. Specifically, and touching upon currently significant critical appraisals of Marx and classical Marxism, Macpherson seemed to establish his position on two bases: a "productivist" or labour model of human fulfilment, and a subject-object conception of human agency.

I think that ultimately Macpherson's position is not necessarily restricted to these assumptions and turns out to be more open to other possibilities than might appear to be the case. But there were certain implications that were not fully pursued here. It is obvious that the economic class relations of a capitalist society, under which capital in its primary social form is the control by one class of access to what is needed to produce utilities, and so those denied access lose control over their ability to labour and the purposes to which it is put, stands at the heart of the critique of the descriptive concept of powers. But we should note what Macpherson saw as the circumstances, material and cultural, that gave rise to this situation. He attributed the emergence of this class relation to the setting up of a virtually unconditional individual right to unlimited appropriation (i.e., private property). The prospect of unlimited acquisition set in motion the play of individual natural capacities, which, because of their inherently unequal distribution, led to the concentration of ownership of the means of labour in the hands of a few. This was, he argued, a product of, and a contributor to, the commitment to unlimited productivity growth in pursuit ultimately of the satisfaction of unlimited desires. Limitless desire, in the face of which there would always be scarcity, was, under the assumptions of competitive individualism, the essence of rational behaviour and thus central to the claim that liberal (democratic) society maximizes utilities. The assumption of the rationality of infinite desire "may be said both to have produced the capitalist market society and to have been produced by that society."[22]

This turns out to be a key point, in part because infinite desire, while real, is not necessarily timeless or transcendent. Macpherson once again demonstrated here the influence of Marx. While the assumption of infinite desire has been necessary to get the level of productivity capitalism has been responsible for generating, the need for it was now receding in the face of the historically unprecedented possibilities for meeting the material requirements of all members of society that capitalist development has spawned. Similarly, scarcity, which existed in relation to infinite desire, and which under capitalism has been "a contrived but useful goad,"[23] could likewise be de-emphasized if not jettisoned altogether.

Macpherson emphasized these questions, as he was to do throughout his later work. But other implications have considerable significance for his more fully developed approach to democratic theory, and they involve powers and needs.

Macpherson's descriptive concept of power makes clear that, as in Hobbes, one's power is very much power over others, or at least the function of the capacity to resist having one's own powers commandeered by others. This sets up what amounts to a fateful dynamic that is ultimately political. In the circumstances of capitalist market competition, one's very possibilities for free agency hinge on success in the competitive struggle. This reality is hidden by and within the claim that liberal democratic society maximizes utilities; it is the other side of the failure to maximize aggregate utilities or to do so equitably. The quest to maximize or exercise one's powers on the descriptive concept of powers is doomed to be frustrated by the very nature and conditions of the quest. The fundamental claim of liberalism, whatever its guise, is to provide the conditions for, and facilitate the exercise of, individual freedom. As Macpherson noted, this promise of freedom was, from the beginning of the transition to a possessive market social order, the spur to move from the authoritative allocation of work and reward to freedom of choice. However, over the course of the development of capitalism, freedom was undermined. This not only took the form of material inequality that was both the product of and reinforced the development of private property and the consequent emergence of distinct classes of owners and non-owners of the means of labour. It was also evident in the requirement to accumulate and exercise power as the beneficiary of the net transfer of powers. Freedom turned into compulsion.

This is obvious for those denied access to the means of labour. But it is also true, if less obviously, for those who command this access and whose own fortunes hinge on the continuing ability to make over the powers of others. Liberal or liberal democratic society always threatens, as Hobbes saw and as Macpherson argued in *The Political Theory of Possessive Individualism*, to turn authoritarian both at the level of the economy and society and at the level of the state. This is another way of highlighting the tension between individualism as freedom from non-consensual subjection to others, and individualism as natural proprietorship of one's person and capacities, with nothing owed to society for them. Or as Macpherson put it, "the transfer of powers which is produced by the assumption of unlimited desire contradicts the moral principle implicit in the value judgement ... that individual freedom is preferable to authoritative allocation of work and reward."[24] Freedom as self-ownership collides with freedom as self-determination.

Freedom as self-determination or self-actualization is at the core of the ethical conception of powers. But the shift to the ethical from the descriptive conception not only points to a different understanding of freedom and a different moral focus, one that challenges the morality of competitive acquisitiveness. It also involves a shift in the nature of theoretical reflection itself. Here again we touch upon what I have called Macpherson's suppressed philosophical dimension. Although he did not identify it and make it an explicit meta-methodological concern, the move is in the direction of a theory both more historical and dynamic, and more tentative. One's powers on this view, recall, are one's *potential* to realize human attributes; and the *ability* to exercise these powers depends upon *access* to the means needed for their exercise, "whatever things outside himself are requisite to that exertion." Such a theory would seem to lose the rigour associated with the formulation of logically connected propositions derived from and consonant with the facts of the situation being empirically investigated and theoretically comprehended. As Macpherson saw, moving from the descriptive to the ethical conception of human powers meant confronting the "physical" facts of a market society, where no transfer or diminution of powers was visible, with what might be called the moral facts associated with what, from an Hegelian perspective, might be called a rational universal: "the proposition that the end or purpose of man is to use and develop his uniquely human attributes or capacities." The former facts seemed much more solid (hence the criticisms of Kenneth Minogue), the latter less so, if indeed they could be called facts at all.

But giving the ethical conception of powers its proper place required that it be articulated in a way that at least matched if not exceeded the power of the given facts. This was the task of theory in the historical setting Macpherson saw himself as inhabiting. This setting generated the problems to be confronted, but it also provided the tools and evidence for this task to be carried out in a manner faithful to the charge Macpherson had already set: to put the justificatory theory of liberal democracy on more secure empirical and normative grounds.

To repeat, Macpherson did not focus systematically or self-consciously on the meta-methodological or meta-theoretical issues involved, nor was he inclined to do so. To be sure he did give us a clue that such issues were not totally foreign to him. To recall, the descriptive concept of powers could identify "no diminution of a man's powers in denying him access in order to use his capacities, for his powers are measured after such diminution has taken place."[25] The given facts did not, as it were, fully speak for themselves. Any claim to scientific exactitude based on them had to, at the very least, be called into question.

In other words, even given the absence of such theoretical self-consciousness, Macpherson's approach and account here point to the distinction between traditional and critical theory. This distinction is central to the work of the Frankfurt School of critical theory and in particular Max Horkheimer. A brief exploration of Horkheimer's position may help clarify and deepen our understanding of Macpherson's concerns.[26]

C.B. Macpherson and Max Horkheimer: Traditional Theory, Critical Theory, Moral Possibilities, and Human Nature

Max Horkheimer's account of the distinction between traditional and critical theory was a core component of the attempt by the Institute for Social Research at the University of Frankfurt to reconsider the philosophical foundations of Marxism in the face of both historical changes in capitalism and the failure of classical Marxism to provide an adequate treatment of subjectivity, class consciousness, and culture, and thus the basis of revolutionary political action and social change. For the critical theorists, theoretical activity, like practical activity, was both embedded in and a product of a changing social and historical reality. Theoretical constructions were elements of concrete social life. Their modification was not a self-contained intellectual decision triggered by the demands of pure reason, but rather a response to objective necessity. While it is usually assumed that necessity stands at odds with freedom, as the critical theorists understood it such necessity was not opposed to freedom, but instead presupposed a form of it that was admittedly yet to be.

When Horkheimer formulated his classic statement of critical theory in his 1937 essay, "Traditional and Critical Theory," and contrasted it with traditional theory, he defined it in opposition to "Cartesianism." For most researchers, theory was "the sum total of propositions about a subject, the propositions being so linked with each other that a few are basic and the rest derive from these. The smaller the number of primary principles in comparison with the derivations, the more perfect the theory ... The general goal of all theory is a universal systematic science, not limited to any particular subject matter but embracing all possible objects ... The order in the world is captured by a deductive chain of thought." Theory, then, was "a systematically unified set of propositions taking the form of a systematically unified deduction."[27]

What separated traditional theory, whether rationalist or empiricist, from the critical approach was its emphasis on theory construction from the standpoint of an external observer. Following the model of the natural sciences, the ideal of pure theory was the subsumption of particular facts under causal laws that in the best case could be expressed mathematically. Applied to the social sciences, this ideal dictated that inquiry would be and had to be "value free." The social context of the theory remained external to the theory itself.

By contrast, critical theory incorporated in its very structure a specific goal: the realization of a rational society. Theory was not value free but constituted "an essential element in the historical effort to create a world which satisfies the needs and powers of men."[28] In this, critical theory drew on the materialist position of Marx, and in particular his critique of political economy. According to Horkheimer, from this perspective social facts are internal to the material life processes within which social actors are always and already embedded as participants. Critical theory so understood aims to grasp its own activity from the standpoint of a member of society. While it takes society as its object, it does so in a way that changes the relation of the "subject" to the "object" of inquiry. Because it conceives facts not as "stand-alone" data but rather as intrinsic to the perspective of the participant in social life, critical theory has to maintain a reflexive relation to the social subjects, who are at the same time the objects of the theory. It seeks to overcome the separation of the role of the detached theorist from that of the citizen. The theorist is both an analyst and a member of society. The goal of theory is not the achievement of systematic purity, but rather the elucidation of the social process in its interconnections and developmental tendencies.

As with Marx's critique of political economy, critical theory is thus a form of immanent critique. That is, critique is tied to material practices and associated meanings as they are experienced by members of society and in terms of which they understand themselves and their actions. Both practices and meanings implicitly possess contradictory dimensions that can manifest perceived threats to the integrity of the self, while at the same time pointing towards the normative conditions for self-fulfilment. The point of view of critique is therefore established from "inside" the structures of social life and meaning themselves. Taking the normative standards proclaimed by a culture on their own terms, immanent critique seeks to demonstrate that these standards are self-contradictory: their actual realization in the structures of social life denies the very claim to normative appropriateness by which they are ostensibly justified.

Critique is not therefore based on an abstract "ought" or norm by means of which society is judged, but begins instead from the "consciousness" of subjects in relation to the ideals and developmental tendencies of the social order. It attempts to show how the rational and emancipatory content of these tendencies cannot be realized within the current (capitalist) social structure.

A more extensive treatment of critical theory generally and its relation to Macpherson's ideas must await my later discussion in chapter 6. However, two of Horkheimer's claims from "Traditional and Critical Theory" warrant attention here, because I believe they reflect key elements of Macpherson's overall approach to the questions at issue in this chapter as well.

The first claim revolves around the question of what might be called critical theory's partisan character. According to Horkheimer, everyday consciousness imbibes of the concepts produced by and reflective of the social process, and in particular the process of work, within which agents are embedded. It is the same social process that provides the (largely unexamined) context and content of traditional theory. These concepts have an intrinsic appeal – they seem transparent, unproblematic, stable, and unchangeable in the same way that society does. On the other hand, the concerns of critical theory and its concepts – Marxist categories such as "class," "exploitation," and "surplus value" – are also the concerns of most people "but are not recognized to be such." They aim at the transformation of the existing social order, not its preservation. "Consequently, although critical theory proceeds at no point arbitrarily and in chance fashion, it appears, to prevailing modes of thought, to be subjective and speculative, one-sided and useless. Since it runs counter to prevailing habits of thought, which contribute to the persistence of the past and carry on the business of an outdated order of things ... it appears to be biased and unjust."[29]

Horkheimer's second claim involves the core justification for critique. As he puts it,

> The critical theory of society is, in its totality, the unfolding of a single existential judgment. To put it in broad terms, the theory says that the basic form of the historically given commodity economy on which modern history rests contains in itself the internal and external tensions of the modern era; it generates these tensions over and over again in an increasingly heightened form; and after a period of progress, development of human powers, and emancipation for the individual, after an enormous extension of human control over nature, it finally hinders further development and drives humanity into a new barbarism.[30]

Both the critical appraisal of the existing state of affairs, including its "unreality" and apparent bias and injustice, and the "existential judgment" are central to Macpherson's political thought, even if he did not give these dimensions systematic philosophic expression. And there is another element of this as well, one particularly germane to Macpherson's ethical conception of powers and its relation to historical forms of human nature. (On this issue Macpherson may well, in certain respects, be the more explicit of the two.) It involves the extent to which both thinkers unfold their critical accounts out of the dialectic of individualism. In this context, questions of ethics and morality and their relation to practical reason are decisive. Here, too, Horkheimer's more systematic philosophically informed treatment of moral questions and their socio-historical roots and dimensions can illuminate Macpherson's concerns. Before moving on to an exploration of the link in Macpherson's position between powers and ontology, I want to take a final look at Horkheimer's contribution to this aspect of Macpherson's work. Two pieces are significant here: "Materialism and Morality" and "Egoism and Freedom Movements: On the Anthropology of the Bourgeois Era." Taken together, these essays link individualism, morality, and moral philosophy with the historical development of capitalist society, a link Macpherson makes as well. In other words, they suggest how an ethical conception of human powers connects with the question of human nature.

Leftist and socialist thought, and especially Marxism, has had a complex relation to questions of morality and ethics. As I noted in chapter 1, it has generally criticized if not dismissed morality – roughly those standards by which individuals ought to appraise their actions as right or wrong – as bourgeois ideology in the service of maintaining the structures, values, and practices of class domination. On the other hand, the radical democratic and socialist critique of capitalism as exploitive seems to clearly express moral condemnation. Certainly there are and have been socialists and socialist sympathizers, even Marxists, who have condemned capitalism and advocated for socialism on the grounds that the capitalist system is unjust and inhumane. And whatever the status of moral claims as such, morality itself is normally understood in materialist terms as a historical form. It is viewed as the product of the development of bourgeois society and the consequent freeing up of the individual, now seen as an autonomous agent capable, as in Locke, of rationally recognizing and acting on the basis of and in conformity with transcendent laws or standards. As Horkheimer puts it, "Autonomously attempting to decide whether one's actions are good or evil is plainly a late historical phenomenon ... The social life process of the modern period has presently so advanced human powers that in the most developed countries, at least the members of certain strata are capable, in a relatively wide range of their existence, not merely of following instinct or habit but of choosing autonomously among several possible aims."[31]

For Horkheimer, morality and moral consciousness, especially in their most advanced form in the philosophy of Kant, express the "spiritual situation" of the bourgeois era. To be sure, morality was shaped by the requirements of maintaining a stable social structure and its class relations. Kant's distinction between duty and interest, and his claim that to act morally required that one follow the dictates of duty, or the moral law, in indifference to one's (self-) interest had a class character. Conformity to duty in denial of interest was demanded of members of the subordinate classes, whose interests were sacrificed to the requirements of social domination, while members of the bourgeoisie were permitted and indeed required to pursue *their* interests. But morality was not simply a ruse, "false," a form of propaganda created by and for the dominant classes and designed to keep the dominated in check. The emergence of morality and the demand that one autonomously judge good and evil, right and wrong, from the vantage point of the universal demands of the moral law and the categorical imperative, and hence act out of duty and not interest, reflected the reality that under capitalism there was a split between particular and general interests. Particular interests seemed clearer, "truer," whereas the demands of the general interest were obscure, because while the social order was reproduced by the actions of individuals, the process of reproduction unfolded behind their backs. The individual "cannot recognize himself in his true connection to it and knows himself only as an individual whom the whole affects somewhat, without it ever becoming clear how much and in what manner his egoistic activity actually affects it."[32] There appears no clear connection between individual choices and actions and social outcomes or the character of the social whole.

Horkheimer describes the overall social context in terms that strikingly recall Macpherson's account of possessive individualism:

> The social whole lives through unleashing the possessive instincts of all individuals. The whole is maintained insofar as individuals concern themselves with profit and with the conservation and multiplication of their

> own property. Each is left to care for himself as best as he can. But because each individual must produce things that others need in the process, the needs of the community as a whole end up being addressed through activities that are apparently independent of one another and seem only to serve the individual's own welfare. The circumstance that the production and maintenance in this order coincide with the subjects' striving after possessions is a fact that has left its impression upon the psychic apparatus of its members ... Even in the most refined form and seemingly remote impulses of the individual, the function he performs in society still makes itself felt. In this era, economic advantage is the natural law under which individual life proceeds.[33]

Under the circumstances where the "life of the general public arises blindly, accidentally, and defectively out of the chaotic activity of individuals, industries, and states," that is, as an apparent fact of nature, and where this state of affairs "expresses itself in the suffering of the majority of human beings," morality is at one and the same time both necessary and ineffective.[34] In response to Kant and his "impossible concept of an eternal command addressed to the free subject" Horkheimer bluntly claims, "Binding moral laws do not exist."[35] Even were all individuals to govern their actions by what they took to be the moral law and the categorical imperative, nothing would change. The irrationality of the social order reproduced blindly by the actions of competitive individuals would trump the best intentions of moral agents.

Nonetheless, morality – even in Kant's work – points towards a future condition of genuine harmony, as opposed to the concatenation of interests under market competition: "In an epoch in which the domination of the possessive instincts is the natural law of humanity, and in which by Kant's definition each individual sees the other above all as a means to his own ends, morality represents the concern for the development and happiness of life as a whole."[36] This could ultimately come about only after the existing irrational "antagonistic economic form" is replaced by "a social life form in which productive property is administered in the general interest not just out of 'good intentions' but with rational necessity."[37] Nonetheless there are covetous anticipations of such development and happiness in the existing society. Horkheimer cites evidence of "moral sentiments," even in the fully developed bourgeois society where individuals are driven by their possessive instincts to treat others as means instead of ends. These can be found in compassion, solidarity with beings, human and non-human, who suffer "as objects of a blind occurrence of nature,"[38] and in politics, the struggle of progressive social forces to realize the classical bourgeois ideals of justice, freedom, and equality in conditions under which these needed to be redefined in the face of the real possibility that the continuing development of the productive forces in a setting of intensifying social antagonisms would bring disaster.[39]

Yet the real presence of these manifestations of moral sentiment still stands as anticipations of a society to come, one that is necessary but not inevitable. Under prevailing social conditions, there is "the unhappy situation that compassion and politics, the two forms in which moral sentiment finds expression today, can only rarely be brought into a rational relationship with each other. Regard for those close at hand, and those far away, support for the individual and for humanity are contradictory in most cases. Even the best harden some place in their hearts." In the end, "morality cannot be proven ... [and] not a single value admits of a purely theoretical grounding."[40]

At the same time, there *is* moral sentiment, which, following Kant, Horkheimer identifies with a kind of love. And

> this love has nothing to do with a person as economic subject or an item in the property of the one who loves, but rather as a potential member of a happy humanity. It is not directed at the role and standing of a particular individual in civil life, but at its neediness and powers, which point toward the future. Unless the aim of a future life for all ... is included in the description of this love, it proves impossible to define. To all, inasmuch as they are, after all, human beings, it wishes the free development of their creative powers. To love it appears as if all living beings have a claim to happiness, for which it would not in the least ask any justification or grounds.[41]

The words here would not be Macpherson's, but they point to what Macpherson undoubtedly had in mind with his ethical concept of powers.

Horkheimer's position raises the problem of normative justification that his successors in the tradition of critical theory, especially Habermas, would take up and attempt to address.[42] I think Macpherson saw this problem as well, and although he did not explicitly deal with it in a systematic philosophic way, he did move beyond the distinction between ethical and descriptive conceptions of power. But before exploring this move and its implications for the issues of productivism and subjectivity, powers, and needs, I want to examine Horkheimer's own account of the historical context in which "unleashing the possessive instincts of all individuals" took place. He offered this account in "Egoism and Freedom Movements: On the Anthropology of the Bourgeois Era." And as was the case with Macpherson, Horkheimer's historical analysis gains its normative significance from a critique of human nature that is itself historically based.

"Egoism and Freedom Movements: On the Anthropology of the Bourgeois Era" is one of Max Horkheimer's most powerful, challenging, and important essays. As with Macpherson's work, the basis for this essay could be put in the form of a question: What is essential (i.e., properly ontological) and what is historical, and therefore potentially changeable, in human beings and human nature as we find them in the current historical period? Horkheimer attempted to provide a detailed account of the emergence of those qualities of individual and collective behaviour that strikingly illuminates the meaning of possessive individualism. The key lay in linking together psychic and social forces against the backdrop of the process of historical development that brought about the rise of the bourgeois social order. At the heart of his approach is the focus on the human "substance" – that is, the drives and needs – at the core of the individualism and individual character that have emerged along with, and in turn facilitated the growth of, modern political and social institutions and the political movements that have accompanied and fostered this process.

Horkheimer brought the distinctive Frankfurt School blend of psychology, especially psychoanalysis, and social theory, Freud and Marx, to bear on the question of how human nature, the character or psychic makeup of individuals, was shaped by the dynamic historical development of productive forces and the social relations within which this occurred; this was the core of the anthropology of the bourgeois era. The increasing command over physical nature that was the hallmark of the development of the productive powers unleashed by capitalist development went along with distinctive forms of social domination and political authority, which were played out in a setting shaped by antagonistic class relations. Horkheimer's focal point is a recurring pattern he detects in mass social and political movements for fundamental change in the context of the historical rise of bourgeois social relations in Europe from the fourteenth century onwards. These "freedom movements" – from the Roman uprising under the tribune Cola di Rienzo "to unite Italy under a democratically disguised dictatorship," through the mass mobilizations under Savonarola in Florence, and then Luther in Saxony, and Calvin in Geneva, to the French Revolution during the Terror under the leadership of Robespierre – were riven with a fundamental contradiction that offered a key to their historical role and significance. The movements and their leaders ostensibly acted in the name of the people and the satisfaction of their interests. But in the end they consolidated bourgeois rule and, just as importantly, the core features of the bourgeois character. At the heart of this character structure was individual self-assertion – possessive individualism. Horkheimer describes the core contradiction in this way: "The needs of the mobilized masses are utilized as a motor for the dynamics of the revolutionary process, but the conditions toward which the movement tends in terms of the historically attainable balance i.e., the consolidation of the bourgeois order, can satisfy them only to a very limited degree." As a result, popular pressures and demands for a new society are turned inward and are spiritualized, with the role of the leader being fundamental to this dynamic. "The historical movements we are speaking of here thus increasingly show the translation of individuals' demands on society into moral and religious demands on the dissatisfied individuals themselves. The bourgeois leader tries to idealize and spiritualize the brutal wishes for a better life, the abolition of differences of wealth and the introduction of real community ... Not so much revolt as spiritual renewal, not so much the struggle against the wealth of the privileged as against universal wickedness, not so much external as internal satisfaction are preached to the masses in the course of the revolutionary process." This process, continuously regenerated under specific historical circumstances, manifests the "necessity to move the greatest part of society by spiritual practice to a renunciation which is necessitated not by external nature but by the organization of society into classes."[43]

Clearly Horkheimer provided here a theoretically drenched historically informed account of the basis of "idealist" (i.e., bourgeois) morality whose chief elements he had explored in "Materialism and Metaphysics." In "Egoism and Freedom Movements," he shows the power and thus the political and social implications – but also the tensions and ambivalence – of bourgeois moral values: their power comes from the very process of turning inward demands and desires for a better life of diminished suffering. So internalized, such impulses are perceived as sinful and individuals must overcome them in order to achieve self-purification. The popular leader, who in reality is "a functionary of the property-owning strata," and who grants surrogate love and recognition to individuals in return for their self-abnegation and self-sacrifice, provides compensatory satisfaction to his followers. He does so by including them as full-fledged members of an ersatz community held together by aggression, a hatred and cruelty, which is turned as much outward against enemies as it is inward against one's own impulses. (This may be thought the eroticized manifestation of that collectivism Macpherson saw as a consequence of possessive individualism, particularly in Locke.) The more intense – and with the development of the productive forces, decreasingly necessary – the repression, the greater the aggressive response. The denial of the egoism of the masses, in a society in which "unrestrained egoism" is nonetheless "an essential trait of everyday life," expresses the contradictions of a recurring political dynamic whereby "the masses, set in motion under the slogans of freedom and justice, and with a tremendously vague or clear urge to improve their situation and to attain for themselves a meaningful existence, peace, and happiness, are incorporated into a new phase of class society."[44]

In the circumstances, the continuous reproduction of class society, in light of the possibility of moving beyond it, threatened ominous consequences, "a reversion to barbarity." According to Horkheimer, this was implicit from the outset of the bourgeois era: "The interests of the bourgeoisie regarding the system of ownership did not agree with those of the masses; despite the progressiveness of the system which the bourgeoisie was trying to establish, from the very start it implied a gap between the owners and the majority of society which grew increasingly wide. The spread of this system ultimately meant an improvement for humanity, but by no means for all people living at any particular time." This situation undergirds the contradictory meanings of key bourgeois political and social concepts and ideals, especially when they are put into service on behalf of the interests of the property-less: "'To make equal' has two meanings: to elevate what is below, to consciously set the highest claim to happiness as the standard of society, or to drag down, to cancel happiness, to bring everything down to the level of the present misery of the masses."[45] (Macpherson would adopt a comparable position in his discussion of how to measure human powers and their maximization.[46]) The latter represented a destructive assault on egoism and its inegalitarian consequences ostensibly on behalf of reconciling morality with the exigencies of social life.

Thus it is not egoism or individualism per se that is the problem. Indeed, under current circumstances, where the market "mediates the reproduction of society only with severe losses in human life and goods," egoism "has actually become destructive, both the fettered and the diverted egoism of the masses as well as the archaic egoistic principle of the economy, which still shows only its brutal side." Change the circumstances, however, and things would be different: "When the latter is overcome, the former can become productive in a new sense. The badness of egoism lies not in itself but in the historical situation; when this changes, its conception will merge with that of the rational society."[47] The two forms of destructive egoism mirror the social and psychological content and impact of possessive individualism.

So both Horkheimer and Macpherson conceived the accomplishments, dangers, and challenges of the historical emergence, development, and triumph of the bourgeois social order in a like manner. For each the focus was and had to be on human nature, the "anthropology of the bourgeois era." The key to transcending the fearsome dialectic whereby each advance in human power over nature, human and non-human, resulted in intensifying domination, even as it also produced opportunities for enhanced freedom, lay in altering the material conditions of existence at the level of both social and psychic structure, with each dimension both connected and separate. A basis and outcome of this process would be for Horkheimer the transformation of destructive into productive egoism, and for Macpherson the realization of the ethical as opposed to descriptive conception of powers.

From the vantage point of Macpherson's analysis the value of Horkheimer's account lay in his taking up Macpherson's project of making theory and philosophy practical, and in expanding its reach and scope. Horkheimer related key concepts that have inspired political and social movements, and shaped as well day-to-day social interactions, in a detailed and dynamic way to concrete historical developments that involved mass mobilizations. He showed how these led to decisive and historically important institutional outcomes that defined the bourgeois era, with the French Revolution being the ultimate example. He did so by in part demonstrating how historically informed individual and social imperatives enter into and mould psychic structure – how, in other words, they become "second nature." No account of social transformation could afford to be indifferent to the power that the given nature of things exerts over those who would have to carry a new project on behalf of freedom and equality. Horkheimer made clear how daunting in the circumstances the task of transformation was.

To be sure, Macpherson was hardly indifferent to the kind of dynamic historical account Horkheimer offered. Indeed, while it obviously lacks the psychoanalytic dimension of Horkheimer's approach, Macpherson's treatment of the Levellers suggests that it, too, harboured important elements of the bourgeois freedom movements that Horkheimer dissected. Nonetheless, perhaps even more powerfully than Macpherson did, Horkheimer demonstrated how essential it was to grasp as fully as possible how historical existence was concretely experienced by those who might be assumed to have a fundamental interest in transforming the conditions under which they lived, conditions that exacted such a toll on them.[48]

So Horkheimer, in my view, offers an important complement to Macpherson's analysis of human nature. In the specific context of my discussion here, Horkheimer provides a way of enriching our understanding of what Macpherson might have had in mind with his conception of distinctively human powers and capacities and what it would mean to transform the conditions of their formation and appropriate exercise.

Yet at the same time, both confronted similar problems in spelling out their respective claims about the transformation of individualism and the move to a more rational social order. To a degree this involved the question of who could and would carry the project of change. For his part, Horkheimer, in "Egoism and Freedom Movements," was committed to a classical Marxist position that stressed the role of the revolutionary working class: the task of raising humanity "to a higher level of existence" was "the world-historical mission" of "the historical persons in whom theory and historical practice became a unity."[49] For both theoretical and historical reasons, Macpherson never took this position. But even without the proletariat as revolutionary agent, both Horkheimer and Macpherson assumed a productivist and subjectivist model of social action in terms of which the overcoming of class domination would allow for the development of society as a collective macro-subject able to rationally organize and direct the process of social reproduction. This "work model" conception of social agency and action, as Seyla Benhabib put it,[50] and the subject-object relation it typically involves, narrows if not occludes those dimensions of social life defined by subject-subject, or intersubjective, ties. These include work relations themselves, which are never restricted merely to technical mastery of an external world of material objects and resources. The productivist commitments that both Horkheimer and Macpherson expressed reflected a dubious traditional metaphysics that both thinkers actually challenged in their writings. They failed to do justice to their distinctive contributions to a critical account of human nature and social analysis: Horkheimer's examination of bourgeois freedom movements, and Macpherson's analysis of human powers in the context of the development of possessive individualism. Both implicitly took issue with reductionist accounts of their positions in terms of social labour, even as they adopted a productivist perspective.

And while Horkheimer provides a richly evocative historical, social, and psychological context for Macpherson's distinction between ethical and descriptive conceptions of powers and how human capacities are shaped by the net transfer of powers, it may be that Macpherson offers the better approach to the matter of how individuals might come to take on board an ethical understanding of powers and what it entails in social relations and self-determination and fulfilment. Whether the psychic barriers to individual enlightenment and social change could ever be successfully surmounted was and remains a key and unavoidable question. For his part, Horkheimer seemed in "Egoism and Freedom Movements" to assume them away – with respect to proletarians "the mechanisms of bourgeois psychology, both as determining forces of their life and as theoretical object, are less important than their world-historical mission."[51] The power of the given, internalized as a repressive idealist morality, would have seemed to counter such hopes, even as Horkheimer acknowledged the potentially progressive possibilities of this morality. (In any event, as subsequent developments indicated, he did indeed lose hope.)

For Macpherson's part, however, there was another way to open up theoretically the question of how to impress upon individuals the need to at least consider the necessity for social and political change. This involved a further refinement in the analysis of human powers and the costs of the net transfer of powers beyond the distinction between the ethical and descriptive conceptions of these powers. For Macpherson, this move had the virtue of more fully clarifying what his account of powers had been intended all along to accomplish, and specifically to indicate more precisely how both the ethical and descriptive concepts were normative – and equally so. In addition I want also to claim something he most certainly would not have intended, namely, that his move to re-articulate the meaning of distinctive conceptions of human powers could well represent a modification if not abandonment of the productivist, subjectivist position and a move in the direction of a more intersubjective, communicative, and politically plausible stance.

The Net Transfer of Powers Revisited: From Ethical and Descriptive Power to Developmental and Extractive Power

Macpherson offered his most fully elaborated treatment of human powers and the net transfer of powers in "Problems of a Non-Market Theory of Democracy," the essay that lays out most completely the theoretical basis for his conception of a radical democratic political and social order. His position built upon the earlier distinction between the ethical and descriptive conceptions of powers but also moved beyond it in response to what Macpherson saw as the problems and limitations of the earlier account.

He identified two key problems. The first was that the distinction between ethical and descriptive conceptions "diverts attention from the fact that a man's access to the means of using his capacities is a component part of his power *whether or not* his power is seen to have an ethical dimension ... The *amount* of a man's power, in the most neutral descriptive sense, always depends on his access to the means of exerting his actual capacities."[52] The second related specifically to the net transfer of powers and involved the question of what exactly was diminished or transferred as a result of the lack of access to what was necessary for the exercise of one's capacities. If the key to the ethical conception was the ability to exercise one's powers under one's control for one's own self-determined purposes, then clearly this is not per se transferable, although it is obviously diminished. So what must be transferred is then "some of a man's ability to use his capacities in a neutral sense, abstracted from any consideration of *whose* purposes that exercise of his capacities serves, his own or another's."[53]

Neither the ethical nor descriptive conception of power captures what is transferred – the former because it is impossible to transfer one's enjoyment of the exercise of one's own powers; the latter because it measures powers after any transfer has occurred and so cannot distinguish for beneficiaries of the transfer their own powers from the use they are able to make of the powers of others they have been able to acquire. So Macpherson suggested the need for a new distinction: between *developmental* power and *extractive* power. This distinction captured two important dimensions of the problem: that there is only one power, although two ways of expressing and examining it; and all power exists in its exercise for purposes, one's own or someone else's. The notion of developmental power captures the idea central to the ethical conception that power involves the ability to use and develop one's capacities. Extractive power points to the ability to use, along with one's own power, the power of others to achieve one's purposes. That is, it is power over others, the power to extract benefit from them.

I suggest that in working up this new framework, Macpherson in effect claimed that power, however it is understood, possesses an unavoidable normative dimension. In his terms, all power is "ethical." The normative element is evident in the new distinction. *Developmental* and *extractive* are inherently normative terms – they entail judgments about what is right, proper, and appropriate from the vantage point of what might constitute human fulfilment.

Moreover, Macpherson made clear that in a capitalist market society almost everyone's power, owners and non-owners of the means of life and labour (i.e., capital) alike, consists of extractive power. Non-owners enjoy no extractive power and little power overall because of the necessity to transfer control over the exercise of their capacities in order to gain access to the means of life and labour.[54] Owners enjoy extractive power and combine it with whatever non-extractive power they have in terms of capacities that can be deployed via the exercise of developmental power.

Macpherson attempted to quantify the differences. He assumed for the purpose of analysis that all capital was owned by 10 per cent of the people (while at the same time noting contemporary efforts to actually measure the distribution of capital).[55] Under these conditions, "Each non-owner's whole power is near zero, and his extractive power is zero. Each owner's whole power is about 9 parts extractive power ['each owner of capital, on the average, having an extractive power equivalent to virtually the whole power of 9 other men'] to 1 part non-extractive power."[56] Indeed, the fact that even the ethical conception of power had a quantitative dimension was a prime reason why Macpherson sought to move beyond the ethical versus descriptive conceptions in the first place, because "the *amount* of that power that men have is what is important in a democratic theory."[57] (The other side of this was that the descriptive concept, which was primarily quantitative, had an implicit qualitative dimension. This was because the very occlusion of the net transfer of powers that the descriptive concept facilitates occurs "because it embodies no standard of essentially human needs or purposes."[58])

So from Macpherson's perspective, both developmental and extractive concepts are simultaneously quantitative and qualitative – they possess what I have called a necessary normative dimension. But the normative properties are not isolable qualities restricted to the concepts taken singly. Rather, they inhere in and significantly define the connection between the notions; they manifest their interactive mutual determination. And this in turn tells us something about the social nature of individual power and capacities.

At one level, it is obvious that power is socially determined via the market. The very definition of extractive power makes this clear: my ability to follow my own purposes depends upon acquiring the use of the capacities of others while avoiding as fully as possible having my capacities acquired by others and exercised for their purposes. And my developmental power is tied to, if not subordinated to, this dynamic. In light of the distinction between developmental and extractive power (or more accurately, what Macpherson seems to claim are developmental and extractive determinations of the same power), Macpherson offered his most fully worked out account of the net transfer of powers and gave it its most specifically social twist, precisely because he provided a fuller picture of the role it plays in shaping individuality and individual agency.[59]

As he presented the net transfer of powers in its most complete form, Macpherson offered his most explicit account of the impact on his thought of both the Marxian critique of capitalism and what he took to be the "democratized" or developmental liberalism of John Stuart Mill and his successors, notably T.H. Green and the English idealists. At the same time it is not fully reducible to either – it is neither pure classical Marxism nor abstract humanist liberalism.

To be sure, the Marxian dimension of the concept is decisive. In a society divided between owners and non-owners of capital, that is, a class-divided society, those who lack access to the means of life and labour transfer "both the ability to work and the ownership of the work itself, and, consequently, the value added by the work." This transfer is structurally determined in that it is "a continuous transfer between non-owners and owners of the means of labour, which starts as soon as, and lasts as long as, there are separate classes of owners and non-owners; not a momentary transfer occurring at the time of that separation." And this is a measurable transfer: "It is the amount of exchange value (whether in money or real terms) that can be added by the work to the materials on which it is applied, and be realized in the value of the product."[60]

Macpherson went further. As noted above, he indicated that what is at stake is not just the *transfer* of powers, but also the *diminution* of powers. He distinguished productive from extra-productive power, that is, the ability to use one's energies and capacities to produce material goods, from the ability to engage in activities beyond the production of goods that provide opportunities to exert one's human capacities for their own sake. He argued that, in the course of transferring one's power, one loses beyond the value of the transfer the fulfilment that comes from exerting one's capacities according to one's own conscious purposes, whether this takes place in one's productive activities or outside them. Where one loses one's ability to direct one's productive capacities, in a society in which production is a central fact, one cannot help but suffer impairment of one's ability to do so beyond the sphere of production. People are deprived of the opportunity to become what they could be: namely, agents capable of exercising their capacities for self-development.

And this deprivation becomes fully clear only when and where *both* the transfer *and* diminution of powers are considered together. As Macpherson put it, "Although the seller [of one's productive capacities] indeed transfers the whole of his labour-power, the whole control of his productive capacities, for the contracted time, he can transfer only part of the value it would have had he had been able to keep it; the rest of that value is lost and is lost by virtue of the fact that he has to sell. If he were able to keep his labour-power and use it himself, its value would be the satisfaction value *plus* the value which its application added to the materials on which it was applied."[61] In other words, Macpherson identified and targeted the pervasive commodification of society characteristic of advancing and advanced capitalism. And the form of social life this process entails, and not the specific fate of concrete purposes understood a priori as such, is the decisive consideration here.

Macpherson connected his account of the net transfer of powers to the claim that a fully democratic society must work to maximize human developmental power, understood as the equal ability of all to use and develop their distinctively human capacities, and argued further that abolishing this transfer (i.e., eliminating extractive power) would lead to fuller maximization of capacities that are ultimately non-contentious. I will have more to say about this later. But given this claim, it is easy to assume that the abolition of the net transfer (and consequent diminution) of powers *means* or *just is* the expression of distinctively human capacities, that the elimination of the class relations of capitalist society means a non-contentious society. But Macpherson did not offer such a concrete picture. What is important is the *transfer* and *diminution* of powers, not the capacities *themselves*. Their specific content presupposes appropriate conditions for their formation. This content cannot be spelled out in advance.[62] This suggests that Macpherson's position can fruitfully be read from the standpoint of intersubjective communicative relations not reducible to a subject-object productivist model.

And what I see as certain tensions or ambiguities in his mature account of powers, capacities, and the net transfer of powers seem to point in this direction – the very ambiguities suggest those implicit but underdeveloped aspects of Macpherson's thought that I have called his suppressed philosophical dimension. As noted above, Macpherson moved beyond the distinction between the ethical and descriptive conceptions of power to that between developmental and extractive notions, in part because the earlier distinction suggested that there were two forms of individual power, whereas there was in fact only one. (In a related move, as noted above, he also now distinguished capacities, which from time to time he had also called powers, from power in the singular, understood as the ability to exercise these capacities and thus as access to the means of life and labour, and as protection against invasion from others.) However, Macpherson did not clearly or consistently adhere to this view. Thus, on the one hand, in appraising contemporary political movements, such as those acting under the banners of "black power" or "student power," he suggested that the power they sought was simultaneously a synthesis and a transcendence of developmental and extractive powers, an overcoming of the division between them that involved "a cross between (i) power as the ability to control others (or not to be controlled by others), so as to increase their share of the satisfactions now available but now distributed unfavourably to them, and (ii) power as the ability to exercise and develop their human capacities in ways and to an extent they believe to be not possible for them, or for anyone, within the framework of existing society."[63] One could say these movements sought both justice and the good life, goals that Macpherson, himself, defended. Yet, on the other hand, this formulation suggested the continuing existence of precisely two distinct powers, even as he seemed to indicate a synthesis of them.

It is worth noting that Macpherson presented this example as part of his broader political analysis of the potential crisis of Western-style liberal, capitalist democracies in the face of global "competition" from alternative democratic systems. As suggested before, this idea is now anachronistic, at least in the form in which Macpherson conceived it. However, the most compelling reason why he presented alternative models and saw a competition between them is now evident: unlike Western liberal democracies, both the communist and non-communist, Third World systems recognized the existence of extractive power and, at least in principle, were committed to its reduction, if not elimination. (And the failure of these alternatives to realize their aims would not from Macpherson's perspective necessarily disqualify them as standards of critique.)

Thus, it seems to me that Macpherson did not fully recognize or conceptualize what he was really after, which was an account of all power as social – that is, embedded in social relations and therefore defined intersubjectively. The question involves what kinds of relations are possible and necessary for powers or capacities to take distinctive forms. What he seemed to be getting at but did not or could not properly theorize was that developmental and extractive power are *both* distinct *and* the same, in the sense that they mutually define each other. Extractive power becomes, as well as being indebted to, developmental power, as Macpherson acknowledged in his efforts to quantify power. Conversely, developmental power becomes defined by its relation to extractive power, either in the sense that I can formulate my purposes only by commanding your power or by resisting your efforts to command mine.[64]

Macpherson more or less moved in the direction of this position when he wrote that, beyond the loss of control over their productive capacities, the transfer of powers meant that members of the class of non-owners of the means of labour also lost control over, and could not properly develop, their extra-productive capacities. But he could not go as far as he needed, because in spite of the intersubjective possibilities of his argument, he was unable to get sufficiently beyond the philosophy of the subject and thus capture the relational nature of power.[65]

Yet at the same time he did connect his view of power to liberty or freedom in a complex way. A fuller discussion of Macpherson's account of freedom must await a more systematic examination of his more explicit treatment of democracy. However, what he will call developmental and counter-extractive liberty (themselves revisions of the now classic distinction between negative and positive liberty) map his two forms of power in a complex, historically developing synthesis. I want to suggest that, in doing this, Macpherson "politicized" power and liberty, which in the circumstances meant that he made them objects of collective will-formation – that is, objects of debate, deliberation, and struggle. I would even go further and suggest that there are echoes of current theoretical concerns around the relation of redistribution to recognition – what I earlier suggested was the presence of justice and the good life in Macpherson's appraisal of contemporary social movements. It would go too far to call Macpherson a theorist of recognition per se. Nonetheless, he claimed that, shorn of the market-based and market-driven competition for power as power over others (i.e., extractive power), our capacities and their exercise would be cooperative and non-contentious. This is a vital element of his account of democracy, and I will revisit it in my more extensive discussion of this account. The point here is that such a claim suggests that something like the idea of recognition might well have fit with Macpherson's purposes.

C.B. Macpherson and Herbert Marcuse: The Question and Challenge of Human Needs

With "Problems of a Non-Market Theory of Democracy," Macpherson brought his evolving treatment of the net transfer of powers to something like a definitive conclusion. But before moving to complete my discussion of Macpherson's ontology by examining explicitly his account of what he saw as two competing conceptions of human nature, I want to explore an additional aspect of Macpherson's work that took shape along with his democratic theory. This involved the question of human needs.

"Any attempt to work out a humanistic political theory sooner or later runs into the question, what are the human needs and wants which ought to be satisfied?"[66] Macpherson is undoubtedly correct in the general sense that all political theory must assume some conception of the human agents whose qualities provide a cornerstone for a theorist's claims about appropriate values, practices, and institutions. Nonetheless certain developments in the 1960s and 1970s brought the issue of human needs to prominence in a particularly visible way. These events shaped Macpherson's work overall, including his own efforts to more specifically and systematically address the issue of human needs and wants. I want to argue here that his account of what he saw as competing ontologies both presupposed and shaped his approach to the question of needs. More specifically, the question of needs and their formation provided for Macpherson, as for other contemporary thinkers, a powerful way of examining the issue of what (if anything) was fixed or timeless, and what was variable, in the human essence – in short, the relation of ontology to history.

The focus on human needs emerged in the context of important and influential socio-political and cultural/philosophical currents that strongly influenced political and social theory and philosophy. Politically the growth of national and international social movements – including civil rights, anti-war, anti-colonialist, feminist, and environmentalist – brought significant challenges to structures of power and authority. There were challenges, not only in the name of democracy, political equality, and political freedom to institutions of formal and informal political and economic power. There was also opposition against what were perceived as more insidious forms of social control and the denial of possibilities for creative self-development and self-expression – even and perhaps especially in advanced capitalist societies that in the post–Second World War period had generated more or less continuous and frequently spectacular economic growth. The focus here tended to be on the ubiquitous presence of bureaucratic norms and administrative values that rendered patterns of social control more subtle than more overt forms of coercion (which, of course, never completely disappeared).

An important element, especially in advanced capitalist societies, if less so in their socialist competitors, of the "management" of consent (and dissent) was the massive expansion of consumption and the celebration of it as the core of the good society or, for many critical of the existing social order, the "goods" society. Freedom, it was argued, came to be increasingly defined as freedom to acquire material satisfactions that could provide pleasure and comfort, which were now seen as important individual and social values.

Many commentators saw in this a fundamental shift in the culture of capitalism, a movement away from the austere bourgeois values of thrift, self-discipline, and self-denial – ultimately the value of work itself – that had ostensibly made possible the very development of the productive forces now being used to cater to an ever-expanding array of consumer preferences. Those sympathetic to classical bourgeois culture and morality were troubled by what they believed to be the undermining of key elements of "Western civilization" and its historical accomplishments.[67]

For their part, however, those who identified with and participated in the new social movements – often comprehensively called the New Left or the counterculture – saw themselves as redeeming the thwarted promises of bourgeois society to provide freedom and the good life. Not just the tyranny of work but the tyranny of (false) gratification had to be overthrown if real possibilities for human emancipation were finally to be realized.

Yet at the same time, the challenge to consumption and consumerism did not entail a repudiation of pleasure and gratification as such. Although rarely formulated explicitly in this way by those active in social movements, both traditional bourgeois morality and its supposed consumerist overcoming represented a repression of, if not denial of, genuine sensuality that could be achieved only in new relations between individuals and, more broadly, between humanity and nature. This would include pleasurable gratification not tied to the hedonistic "calculus" whereby the quest for sensual fulfilment remained bound to possessive individualism, market competition, and extractive power (i.e., it would de-emphasize, for example, what Fred Hirsch called "positional goods" whose capacity to produce "pleasure" was rooted in the fact that others lacked access to them). In other words, repression could take the form not only of direct coercion but also of more subtle kinds of manipulation and control – it operated at the level of both social facts and social values, and had to be fought in both dimensions.

As indicated above, Macpherson took note of these emerging social movements, particularly in Western liberal democracies, although with analogues elsewhere, in the context of his discussion of powers and capacities. And he recognized the comprehensive nature of the political challenge they posed and the necessity to take it on board in any meaningful analysis of contemporary political questions: the members of the new movements did not believe it was possible to fully exercise and develop their distinctively human capacities "within the framework of the existing society, whether they designate existing society as the consumer society, or as capitalist, imperialist, technocratic, bureaucratic, gerontocratic, or (more comprehensively) alienated. They may be derided as wishing to opt out of society, or resisted as threatening to disrupt or take over existing societies. But they cannot be disregarded by any realistic political science."[68]

In addition to political and social developments, there were also cultural/philosophical and theoretical factors at work. For one, the writings of the Frankfurt School, including those of Max Horkheimer and, especially, Herbert Marcuse, became more widely available about the same time the New Left and the counterculture emerged. In his own essays from the 1930s, notably "The Affirmative Character of Culture" and "On Hedonism," as well as his later, better-known, and widely read books *Eros and Civilization*, *One-Dimensional Man*, and *An Essay on*

Liberation, Marcuse carried forward the themes Horkheimer had laid out in "Materialism and Morality" and "Egoism and Freedom Movements." He developed the idea that the repressive side of bourgeois morality was a vehicle for class domination and that consequently the interest in happiness and pleasure as values in themselves needing no further justification had to be articulated and defended. The task was to unlock the emancipatory potential of sensual gratification as a means of bringing into view the shared nature and fate of humans as natural, suffering beings. A "new sensibility" could provide the erotic basis of new forms of human community.

For Marcuse the capacity of advanced capitalism to legitimate itself had expanded dramatically, precisely because it could now offer pleasure to ever more people in the form of a dazzling array of commodities. Ideology – for classical Marxism, a feature of the superstructure that made it both immediately accessible intellectually and, once the revolutionary proletariat was ready to take power, easily "hosed off along with the grime of capitalist industry"[69] – had come to assume a new, more intensive, and entrenched form as the common sense of everyday life experience in a setting of high-intensity consumption.[70] The claim that society had been perfected because it now met, or with social engineering could meet, the needs of all was simultaneously true and false. It was true in that the system fulfilled the needs it had itself generated and culturally legitimized. But it was false in that these were just those needs that reinforced the existing structures and values of social domination, which promised autonomy but maintained heteronomy – even if individuals were "willingly" complicit in their own subordination. The result, as Marcuse provocatively put it, was a social order characterized by a "comfortable, smooth, reasonable, democratic unfreedom."[71]

Yet even as the quest for pleasure and the satisfaction of desire functioned as instruments of social control and the maintenance of a class-divided society, they suggested other possibilities. Building on Horkheimer's dialectical critique of morality, Marcuse argued that, as with Horkheimer's conception of egoism, hedonism contained contradictory elements. Tied to the repressive demands of bourgeois society, the hedonistic "calculus" served as an instrument of social control. However, to the extent that hedonism reflected the material, instinctual quest for gratification, for happiness and pleasure, which, "unlike 'higher' motives, requires no reasons, excuses, or justifications,"[72] hedonism harboured the seeds of new forms of desire that could overshoot and call into question the existing order of things; that could, in other words, hold a key to a more rational society in which the massive development of the productive forces would be put in the service of freedom and happiness. In this respect it represented a kind of concave mirror image of (repressive) morality itself.

Marcuse put it this way:

> In a social organization that opposes atomized individuals to one another in classes and leaves their particular freedom to the mechanism of an uncontrolled economic system, unfreedom is already operative in the needs and wants themselves ... Critical theory comes to the question of the truth and universality of happiness in the elucidation of the concepts with which it seeks to determine the rational form of society. One of these determinations circumscribing the association of free men contains the explicit demand that each individual share in the social product according to his needs ... Here reappears the old hedonistic definition which seeks happiness in the comprehensive gratification of needs and wants. The needs and wants to be gratified should become the regulating principle of the labor process. But the wants of liberated men and the enjoyment of their satisfaction will have a different form from wants and satisfaction in a state of unfreedom, even if they are physiologically the same ... The bogey of the unchained voluptuary who would abandon himself only to his sensual wants is rooted in the separation of intellectual from material productive forces and the separation of the labor process from the process of consumption. Overcoming this separation belongs to the preconditions of freedom. The development of material wants must go together with the development of psychic and mental wants. The organization of technology, science, and art changes with their changed utilization and changed content. When they are no longer under the compulsion of a system of production based on the unhappiness of the majority, and of the pressures of rationalization, internalization, and sublimation, then mind and spirit can only mean an augmentation of happiness. Hedonism is both abolished and preserved in critical theory and practice.[73]

In the measure that morality and hedonism contained elements that could be carried over into the construction of a rational society, each could be played off against the other. Morality was right against hedonism in that autonomy requires rational judgment about and discrimination between pleasures. But hedonism was right against morality in that rationality and happiness as gratification should not be kept separate.

Marcuse and his colleagues clearly drew upon Marx (as well as Freud) for their analyses, but especially in Marcuse's case with a difference. Insofar as it dealt at all with questions of pleasure and happiness, traditional Marxism had been largely ascetic, as had revolutionary regimes ostensibly based on Marxist principles, which adopted a work ethic that might have made John Calvin blush.[74] But Marcuse took up the long-unavailable unpublished early writings of Marx, with their emphasis on alienation and the distortion of the human essence under capitalism, as well as his critique of political economy.[75] The combination challenged any notion of an absolute separation between an economic base and a political, cultural, and ideological superstructure. Base and superstructure dialectically interacted in a complex system, which reproduced itself as a totality that shaped not only the structure of social life but the nature of individual experience itself. The critique of morality and hedonism clearly reflected the impact of the early manuscripts. And the combination of critical theory with the writings of the young Marx proved potent in the circumstances under which the New Left and the counterculture emerged, as both became much more widely available.

Clearly much more that is beyond the scope of this study could be said about these theoretical and philosophical currents and issues. Many of the claims of Marcuse (and others) were and are controversial. Marcuse, himself, famously, or notoriously, distinguished between true and false needs, that is, needs that were genuinely fulfilling and made individual autonomy possible, versus those that served to secure social domination. The question then was how this distinction might be established, and who would (or could) establish it. And in the measure that under the sway of advanced capitalism and the culture industry individuals were too thoroughly conditioned to conceive an alternative more suited to their real interests, the only way out, as Marcuse saw it, was an educational dictatorship that, following Rousseau, forced people to be free. For many, this smacked of authoritarianism or even totalitarianism.[76]

But whatever the merits, or otherwise, of the discourse around needs, Macpherson in the circumstances felt compelled to address its significance for his position. While ultimately he followed Marcuse and upheld the distinction between true and false needs, he did so in a way that reflected his own distinctive concerns on the issue of needs and its relation to questions around ontology and democracy.

Macpherson provided his most explicit and systematic account of human needs in a short paper entitled "Needs and Wants: An Ontological or Historical Problem?"[77] This is a lucid if schematic treatment of what Macpherson saw as the dominant models or accounts of human needs and their relation to politics that were developed by the main currents of modern political thought. His analysis reveals his approach to questions of human nature and the place that needs occupies in it. But it also has the virtue of crystallizing the key concerns and goals that animated his political thought overall: the discourse on needs provided him with an opportunity to indicate with telling clarity what was at stake in the critique of possessive individualism and liberal democracy. It is noteworthy in this respect that it represents perhaps Macpherson's most explicit attempt to contrast Continental with Anglo-American political thought.[78]

Macpherson argued that any consideration of human needs in the context of political theory has to be both ontological and historical at the same time because the problem of needs is both. Such a consideration must address ontological questions, because an analysis of human needs assumes some conception of what is distinctively human, or what is the human essence. This is inherent in the very language of needs. The term unavoidably carries with it a sense of what is or is not appropriate for human beings, and for this determination a concept of the human essence is indispensable.

But the human essence may also be seen not as fixed for all time but as changeable. There may be evidence that it has changed over time, and further evidence of the possibility or potential that it might change again. Thus the question of needs has a historical as well as an ontological dimension.

For Macpherson, the success, or lack of it, of a particular tradition of thought in combining ontological with historical considerations served as the standard for appraising their conceptions of human needs. Without history, ontology was abstract and inert. Without ontology, history offered no basis for judging and thus discriminating the good from the bad, the human from the inhuman – it descended into relativism.[79] Only a dynamic fusion of both history and ontology would be able to capture what any discourse on needs had to address. Only then could one confront the normativity inherent in any attempt to say something meaningful about human desires. It is the same normativity that unavoidably characterized power and capacities.

For Macpherson, the attempt to address human needs as both an ontological and historical problem involved in the first instance the commonly held distinction between needs – "things absolutely necessary to sustain human life" – and wants – "things gratifying but not necessary."[80] But as commonplace and straightforward as this distinction is taken to be, Macpherson rejected it. It was insular in that only English as opposed to other languages, notably French and German, actually draws it; and it was ideological in that not every modern tradition of political thought makes it. The two criticisms are in fact connected, and this opened the way for Macpherson to lay out what the different traditions, Continental and Anglo-American, have to say.

Macpherson identified four distinctive traditions of thought, each with its particular take on the question of needs. He associated them with, respectively, Rousseau; the classical political economists and Benthamist utilitarians (liberal individualism); John Stuart Mill, T.H. Green, and their successors (ethical liberalism); and Marx. (Roughly, these perspectives might be identified as phenomenological, analytic, and Marxian.) Each conception of needs is in turn linked to specific approaches to ontology, history, and the relation between them. In other words, the cogency, truth, and normative consequences, and thus appropriateness, of these traditions in this case turn significantly on how they understand the issues involved.

Not surprisingly, Macpherson singled out the liberal tradition, particularly its utilitarian (i.e., its most explicitly possessive individualist) dimension, for his sharpest criticism. Insofar as liberal individualist thinkers such as Bentham treat humans as creatures of infinite and insatiable desire, which in turn "provides the incentive that propels the market economy,"[81] they offer an unhistorical view of a fixed human nature. They improperly collapse history into ontology. Humans as infinitely desirous creations of a market social order are assumed to be humans as such, as we would find them in all times and places.

The price of doing this is not simply an impoverished understanding of history and historically distinct societies, whereby infinite desire and the emulative ethic are seen as enduring features of all societies, whatever other differences characterize them. It also involves the inability, along with the unwillingness, to evaluate desires or wants: every want is as good as any other. Ontology is impoverished, certainly because it is viewed as fixed and unchanging, but also and just as decisively because it is stripped of its normative dimension – or, more precisely, its normative dimension is collapsed into the justification of the possessive market social order as the only plausible and acceptable one. From the point of view of needs, one ironic consequence is that society as a factor in the development of needs disappears and so the cultural determination of wants is obscured. This is why the equality of all wants is taken for granted, so that what is lost is the capacity to "make a distinction between (a) wants that develop out of new possibilities opened up by cultural and technological advance and (b) wants inculcated by the controllers of a system of production for their advantage."[82] It is possible to see in Macpherson's claim here a key element in the distinction he drew between the ethical and descriptive, and subsequently the developmental and extractive, conceptions of power.[83]

The ethical liberalism of Mill, Green, and others represented an improvement, in that it rejected the idea that wants were and should be infinite and that all were equal. "For them, the *quality* of want-satisfaction, and therefore of wants, was as important as the quantity ... Wants might and should change in quality, away from material desires and the desire to have more than the next man, to intellectual, moral and aesthetic wants."[84] Ethical liberals restored the distinction between ontology and history. There were normative standards by means of which wants could be appraised. These were tied to a developmental conception of human nature, whereby creative self-realization rather than unlimited acquisition was the decisive and even definitive quality.

However, for Macpherson, the ethical liberals failed, because while they deplored the existing range and nature of wants that were the product of a hard-driven capitalist market society, essentially they accepted this society and its institutions. As a result, the separation they forged between ontology and history was abstract and hence "false." With little purchase on the historical situation, the ontology of the ethical liberals was "idealist" in the pejorative sense. It expressed an abstract "ought" confronting an intractable reality. The demands of this reality in turn were mystified to the extent that the requirements of the historically evolved social order were, if not denied, downplayed as barriers to the realization of the developmental potential the ethical liberals sought to promote. "Thus even the ethical or developmental liberalism of Mill and Green and their successors is not historical enough to provide a morally acceptable account of human wants and needs."[85] If classical utilitarian liberals were historically accurate and thus ontologically accurate, given existing reality, in spite of (or perhaps because of) their collapse of ontology into history, the ethical liberals in a sense failed on both grounds, even as they sought to provide a normative critique of the existing state of affairs.

The alternatives to the liberal tradition, the ideas of Rousseau and Marx, highlighted for Macpherson the limits and failures of liberalism. Rousseau and Marx, correctly in Macpherson's view, saw needs as both ontological and historical, while maintaining the necessary distinction between ontology and history. For his part, Rousseau offered an explicitly developmental account of the human essence and thus human needs. There is a historical trajectory to the development of humans as they emerged from their "natural" state characterized by simple physical wants for food, sex, and rest, and became more recognizably human (i.e., bourgeois). Over the course of millennia, members of the human species, driven by their passions and the knowledge and tools acquired as a result, became increasingly creatures of desire. This process gradually brought them into a fatal dependence on one another. Dependence simultaneously fuelled the infinite expansion of wants and defined them competitively, so that they came to consist in superiority to others. In Rousseau's terms, *amour de soi* was transformed into *amour-propre*. As a constitutive core of this development, the ever-expanding array of wants degenerated into "true" needs, and the conveniences to fulfil them became more painful to lack than pleasant to have. This was at the heart of the transformation of natural into civilized or socialized humanity. Human development turns out to be progress in alienation – "*from* natural wants, that are consistent with equality and freedom, *to* artificial ones, that bring inequality and unfreedom."[86]

While, as we have seen, Macpherson was generally quite critical of Rousseau, in this respect at least he found considerable value in his approach. Rousseau offered a historically dynamic take on need formation and put this at the heart of a developmental account of human nature and its changes over time. Where he fell down, in Macpherson's view, was in distinguishing natural from artificial wants. By contrast, the more revealing and critically important focus should be on "the cultural determination of wants, and its distinction between wants that people may freely develop and those in effect imposed on them by a predatory culture."[87] Thus Rousseau correctly distinguished ontology (nature) and history from within history itself, but undermined his own insight by abstractly casting nature as the one-sided negation of this history, which was defined by the emergence of artificial wants. From Macpherson's perspective, a society made up of what Rousseau supposedly saw as "natural" humans would be the equivalent of what Marx defined as "crude communism."[88]

Marx provided for Macpherson the best approach to the question of needs and their ontological and historical character. Like Marcuse, Macpherson looked for the most part to Marx's early writings, in particular the *Economic and Philosophic Manuscripts of 1844*, for insight. These writings offered a striking picture of capitalism as a system of comprehensive alienation, where private property reduced needing to possessing and where labour, which, as the exercise of the full spectrum of human creative activities, should be the truly human need, turned as wage or alienated labour into oppressive and degrading drudgery barely able to secure subsistence. With respect to needs, it was a matter of quality as well as quantity. The "system of private property creates divisive and predatory wants: everyone speculates on creating a new need in another in order to force him to a new sacrifice, to place him in a new dependence, and to seduce him into a new mode of gratification and therefore economic ruin."[89]

For Macpherson, Marx offered "a great advance over any of the other analyses of needs and wants. It is both ontological and historical, and its strength lies in that combination. It makes no use of the natural/artificial distinction ... What, then, was Marx's concept of fully human needs and wants? What would needs and wants be in an unalienated society? On this Marx was not very specific ... [But] Marx's whole point about the future good society was that it would be a realm of *freedom* – freedom for people to develop their own needs and wants in whatever ways they liked."[90] The solution lay in abolishing alienated labour as private property, now possible on the basis of the general industriousness that capitalism had bred and the consequent massive expansion of human productive powers.

Macpherson treated one additional attempt to identify appropriate human needs, no doubt because it claimed to offer a critical (i.e., ontological) standard for appraising social arrangements. This was the psychologist Herbert Maslow's hierarchy or rank order of needs, ranging from survival needs to self-development needs, which Macpherson's fellow political theorist, Christian Bay, had used for his own account of needs and politics. Macpherson's analysis here was brief, but in effect it claimed that Maslow's position as taken up by Bay represented a combination of ethical liberalism (because it held self-development to be the highest need) and the ideas of Rousseau (because it seemed to represent a version of the natural/artificial distinction). Aside from its focus on the individual psyche, this approach to the question seemed to assume an unchanging human nature and an ahistorical conception of needs and wants. In other words, it fell behind the achievement of Marx and so was deficient as a critical theory of needs and need formation in a possessive market society.

That Macpherson championed Marx's account over and against those offered by other traditions of modern political thought is hardly surprising. Yet it is worth noting that in using Marx, Macpherson did not lay out any specific set of needs as *the* most fully human ones; indeed this was his primary criticism of Maslow and Bay. In this respect he reiterated in a new context what I have argued was his position on the net transfer of powers: that it was the transfer and diminution of the powers themselves that mattered, not any specific capacities, capacities he was not prepared to lay out in particular detail. The idea that needs formed in a society characterized not by the triumph of possessive instincts but by free cooperation and self-determination would differ from those taken for granted in the current social setting was central to Macpherson's position, as he took it to be to that of Marx.

Macpherson offered an additional wrinkle on his approach to needs and what I have argued is the open-ended articulation of them in a response to criticisms of his position in "Needs and Wants" by his University of Toronto colleague Alkis Kontos. It was here that Macpherson specifically defended the distinction between true and false needs. But he suggested that such a distinction could not be based on a rigid dichotomy between "ought" and "is," between ontology and history.

Kontos's critique has the virtue of relating Macpherson's position on needs to his general account of human nature, and beyond this to the issue of ontology in general and the necessity to address metaphysical and meta-methodological questions explicitly and systematically in the course of explicating and justifying one's ontological assumptions. In this respect Kontos sought to draw out and illuminate what I have called Macpherson's suppressed philosophical dimension; indeed his approach has strongly influenced and inspired my own. In doing so, he offers a powerful defence of thinking in terms of ontology – which he takes to be "a set of essential attributes which disclose the essential human being in his/her membership in the species" – that avoids identifying the human essence either with a fixed, unalterable quality that exists in a kind of a priori pure form above history and time, or with a supposed pattern of historical events that suggest an ineluctable telos to human development and is accorded a dubious justification by the selective use of partial historical evidence. Rather, ontology "suggests an orientation, a propensity or proclivity of a certain quality" whereby ontological capacities are seen as "inherent and dynamic, in constant dialectical relation with historical time and its emergent structures, material and mental ... It is this dialectic which discloses ontology and renders it simultaneously empirically inferable and intellectually-imaginatively visible."[91] Self-confined within the framework of his project of rehabilitating liberal democratic theory, and thus eliding the philosophical issues involved, Macpherson, according to Kontos, was not able to sufficiently establish and secure his critique of needs.

Specifically, Macpherson's criticism of classical liberalism's assumption of the naturalness of unlimited need and desire was incisive, and he used it to sustain the claim that liberalism held human beings to be infinite consumers and appropriators – which he then contrasted negatively with the ontological assumption that emerged from Marx's account of needs, namely, that humans were active doers and creators, exerters of their distinctively human capacities. For Kontos, while this opposition might make sense within the context of liberal democratic theory, it fails as stated to sufficiently justify Macpherson's preferred alternative: "The negation of the one postulate does not necessarily support the other except in the context of liberal democratic theory."[92] Historical explanation and justification is not ontological justification, although history is the inescapable medium of ontology. Macpherson needed to more systematically consider what constituted the core commitments of any argument about human nature and why they mattered – the "essence" of essence, if you will. He needed to relate "is" to "ought" in a more self-reflexive manner. In failing to do this, Macpherson in effect repeated what he had himself criticized in Rousseau: he abstractly and one-sidedly contrasted "natural" with "artificial" (or false). This in turn reflected the fact that Macpherson continued to utilize the liberal language of needs versus wants, even as he criticized it. However, that he recognized the ahistorical and thus a-ontological character of Rousseau's argument indicated that, if prodded, Macpherson could well have taken on this task.[93]

I will examine Macpherson's explicit ontological assumptions in greater detail presently. My point here is to indicate how, in responding to Kontos, Macpherson further elaborated on his view of how best to consider the question of needs.

Macpherson offered this elaboration in response to Kontos's claim that Macpherson continued to use liberalism's needs/wants distinction even as he quite properly rejected it. I have suggested that Macpherson's continuing resort to the distinction could be seen as an attempt within the language of liberalism to demonstrate how the liberal, especially utilitarian liberal, conception of human nature as infinitely desirous prevents a critical evaluation of desires. Macpherson, indeed, here did take this position: while the distinction between needs and wants is "insular and ideological ... I was chiefly addressing an insular and ideological audience *i.e.* English-speaking liberal democrats, who are best addressed in terms familiar to them."[94]

He went on to suggest that, on second thought, the distinction might be useful for drawing attention to the changing nature of our "wants" over time, as civilization becomes more complex and there consequently emerge real changes in the requirements of life and social organization. However, on further thought, he questioned how useful the distinction might be after all. His reasoning here is interesting. Because for any society beyond the most "primitive," some "wants" become "needs," or "needs" change and increase given technological developments, "there is really no difference in saying 'some wants become needs' and saying 'needs change and increase.'"[95] Given the historical changeability of needs, it would make more sense to distinguish among three conceptions of needs: narrow, intermediate, and (comprehensively) broad. Narrow needs are basic survival needs and might be considered unchanging over time. Intermediate needs are required for the conduct of work under prevailing conditions of production. They do change historically, according to changes in the focus and organization of work, and are both social and individual (e.g., more complex food, drink, and other means for securing reproduction under ever more complex conditions). Broad(er) needs, by contrast, are those whose fulfilment is demanded by the commitment to the fullest possible development by individuals of their human capacities, given the prevailing level of the technical mastery of nature. These change with new (and potentially liberating) technological possibilities.

The distinction between, on the one hand, narrow and intermediate needs and, on the other hand, broad needs – we might, without doing violence to Macpherson's position, call these needs for full, rational self-development – suggests a move from a quantitative to a qualitative understanding of needs that raises the question of the type of society required for full human flourishing. This brought Macpherson close to critics of capitalism and capitalist technology such as Marcuse. It included a defence of the distinction between true and false needs.

On the basis of his broad definition of needs, Macpherson argues that "some needs that emerge at successive levels of social organization will be truly necessary (those which would need to be incorporated into the most advanced human society), and some will be falsely necessary (those which are required only by an exploitive class-divided society, whose maintenance economically requires the endless creation of artificial needs, and politically requires an ideology which legitimizes both those needs and the state which upholds that economic system)." Later, duly noting Rousseau's view of how increased technical mastery, coupled with expanding wants, has, over the course of human species development, generated dependence and unfreedom, Macpherson suggested we could move beyond Rousseau's insight by using the distinction between true and false needs. He argued that false needs "are those imposed by relations of production which require domination: these are false in any circumstances, such as our present ones, where it is possible to envisage meeting a civilised level of needs without domination." By contrast, true needs "are those which could be met by a rational, non-class-dominated, organization of production (work and leisure), given the presently available technology; and these can be seen as increasing indefinitely with future improvements in technology, provided that those improvements are no longer harnessed to the right of unlimited private appropriation."[96]

Again, Macpherson never really more fully developed his account. It certainly is exposed to the sorts of criticisms mounted against the whole idea of true and false needs, indeed the use of needs in general as a tool of radical, critical social analysis. Insofar as it has been, and remains, tied to the Marxian critique of capitalism and suggests a radical reduction, if not outright elimination, of the commodity form and market institutions and exchanges, it can be accused of failing to fully respect evolved complex forms of social relations and social communication that represent genuine accomplishments on behalf of the realization of human potentials, in spite of the distorted impact of capitalist domination.[97] In any case, I would only note here a point that is easily missed. Macpherson seemed to use the distinction between true and false needs not to lay out a specific schedule of needs (although as anyone, regardless of how one might view the question of needs, or indeed even whether one has thought theoretically or philosophically at all about it, will have some conception of genuine/desirable versus dubious/undesirable needs, so undoubtedly did Macpherson), but rather to raise the question of desirable and appropriate forms of society. It is no doubt true that there have been radical social critics whose opposition to capitalism masked or masks an ascetic distaste for consumption. But Horkheimer and Marcuse were right: sensual gratification as such needs no defence. The current urgent necessity to address environmental crises and challenges should not obscure this point. A radical challenge to capitalism need not descend into destructive levelling. I think Macpherson would have agreed.

The critique of needs joins together with the analysis of powers and capacities to forge the context, basis, and content of Macpherson's explicit ontological postulates. These partake of the features of what I have called a constellation, suggesting a force field of conceptual elements that identify concerns we should acknowledge, want to acknowledge, and in fact already address insofar as we are agents of a certain sort. I believe Macpherson did want to open up these issues with his approach to human nature, even if he did not fully or adequately conceptualize what he was doing. In other words, as I have tried to argue, Macpherson provides potential resources for communicative engagement with the challenges of social life and individual self-development, and not fixed and fast-frozen standards of judgment or truth.

Liberal Democracy and Its Dual Ontologies

Macpherson referred to the idea of competing ontologies within liberal democratic theory throughout his writings.[98] But in my view he provides his most thorough treatment of this point in "Democratic Theory: Ontology and Technology." That he would do so here is perhaps not surprising or coincidental, given his position on human needs. The essay clearly reflects the concerns of the Frankfurt School and especially Marcuse. It also carries with it a sense of urgency about coming to terms with a philosophical issue, ontology, which for many people might otherwise seem abstruse, remote, or even rebarbative.

The starting point for Macpherson's analysis is the now familiar idea of Cold War–era competition between East and West on political, technological, and ethical grounds. This last could in turn be viewed as a competition between two ontologies. Again, it must be noted this idea of a world-historical conflict between alternative systems has been outwitted by historical developments.[99] However, although the conflict remains a reference point for his account, Macpherson focused his attention primarily upon the tension or contradiction between the same two ontologies as they exist *within* the justificatory theory of liberal democracy, and thus as they affect the economy, politics, and culture of liberal democratic capitalist societies.[100] What makes this contradiction decisive is that it is thoroughly implicated in a "race" with technological change. As is the case with existing technology, the life-altering impact of new technologies, for good or ill, would be shaped by the resolution, or lack of resolution, of the ambivalence embedded in the ontological assumptions that undergird both political theory and institutional practice in contemporary liberal democratic states.

Liberal democratic theory has been shaped by the presence of two incompatible assumptions about the human essence. Each emerged at a different stage in the development of liberal society and reflected both relations of power within the existing social structure and prevailing assumptions about what was morally and materially possible. "One of these is the liberal, individualist concept of man as essentially a consumer of utilities, an infinite desirer and infinite appropriator. This concept was fitting, even necessary, for the development of the capitalist market society, from the seventeenth century on: it antedates the introduction of democratic principles and institutions, which did not amount to anything before the nineteenth century." By contrast, the other assumption involves "the concept of man as an enjoyer and exerter of his uniquely human attributes or capacities, a view which began to challenge the market view in the mid-nineteenth century and soon became an integral part of the justifying theory of liberal democracy."[101]

Clearly Macpherson here revisited, recapitulated, and elaborated his analysis of possessive individualism and its fate in light of a process of historical development both theoretical and empirical (or, put otherwise, a process involving both philosophical history and empirical history). To return to my earlier discussion, the emergence of competing assumptions of the human essence occurred when the two conceptions of individualism at the core of liberalism almost from its birth – namely, as both self-ownership and self-direction – began to simultaneously mature and come apart with the historical development of capitalist socio-economic and political relations.

The liberal individualist (or market) concept of the human essence dated primarily from the seventeenth century, when it was introduced by the emerging capitalist society. It made unlimited desire and the acquisitiveness that supported it empirically actual and morally acceptable. These were behavioural requirements of a new system of social reproduction and its core institutions. Echoing his account of the transition to a full possessive market society, Macpherson identified these new institutions as freedom of contract under which individuals are able to most gainfully deploy their persons and properties, increasingly pervasive market relations of exchange within which owners of commodities, be they land, labour, or capital, could be induced by market prices to enter them into the productive process, and a legal order that secures for individuals the right to unlimited appropriation. This last is especially important, because for a full possessive market society to take hold, it is not sufficient that individuals seek the best return for the use of their properties. "What is needed, in a society which by definition cannot rely on traditional, patriarchal, or feudal obligations to work, and whose supporters, besides, see prospects of untold wealth under the new market arrangements if only people can be induced to exert themselves, is an institutionalized incentive to setting up a right of unlimited individual appropriation. The establishment of that right could be expected to move men to continuous effort by giving them the prospect of ever more command over things to satisfy their desires."[102]

The entrenchment of the morality of unlimited appropriation was, according to Macpherson, profoundly consequential, indeed revolutionary, for both social relations and individual conceptions of rationality and the self. Once it triumphed and facilitated the maximization of productivity in support of infinite desire, it swept away, as Hobbes saw, traditional conceptions of commutative and distributive justice, that is, the very idea that acquisition should be limited by traditional standards of allocation. And further, it also transformed the nature of scarcity: from an absolute barrier to the satisfaction of needs that confronted humans as inevitable fate to a historically determined but equally fateful and insurmountable challenge in the face of infinite desires, which by definition could never be fully satisfied. And with infinite desire itself now viewed as moral and rational, so, too, was the struggle against scarcity; indeed, infinite desire was the spur to the mastery of nature as a rational (and thus scientific) project. This will turn out to be tremendously significant for Macpherson's conception of technology and its relation to ontology.

There is one other element of Macpherson's account of the liberal, individualist conception of the human essence that deserves some comment. Macpherson did not really develop it and commentators have not paid much attention to it. While according to Macpherson the liberal, individualist concept defined the human as "essentially a consumer of utilities, and infinite desirer and infinite appropriator," he acknowledged that in principle a consumer of utilities need not be by definition an infinite desirer or appropriator. But the circumstances, material and ideological, under which capitalism got going and was firmly established required that "man" the consumer of utilities become an *infinite* consumer because of the pressure of infinite desires seeking gratification. And in the measure that humans were understood as both infinite consumers and desirers, it became possible and necessary to conceive of them as infinite appropriators as well, once it was assumed, as in Locke, that, in order to be productive, land and capital needed to be privately owned. This is another way of laying out the way in which ideas and institutions shaped each other in the rise of capitalism.

Macpherson argued that, under these circumstances, theorists in search of a suitable justificatory account of the new order found the idea of humans as infinite consumers of utilities more useful for the kind of *general* account of human nature they sought and needed. It was both more intellectually defensible, because more capable of being plausibly applied to all human agents, and morally defensible than what theorists actually were after: the justification of infinite, or unlimited, appropriation. Even given the forces at work transforming societies into capitalist market social orders, such a bald assertion of human purpose flew too much in the face of traditional natural law and morality, which had condemned the unlimited pursuit of wealth as unsuitable and even indefensible for rational beings. Presenting the human essence as consisting in the unlimited quest for material gratification represented a more acceptable picture, one, moreover, that could be more readily defended as true of individuals as such, wherever and whenever they lived. (I think one could see what Macpherson was getting at by considering everyday discourse in contemporary society. References to the "consumer" are ubiquitous and largely positive, because consumer behaviour is seen as an essential feature of economic life. By contrast, no one refers to the "appropriator." Owners of capital are presented as benefactors and thus drivers of economic well-being, never as appropriators.)

But there is another way to read the distinction between infinite consumption of utilities and infinite appropriation. Macpherson did not offer this reading, but I believe it is consistent with, if not entailed by, his analysis of needs. In a sense, consumption *can* be considered a general human property in any imaginable setting. As discussed earlier, gratification of desires per se, including the complex "wants" that emerge with the process of social and economic development, expresses the drive for hedonistic fulfilment and sensual happiness that, according to the Frankfurt School, needed no extrinsic justification. So it may not be consumptive desire for utilities as such that is the problem. Rather, it is the way in which historically and institutionally maximization of utilities became intertwined with the values and institution of unlimited appropriation of wealth as private property. Unlimited accumulation could be justified on the basis that it permitted the fullest range of material satisfactions, while understanding and justifying desires as infinite permitted and facilitated unlimited accumulation.

Macpherson hinted at this reading when he argued that theorists were reluctant to define the essence of man as an infinite appropriator. He held that "it was more fitting to the needs of a general moral theory to describe him, instead, as an infinite desirer of utilities, which could be taken to mean only a desirer of things for consumption. This would entitle him to unlimited appropriation of things for consumption. And by failing to make, or emphasize, the distinction between property in things for consumption and revenue-producing property, the theory could be taken to justify unlimited appropriation of the latter as well."[103] Clearly, Macpherson intended with this claim to suggest that unlimited desire for utilities functioned as an ideological cover for infinite appropriation. But he did not develop the point at any length, and this precluded him from perhaps following up in the manner I've suggested: to separate desire from appropriation in the context of a critical theory of needs. In any event, I would argue that this move is at least implied by Macpherson's claim that the needs associated with the development and exercise of distinctively human capacities are, in principle, non-contentious. Since this was a core component of Macpherson's conception of a fully democratic society, the relation of desire to appropriation is of more than passing interest. It certainly suggests what is at stake in the contrast Macpherson drew between the liberal, individualist and democratic, egalitarian accounts of the human essence. Nonetheless, it should not be assumed that separating maximizing utilities or satisfying desires that are no longer necessarily infinite from appropriation would alone do the job of highlighting and getting us clear of the compulsions and compulsiveness of capitalist market relations. We still need a more comprehensive alternative account of individual development: recall that the maximization of utilities was not for Macpherson the same as the maximization of human powers.[104]

What Macpherson called in "Democratic Theory: Ontology and Technology" the egalitarian complement to liberal individualism in Western democratic thought emerged in the nineteenth century, partly as a consequence, as noted earlier, of political pressure from an increasingly class-conscious and organized working class demanding democratic rights, and partly as a result of the attack on the morality of the market and its more hideous social consequences and human costs "by moralists as different as Mill and Marx, Carlyle and Saint-Simon, Ruskin and Green, the German romantics and the English Christian socialists."[105]

In different ways and with varying conceptions of the social changes required, thinkers came to stress a new morality that asserted the right of all individuals equally to make the most of themselves. They needed to be seen as exerters and enjoyers of their distinctively human capacities – neither infinite consumers nor infinite appropriators, but infinite developers of their human attributes.

Macpherson put the alternative ontological position this way: "Life was to be lived, not to be devoted to acquiring utilities. The end or purpose of man was to use and develop his uniquely human attributes. A life so directed might be thought of as a life of reason or a life of sensibilities, but it was not a life of acquisition. If we wished to express this concept of man's essence in terms of maximization we could say that man's essence is not maximization of his utilities but maximization of his human powers." This was both new and old. The theorists who mounted the challenge to market morality "were reasserting the old values [of life as activity, not acquisition], and on a new and more democratic plane," and thus "were, in a sense, exposing Locke-to-Bentham as a deviation from the Western humanist and Christian traditions that go back to the Greeks and to medieval natural law."[106]

Macpherson obviously believed that this alternative conception of the human essence was not only morally superior to the utilitarian picture, but absolutely essential for a fully democratic society. As it played out in practice, the utilitarian or possessive individualist conception of human nature sustained and was in turn sustained by those market and property institutions that entrenched the net transfer of powers. As we have seen, this meant that in a setting of market competition driven by the pursuit of unlimited acquisition, the majority of individuals will have to sell their ability to labour and so will be denied access to the means of life and labour, save on terms set by owners of capital. They thus lose the ability to utilize their productive (and extra-productive) capacities under their own control and for their own purposes – essential elements of the right to make the most of themselves as doers and exerters of their distinctively human attributes.

But the idea that the alternative democratic and egalitarian conception of human nature was both old and new provides another clue about Macpherson's approach, one that challenges the view that he abstractly juxtaposed to each other the liberal individualist and democratic egalitarian ontological postulates. Given that it embodied a normatively charged standard that was once widely accepted and may be again, the conception of the human essence as free, creative activity indicated for Macpherson the plausibility of assuming that human nature was not fixed but historically changeable. He felt he needed to make this clear, not only because of his Marxian-influenced normative judgment about necessary and possible human behaviour under the impact of capitalist social institutions and the consequent need for a more morally defensible alternative to possessive individualism. He also knew that he had to address the reality of infinite desire and thus the concomitant right to infinite appropriation. Evidence of the apparently limitless expansion of desires over time was strong and rendered moot any meaningful distinction between innate and acquired desires, or any moral criterion for selecting among different patterns of desires. This would seem to make the idea of an alternative account of the human essence at best an abstract "ought" – "If you start from the assumption that there is a permanent unchanging nature of man, then you are forced to subsume all changes, such as increase of desires, under his innate nature. If you drop that assumption and assume instead that man changes his nature by changing his relation to other men and the material environment, the difficulty disappears. It can then be seen that man can in principle choose and impose what moral rules he wishes, and can change them as circumstances seem to call for."[107] Macpherson went on to argue that this is what humans have done in different historical epochs: they created an image of human nature as infinitely acquisitive in the context of the rise of possessive market society, and later established and/or restored a developmental account as an element of the nineteenth- (and twentieth-) century reaction against the moral and material consequences of capitalist development. But can ontological assumptions be created and transformed, or even discarded, so readily?

Here again the issue of Macpherson's suppressed philosophical dimension emerges. But while not undertaking a systematic, metamethodological, or theoretical exploration, he did offer the elements of a justification, which had two prongs: the relation between ideas and material conditions, and the special nature of ontological postulates.

Macpherson's general approach to the first matter is clear. Commenting on the significance of the place of unlimited desire in the rise, entrenchment, and justification of market society and his emphasis on it, Macpherson argued that in according first place "to the acceptance of the assumption about unlimited desire I do not mean to say that this change in ideas was the sole motivating force. I do not enter into the general question of the primacy of ideas or material conditions. It is enough to argue that the acceptance of the assumption about unlimited desire was a necessary condition of the establishment of the right of unlimited appropriation."[108] He further elaborated on this point by claiming that "I do not attempt to deal here with the question whether this concept was a conscious invention of thinkers who saw clearly that the market society could not be justified without such a concept. I simply propose that the need for such a concept did exist, and that this was met in the body of liberal theory from Locke to Bentham."[109] Changing material conditions called forth a new understanding of human purpose (or, rather, a new morality under which acquisitiveness was granted positive status) and it was provided, while the new ontological postulate supported the new institutions and gave meaning and justification to the practices that sustained them.

What saved this claim from being merely functionalist, or as one of Macpherson's critics had it, an example of "sociologism,"[110] was his position on the second issue. For Macpherson, ontological assumptions or postulates were a complex combination of fact and value (the link to his position on Hobbes's deduction of value from fact is, I think, evident here, although he did not address it). They can be and frequently are linked to empirical claims but they are primarily value concepts whose "basic assertion is not that man *does* behave in a certain way (although it may make this assertion), but that his *essence* can only be realized by that behaviour."[111] As such, an ontological postulate can be replaced by an alternative, should new value judgments about what is possible and desirable, and correspondingly new conceptions of human purposes and behaviour, emerge in the context of historical/material developments. In response to possible criticisms that shifting from one postulate to another seems to avoid the demands of truth and verification and would thus be at best arbitrary and at worst irrelevant or irrational, Macpherson claimed that because ontological postulates were primarily evaluative, questions of truth or falsity were not at issue. He wrote, "All we have demonstrated is that the postulate of man as essentially consumer and appropriator was brought into Western theory and ideology at a certain historical period and that it did fill a certain need (in that it provided a justification of capitalist market relations)."[112]

There, essentially, is where Macpherson left matters. As it stands, his justification is pretty sketchy. It is not helped by his resort to a conception of truth as propositional. This flies, however, in the face of what I think he was really doing. He sought to provide conceptual tools for individuals who face the challenges of living well in the context of market relations. These are individuals who have come to view well-being in terms of consumption, but who can and do recognize and acknowledge *both* the pleasures (and pressures) of consumption *and* the quest for meaningful self-expression and self-direction. In Axel Honneth's terms, they can achieve coherent identities and senses of self only via robust relations of civic and legal respect, egalitarian cooperation in labouring in the service of social production, and personal affirmation through love and intimacy – qualities that also resonate with Macpherson's account of general human capacities. In other words, Macpherson's approach to ontology may best be seen as interpretive, more fully at home, as I argued in the introduction, with Hegel's "objective spirit," or Wittgenstein's "form of life," as well as the work of Horkheimer, for whom the content of ideas "is not eternal, but is subject to historical change – surely not because 'Spirit' of itself capriciously infringes upon the principle of identity, but because the human impulses which demand something better take different forms according to historical material with which they have to work. The unity of such concepts results less from the invariability of their elements than from the historical development of the circumstances under which their realization is necessary."[113]

Viewing Macpherson's analysis in this way also helps, I think, put into perspective his well-known and controversial claim that the justificatory theory of liberal democracy has, over the course of its development, come to incorporate the two conceptions of the human essence – "the concept of man as maximizer of utilities or infinite consumer and the concept of man as maximizer of individual human powers or as exerter, enjoyer, and developer of his human capacities"[114] – both of which are essential insofar as our societies are and remain capitalist democracies, but which are in the circumstances fundamentally incompatible. Citizens of liberal democratic states "live" both sets of ontological attributes and refer to both to make sense of their lives. Viewing them as interpretive or hermeneutic tools or standards suggests that they function not just as qualities that may be attributed to individual agents but also as vehicles of critical self-awareness and communicative interaction. They may be thought to open up questions that we always and already have about ourselves and our world, and to do so in a distinctively revealing way. While Macpherson might not have found such an account of his project particularly congenial, I believe he would have assented to what I have taken to be his desired impact. He would himself later sharpen and render more stark the stakes involved in the argument about the incompatibility of the two postulates, when in *The Life and Times of Liberal Democracy* he argued that the liberal or possessive individualist conception of the human essence, and the particular model of capitalist, inegalitarian democracy it sustains, would remain dominant "as long as we in Western societies continue to prefer affluence to community (and believe that the market society can provide affluence indefinitely)."[115]

The urgency Macpherson conveyed throughout his account of the need to confront these ontological questions was particularly relevant for the issue of technological development and change. Macpherson did not address the question of whether the challenges and problems flowing out of technological change resulted from the use of technology to reinforce capitalist market values and relations or from the intrinsic properties of technology itself (Marcuse, strongly influenced by both Marx and Heidegger, had suggested it was both, a position Macpherson likely would have accepted). What he did argue was that in the measure that the conception of humans as infinite consumers and appropriators remained dominant, present and future technological developments would be harnessed to the market-driven dynamic of unlimited production and consumption in the service of infinite desire. And while he did not specifically address it here, technological development under these conditions would also, from his perspective, maintain and even intensify compulsive labour and thus the net transfer of powers, even as such development made possible a reduction if not outright elimination of both. In his words, "The technological revolution in Western nations, if left to develop within the present market structure and the present ideology, would have the immediate effect of strengthening the image of man as infinite consumer, by making consumption more attractive. As technology multiplies productivity, profitable production will require the creation of new desires and new amounts of desire ... Thus in the West the immediate effect of technological revolution will be to impede the change in our ontology which it otherwise makes possible and which I have argued is needed if we are to retain any of the values of liberal democracy."[116]

For Macpherson, then, the critique of ontology represents an attempt to put into focus, if not indeed on the agenda, pressing questions about the direction of human societies as they face momentous challenges, opportunities, and dangers simultaneously. As Kontos notes, Macpherson explicitly defined the question of ontology within the framework of the contradictory developmental logic of liberal democracy. However, it may be that he also offered a kind of implicit "meta"-ontology: an "ontology" of ontology, if you will. There is evidence of this approach in the roster of distinctively human capacities that he provided in "The Maximization of Democracy" and referred to in subsequent discussions, and whose concrete content he did not spell out. But it may be even more powerfully present in what he seemed to assume about the individual agents he addressed. These were (putatively) rational beings who were *both* desirers (if not necessarily infinite desirers) *and* doers. As I have already suggested, they could potentially (and he thought many could already actually) grasp the issues he raised because they constituted the human substance of liberal democratic society – they were "living" the contradictions of this society. To be sure, powerfully influenced as he was by Marx, he likely thought that recognition of the contradiction between the two competing conceptions of the human essence and the commitment to do something about it would emerge most fully and strongly from members of the subordinate classes in capitalist societies, who suffered the most destructive consequences of the net transfer of powers – a kind of ironic reversal of Locke's class-based differential rationality. (Or, perhaps more accurately from Macpherson's perspective, this would mean the transfer of the most historically advanced form of social rationality to those now most fully able to realize the goal of free self-development that had once provided the promise and justification of the bourgeoisie.) But there were no guarantees this would occur or would occur in a way that would foster the kind of social and political transformation he thought necessary. Ontological reflection provided questions we needed to answer, not answers we simply needed to apply.

I think that, ultimately, Macpherson's ontological position was a complex synthesis of the critique of the net transfer of powers and the critique of needs. It shifted the focus from the challenge of political obligation that he had identified in *The Political Theory of Possessive Individualism* to the question of the good life as one in which individuals would be able to make the most of themselves. It was a way, for Macpherson a particularly powerful way, of asking how we should live and live together with others.

The answer to this question turned out to be a richer democracy, liberal *and* socialist, individualist *and* communal, democracy as a way of life or kind of society, and not a mechanism for choosing and authorizing governments. But like the account of ontology that provided its foundation, and even its impetus, the theory of democracy would turn out to be more about questions and ongoing challenges, rather than answers and definitive solutions.

Chapter Three

Capitalism, Socialism, and Self-Development: Macpherson and / on Marx

> Let me say ... what I think is valuable in the liberal tradition. At the level of abstract theory it is something like John Stuart Mill's view of human nature as developmental ... A socialist theory and practice which was faithful to Marx's humanistic vision would already embody that valuable element of liberal-democratic theory ... [I]f what I consider the basic liberal and the basic Marxist value of individual self-development is not made the mainstay of the whole attempt at transition to a good society, then there won't be any transition; it won't even get started.
>
> C.B. Macpherson

It might seem redundant to devote a separate chapter on the political thought of C.B. Macpherson to the relation of Macpherson's ideas to those of Karl Marx. As should be evident from my previous discussions, Marx's influence on Macpherson was considerable and obvious. I have argued that not only was the theory of possessive individualism a strongly Marxian reading of the social history of the origins and development of English liberalism, but that the methodological structure of *The Political Theory of Possessive Individualism* itself owed a significant debt to volume 1 of Marx's *Capital*. The key elements of Macpherson's ontology – the net transfer of powers, the critique of needs, and the idea that free, creative activity is *the* essentially human attribute, an expression of the historically changeable character of human nature itself – likewise manifest a clearly Marxian reading of the impact of capitalist development and its core institutions on human possibilities for a life of freedom, reason, and fulfilment. And his approach to democracy as a kind of society in which individuals would be fully able to use and develop their distinctively human capacities clearly represents Macpherson's attempt to spell out core features of what he took to be Marx's conception of socialism.

Moreover, although from time to time he did address issues emerging specifically from Marxian thought, and the impact of Marx himself, Macpherson never undertook a full-scale and systematic treatment of Marx's work. No doubt this had a good deal to do with the fact that the Marxian critique of bourgeois politics and society provided the basic framework, the taken-for-granted commitments and assumptions, that undergirded Macpherson's approach to the liberal tradition and its development. He likely felt little need to subject Marx's work, or Marxism generally, to the same kind of overarching critical evaluation he brought to liberalism.

Yet Marxism does itself represent one of the great traditions of modern thought. That Macpherson believed it provided the most compelling account of human possibilities and aspirations, along with a powerful method for making sense of historical development and change, should not put it out of bounds for critical appraisal or critically self-aware, immanent reflection. Indeed Marxism's very commitments would seem to make this a core dimension of Marxism itself.[1] However central and indispensable he might have believed the Marxian framework to be, I think Macpherson did offer elements of such a critical stance, or at least provide resources for the task. Certainly the evident willingness of Marxist thinkers and scholars to identify him as one of them, or at least as someone who made a serious contribution to Marxist analysis (and, in the eyes of some, could have and should have gone even further), suggests that an attempt to systematically explore and, where possible, further develop the explicitly Marxian dimension of Macpherson's work could facilitate a richer appreciation of that work and its potential to offer insight into contemporary questions. This would seem all the more worthwhile, given that in the current global political and economic uncertainty in the wake of the financial crisis of 2008 Marx himself has been experiencing a revival of interest in many quarters.

In this chapter I explore more systematically what I take to be the impact of Marxian ideas and concepts on Macpherson's thinking – and what in turn Macpherson brought to Marx's work that both further developed key ideas and offered a critical vantage point from which to appraise its strengths and weaknesses. Part of his contribution involved affirming the core elements of historical materialism as Marxists have traditionally conceived it, that is, the conception of history as a successive series of modes of production whose dynamics revolved around the combination of class struggle and the development of social labour, and thus the view that thought is socially and historically conditioned. But I want to argue that Macpherson's main contribution lay in developing Marxism as critique: a self-reflexive, hermeneutic engagement with the meanings and purposes intertwined with our historically and dynamically developed social practices with a view to clarifying the situations of social agents experiencing the contradictions Macpherson identified with the presence in liberal democratic societies of the twin competing ontological commitments of consumerism and self-development. In part, this involves what some critics have identified as Macpherson's attempt to construct a "liberal" Marxism; here his emphasis on a transformed and enriched individualism stands out. This commitment has prompted criticism by some Marxists that he conceded too much to liberalism and thus capitalism, when the point of Marxism was to overthrow both. Such criticisms offer a concave mirror image of liberal claims that Macpherson conceded too much to Marxism at the expense of liberal values.

But once again I would suggest that Marxist criticisms, like liberal ones, miss what is valuable in Macpherson's synthesis of liberalism and socialism. To be sure, he insisted that each needed the other (the "need" was, of course, greater on the liberal side) if both were not only to be realized but realized in a way that fulfilled the normative aspirations associated with them as much as humanly possible. To that end, I want to argue that what Macpherson demonstrated was that to get to the kind of society entailed by his critique of ontology one had to hold the claims of liberalism and socialism or Marxism together in an ongoing way. What he called democracy represented this kind of dynamic synthesis. This is why, if a specific label could be applied to Macpherson, it would be that of a theorist of radical democracy, or more appropriately the conditions for its achievement.

In what follows, I do not pretend to have satisfactorily clarified in my own mind all of the elements of my reading of Macpherson's relation to Marx, or indeed grasped all of the issues my approach would require me to address. I offer it here as one response, and a tentative one at that, to the question that has animated my examination of Macpherson's work all along, namely, what is of value in Macpherson's work today, here particularly in relation to what *he* took to be centrally significant to that work: the legacy of Karl Marx.

My efforts here, in other words, are intended to once again get at the submerged dimension of Macpherson's thought, or what I have called his suppressed philosophical dimension. In a sense this is the acid test, because the very approach I have tried to use is itself indebted to Marx and the tradition of Continental philosophy more broadly. It matters, I think, that we explore the issues involved, not to offer Marx as a sacrosanct icon but rather to preserve the kind of thinking that he represented and that continues to deserve a hearing. In this context my goal here is to show, as I have already tried to do in the previous chapters, what I take to be the relation of Macpherson's ideas to the critical theory of the Frankfurt School. With respect specifically to Macpherson's relation to Marx, aside from the impact already noted of Horkheimer and Marcuse, I want to argue that the efforts of the so-called second- and third-generation critical theorists, Jürgen Habermas and Axel Honneth, to rethink the Marxian project and historical materialism as social critique help us identify and grasp the issues involved. These once again turn on questions of self-development and intersubjectivity, from Habermas's efforts earlier in his career to separate the dialectics of work and interaction as key components of a revised historical materialism, to Honneth's more recent attempts to relate social reproduction to individual identity formation in the context of the vigorous contemporary reassertion of capitalist market values in the form of the "normatively charged economization of social contexts."[2]

At the same time, Macpherson very much identified with key elements of classical or so-called orthodox Marxism (sometimes to his detriment). Nonetheless, he never fit fully into the orthodox camp, in large measure because of his reservations about the Leninist model of the revolutionary vanguard party, reservations that in turn reflected his own fundamental theoretical commitments. Assessing the relation between Macpherson and Marx, then, requires an account of both dimensions of what I see as the nature of this relationship, although I take the elements of critical theory in his outlook to be the more distinctive and valuable.

There is another issue in any attempt to treat Macpherson and Marx that seems to me to be suggestive and important. This relates to my claim that Macpherson's work in a fundamental way turned on working out the dialectic of possessive individualism in terms of which it functioned as a category of critique and not simply a commitment attributed to classical liberal thinkers. In chapter 1 I noted Macpherson's analysis of the relation of individualism to collectivism in the context of the tension at the core of possessive individualism between individualism as self-direction and as self-ownership, and how in the historical circumstances this meant that individualism and collectivism, although typically treated as polar opposites, in fact entailed each other. I concluded from this that, in effect, Macpherson held that collectivism likely represented the highest form of community of which a possessive market society was capable.

I think this is a vitally important issue in appraising Macpherson's contribution, and no more so than with respect to his relation to Marx. For him, to transcend possessive individualism meant to get beyond both (possessive) individualism and collectivism in a new social order in which individuals could be both with themselves and with others – both self-determining persons and citizens. To the extent that both classical liberalism and classical Marxism remained locked into the individualism versus collectivism continuum, they failed to realize the potential that the development of both human species' productive capacities and normative insights and possibilities for a fully human life had historically opened up. I think this problem and challenge is a little-recognized but decisive implication of Macpherson's work that merits further attention, especially in dealing with the impact of Marx. Here Macpherson's extensive discussion of property and its changing historical and social forms, along with his account of human rights, might well give us important clues about his position, in addition to paving the way for a systematic treatment of his democratic theory.

Macpherson on Marx: How to Read Marx Today

Although Macpherson referred specifically to Marx and Marxian theory in many places throughout his work – articles, book reviews, review essays – the most specific and systematic discussion of Marxism I have found is an interview conducted in 1983 by Frank Cunningham to commemorate the hundredth anniversary of Marx's death. Macpherson reiterated, as he did frequently, the enduring and even expanding value of Marx and Marxism for understanding the contemporary situation. While Marx was perhaps mistaken in his expectations about when a revolutionary transformation might occur (there has certainly been debate about how predictive he intended his analysis to be), according to Macpherson his account of the long-run dynamics of capitalism as a system have stood up rather well. This was particularly so with his analysis of the alienating effects of capitalist development on labour. Here Macpherson was influenced by the work of Harry Braverman, whose study, *Labor and Monopoly Capital*, offered a powerful account and critique of the complex ways in which the labour process under capitalism had been historically organized to maintain in the face of working-class challenges authority relations in industry as well as the broader society. Braverman particularly emphasized the de-skilling and thus degradation of work and of workers. The knowledge of the demands of production that workers had acquired through their intimate association with the tools and materials needed to produce commodities was stripped from them and lodged with management, in the process enhancing the everyday power of capital in the workplace. Among other things, Braverman demonstrated that work processes and relations were not given in the nature of things – they were not merely responses to objective technical demands and requirements. Power and control were at the heart of these demands and requirements, and so made them potentially and often actually objects of resistance and struggle.

But there was another aspect to this reality. In the measure that workers were stripped of their power to direct the labour process and thereby occupy strategic vantage points in the process of production, they lost the capacity not only to counter the power of management with their ability to shape and even cease production. They also lost sight of the overall purposes achieved through their collective efforts. This limited their capacity to generate class consciousness and therefore reduced their potential to challenge the capitalist system as a whole. For Braverman and those who stood alongside or followed him in analysing the labour process as a whole from a radical or critical perspective, power trumped, or perhaps more accurately defined, efficiency in the organization of industry, even as capitalism has typically been defended on the basis that it is the most technically efficient form of social production, a system beyond power.[3]

Macpherson saw in the degradation of labour, along with the ongoing tendency towards economic crisis, proof of the continuing validity of Marx's account of historical change and the laws of motion of capitalism. However, at the same time Macpherson questioned "the adequacy of his consequent prescription of a proletarian revolution as the only possible mechanism of a transition to a good society." The proletariat in advanced capitalist countries had not become a revolutionary "universal class … whose consciousness of its own alienation would turn into a revolutionary consciousness and into revolutionary action." Instead, and to a significant extent, because the "working-class, both male and female, have to devote their efforts largely to maintaining their real material interests," the class has been largely dedicated "to fighting to maintain or increase its share of the capitalist pie, without ... questioning the methods of the bakery."[4] In effect, the development of capitalism along the lines Marx forecast had entrenched the image of humans as infinite consumers with the very individuals who, according to Marxist theory, would be most likely to bring capitalism down.

Moreover, Macpherson went on to note that in the *Grundrisse* Marx suggested that with technological developments and the increasing role of science in production, the extraction of surplus value from living labour could potentially give way to science and technology as the key source of profit and that this would alter significantly the process of working-class formation. Workers under this scenario could become less oppressed, better educated, and more versatile. "If the working class is likely to change in that direction, then one would no longer count on the utter grinding down of the proletariat, which is what we usually thought Marx was relying on in all that talk about the universal class turning to revolution just because it was so totally exploited, totally alienated."[5]

But whatever the explanation for the actual or potential political role of the working class under capitalism, for Macpherson the classical Marxist model of social transformation had to be reconsidered and reconstructed. Specifically it was time to question the relevance of the idea of proletarian revolution and the revolutionary dictatorship of the proletariat. And for Macpherson this was not just a matter of responding to historical changes to capitalism and class formation. It also involved issues of political theory and practice raised by the emergence of liberal democracy.

As we have seen, Macpherson made the case that a democratized liberalism was rooted in a conception of humans as doers and exerters of their distinctively human capacities rather than, or only, as infinite consumers and appropriators. While this developmental ethos created a tension or contradiction within liberalism because of liberalism's possessive individualist roots, for Macpherson it constituted from the outset Marx's core ontological commitment, a central feature of his "humanistic vision." This gave Marxism an advantage in the quest for a more humane, just, and egalitarian democratic society, which was why Macpherson believed that humanistic liberals should consider carefully what Marx had to say.

But that Marx was essentially correct in his understanding of the dynamics of liberal capitalism and so most powerfully revealed the limitations of classical liberalism and its reformist successor that remained too much in the thrall of the market did not mean that the gains liberalism historically represented should be diminished or set aside. Macpherson attributed Marx's prescription for proletarian revolution and dictatorship, as well as his tendency to dismiss civil liberties as merely covers for capitalist domination, to the absence in his time of developed democratic liberal states. Macpherson claimed that had there been such states, Marx might well have emphasized instead the value of both liberal rights and democratic political institutions in providing vehicles for the formation and expression of a popular majority in favour of social transformation, in the process moving society along a more developmental path. He saw Marx's prescription for revolution and dictatorship as instrumental, a matter of means not ends.

By contrast, Macpherson argued that a socialist society realizing Marx's humanistic vision should maintain core liberal values: "freedom of speech, association, publication, etc; freedom from arbitrary arrest and imprisonment; freedom to exert political pressures whether by the vote or in other ways, and in general, civil and political liberties at least of the degree that we have them now in the liberal democratic states."[6] This seemed for Macpherson to be a matter of both pragmatism and principle, means and ends. Without liberal freedoms, workers would be far less able to successfully organize and pursue change towards socialism. But it would also mean that the presence or absence of liberal freedoms would profoundly affect the kind of socialism sought, because it would powerfully determine the qualities of agency of those carrying the project of transformation. In Macpherson's words, "Marx was surely right in assuming that wide participation would be needed in order to replace capitalism and the capitalist state, and he was right in thinking that this participation must be a kind in which people begin to change themselves, begin to attain a new consciousness of their own possibilities."[7] He saw the social movements of his time that had essentially sprung up on the basis of liberal and democratic institutions (and by inference, those of our own) – feminist, ecological, urban neighbourhood, anti-nuclear and disarmament, workers' control, and industrial democracy – as clear demonstrations of this dynamic, a dynamic of self-education and self-development. A vanguard-led revolution and subsequent dictatorship could not accomplish this and would even preclude it: "A vanguard claiming to know our needs better than we do … endangers the whole prospect of transition to a good society …

And you can't make individual self-development a central value if you resign your judgment to a vanguard at the beginning."[8]

Macpherson's position here reflected a fundamental distinction he detected within the body of liberal thought itself: the distinction between, and contradiction between, *economic* liberalism and *political* liberalism. As he succinctly put it, the term *liberal* "can mean freedom of the stronger to do down the weaker by following market rules; or it can mean equal effective freedom of all to use and develop their capacities. The latter freedom is inconsistent with the former."[9] At one level this obviously parallels the contradiction between the competing ontologies characteristic of liberal democratic theory. Economic liberalism is the liberalism of infinite consumption and appropriation. Political liberalism is the liberalism of self-development. Yet at another level it lays out a vital element of the transformation to a society of free and equal, self-developing individuals. Self-development involves and may be said to require the appropriate institutions of political liberalism. Throwing these out along with capitalist economic institutions, the carriers of economic liberalism, in pursuit of a society consistent with Marx's socialist vision, would be discarding the baby with the bath water. Self-development required preserving liberalism as the "equal effective freedom of all to use and develop their capacities."

I believe Macpherson remained consistently committed to this position. While he suggested that Marx might well have changed his mind about proletarian revolution and dictatorship, had there been widespread, functioning, liberal democratic states, Macpherson was aware that, in the circumstances, this would have meant a liberal democracy with a dominant, politically conscious, working-class majority able to resist the power of capital in the democratic pursuit of socialism. On the basis of his Marxian-influenced account of the historical development of liberal democratic states and societies, democracy and liberalism – to be sure, the liberalism of possessive individualism – became compatible only because democracy was "domesticated." Workers were admitted to formal political power under conditions that muted radical or socialist class consciousness and integrated workers into capitalist institutions such that universal suffrage only sporadically threatened the stability of the system, if it did at all. Since a key element of the integration of the working classes of advanced capitalist societies was the entrenchment of consumer consciousness and a preference for affluence over community, the lure of a vanguard solution to the problem of how a revolutionary class consciousness could emerge was considerable, as with Marcuse and his claim on behalf of an educational dictatorship. Macpherson himself was seen as at least potentially tempted for these reasons by the vanguard model.

But Macpherson held fast in his resistance to the vanguard alternative and thus the idea of proletarian revolution and dictatorship. He remained committed to Marx's vision but not to a traditional Marxist political strategy. His version of Marxism was open-ended and tentative in the same way as that of the Frankfurt School. Socialism might have been necessary but not necessarily achievable. History offered possibilities, not certainties. This, I think, remained true of Macpherson's relation to Marx even where, as was the case from time to time, he seemed to be "orthodox" in his Marxism.

Beyond the brief interview devoted specifically to the legacy of Marx and his work, Macpherson did address Marxian themes in other writings with varying degrees of explicitness. He undertook these discussions with his overall project of setting out a radical theory of democracy always in mind, and they were clearly intended as a contribution to that task. Nonetheless they can be considered and appraised apart from this overarching project, although their relation to his writings on democracy should be kept in mind. In this light, the following discussion focuses initially on the essays included in his final published work, *The Rise and Fall of Economic Justice and Other Essays*, as well as his essays on property, which were published in a number of works, most notably *Democratic Theory: Essays in Retrieval*. From there I intend to move to a discussion of Macpherson's *first* published book, *Democracy in Alberta*. In this context, reading Macpherson backwards, as it were, has the virtue of demonstrating the continuity of concerns – liberal democracy and socialism, Mill and Marx – that occupied his attention over the course of his career. It makes good on his claim in 1975 that revising liberal democracy on the basis of the Marxian critique of capitalism had always been his goal.

But a discussion of Macpherson's account of the challenges, accomplishments, and contradictions of Alberta populism, rarely discussed these days, is particularly fitting as a way of demonstrating a different facet of the relations he saw among Marxism, liberalism, and democracy. *Democracy in Alberta* was his most sustained exercise in empirically and theoretically informed social science. It also offered in key respects his most explicitly Marxian analysis. This was no accident. Like Max Horkheimer, Macpherson believed that to take the longer, empirically informed view of social phenomena, including liberalism and democracy, required an approach that saw the present as history. This was a present that bore the hallmarks of the politics and culture of capitalism as a historically dynamic but contradictory socio-economic form of life. It was a present pitched between past and future and thus best grasped by a theory that says that "the basic form of the historically given commodity economy on which modern history rests contains in itself the internal and external tensions of the modern era."[10] Marxian ideas thus provided the best vehicle for understanding the limits of, but just as importantly the strengths of as well as the necessity for, the values and institutions of liberalism and democracy.

And I would note as well that the work I intend to examine in this chapter deals in one way or another with the state, class, and property – what Macpherson himself labelled the essential constituents of the theory of possessive individualism. I earlier argued that Macpherson's political theory, and in particular his democratic theory, represented the immanent development of the meaning and significance of possessive individualism. It could now be said that this same dynamic manifested for Macpherson the meaning and significance of Marx and Marxian ideas. I hope to demonstrate that, with respect to both, what emerge are not so much models but rather critical vantage points, questions and not answers.

Macpherson and Marx: The Critique of Political Theory

With Marx and the tradition of German idealism out of which Marx's thought emerged, Macpherson viewed theoretical analysis and social critique as intimately connected. Theory provided access to the structure of experience; it was not simply a body of mental constructs whose ties to reality remained in a fundamental way obscure (and therefore always haunted by the threat of scepticism). It represented a kind of articulation with more than merely academic interest and so potentially provided means of self-understanding and social connectedness for individuals embedded in a form of life. It offered insight into the distinctive properties of a specific historically developing set of social relations defined by contradictory possibilities for both individual and social fulfilment, and new intensified forms of domination. To borrow from Axel Honneth, theory offered a way of developing the connection between social reproduction and individual identity formation.[11]

As usual Macpherson did not specifically and self-reflexively engage the meta-theoretical questions involved. His task was more modest: to persuade political theorists, primarily liberal theorists, to (re)consider the proper task of humanist political thought. This meant addressing the core factors shaping the emergence and significance of dominant strains of political thinking. For him these factors had a powerful economic component. His most explicit and systematic attempt to account for the historical and analytic structure of thought in the context of its determining forces was his "Economic Penetration of Political Theory: Some Hypotheses."

"The Economic Penetration of Political Theory" was published late in Macpherson's career, first in 1978 as a journal article and then in 1985 as a chapter in his final book, *The Rise and Fall of Economic Justice and Other Essays*. It thus would seem to be the product of extensive reflection by Macpherson on the central concepts and principles of critical political reflection as he had come to view them on the basis of his overall body of work and what he took to be its meaning. Reflecting the role that possessive individualism played as the anchor and product of his thinking, Macpherson sought to demonstrate that no serious or insightful exploration of core political values, principles, actions, and institutions characteristic of liberal democratic capitalist societies could be indifferent to the impact of capitalism on theory and reality. This went beyond the obvious need for theorists to keep in mind and address the relation of state and market, polity and economy. How theorists had to conceive the nature of politics, the political, and their tasks was unavoidably and fundamentally shaped by the ways in which capitalist or possessive market institutions defined the boundaries of the conceivable and rational and thus the questions they took to be central to their efforts.

Macpherson laid out his position as a series of propositions or hypotheses that were intended as a comprehensive summary of issues to which political theorists had to attend. He wanted to indicate necessary relations between economic phenomena and conceptions of justice that would open up space for social and political critique. A key question his analysis raises is whether the relations between economic and political phenomena he identified and explored are timeless, relevant in all historical periods, or historically generated and situated, a product of the transformative impact associated with the development of capitalism. In short: is Macpherson's critique transcendent or immanent?

Marx's critique of ideology provided the architecture for "The Economic Penetration of Political Theory" (as well as for his "Deceptive Task of Political Theory," which may be seen here as a companion piece). Macpherson saw political theory, in particular liberal theory and modern liberal or market economics, as having undergone from the nineteenth century onward a noticeable decline in its capacity to provide an accurate picture of the social relations of a capitalist society. The key failing was its inability or unwillingness to take into account the nature of power as a pervasive social phenomenon not restricted to the state. This, of course, was why the net transfer of powers was both so significant and so elusive theoretically. Macpherson sought to "de-reify" the economy as an object of analysis, by restoring its dynamic qualities as a set of social relations of control and dependency, as opposed to the tendency of dominant paradigms of thought to view it as a "natural" external force governed by its own laws and operating independently of human direction and control. The roots of critique in Marx's account of commodity fetishism are obvious: "Economic relations between people have in effect been reduced to relations between things: the underlying economic relations of dependence and control between people have dropped out of sight ... Economic ideas which are confined to relations between things, or to relations between disembodied persons who appear only as the holders of demand schedules, cannot enter into political theory at any fundamental level, since political theory is about relations of dependence and control between people."[12] And in the measure that economics has "penetrated" contemporary political science, it has extended its propensity to abstract from relations of dependence and control to a form of inquiry for which these relations should be fundamental. Both economics and political science are diminished as a result.

Placing questions of dependence and control, that is, power, once again at the heart of both economic and political analysis meant for Macpherson addressing the extent to which economic ideas – "assumptions about the necessary or possible relations between people in their capacity as producers of the material means of life" – established the inescapable requirements of a political order, i.e., justice and political obligation, as well as, more indirectly, the essential attributes of human nature and thus appropriate and necessary relations between people. In turn the focus on humans as participants in dynamic relations, by which in turn they are shaped, rather than as abstract, atomized, and reified individuals whose behaviour can be deterministically modelled, required attention to questions of class and property. A sound political theory thus provided a self-reflexive, critically detached, and robust account of both, because the penetrating quality of theory is dependent upon its capacity to realize the very extent to which it is itself penetrated by economic assumptions. Such awareness transforms the very ideas that come under scrutiny by calling into question what is taken for granted. Macpherson defined the economic penetration of political theory as the extent to which economic ideas or assumptions entered into and shaped such theory. He noted rather offhandedly that if "there is also in the title an implication that the penetrating quality of a political theory, its ability to get us to the root of the political problems it is concerned with, depends somewhat on its economic grasp, I shall not disavow that position." He implied this was a secondary consideration. In fact it was central, indeed decisive, for his analysis. In this respect his debt to Marx was once again clear. Adapting Marx's claim from his famous preface to the *Contribution to the Critique of Political Economy* that political economy provided the anatomy of civil society, Macpherson argued that the anatomy of *political* society had to be sought in political economy.[13]

This consideration might well have been buried, even to some extent for Macpherson, because of the unusual structure of the argument. He offered five hypotheses about the relation of economic assumptions (or political economy) to political theory and drew from the history of political thought examples in support of them. This would seem to make this analysis a straightforward instance of traditional theory. Yet things are not so straightforward. The hypotheses do not stand alone. They are structured in such a way that their impact is cumulative, with their meaning and significance tied to their contribution to the concluding argument Macpherson strove to defend. Indeed one of the hypotheses was advanced only to be subsequently discarded; all of them are implicitly modified or more fully explicated only in the context of the completed analysis. In short it is yet another example of Macpherson offering an account indebted more to critical than traditional theory. However, I would argue that in this case Macpherson was even more disinclined than usual to pitch his argument on an explicitly metamethodological plane, to bring to the surface his suppressed philosophical dimension. His analysis appeared to have been intended to establish the extent to which political theory has at different times been penetrated by economic assumptions and to explain the variation. In fact its purpose was prescriptive: to encourage contemporary political theorists to deliberately theorize in a way that specifically demanded that their reflections be "penetrated" by economic assumptions, that is, by the recognition of how and to what extent relations of control and dependency between individuals as producers of the material means of life shaped their understanding of political questions. But this resulted in something Macpherson only hinted at: that the very nature of that penetration, indeed the meaning of economic versus political assumptions, would necessarily change.

It is clear that, for Macpherson, political theory everywhere and at all times was strengthened in both its realism and its critical potential by taking on board necessary and possible relations among individuals engaged in producing and reproducing the material conditions of life. But it could be argued that awareness of this requirement did not necessarily entail "penetration" as Macpherson wanted to explore it in this context. His concern appeared to be focused in an almost Aristotelian sense on the "unnaturalness" of the ways in which economic relations determined political ones and the tendency in the historical circumstances he addressed for this relation between the economic and the political to be simultaneously fundamental and obscure. That is, the historically evolved connection has been, in Marxian terms, ideological – the real relations hiding, as it were, in plain sight. Taking hold properly of this relation and thus critically evaluating it – as with Marx and the Frankfurt School, explanation and evaluation are necessarily linked together – is at the core of the identification of the extent of the economic penetration. Without specifically stating it, Macpherson clearly believed the fullest manifestation of penetration was the result of the triumph of capitalism, or pervasive possessive market relations. Hence his initial, and in many ways most fundamental hypothesis: that the economic penetration of political theory varies with the extent of the market. "More accurately this should be, varies with the extent to which market relations have permeated the society, or, the extent to which the relations between people as producers are market relations."[14] While there were periods historically in the ancient world in which market relations assumed considerable prominence – Macpherson viewed ancient Greece in its later stages in this light and saw Aristotle as a critic of a fairly commercialized society – it was clearly in the modern era, the era of Hobbes and his successors, in which pervasive market relations triumphed. Echoing the arguments he made continuously throughout his career, Macpherson suggested that the move to a society that freed individuals from previous constraints and demanded of them self-interested, rational maximizing behaviour posed unique new problems for political order and stability. Perceptive theorists came to recognize the economic basis of the new problems, and the best political thinking therefore took this into account. Where this occurred, it established the penetrating quality of a political theory aware of economic penetration and its extent.

Given the momentous changes the emergence of capitalism wrought, Macpherson then proposed a second hypothesis: that the economic penetration of political theory varies with the extent of recent or current change in actual economic relations. But just as quickly he discarded it. His argument here is not as clear or as systematically laid out as it might have been. However, as I see it, the intersection of history and ontology that I attempted to analyse in chapter 2 is the key here. While theorists might have been aware of the specific features of a possessive market society, not all of them saw this society as "new." Hobbes was the classic prototype of a theorist with a profound grasp of market society who nonetheless saw it as an expression of a timeless and permanent human nature. By contrast later theorists, such as Rousseau, saw human nature as having changed and in principle as capable of changing again.

This led Macpherson to a modified version of the hypothesis. It was not the newness of markets or market relations, even fairly pervasive ones, that proved decisive in accounting for fundamental social change. Rather, it was the extent to which commodity relations more generally – including and especially the widespread and, for a majority of the population, increasingly decisive commodification of labour – weighed heavily. This was, on Marxian grounds, the factor that most fundamentally distinguished capitalist market relations from previous societies with extensive market institutions (or, to use Macpherson's analytic models, what distinguished a possessive market from both a customary and a simple market social order).

In other words, the key issue here was yet again the net transfer of powers consequent upon the emergence of a new kind of class-divided society. Macpherson's third hypothesis incorporated it: "*The economic penetration of political theory varies with the theorists' recognition of the necessarily exploitive or extractive nature of market relations in a society divided into owners and non-owners of productive material property.*"[15]

There are two points to note here. First of all, Macpherson, in a highly condensed fashion, recapitulated the argument from *The Political Theory of Possessive Individualism* about the movement in liberal theory from Hobbes through Harrington and the Levellers to Locke, in terms of which the increasingly obvious class nature of the society became front and centre a political problem of the first order and so called forth a modification of Hobbes's position (without, of course, an abandonment of it, even if the debt often went unacknowledged). Here Macpherson made the claim that one might be tempted "to the simple hypothesis that, with the increase of scale of the full market economy, political economy got an increasingly better grasp of the essentials of the economy, and that, correspondingly, political theorists were more influenced by political economy." Such an improvement in political economy "was due to its increasing recognition of a class of industrial and agricultural (rather than mercantile) capitalists, whose share of the whole annual produce of the nation, i.e. profit, was seen to be not wages of superintendence, nor akin to rent or interest, nor merely from taking advantage of momentary terms of trade. Instead, it was seen to be the excess of value added by the current labour, which capital employed over the wage paid."[16] In the measure that profit was so understood, it reflected the increasing and increasingly salient impact of class relations on the dynamics of the economy and thus on the political system. This was recognized by theorists such as Locke, Smith, and Bentham, for whom the economic penetration of political theory was central.

This leads to the second point. It was one thing to acknowledge the presence of class relations and even the net transfer of powers, and on this basis also acknowledge the necessity for political theory to address issues of justice and stability in light of the challenges posed by a possessive market economy. It was quite another to see this as representing a historically new social order that had been the product of historical change and could in principle change again into something else. While classes and a class-based distribution of the social product might well be recognized, as it was indeed by Adam Smith, it did not follow that such a distribution would be seen as necessarily exploitive, even if Smith himself acknowledged the consequences of class-based inequality and the need for civil government to protect owners from non-owners. "The reason for this is plain. *Given* the pattern of ownership which they assumed, everyone got a fair reward for what he put in. [Theorists] assumed the necessary and permanent division of all modern and progressive societies into three classes: those whose income derived from (a) ownership of land, (b) ownership of capital, and (c) ownership only of their capacity to labour."[17] If one assumed either that the possessive market society was, as Hobbes believed, natural and timeless, or as representing the end result of a process of historical development and the achievement of individual freedom for all, then it could well become difficult if not impossible to see the society as exploitive or extractive, or even if this were seen, to imagine any alternative to it.

If I am right about this, then for Macpherson the penetrating quality of political theory, its critical and scientific character, requires that the assumptions of the theorist involve *both* the recognition of the class character of the society and consequently the need for a political authority capable of maintaining order in the face of conflict between the propertied and the non-propertied *and* the possibility, if not necessity, of historical change rooted in the potential changeability of human nature. Of course from Macpherson's perspective, the great thinkers in the tradition of English liberalism, political theorists or political economists, held to the first but not the second.

Macpherson did not lay out here this line of argument. But I believe it captures what he wanted to say; moreover it helps make sense and put into context the final two hypotheses he advances.

Macpherson's fourth hypothesis held that the economic penetration of political theory varied with the political strength of an exploited class – directly in socialist theory, and inversely with liberal theory. The fifth claimed that economic penetration varied with a theorist's confidence in the ability of an emerging or established economic order to maximize human well-being or maintain political dominance. The two are clearly linked. If exploitation, or, in Macpherson's terms, the net transfer of powers, is the decisive factor, the recognition of it requires both subjective and objective elements. The theorist must recognize such exploitation (and believe it can and should be ended). But there also must be an objectively present or embodied manifestation of it in the form of some social force, an exploited class, whose presence and behaviour demands that relations of exploitation be abolished. Where such a class is present, an honest theorist cannot seriously avoid addressing its claims – cannot, in other words, undertake theoretical reflection without taking on board the extent to which economic relations of dependence and control shape the political system and the nature of the problems of justice and political obligation. Macpherson saw John Stuart Mill as the classic example of a thinker both personally appalled by the evident exploitation visible in his time and acutely aware of the political challenge mounted by a growing and increasingly militant working class. However, as a liberal fundamentally committed to capitalism, he was unable or unwilling to throw his support behind radical and transformative social and economic change.

Thus for Macpherson, as sensitive a liberal as Mill was, he nonetheless represented a turning point in liberal thinking about the relation of political economy to political theory. From Mill onward, there was a decline in the level of insight into the economic penetration of political theory, because the threat posed by a potentially revolutionary working class undermined any claim to permanence of possessive market relations and the individualism they reflected and reproduced. Henceforth the nature of the political problem, indeed the definition of politics and the political, had to change so that new conditions for social harmony, apart from the market seen as the fount of natural liberty, could be identified. I will return to this issue presently.

By contrast, socialist thinkers, and especially Marx, "may fairly be regarded as the high point of economic penetration of political theory, and his was the period of maximum political strength of class-conscious working-class action in the Western nations."[18] Socialism emerged as the voice of working-class political action, its fate tied to both its capacity to articulate the situation of those social forces carrying the socialist project and the ability or inability of those same forces to bring about the required change. On the other hand, according to Macpherson, as the twentieth century unfolded and, at least in Western countries, the revolutionary impetus was stilled and class conscious political action weakened, social democratic and democratic socialist theory tended to manifest a declining economic penetration.[19] However, the diminishing economic penetration of socialist theory was not matched by a reinvigorated economic penetration of liberal theory, as one might have anticipated, given the diminished strength of a class-conscious working class. Liberalism remained, and has remained, incapable of accurately capturing the link between economic relations as relations of power with political relations and political power.

Macpherson's analysis on this point is pretty shaky. The analysis is particularly unsatisfactory when applied to the continuing inability of liberal theorists – and here Macpherson included thinkers running the gamut from Ernest Barker to John Rawls – to properly allow for the economic penetration of their theories. He once again identified as the decisive factor "the global threat of the socialist and Third World societies. It would be astonishing if liberal theorists in countries which, either directly, or indirectly as client states or nostalgic states, rely on global exploitation, did not respond, even if only subconsciously, to the threat. I see them as having done so."[20] As in other contexts in which Macpherson played up the idea of a competition between social and political systems, this claim does not stand up well. The case for the decline of economic penetration in socialist theory, which Macpherson in any event defined quite loosely here, seems equally unconvincing; certainly the diminution of penetration, even in mainstream social democratic theory, would seem to have been less complete in the measure that even the mildest forms of socialist thought have continued to bear at least some connection to a more egalitarian and democratic social order.

Essentially acknowledging the problems here, Macpherson moved on to identify what was in fact his real point all along: that the extent of the economic penetration of political theory ultimately comes down to the historical viability of capitalist society. It is this element that moves the whole argument from a set of hypotheses about the relation between political economy and political theory to a form of social critique whose plausibility and fate rests on a wager about the possible transformation of capitalism – that is, to a form of critical theory. This I take to be the significance of his fifth and final hypothesis, which relates the economic penetration of political theory to the theorist's confidence in the ability of a new or emerging economic order to maximize well-being and to become or remain politically dominant. Although stated as a separate hypothesis, it really incorporates and represents the transcendence of the previous four. Only from this vantage point do the previous four reveal their meanings, insights, and limitations. The extent of the market, especially as the product of changes in economic relations, the recognition of the exploitive character of market relations, and the strength of those class forces opposing the system and pressing for a new kind of society all point towards the key questions about whether a particular social order, either established or emergent, is politically plausible or viable and maximizes human fulfilment. This is a matter both subjective and objective: "To put the point most generally, confidence in an established or emergent economic system is not reducible to any external factor because the possibility of an emergent one depends partly on people's perception of such new possibility."[21] It is the wager Macpherson made that I noted above.

The wager would pay off if the costs of largely unregulated economic growth, the deterioration of living standards, and a general decline in the quality of life triggered a "move away from a society permeated by market behaviour and material maximization."[22] If market relations and the scarcity with which, according to Macpherson, they have been associated were eliminated altogether – an admittedly limiting case – the economic penetration of political theory would disappear entirely – and so might political theory, at least as a theory of justice and obligation, along with it. "That is the logical conclusion that would follow from the postulates of classical liberal theory, which tied political obligation, rights, and justice to scarcity."[23] Short of this state of affairs, "any move from a market-dominated society to a non-market-dominated society will clearly need the services both of political theory and political economy. And it will need a political theory that recognizes the determining role of necessary and possible relations between people as producers ... indeed a revival from the present low point in Western political theory, of economic penetration ... The conclusion which seems inescapable is that ... political theorists will have to ... take the lead in restoring to political theory the economic insight it once enjoyed."[24]

The point of Macpherson's analysis is clear enough. It is indeed the point of his work as a whole: to establish the full meaning, critical potential, and critical limitations of liberalism and liberal democracy by means of an immanent critique indebted to Marx and thus rooted in the wedding of political economy to political theory. Only in this way would political theory be faithful to its humanist charge and be able to address the challenges of the dynamic historical epoch that characterized the rise of capitalism and its social contradictions. Conversely a political theory informed by political economy would also help ensure that economic analysis would maintain a historical focus and an explicit sensitivity to economic power. This is why in "The Economic Penetration of Political Theory" Macpherson carefully distinguished economic ideas as assumptions about necessary and possible relations between people as producers of the material means of life from both economic theory and modern economics. For Macpherson, the separation of political economy from political theory reflected the inability or unwillingness of nineteenth- (and twentieth-)century liberalism to take on board social and political developments that at least potentially called into question the permanence, stability, and harmony of possessive market societies. Political economy became economics. Political theory, a complex, dialectical intertwining of the descriptive and the normative, with Hobbes and his derivation of value from fact the classic prototype, split off into (descriptive) political science and (normative) political thought. The driving force in each case was the same: a retreat from class and potentially transformative social conflict to a (timeless) individualism and the rationality of self-interested maximization that ideally could be explored and explained by social scientific covering laws, i.e., as traditional theory. The achievement of supposed rigour came at the cost of critical insight and humanistic commitment.[25] The task for political theorists was to make this an issue and develop alternatives.

While Macpherson's purpose in "The Economic Penetration of Political Theory" was relatively straightforward, overall his analysis seems a bit muddled and without the incisiveness of his best work. The core of the problem is the concept of penetration itself. Macpherson's use of it was ambiguous. On the one hand, he measured the quality of a political theory by the extent to which it was penetrated by economic assumptions, and he urged political theorists to ensure their work was duly and properly penetrated. On the other hand, although Macpherson did not explicitly put it this way, all political theory under modern conditions is necessarily and pervasively penetrated by economic assumptions, *whether theorists are consciously aware of it or not*. This reflects the impact of the market – extensive commodification – and thus market-based relations of power. In this respect the economic penetration of political theory is not to be encouraged. Rather, it is to be resisted or, more accurately, subjected to critique.

That Macpherson wrestled with this ambiguity was, I think, evident in his claim that the goal of moving away from a society permeated by market behaviour would seem at the extreme to entail the elimination of the economic penetration of political theory, because the endpoint of such a process would be the abolition of the market, that is, the commodity form. His reference to Hume notwithstanding, this seems implausible, if not undesirable.

The problem, I think, is that his categorical framework did not quite fit with the core of his analysis. He wrote of the economic penetration of political theory. But what he was really after was something else that his resort to this idea did not properly express. To make use of a chiasmus, a figure of speech often deployed by members of the Frankfurt School, and particularly Marcuse, Macpherson wanted not so much the economic penetration of political theory, but rather the political – that is to say, the communal and solidaristic – penetration of the economy. Theory needed to be linked to praxis in a project that would reduce the blind and compulsive forces of a nature-like market social order and realize the conditions necessary for a good society of freely self-determining and rational individuals that, at its best, liberalism and its institutions promised but could not deliver. It is the project laid out in *The Political Theory of Possessive Individualism.*[26]

The issues posed by "The Economic Penetration of Political Theory" are not just Macpherson's alone. They also speak to ambiguities in the Marxist tradition itself, and in particular its more orthodox manifestation, to which many of Macpherson's explicit theoretical claims bore considerable affinity. For both Macpherson and Marxism there is frequently a tension between theoretical and empirical claims and philosophical and methodological commitments. The latter are often more dynamic, incisive, and relevant than the former – a point made tellingly by Georg Lukács in his essay "What Is Orthodox Marxism?"[27] The substructure of "The Economic Penetration of Political Theory," or what I have called Macpherson's suppressed philosophical dimension, is more suggestive than his specific arguments.

Although the analysis in "The Economic Penetration of Political Theory" was clearly indebted to Marx, and even a fairly orthodox reading of the Marxian legacy, it did not explicitly take on board the relationship. By contrast there is a much earlier essay that did explicitly model itself on Marx's analysis, and it turned out to be one of Macpherson's most significant pieces, although surprisingly neglected in appraisals of his thought. This is "The Deceptive Task of Political Theory," an incisive and important writing that, among other things, introduced the concept of possessive individualism and clearly demonstrated its Marxian roots. Perhaps this neglect reflects the view that the essay is now antiquated, "too" Marxist in a way that is no longer fashionable or credible. But I believe it harbours value, not only for what it says about Macpherson and his relation to Marx, but also what it says about the task of political theory, a theme we have already pursued.

"The Deceptive Task of Political Theory" attempted to do for (and to) the classical tradition of liberal theory what Marx's argument in volume 1 of *Capital*, whose impact on Macpherson's account of possessive individualism I have already attempted to demonstrate, had done for the classical tradition of political economy. Macpherson sought to systematically show how and why liberal thought was impelled by both the pressures of a changing historical reality and the internal character of its own categories to shift from a "scientific" account of the foundation of political obligation, valid for all humanity, to a thinly veiled apology for class society and the political dominance of the bourgeoisie. Marx had understood this transformation in the realm of economic theory as the movement from "classical" to "vulgar" political economy. He argued that it signalled an ultimately futile attempt to preserve the essentials of bourgeois economic science, with its assumption of inevitable social harmony, in light of the reality, no longer to be ignored, of the rise of the industrial working class and the growth of class conflict. As Macpherson noted, "There was more than name-calling to the epithet 'vulgar.'"[28] There was no suggestion that, at least in most cases, theorists had conspired to distort reality or had consciously falsified their evidence. Rather, the assumptions that political economy could be (and was) scientifically concerned with a determinate system in permanent equilibrium and that, because of the "natural" character of the economy, it could be morally impartial in its assessment of the system were no longer tenable. Powerful social forces, carrying with them a new conception of society and its future direction, had emerged to challenge the foundations of the social and economic order. Capitalism no longer appeared permanent. "Yet while political economy could not go any further on the assumption that capitalist social relations were the final form of social relations, at the same time the economists could not abandon that assumption without abandoning their whole conception of the world ... So the material of classical political economy (the economic relations of production and distribution of a capitalist society) had from then on to be dealt with in a less scientific way: economics became apologetics or a search for terms of accommodation between the old theory and the new facts which could not be fitted into it." Put another way, explanation and justification parted company. Apologetics or syncretism followed suit: "If classes destroyed the vision of equilibrium, it was classes that had to go and equilibrium be kept."[29]

Carrying the argument further, Macpherson suggested that a comparable process was evident enough in the body of classical liberal thought, if two factors were kept in mind. In the first place, like classical political economy, "classical" liberalism was both descriptive and justificatory, with the justificatory dimension more obvious. Here again, Macpherson's account of Hobbes and the general affinity Macpherson's work shares with that of the Frankfurt School stands out as an important element of his thought. In the second place, the tradition of classical liberalism, which stretched from Hobbes to Jeremy Bentham and James Mill, provided a body of scientific material suitable for vulgarization. Since the concern of any political theory that is also a political science – and Hobbes, for one, would not have distinguished the two – is the kind of state most congruous with human needs and capacities, the scientific substance of classical liberal thought lay in "an essentially utilitarian theory of political obligation based on postulates of human nature which, within the limits of the then bourgeois vision, were profound." At the heart of this theory and vision was an individualist assumption, going back to Hobbes and Locke, that "was the strength of the liberal theory in the seventeenth and eighteenth centuries (when it corresponded with the social reality), and became the defect of that theory about mid-nineteenth century (when it ceased to do so) ... It will be convenient to call the assumption 'possessive individualism.'"[30]

Possessive individualism became a defect because the rise of a politically conscious working class equipped with an alternative conception of human possibilities undermined the central claim of classical liberalism: "that bourgeois human nature is the final form (or, more usually, the universal form except for some supposed primitive age) of human nature." The same historical developments that outwitted classical political economy challenged liberal thought. In each case, working-class consciousness "made the old theory invalid and made it obvious that it was invalid." Once an "articulate working class" developed unorthodox ideas about human needs and capacities, it became "impossible to make politically meaningful statements about human nature as such, with anything like the previously possible degree of scientific validity. It has become necessary to recognize a class difference in human nature, or at least in concepts of human nature."[31]

Because the justificatory dimension of political economy is always more or less explicit and clear, thinkers in the "vulgar" or revisionist tradition of liberalism sought not so much to accommodate (or deny) the claims of the working class in light of the requirements of capital, but rather to reconcile possessive individualism with social democracy, i.e., two competing conceptions of political obligation. From John Stuart Mill to T.H. Green to the idealists, neo-idealists, and pluralists of the twentieth century, English liberal theorists gradually "solved" the problem of class by stressing the role of the liberal democratic state in harmonizing the demands of the individual with those of society. Indeed the state was seen as the only institution capable of doing so, because of its unique capacity to embrace the claims of both. So understood, twentieth-century liberalism provides the foundation of the "equilibrium" model of the political process long dominant in conventional academic political science, very much in the same way that neoclassical economic theory laid the basis for the equilibrium analysis at the centre of modern economics. Macpherson would later carry this argument forward into his account of liberal democracy and its various forms.

Macpherson's analysis was thus at one level a Marxian critique of the ideological character of nineteenth- and twentieth-century liberal thought, with "ideology" understood as partial claims masked as universal values. What ultimately limited both the classical political economy that Marx tackled and the liberal theory Macpherson analysed is that neither could account for either the existence of exploitation or the historically changing character of social relations. Only a new, more comprehensive, and therefore truthful science could both rationally comprehend the exploitation and inequality whose manifest existence had so sorely vexed the most honourable of the "vulgar" thinkers, and also point to those historical tendencies that would eliminate the problems. This new science was linked to the actions and aspirations of an emerging social group: the industrial working class.

To suggest that Macpherson adopted a certain Marxian conception of science is to return us to the issue Horkheimer raised in his account of critical versus traditional theory: the unavoidable partisanship of critical theory whose fate is tied to the prospects for an emancipatory politics and a transformed society. Such partisanship must always show why it should not be dismissed as simply biased and unrealistic.

As a thinker sharing what I have argued is common ground with Marx and the Frankfurt School, Macpherson had to confront similar criticisms. In the circumstances, these involved the claim that his very critique of liberal ideology was itself ideologically motivated and therefore one-sided. But if I am correct in reading his suppressed philosophical dimension, the question posed by Macpherson's interpretation of the liberal tradition in the context of "The Deceptive Task of Political Theory" is not whether his position is "ideological" in the negative sense of the term, but whether the (largely implicit) assumptions about the character of science and philosophy found in that tradition and the work of its defenders are adequate. He examined this issue of adequacy in his treatment of two themes we have seen at play in his work: the relation of explanation to justification, and the historical character of political analysis.

Recall that the relation between explanation and justification, or "fact" and "value," was central to Macpherson's treatment of Hobbes and thus possessive individualism. Macpherson believed that Hobbes had revolutionized political philosophy, not so much by abandoning value claims of the sort evident in ancient political thought, but rather by attempting to demonstrate that the facts contained and expressed their own morality, so to speak. The ancient concern with the *Summum Bonum* could be dismissed, because it had now become possible *for the first time* to put ethics on a strictly materialist basis. Since the validity of this new morality was not altogether self-evident, it was necessary for Hobbes to show how and why it was now possible (and necessary) to proceed in the way that he did. Crucial to this issue were the changing historical relation of fact to value, and the changing conceptualization of that relation.

Macpherson had begun his analysis in "The Deceptive Task" by noting that it might seem odd to draw a parallel between the development of political theory and that of political economy. Unlike political economy, political theory had always been "apologetic." There seemed no basis in it for a transition from science to overt justification. For Macpherson, however, this distinction between political theory and political economy was superficial and relative, "conditional on the way in which each, during any phase of its own development, is related to the society in which and for which it is written." It turned out that political economy was, even at its most "scientific," a justification of market society. "The explanation of 'the system of natural liberty' was itself a vindication of it, in the circumstances; to explain the system was to demonstrate its superiority to the previous system in liberating man by increasing his ability to dominate his natural environment."[32] Only with the emergence of a new vision of society did explanation and justification part company. Hence political economy and political theory had a strikingly similar character *as* thought.

Macpherson intended this analysis to show that political theory could be understood in light of political economy which, given Macpherson's Marxian assumptions, could necessarily penetrate social reality more thoroughly than did political theory. To demonstrate that each shared the same structure was in this context to validate political theory as the basis for the kind of critical account of society that Marx had undertaken using the material of classical political economy. Thus Macpherson sought to demonstrate the scientific character of political theory in light of the scientific character of political economy – and more particularly the Marxian reconstruction of that science.

But he did something else as well. He suggested, in effect, that while the scientific character of political theory could be illuminated by a comparison with political economy, it was also true that political economy *as a science* could be properly clarified only in light of the normative concerns of political theory. Explanation and justification (science and ideology) were not absolutely and irrevocably distinct qualities of social analysis, but rather alternative ways of pinpointing important features of a dynamic social order. What provided the context and content of explanation and justification, science and ideology, "fact" and "value," was history. To be properly scientific was to be able to establish the object of inquiry – society – as it actually appeared to exist *now* and as it might *become,* given its manifold historical possibilities. The capacity to specify these possibilities was always limited, because history is multivalent; thus science itself had a historical nature. Explanation and justification come apart, or science becomes ideology, when the actual is "frozen" or accepted as permanent, even in the presence of genuine and comprehensible alternative possibilities. There was nothing inherently scientific or ideological in any specific claim about the social order, whether that claim was "descriptive" or "normative." Its character must be judged in relation to the character of society as a whole. Thus "the position that society consisted of free market relations"[33] was (relatively) scientific at one stage in the development of market society, (relatively) ideological at another stage. The historical basis of this shift was to be found in the increasingly central, and evident, class character of the society.

One need not in light of this position adhere to a teleological conception of history, to the fulfilment of which all historical developments inevitably lead. Certainly evidence that Macpherson held such a conception is scant at best. But the real issue is the breadth of the comprehension of society in its actuality and its potentiality that is to be found in the work of a theorist. Hobbes and Marx, the key thinkers for Macpherson, were on his assumptions both scientific, indeed *equally* so. Such an understanding of science is not "historicist" but historical. To claim that a thinker's writings are historically determined is not to diminish their stature, but in fact to do the opposite: to acknowledge their immersion in and relevance for the only forum in which human capacities are developed and exhibited.

It is instructive to consider "The Deceptive Task of Political Theory" and "The Economic Penetration of Political Theory," two pieces a quarter of a century apart that essentially book-ended Macpherson's most creative period as a theorist, for what they reveal about his fundamental commitments, especially as they reflect his debt to Marx (and also, interestingly, to Hobbes). On the one hand, they make clear the extent to which Macpherson embraced an explicit and relatively orthodox conception of Marxism as the critique of bourgeois ideology. It is framed by what on the surface appears to be a historicist or relativist view of thought as a direct if distorted reflection of the material conditions of society. In this view all thought is "ideological," and claims about the autonomy of thought are themselves ideological, examples of false consciousness. Dominant political ideas reflect the material and thus cultural power of dominant classes. The "deceptive" task of political theory, or the decline in the economic penetration of political thought, took shape as the apparently universal ideas of a heretofore unchallenged bourgeoisie began to give way to those of an emerging working class representing human progress in the mastery of nature and the achievement of freedom. To generate non-deceptive political theory or to restore the appropriate level of economic penetration required that thinkers become partisans. They had to adopt the perspective of the working class, "the historical persons in whom theory and historical practice become a unity.[34]

But as with Horkheimer and the early Frankfurt School, this partisanship for Macpherson was not blind. The normative basis for it involved the kind of immanent critique, the commitment to critical versus traditional theory, that I have been arguing forms what I have called Macpherson's suppressed philosophical dimension or what Erica Sherover-Marcuse called the disengaging of a political theory from the body of political thought.

Bringing this dimension to light not only reveals more fully the normative aspect of Macpherson's thought and therefore the extent to which he accorded theory an autonomy denied by claims that all thought is merely an ideological reflex of supposedly transparent "material" conditions and relations (which, after all, require conceptual mediation in order to be "visible"). As with Marx, the method both undergirds and overshoots specific empirical and theoretical claims. Its power and value lie in its articulation of social possibilities in the context of the ongoing dynamic relation between thought and lived experience. But exploring Macpherson's suppressed philosophical dimension demonstrates that, while Macpherson remained faithful to Marxian ideas and was inclined to adopt explicitly an overtly orthodox conception of these ideas, their relation to his overall work did subtly shift.

I think we can detect this in the differences between "The Deceptive Task" and "The Economic Penetration of Political Theory." To be sure, they make comparable points about the historical development of liberalism and its decline as a carrier of the most progressive values and commitments, as it was transformed into the defender of a contradictory social order that promised freedom for all while denying it to most. However, the titles of the two pieces tell us something about how Macpherson conceived the nature of a critical theory of society. "The Deceptive Task" has a clarity and cogency that make it powerfully insightful and one of his best writings. By contrast, "The Economic Penetration of Political Theory" is more loosely argued and suffers from gaps in the analysis that I earlier attempted to examine and explain. While this can be seen as evidence that the later essay lacks the analytic acuity of the earlier one – and this may be part of the story – it also indicates a tentative quality to the analysis absent from the initial work. This I think reflected in turn Macpherson's decreasing commitment to the idea that a politically conscious working class would lead the way towards a more fully democratic society, coupled nonetheless with the continuing commitment to a socialist critique of possessive individualism and capitalist society.[35] The task of the critical, humanist political theorist, then, was not so much to uncover the ideologically driven distortions of social theory in the interests of the working-class project as to articulate the pathologies of a social order built upon exploitation and the net transfer of powers, with no specific agent of transformation, although it was assumed that a politically conscious working class would necessarily play a key role. I argued that the idea of economic penetration, as Macpherson sought to develop it, did not successfully capture what he was really after.

In the end, the tension between overtly classical Marxist claims and assumptions and an implicit but powerful open-ended, dialectical approach that goes beyond those claims and is a source of continuing theoretical vitality plays itself out throughout the body of Macpherson's work, and in particular his explicit invocation of Marxian themes. His distinctive combination of liberalism and socialism as expressed in his richly mediated understanding of individualism testifies to this ongoing tension.

The chief vehicle by which Macpherson sought to work out this tension in the mediation of social critique and social institutions was his critical/historical analysis of property. Macpherson viewed his attempt to develop what he called a political theory of property as the linchpin connecting his critique of possessive individualism, his conception of ontology, and in particular his account of human powers, and his theory of democracy as a kind of society. The impact of his analysis of property on the theory of democracy will become evident in the next chapter. Here, my interest lies in exploring the ways in which this analysis simultaneously reflected and developed his relation to Marx and the Marxian legacy.

The Political Theory of Property: Human Rights and Self-Development

Part of the rationale for working up a theory of property was that this institution and the values associated with it occupied a key place in the everyday culture of a liberal democratic capitalist society. Breaking property out of its possessive individualist integument and reformulating it in a way that respected the normative weight it holds for individuals, while at the same time having it serve as a critical standard for the appraisal of capitalism, was a core purpose. He did this by combining "a straightforward historical account of the successive theories justifying or criticizing the various types and amounts of property" with "a logical classification of the grounds on which property has been or may be justified, and to subject each to tests of logical consistency and adequacy." The result was what he specifically identified as his own approach: "to start from the observable changes in the very concept of property, that is, in the content put into the definition of property itself, in successive eras in the Western tradition, and to relate those changes to changing requirements of dominant and rising classes."[36] This approach is obviously indebted to the Marxian (and Hegelian) tradition.

Nonetheless, in examining Macpherson's account of property I am abandoning my stated intention that this chapter be restricted to his writings that explicitly addressed Marx or the Marxist tradition. As with most of what he wrote, the impact of Marxian ideas on his theory of property was evident but rarely explicit. While he did include extracts from Marx's writings in his edited collection, *Property: Mainstream and Critical Positions*, which he intended as a comprehensive survey of key analyses of property in the modern bourgeois era,[37] in his central essay, "A Political Theory of Property," he developed his argument on the basis of the immanent dialectic of liberal individualism and nowhere specifically referred to Marx.

Yet I would justify including this account here because I believe it best represents Macpherson's response to the dilemmas and challenges of Marx and Marxism that I have argued characterized his relation to both. In particular it highlights his attempt to demonstrate that a revision of liberal democratic theory that owes a massive debt to Marx can and must be based on an ethic of individualism and not its denial or suppression. It therefore represents a point at which the intersection of political theory and political economy, a key focus of both "The

Deceptive Task of Political Theory" and "The Economic Penetration of Political Theory," comes to fruition around an institution that not only plays a critical role in sustaining the social relations of a possessive market society but also crystallizes for most people the values of freedom, fulfilment, and normative recognition. It thus expresses in a particularly important way the relation of theory to practice that is the cornerstone of the work of both Marx and Macpherson. If we are to move from a constrained liberal democracy based on and reproducing a now historically inadequate conception of the human essence to a more fulfilling liberal democratic social order founded on a richer and now historically possible account of human possibilities, a focus on property is essential – indeed, for Macpherson "all roads lead to property."[38]

In this sense it reflects nicely the critical dynamic of a form of Marxism not tied specifically either to the reification of the working class as a revolutionary agent or to a vanguard model of revolutionary change, yet committed to a radically democratic and socialist transformation of a capitalism that manifests structurally unavoidable social pathologies. Moreover, we can, I think, see in Macpherson's theory of property a clear if implicit acknowledgment of Marx's powerful claims in his *1844 Manuscripts* about the baleful impact of private property as the cornerstone of a political economy whose "truth" lies in its expressing the realities of alienation.[39] So I think there is value in exploring Macpherson's account of property in the context of his engagement with Marx and Marxian ideas. And as I hope will also be apparent, property provided a key element of the argument Macpherson offered in *Democracy in Alberta*.

The springboard for Macpherson's account is the conception of property that has come to dominate Western liberal capitalist societies. At the heart of this conception, which has profoundly shaped and in turn has been shaped by the institution of property itself, is the idea that all legitimate property is private property, whereby one has the virtually absolute right to exclude others from the use or benefit of something, while enjoying the virtually unlimited right to alienate what one owns. Important implications have followed from this fundamental idea. In the first place, while property is understood as a right – indeed in a liberal democratic capitalist society among the most basic of rights requiring political support and enforcement – it has been seen for the most part as a right to things, and even the things themselves. And carrying forward his earlier account of how unlimited appropriation became more acceptable morally, because domination over people could be masked and transformed into domination over objects, Macpherson argued that the institution of property provided an incentive to labour in pursuit of continuous acquisition, a limitless desire for command over things.

The most important conclusion Macpherson drew from the dominant role of this conception and institution of private property under capitalism was that, while, like any form of property, it involved a relationship, it obscured it with the emphasis on exclusive command over things. A legal relation between individuals took the reified form of a relation between an "owning" subject and "owned" objects. An owner stood apart from other owners, so any connection between these owners was purely external – in effect a relation between two objects governed by their desires, which, as Hobbes saw, made them equivalent and thus subject to the determining "laws" of the market. And in the measure that owners, including corporate owners treated in law as if they were individuals, related to each other (and indeed themselves) as objects, they masked the reality that domination over objects was in the end domination over the powers and capacities of others, and even over oneself. While Macpherson did not offer so explicit or systematic an account along these lines – although it is another way of defining possessive individualism – it provided the critical context of his treatment of different and alternative forms of property, their historical roots, and the prospects they could hold for an alternative society more attuned to the potentialities of individuals as doers and exerters of their distinctively human capacities. The issue of property puts into particular relief the need to move from a subject-object to an intersubjective mode of social interaction.

Macpherson's account offers a lesson in how social meanings can change – and institutions along with them – even if concepts and categories do not. Throughout his discussions of property, both as a concept and a socio-historical institution, and the ways in which each shaped and was shaped by the other, Macpherson stressed a pattern of development that focused on how pre-capitalist and capitalist societies have understood property, and how an institution of property that would be consistent with what might broadly be called a post-capitalist social order could be logically and empirically defined and defended.[40] And in this context I use the term *post-capitalis*t rather than *socialist* deliberately, although the sort of concept and institution Macpherson envisaged was tied closely to the common and cooperative ownership and management of society's productive resources, obviously a key socialist position.

Macpherson focused on property for two important reasons. First, as a value and institution it was deeply anchored in the culture of existing liberal democratic societies and in the psychic make-up of individuals. Second, a sufficiently broad historical view of property demonstrated that it was expansive enough to accommodate the aspirations and potentialities of individuals understood as autonomous and active doers and exerters of their distinctively human capacities and therefore entitled to access to the resources and conditions required for the exercise of those capacities. Indeed, as we shall see, in this light Macpherson even argued that human rights associated with autonomous, non-possessive individualism, and therefore often seen as antithetical to (private) property rights, could plausibly be defined and defended as individual property rights.[41]

Just as the Locke-to-Bentham conception of human nature as infinitely appropriative represented a deviation from the long-standing Western humanist and Christian traditions that stressed a developmental account of human nature where one's powers were to be rationally exercised in conformity with the demands of the good life, which was not a life of unlimited acquisition, so too is the assumption that all property is and must be *private* property. Both are tied together and jointly owe their origins to the rise of a fully capitalist market society. Coupled with the equally modern and overwhelmingly dominant view that property consists of things as opposed to the right to things, these assumptions ground and solidify key dimensions of individuality, as this has been reinforced by and in turn reinforced the relations of a possessive market society. In short, for Macpherson, property as a concept and institution crystallized the core elements of possessive individualism and the possessive market social order. Macpherson focused on property because he saw it as simultaneously the most significant bulwark and the most vulnerable pressure point of capitalist life and the relations through which it was reproduced in an ongoing way. The key was to show that another institution more adequate to a liberal democratic society dedicated to the fullest realization of human capacities was both necessary and possible.

He started out by making clear that the view that one could be said to possess property only where one had the right enforced by political authority to exclude others from the use or benefit of something, was excessively narrow and one-sided. It left no room for the idea of common property, property available for use by all on terms set by the state, which involved not the right to exclude but rather the right *not* to be excluded from the use or benefit of something. Or, more precisely, it left no room for the idea that the right to common property was an individual right, every bit as much as the (individual) right to private property. Both private and common property are based upon rights created and enforced by the state, and thus it "therefore does not follow, from the fact that all property is enforceable claims of (natural or artificial) individuals, that property is logically confined to private property (the right to exclude others)."[42]

It is clear, I think, that the complex and contradictory meanings of individualism occupy a central place in Macpherson's account. And while it appears to be strictly a legal albeit significant distinction, the difference between the right to exclude and the right not to be excluded has a much greater significance, because each is necessarily defined by the other. What is at stake is the nature of individual agency itself. The right to exclude reinforces, indeed defines, an atomistic understanding of individualism. To exclude or repel seems to put an absolute barrier between self and other. Agents equally armed with the right to exclude can yield it and permit others to penetrate their exclusive space only by individual agreement – by contract. The implication is that we can and should have the right to "choose" our bonds. The flip side, as I argued in chapter 1, is that in a society of private property owners, the only workable community is a collectivist one sustained by the state. The key political question for generations of liberal analytic political philosophers is: why should one obey? This view of politics and the state presupposes private property as the individual right to exclude. It is why I argued that, for Macpherson, the problem of political obligation he identified in *The Political Theory of Possessive Individualism* was a placeholder that opened up to his real interest: the possibility for a fully human life.

By contrast, the right not to be excluded is, as it were, always and already "social." It explicitly identifies an unavoidable association, whatever individuals might think about the matter. It defines the "common." This may be a right to things that is available to all. But the thing-like character of that from which no one should be excluded takes a back seat to the question of access. As we've seen for Macpherson, access – to the means of life and labour – was decisive for realizing the democratic potential of a society capable of unleashing enormous productive capacity that could sustain the ability of everyone equally to use and exercise their distinctively human capacities. In terms of the spatial metaphor here, access entails an enduring connection or roadway – an ongoing relationship. To challenge what Macpherson saw as the twin misunderstandings associated with the capitalist property regime – that property consists of things and that the only coherent and legitimate form of property is private property – is to engage in an exercise of de-reification: to restore the meaning of property as a set of relationships. This is what Macpherson did and it threads together his discussions of the issue.

"That property is *political* is evident. The idea of an enforceable claim implies that there be some body to enforce it ... and in modern (i.e. post-feudal) societies the enforcing body has always been the state, *the* political institution of the modern age ... That property is a political *relation* between persons is equally evident. For any given system of property is a system of rights of each person in relation to other persons."[43] Macpherson sought to demonstrate how, during different historical epochs and under different systems of material production and reproduction, the recognition of the political, relational, and thus power-laden qualities of property varied; it was at times more, at times less, conscious and explicit. A common element of different property systems and the responses to them was the always complex relation among the purposes a particular institution of property is designed to fulfil; conceptions of how the institution actually operates; and judgments about the normative appropriateness of both. Neither has typically been static or uncontested. Each has been shaped and in turn shaped the others. The extent to which property is seen both as historically changeable and as a set of power relations profoundly influences the degree to which the institution itself, and not just its effects, becomes an object of political attention, contestation, and, potentially at least, social change.[44]

As noted above, for Macpherson the emergence of a fully capitalist market society brought about a historically specific and unique conception of, and institution of, property that had three decisive features: that all property was private property as the individual right to exclude others; that property was a right to things that in popular consciousness easily became the things themselves; and that property provided a necessary incentive to undertake socially necessary labour, i.e., labour provided the justification for legitimate acquisition. What knitted these features together was the transformation of both material things and individual productive capacities into marketable or alienable objects – the essential formula for possessive individualism and its social institutions. And as was the case with possessive individualism generally, Macpherson developed his analysis of property on the basis of a critique of the immanent logic and thus historical specificity of its capitalist form. This meant exposing its contradictions and limitations, and thus the claim that it was – or should ideally be – universal and potentially timeless, that is, the one institution that truly reflected human nature as such.

To the claim that all property as an individual right had to be private property, and that therefore the concept of common property was incoherent, Macpherson responded that, in fact, since all property was politically created and enforced as rights of individuals, there was no logical or historical reason to deny to common property the same status as an enforceable individual right. The reason why the idea of common property had slipped from view (and, one might add in a more contemporary vein, common property has been transformed into private property via privatization) was that the individual property right was understood as the right to exclude; indeed the right to exclude defined individual agency and freedom.

> But it does not follow from this that an individual's property is confined to his right to exclude others. An enforceable claim of an individual to some use or benefit of something equally includes his right *not to be excluded from* the use or benefit of something which society or the state has proclaimed to be for the common use ... The fact that we need some such term as *common* property, to distinguish such rights from the exclusive individual rights which are private property, may easily lead to our thinking that such common rights are not individual rights. But they are. They are the property of individuals, not of the state. The state indeed creates and enforces the right which each individual has in the things the state declares to be for common use. But so does the state create and enforce the exclusive rights which are private property ... The state *creates* the rights, the individuals *have* the rights.[45]

That individuals have enforceable claims to property does not mean that all property is necessarily private. The right not to be excluded is as logically defensible as the better-known right to exclude. At stake once again are related but distinct conceptions of individual agency: as self-direction and self-ownership.

The common tendency to view property as (unlimited) rights to things, and even as the things themselves, was the product of the transformation of rights to revenues characteristic of pre-capitalist societies. These were typically tied to limited claims to land and its uses, and to various corporate charters, monopolies, and the like. The transformation

> came with the spread of the capitalist market economy, which brought the replacement of the old limited rights in land by virtually unlimited rights, and by the replacement of the old privileged rights to commercial revenues by more marketable properties in actual capital, however accumulated. As rights in land became more absolute, and parcels of land became more freely marketable commodities, it became natural to think of the land, itself, as the property. And as aggregations of commercial and industrial capital, operating in increasingly free markets and themselves freely marketable, overtook in bulk the older kinds of moveable wealth based on charters and monopolies, the capital itself, whether in money or in the form of actual plant, could easily be thought of as the property. The more freely and pervasively the market operated, the more this was so.

While these developments made it appear that land and commercial capital were themselves now being exchanged in the market, "the difference was not that things rather than rights in things were exchanged, but that previously unsalable or not always salable rights in things were now salable." The expansion of capitalism entailed and was furthered by the increasing and expansive marketability or commodification of what formerly had been limited rights in things. Property as the "exclusive, alienable, 'absolute,' individual or corporate rights in things was required by the full market society because and in so far as the market was expected to do the whole work of allocation of natural resources and capital and labour among possible uses."[46]

Property as an incentive to necessary labour completed, for Macpherson, the account of the historically distinctive characteristics of the institution as it developed with and made possible the achievement of the fully capitalist market society. Here the Marxian influence and implications were decisive. The advent of the market society freed individuals from traditional ties and put them on their own as free contractors subject to the market's power of evaluation. This fact was matched by a value: individuals equally had the right to make the most of themselves and thus had to be accorded an equal right to the property they needed for this. Such property was necessarily private property. This was to be property of individuals who had become free not only in fact but in theory and ideology – "all men were now asserted to be capable of a fully human life (clearly, by the Levellers; grudgingly and ambiguously by Locke)."[47]

What was then needed was a quality shared by all upon which an equal, individual property right could be based. Labour filled this role. Moreover, since one's labour was necessarily and exclusively one's own, any property acquired by it – by mixing one's labour with what one worked on, as Locke argued – was necessarily exclusive, individual, and thus private. "The concept of property as nothing but an exclusive, alienable, individual right not only in material things but even in one's own productive capacities was thus a creation of capitalist society: it was only needed, and only brought forth, when the formal equality of the market superseded the formal inequality of pre-capitalist society."[48]

The sentence cited above captures the central place that Macpherson, again following Marx, assigned to the self-ownership and alienability of labour as private property, the core of possessive individualism. As noted, the exclusivity of the individual right to private property is clearly tied to the labour justification. But so, as well, is the tendency to identify property with things themselves rather than the right to things. Two points are significant here and they speak to key issues in the transformation of property and the move towards a more fully democratic society.

In the first place, property is controversial, a source of contention about both what it is and what it should be. It requires justification, because it is an enforceable legal right only insofar as it is widely held to be a moral right: "Property is not thought to be a right because it is an enforceable claim: it is an enforceable claim because it is thought to be a human right."[49] Once the question of justification is opened up, debates about human purposes, indeed human nature itself, come into view. As we have seen, for Macpherson this was both an ontological and historical issue. Making labour the basis of property and thus a core feature of individual agency represented a step forward in the development of human capabilities and their normative manifestations and possibilities, because it expressed the entrenchment of formal equality, versus inequality, as a core value of a capitalist market society.

Nonetheless, if formal equality was now central as a value, substantive inequality remained decisive. And for Macpherson, this was acknowledged from the outset. While the idea that all were now capable in principle of a fully human life and thus needed morally and legally an equal, individual right to property, "it was impossible to derive, from human needs alone, an exclusive individual right, open to everyone, in land and capital. For it was assumed that land and capital always necessarily would be, as they always had been, held by less than all men, and on that assumption need alone could not confer on everyone an exclusive right."[50] Labour, which could plausibly be seen as universal, filled the bill. In principle, all had an equal need to labour, so labour could serve as an egalitarian justification of property.

However, if labour in the abstract could serve as a universal justification, the specific conditions under which it was performed – in a possessive market society, those involving a net transfer of power – were typically obscured by the apparently equal subordination of all to the evaluations of the market. And this leads to the second point. All individuals were equally entitled by their labour to the means by which they could live a fully human life. Such a life required not only those consumables necessary for survival but also access to the *means* of producing those same consumables. The two are not identical. But starting with Locke, the tendency has been to efface the distinction. If one has access to consumables – or, to put it another way, was equally free to labour in order to acquire them – one is seen to enjoy the same equal property right as those who hold access to the means of producing consumables, that is, the means of life and labour. From Macpherson's vantage point, the net transfer of powers, under which some control access to the means of life and labour and so are able to control the lives of others, is occluded. But it was precisely access, or lack of access, to the means of producing what is needed for life that raised the critical questions of justification of the institution of property.

These two issues – the question of normative justification and the relation between access to consumables and access to the means of life and labour – defined, for Macpherson, the context within which he believed fundamental changes to the concept and institution of property would likely occur. And as was the case with the possible (and necessary) transformation of human nature, the changes with respect to property would represent both a retrieval and an advance.

The retrieval involved the return to the idea that property was a right to a revenue or an income, a dominant form of return prior to the entrenchment of market capitalism. By the mid-twentieth century, at least in the advanced capitalist world in which corporations dominated the economy and welfare state intervention had reached new levels, claims to monetary returns or state-subsidized services had become widespread. This was most obviously the case for *rentier* investors. But it was also true of elements of the organized working classes fortunate enough to enjoy company pension plans and public goods in the form of state-provided services in education and health care. To a considerably lesser extent, the poor, the unemployed, and the retired reliant upon state-provided retirement benefits also enjoyed access to income assistance and supplementation.

Of course the reality was that owners of financial wealth were the only ones who could rely extensively or even exclusively upon *rentier* income, even where and as revenue-consciousness had penetrated all classes. And this, for Macpherson, was the point. Classes had not disappeared, even if class consciousness had been muted by a shared interest in maintaining the capitalist growth necessary for generating revenue in its various forms. Since the overwhelming majority of the populations of capitalist market societies had to work for a living as wage or salary earners, the right to a revenue became more thoroughly modernized and extended as the right to employment – in effect the right to access to the means of labour, without which property in one's own labour was virtually without value.

For Macpherson this represented a significant change in the concept of property. This was because "to see one's property as a right to earn an income through employment is to see (or come close to seeing) as one's property a right of access to some of the existent means of labour, that it is, to some of the accumulated productive resources of the whole society (natural resources plus the productive resources created by past labour), no matter by whom they are owned."[51] Macpherson saw this move as both necessary and possible in the circumstances. It would involve a de-reification of property, both a move away from a conception of property as things and a move towards the recognition of property as a political and social relation. The individual right to exclude others from the use or benefit of something would have to give way to the equally individual right not to be excluded from the use or benefit of society's accumulated productive resources. This development would parallel the transformation at the level of human possibilities from the no longer necessary possessive individualist conception of humans as infinite appropriators to the democratic and egalitarian view of humans as active doers and exerters of their distinctively human capacities. Institutionally, at the level of property rights and relations, it would entail a fundamental shift from the dominance of private to common property.

Macpherson saw the potential for such a shift in a couple of different ways. Originally writing from the vantage point of the 1970s, he argued that there had emerged what he called the "quasi-market" society. This involved an increasingly significant role for the state in allocating resources via fiscal policy, state ownership, and regulation. In the process, the state supplanted the market, which was no longer expected to do the whole work of allocation. Where this occurred, it represented a move towards de-commodification – in other words, an increasing role for common as opposed to private property. And this obviously included those welfare state measures that reflected a partial de-commodification of labour with, on the one side, the provision of a "social wage" and, on the other, the increasing emphasis on the right to employment.

To the extent that the emergence of a quasi-market social order reflected the strength of working-class and other pressures for a more democratic, economically equitable, and environmentally sustainable social order, such democratic pressures would be needed to push forward the claims for a new institution of property understood as the equal individual right not to be excluded "from the use or benefit of things, and productive powers, that can be said to have been created by the joint efforts of the whole society." Macpherson argued that such a development, the only one consistent with the expansion of democratic rights and values, would in fact build on what he claimed were the three principles upon which the individual right to property had always been constructed: "the right to the material means of life, the right to a free life, and the right to the (current and accumulated) fruits of one's labour."[52] The strength and legitimacy of the capitalist institution of private property rested on its being justified on these foundations; its (increasingly evident) weakness and decline in legitimacy rested on its denial of them in practice for the overwhelmingly large majority of individuals.

As Macpherson saw things, there was clear evidence of expanding democratic pressures, not simply for an expansion of common property in society's collectively produced resources, but for a further broadening of the concept of property itself. The right not to be excluded would be extended, initially to the right to an equal share in political power, and beyond this to what he called "a right to a kind of society or set of power relations which will enable the individual to live a fully human life." This is, I would claim, Macpherson's version of the classical Marxist account of the nature of and difference between socialism and communism, and the transition from the one to the other. And as was the case for Marxists, for Macpherson this transition hinged on the extent to which enhanced productivity, the outcome of technological development, made possible the reduction of socially required labour to the point at which income would no longer depend upon the expenditure of labour. Aside from his rejection of the vanguard-led revolutionary model, what distinguishes Macpherson's version of the two "stages" approach to the achievement of a society beyond possessive individualism was his very attempt to root them in the concept of property as an enforceable individual right. He did this because "the broader claims will not be firmly anchored unless they are seen as property. For, in the liberal ethos which prevails in our liberal-democratic societies, property has more prestige than has almost anything else. And if the new claims are not brought under the head of property, the narrow idea of property will be used, with all the prestige of property, to combat them."[53] In the currents circumstances, this is at least suggestive, if not prescient.

Even acknowledging this point, Macpherson admitted that it might seem far-fetched to consider as property the right to participate in a satisfying set of social relations that facilitated the fullest development and exercise of one's human capacities. But here as well he thought that the past could shed light on the future. Just as the pre-capitalist conception of property stressed the right to a revenue, so the idea of property dominant prior to the emergence of a fully capitalist market society – including among thinkers such as Hobbes and Locke – was significantly broader than rights to material things. Tying the two together, he even suggested that with the prospective overcoming of scarcity, "property must become rather a right to an *immaterial* revenue, a revenue of enjoyment of the quality of life." This is, to be sure, an odd formulation, undoubtedly designed to detach material well-being from an exclusive focus on consumption and appropriation. Thus, aside from the right in material things and revenue, property should include an individual's "life, his person, his faculties, his liberty, his conjugal affection, his honour, etc."[54] Of course these would be goals for the future in the measure that they reflected liberalism's greatest triumph, namely, the assertion of the moral equality of all individuals.

Macpherson was understandably reticent about what a society based on an individual property right to a satisfying set of social relations might look like, although one obvious clue lay in the distinction he drew between competing conceptions of the maximization of one's ethical/developmental versus descriptive/extractive powers. The most charitable interpretation is that, although it would represent a revolutionary transformation (without necessarily requiring "traumatic revolutionary action"),[55] it would not be a "stand-alone" condition. Rather, it would incorporate what Macpherson had presented as the content of the right not to be excluded: access to the means of life and labour to the extent there remained the need for current individual labour; and access to political power as the right to participate in determining the use of society's accumulated productive resources. And as will become evident through an examination of his account of democracy, it would also include means for ensuring personal security or what he called counter-extractive liberty. But obviously we need to know more about the alternative. Perhaps Macpherson's sketch, which presumably he intended as his version of Marx's claim that no blueprint for the future was possible, since we cannot determine in advance what free individuals would do, could best be understood as a Kantian regulative idea.

In any event, Macpherson assumed an intensification of the political efforts of democratic forces armed with democratic ideals to push demands for fundamental reforms that offered the potential for significant change. This took the form of the dialectic of a partial breakdown of the political order (i.e., crises of managed capitalism) and a partial breakthrough of public consciousness (i.e., continuing challenges to the image of individuals as infinite consumers as opposed to exerters and developers of their human capacities).[56] From his vantage point in the early 1970s, this seemed eminently plausible.

As the decade unfolded and radical political forces were muted if not fully stilled, and in the realm of political theory John Rawls's theory of justice and the related emphasis on human rights came to dominate the mainstream, Macpherson shifted his focus. He remained committed to the need for a radically transformed conception of property. But now he sought to relate it to the emerging discourse on human rights. He saw here a sharp theoretical and ideological division between those for whom the right to property, typically understood as the unlimited individual right to exclude, was a fundamental human right, and those for whom property rights, or at least the existing rights, were opposed to human rights.[57] The origin of this division was in the contradiction between the excessively narrow conception of property entrenched along with the triumph of capitalist market relations and the broader conception held by theorists of the early seventeenth century, which ought to be restored under contemporary conditions as an essential feature of a fully democratic, non-market social order. As Macpherson put it in this context, "Property as an exclusive right of a natural or artificial person to use and dispose of material things (including land

and resources) leads necessarily, in any kind of market society (from the freest, most perfectly competitive one, to a highly monopolistic one), to an inequality of wealth and power that denies a lot of people the possibility of a reasonably human life."[58]

This is familiar. But now Macpherson argued that a shift from the narrow to the broadened concept of property, that is, to "an individual right both to some exclusive property and to some non-exclusive right of access to the remaining natural resources and the accumulated capital of a given society," could be and should be expressed in the language of human rights. The move was vital. "If we continue to take it in the modern narrow sense, the property right contradicts democratic human rights. If we take it in the broader sense, it does not contradict a democratic concept of human rights: indeed, it then may bring us back to something like the old concept of individual property in one's life, liberty, and capacities."[59] And as we have seen, this could be an enforceable individual right.

For Macpherson, humanist liberal and socialist defenders of democratic rights as human rights should resist discarding property rights, indeed should conceive human rights as property rights insofar as there was a move to the broadened conception of property. This was not only strategic. It also recognized the reality that both human rights and property rights have been tied to human flourishing, to a full and free human life. Even the narrow right to property, however inadequate, was so understood and defended. "So I think that, given our present scale of values, it is only if the human right to a full life is seen as a property right that it will stand much chance of general realization."[60]

Macpherson's account of property may well appear to be the most anachronistic part of his theoretical work. To be sure, a good deal of it is the product of the virtual disappearance of significant alternatives to a neoliberal capitalism that has vigorously reasserted possessive market values – including the idea that property means private property as the right to exclude. Ironically Macpherson's claim that property had been and would continue to be increasingly understood as a right to a revenue has been borne out. However, at least in the advanced capitalist societies, this has come to mean the diffusion of the *rentier* outlook across broad sections of the population. Quite apart from the ideological strength of possessive market values, which Macpherson had seen as diminishing in importance, there is an objective basis to this shift. As unemployment has increased and job security withered (and with it, property as the right to access to the means of labour in the form of a right to a job), individuals have been forced to view themselves as, and behave as, "entreployees": agents in a process of "self-securitization" whereby one treats oneself as a complex of investable assets in employment settings characterized by what Hartmann and Honneth call "desolidarizing tendencies insofar as employees are less and less in a position to develop longer-term connections with firms or colleagues."[61] On the other side, with the reduction if not elimination of state-provided social supports, individuals are expected to look after their own needs, in particular retirement income, by investing in the stock market, either directly or indirectly by means of various financial instruments. Beyond this, in the wake of a prolonged period of wage and salary stagnation, many workers have had to rely on debt to finance consumption, as well as the purchase of housing.[62] In the context of the increasing financialization of capitalism, under which finance, insurance, and real estate capital have bulked ever larger as sources of profit, broad segments of the population have their economic fates tied to financial growth and expansion.[63] There is little pressure to pursue the broadening of the concept and institution of property along the lines Macpherson had urged.

And to pile on an additional bit of irony, if the idea of property as the right to a revenue has been restored in a way that has reinforced and not challenged the dominance of capitalist market relations, so too has Macpherson's hope that property as the right to an immaterial revenue, that is to a quality of life not reducible to material goods or commodities, been "realized" in a "digital" world.[64] The increasing central role and emphasis on acquiring financial assets has contributed to this; so has the supposed levelling of work-related hierarchies in contexts of "entreployeeship."

So perhaps we should set aside Macpherson's political theory of property as in essence a piece of orthodox Marxism whose plausibility has withered. Yet I think this would be a mistake. Property has the potential to resurface as a political question whenever the claims in which it is anchored come to be seen as violated by the very institutions that should be defining and enforcing them. However triumphant the possessive individualist conception of property might be, this cannot be ruled out – even among those who might be most committed to the institution. Indeed Macpherson early in his career had explored just such a development. This was *Democracy in Alberta*, his account of the rise to power of the Social Credit movement in that Canadian province and what it told us about the nature and limits of democracy in a capitalist society.[65]

Democracy in Alberta: Populism, Property, and the Limits and Contradictions of Liberal Democracy

In the agricultural heartlands of both Canada and the United States during the early decades of the twentieth century, independent commodity producers faced threats to their continuing viability from the emerging structures of oligopolistic corporate capitalism. Whether small proprietors, or what has been called the agrarian petite bourgeoisie, could survive in a world increasingly dominated by large-scale, organized capitalism formed the context within which political consciousness, political and social institutions, and patterns of political action took shape. Agrarian political and social movements took root in the face of the predicament confronting the independent producers. These "farmers" movements typically promoted an alternative populist vision of society, one forged in opposition to the new capitalist order. To varying degrees members of these movements believed they spoke and acted not just on their own behalf but also for all who toiled. They conceived a society of freedom and justice, prosperity and security, where cooperation triumphed over competition. Such a society would realize the promise of democracy as a political system expressing and carrying out the will of (all) the people in the face of those economic forces that blocked or distorted the expression of democratic demands and possibilities.

It was this vision and curiosity about those who struggled to make it a reality that in the early 1950s lured C.B. Macpherson to the Canadian west and the province of Alberta, where two populist political movements, first the United Farmers of Alberta (UFA) and then Social Credit, had swept to political power, armed with a fundamental commitment to what they viewed as a richer, more authentic democracy. How in the face of the changing requirements of capitalist production agrarian producers were forged into a distinctive social force and the political responses their situation generated formed the core of *Democracy in Alberta*. While not well-known outside of Canada, or for that matter particularly well-remembered inside the country, the book represented a landmark account of the emergence of the Social Credit movement and its impact on the political institutions and political culture of Alberta in the first half of the twentieth century. Specifically, Macpherson sought to make sense of what happened when "a people" took up and tried "with some success to put into effect, within a few decades, two new theories, each demanding abandonment of the orthodox party system," each "based on a novel theory of democratic government ... carried into effect by a popular movement broader than a political party."[66]

But as significant as it was, Macpherson's study did more than this. Anchoring his account in an analysis of class and property, Macpherson offered largely neglected insights into three concerns central for the kind of critical political theory he attempted throughout his work to develop: the continuing significance of class for democratic theory and practice in advanced capitalist societies, even in the face of developments that complicate processes of class formation and identification; the necessity and possibility of embedding theoretical claims around democracy in historical forms of social life; and the seemingly inherent tendency of political systems that are liberal democratic and capitalist to embrace or manifest populist impulses. In this respect, *Democracy in Alberta* offered a unique, early version of the complex relation of possessive individualism and democracy before Macpherson had, in a manner of speaking, developed his distinctive conceptualizations – while at the same time addressing issues that retain considerable salience for contemporary political thought.

Working within a broadly Marxian framework, Macpherson sought to demonstrate the continuing and critical role played by social class in shaping political consciousness and behaviour, even in contemporary "pluralistic" societies in which other forms of identity and patterns of social division were (and are) at play. As he succinctly summarized it, the "concept of class which finds its significant determinant of social and political behaviour in the ability or inability to dispose of labour – one's own and others' ... may be thought ... the most penetrating basis of classification for the understanding of political behaviour. Common relationship to the disposal of labour still tends to give the members of each class, so defined, an outlook and set of assumptions distinct from those of other classes."[67] On the other hand – and this proved decisive for Macpherson's analysis – class position as an outside observer might see it does not necessarily mean that members of a class so understood consciously make their political choices in terms of class interest, and this gulf between social location and political consciousness has been particularly decisive for the petite bourgeoisie.[68] This turned out to be vital for the forms of political action Alberta's agrarian producers pursued, the consequences favourable and unfavourable that they generated, and, ultimately, the kind of democratic theory and practice that emerged and left a profound imprint on the province and the country.

In developing his analysis, Macpherson stressed the essential role of the system of political parties in a liberal democracy in mediating at the level of the state the class relations of a capitalist market society. He claimed that both the United Farmers of Alberta, first elected in 1921, and the Social Credit movement, which succeeded it in office in 1935, represented a distinct and conscious break with the orthodox alternate party system associated with British parliamentary democratic government. Both believed the party system, especially as it operated at the federal level in Canada, where major powers over the economy were constitutionally lodged, was an instrument of privilege. It was a vehicle by which the dominant interests in the state and the economy cemented their control over the society. It thwarted the popular will and blocked the achievement of the prosperity, security, freedom, and dignity to which the people were entitled.

These movements thus condemned the existing system as undemocratic. They offered instead what they believed to be a superior alternative, one founded on the theory and practice of delegate democracy. For the UFA, this was group representation in the legislature. For Social Credit, this involved the assembly representing a general will of the people for freedom and plenty, which the productive heritage of the society had made possible. For both movements, there was a desire and an attempt to go beyond normal party competition, party discipline, and Cabinet dominance of the legislative body.

In each case, however, the attempted break with orthodoxy was only partial and ultimately unsuccessful. While in power, both the UFA and Social Credit increasingly became more conservative, reconciling themselves to the realities of party government in a capitalist liberal democratic society.

But neither movement reverted totally to the alternate party system. According to Macpherson, this persistent deviation from orthodoxy represented a new species of democratic government. It had to be explained by the peculiarities of Alberta society. As Macpherson saw it, the population of Alberta during the period he studied was predominantly made up of independent commodity producers. Faced with unfavourable terms of trade and thus a threat to their economic security in the period immediately following the First World War, and then during the Great Depression, the class of independent producers rebelled against their situation in the Canadian political economy. The UFA and then Social Credit were the result. This was a revolt of the petite bourgeoisie, a rebellion mounted by the most substantial class in a society that politically and economically was a semi-colonial, subordinate part of a mature capitalist economy.

As Macpherson saw it, targeting the federal party system and the Eastern Canadian financial interests that dominated it by the UFA and Social Credit made sense for them. The decisions of both clearly affected the economic well-being and political efficacy of the independent producers. Insofar as these forces were seen as expressions of power relations that ought to be transformed to make them responsive to the interests of the majority, both the UFA and Social Credit developed a thoroughgoing critique of the political economy that was reasonably incisive and, within limits, effective as a basis for policy initiatives on behalf of the "people."

Nevertheless, according to Macpherson, the class position of the independent agrarian producer set "inherent limits" on their radicalism.[69] While opposed to outside domination in the form of central Canadian economic interests and the political structures that in their eyes secured this domination, the agrarian petite bourgeoisie accepted and even celebrated private property and the logic of capitalist market relations. Indeed they believed that genuine and legitimate private property consisted of the kind of smallholdings they themselves possessed, holdings sufficient in size to guarantee personal independence. A community founded on private property in this sense would be one of free and equal (possessive) individuals able to regulate their ties through non-exploitive relations of exchange, that is, a price system that treated all individual owners equally and fairly and was not tilted against them on behalf of monopolistic interests. This was a vision, in other words, of a simple market society.

As we have seen, once the logic of capitalist market relations takes hold, a simple market society is unsustainable. Market competition, reinforced by political power as the populists recognized, doomed petty holdings as anything other than marginal. Thus, for Macpherson, what the independent commodity producer failed to see was that the normal operations of the capitalist market economy and its price system tended towards the concentration of wealth. Relations of exchange could never, on the whole, involve equal, individual proprietors. The independent commodity producer celebrated independence as both an existing reality and as an ideal to be achieved, often both together, but usually one or the other, depending upon the degree of economic and financial success and the accompanying sense of social security available to members of the class at any one time.

This conception of independence, which was a fundamental aspect of an agrarian consciousness, was realistic to the extent that it reflected the farmer's general freedom from the requirements of wage labour as either an employee or employer. Typically, the small proprietor's livelihood did not depend on a wage or on profit generated by the employment of the labour of others. "But while in his own productive activity the farmer does not stand immediately in either of these relations of dependence, yet he is producing in an economy which, on the whole, and increasingly, operates by means of these relations and is dominated by those who do stand in these relations ... More specifically, the farmer produces in an economy determined by the decisions of entrepreneurs of a somewhat different order than himself ... yet not generally seeing how wide the gulf is between him and them, the farmer is apt to class himself with them, or at least to feel that he has an independent position in the economy akin to theirs."[70]

The independent producer's sense of independence was thus real but also illusory: it masked a more fundamental dependence on the structural forces of a mature capitalist political economy. This was the reason why the producers could not totally break clear of the relations of a mature capitalism, even as at the same time they were unable to reconcile themselves totally to those relations, either. As a result, their response was anomalous and contradictory. It oscillated between radicalism and conservatism, between a challenge to the system on behalf of those who toiled and with whom at times they identified, and a defence of their interests as owners of private property, frequently over and against erstwhile allies interested in fundamental change. This is the hallmark of a distinctively agrarian consciousness, as opposed to a cohesive class consciousness. For Macpherson, it represented the classic pattern of petit bourgeois radicalism.

What Macpherson ingeniously called the "quasi-party system" was directly traceable to this radicalism and its impact on political consciousness, action, and institutions. His account was intended to capture the political implications of this complex array of forces and pressures, and in particular the status of democracy as the key value in terms of which they were played out. In a capitalist society with liberal political institutions formed in the pre-democratic era, the struggle for democracy revolved around demands for a universal franchise. Once achieved, universal suffrage made necessary the organization of a mass electorate and the channelling of at least potentially antagonistic social interests in ways compatible with liberal institutions in a capitalist society. For this purpose, the system of political parties was indispensable. To the traditional and long-recognized task of providing protection against arbitrary government by offering viable electoral alternatives to the party in power was added an additional, even more fundamental responsibility: the moderation and containment of opposing class interests. Alternate parties were either organized explicitly along class lines or structured as brokerage mechanisms for interest groups with class bases of support.[71] As Macpherson saw things, this role has tended to go largely unrecognized, particularly in North America, as the advent of universal suffrage seemed to do away with the class problem.[72] This was replaced by the "pluralist" task of reconciling the needs of an increasingly diverse array of social groups with overlapping memberships from all classes, a task made easier by the massive expansion of capitalist production, at least in the core capitalist countries, over the course of the twentieth century. Yet insofar as the society remained capitalist, and indeed capitalist market relations became ever more decisive for the life prospects of those living in these societies, the class question remained on the agenda.

And so it was in Alberta under the UFA and Social Credit. There, however, where one class, or at least the outlook of a single class, was overwhelmingly predominant, an alternate party system seemed both divisive and unnecessary. What was needed was the protection of the class of independent commodity producers against outside interests. On the other hand, there was no basis for an outright one-party state, which, according to Macpherson, "is only thrust up as part of a revolutionary (or counter-revolutionary) transfer of power in a strongly class-divided society."[73] The overwhelming dominance in Alberta of the UFA and then Social Credit, which together held power for fifty years in the province, expressed the logic of the quasi-party system. And it is worth noting that until swept out of power in May 2015 by the centre-left New Democratic Party, the Progressive Conservative Party held office uninterruptedly after Social Credit was finally defeated in 1971. (It will be interesting to see if the triumph of the NDP ushers in an era of more vigorous partisan competition and as a result the end of extended one-party government.) A single party was overwhelmingly dominant while other parties, though never formally proscribed, were marginal. The system represented "a middle way between an alternate party-system which had become unreal or harmful and a one-party state which would be unacceptable and for which there is not the requisite class basis," an uneasy compromise that carried out at least tolerably well the functions of a "normal" party system.[74] Less democratic than a fully competitive system, it was nonetheless more democratic than a one-party dictatorship. Not a completely satisfactory state of affairs, but then, as Macpherson indicated, "beggars cannot be choosers."[75]

However insightful this account of Social Credit and prairie populism, it might seem to be of purely historical interest at best, an account of a society and its political system that has now left behind its predominantly agrarian past and become a highly urbanized, albeit resource-driven, capitalist society in which the class divisions one would anticipate have indeed taken shape. Yet such a judgment would be too hasty. For one thing, although provincial elections are typically competitive, as noted above, the Conservatives comfortably held power from 1971 until 2015 – longer than either the UFA or Social Credit. For another, for all the social and economic changes that have taken place in the province, the values of competitive individualism and free enterprise remain strong.

However, I would suggest that the analysis has even greater breadth and explanatory significance than has normally been attributed to it, or that even Macpherson might have seen or intended. We are once again on the terrain of his suppressed philosophical dimension. In part, this reflected the sweeping nature of his approach, one that combined political economy, political theory, and empirical political sociology to present a picture of a body of people struggling in and against political, social, and economic conditions local in their impact but national and international in their scope: the wrenching forces of capitalist development and crisis, depression, and war – the fateful and seemingly uncontrollable processes that produced both prosperity and misery, each equally arbitrary and unpredictable. But what caught Macpherson's attention in his attempt to grasp the significance of the Alberta experience was not just that this experience could be analysed from the "outside," from the vantage point of a critical theory of capitalist democracy and its implicit and explicit tensions and contradictions. Of course he did exactly this, and the framework he deployed was fundamentally shaped by what he would later call the political theory of possessive individualism and the theory of democracy interwoven with and developed out of it.

Beyond this, however, Macpherson was interested not only in the political practice of the prairie populists but also in the ways in which that practice was shaped by theories of democracy and society. These theories revolved around the requirements of group government for the United Farmers of Alberta and plebiscitarian leadership under a general will for Social Credit. Within its respective limits, each was remarkably self-conscious, coherent, and sophisticated (although, particularly in the case of Social Credit, ultimately delusory). To be sure, for Macpherson such theories necessarily combined the rational and insightful with the irrational and misleading, for such was the impact of class location on political and social consciousness. Nonetheless, for the populists, their practice was shaped by theories, including a theory of what constituted an appropriate practice, such that these theories *did* more or less capture key dimensions of the social reality within which these social actors found themselves.

In other words, Macpherson brought forward the class question and the social basis of political action in a way that situated his analysis in a context shaped by history as a living and vital force. In doing so, he did something important and suggestive, but largely unappreciated: in effect he made political ideas, in this case democracy, a matter of what Hegel called "objective spirit." That is, he showed how the theory and practice of the UFA and Social Credit interwove normative commitments with organized empirical practices in a way that both demonstrated the living reality of thought and the roots of thought in the dynamics of social life, and made visible the extent to which those practices could be judged as rational in light of the essential purposes they embodied and sought to achieve: the independence, freedom, and, ultimately, dignity of the producers themselves.[76] Viewed through the prism of property, the UFA and Social Credit represented an attempt to broaden the concept by emphasizing the right to the full fruits of one's labour, and even beyond, "the idea that individual property is much more a matter of property in life and liberty, in the use and development and enjoyment of human capacities, than it is merely a matter of rights in things or revenues."[77] The attempt was doomed to fail because their steadfast commitment to private property undermined their aims.

Macpherson argued that both the UFA and Social Credit responses to the predicament of the agriculture petite bourgeoisie were rooted in a faulty understanding of the real situation and were thus fated to be defeated, although at times partially successful in moderating the impact of the unfavourable circumstances within which the class of independent producers lived and worked. As earlier noted, the quasi-party system was the result of the desire to break clear of the limits of political institutions, coupled with the necessity to reconcile to them and to the requirements of the capitalist market society that underpinned them.

Yet at the same time, although it is easy to miss this, Macpherson also made clear that this reconciliation was not a coming to terms with a rational reality that "naturally" ought to prevail. The UFA and Social Credit sought to distance themselves from the dominant forms of the party system and liberal democracy because they viewed these as the tools of privileged elites who used them to oppress the people. And they were right. In Macpherson's eyes, the failure of their preferred alternatives did not diminish the force or justice of their critique. Their responses may have been inadequate, even delusional and ominously paranoid (as with the anti-Semitism of certain currents of Social Credit doctrine and some Social Creditors). Yet these were not only, or even necessarily, utopian in the pejorative sense of that term. The dominant political forms were not, and are not, simply the best of all possible worlds. The failure of the Alberta experiments with unorthodox democratic practices did not signal the elimination of the gap between the democratic claims of the existing order and the undemocratic realities. These experiments responded to ongoing social dynamics and spoke to a real need.

In his account of the quasi-party system, Macpherson saw the contrast between the class and pluralist conceptions of the function of a party system in a liberal democracy as reflecting alternative understandings of the meaning of democracy itself. From the perspective of the class conception, "democracy is an affair of the presently underprivileged; it means government responsible to and suffused with the will of the 'common people,' those whose claim to consideration is their common humanity rather than their estates, their life and labour rather than accumulated wealth or hereditary status."[78]

In the twentieth century, however, this classical conception of democracy was largely supplanted by the pluralist one, which "assumed that with the establishment of popular suffrage the class function of democracy is no longer sufficient. The primary problem of democratic government is taken to be the representation and reconciliation of a multitude of diverse and conflicting group interests ... which cut across and blur class lines. In this view the machinery of government is, in itself, neutral; it has no inherent class content, but operates in response to pressure from all groups."[79]

Hence the differences between these two accounts were not merely descriptive, but normative. This distinction between the normative and the descriptive – or more accurately, two different normative visions, since the pluralist model, by virtue of its emphasis on the free competition of social interests, carried in its commitment to the responsiveness of democratic government to the forces of the political marketplace and an ensuing social stability its own implicit normative assumptions – shaped much of Macpherson's later work. It was to be developed more systematically in his distinction between democracy as a kind of society in which individuals were free to use and develop their human capacities versus democracy as a method for choosing and authorizing governments; and in his account of a model of participatory democracy versus what he saw as the dominant pluralist-elitist-equilibrium paradigm.

So the class question was not simply, for Macpherson, an arbitrary Marxist description of a social reality understood by its constituents in other, less insightful or accurate terms. Rather, it spoke to aspirations for equality and dignity that the achievement of universal suffrage on its own was unable to meet. The periodic resurgence throughout the history of mass democratic institutions and down to our own time of the demand for a fuller, richer, and more comprehensive kind of democratic practice beyond the electoral process suggests that Macpherson was right to assume that the class concept, with its humanistic aspirations, addressed a need that the pluralist notion could not. This need was for social relations not mediated by the commodity form.

As Macpherson saw it, in spite of their limitations, the prairie populists stood in the tradition of class movements for social and economic as well as political democracy. However, their commitment to the existing system undermined their purposes. They were the victims of a false consciousness about society and their place in it that followed from the petit bourgeois notion of independence they saw as the ultimate political and social value. Just how valuable this dimension of Macpherson's account remains can be seen from the fact that, while possessive individualist values have in recent years come to be asserted with a vigour not seen in decades, the real possibilities for the kind of independence the populists cherished are more remote than ever.[80]

We can see this dynamic played out in the trajectory of the transformation of the quasi-party system and the character of democratic will formation in the passage from the UFA to Social Credit. In Macpherson's view, the UFA was more realistic in its response to the plight of its social base, Social Credit more delusory. This was no accident. The petit bourgeois vision became progressively more unrealistic as the process of capitalist development accelerated with the widespread concentration and centralization of capital and the consequences of the Great Depression, a process that has continued. Macpherson saw, as a result, a significant shift in the theory and practice of democracy from the rise of the UFA to its collapse and replacement by Social Credit. The UFA sought the representation in the legislature of the concrete interests of the different elements of the population; this was the essence of its model of group government. By contrast, Social Credit promoted the idea of the permanent plebiscite, where an all-powerful leader expressed and put into effect the popular or general will. This was claimed to be a richer form of democracy than the group government model. In fact, it was more superficial and hollow.

This "hollowing out" of democracy has contemporary resonance, as Macpherson surmised it might have. Governments emphasize "leadership," seek from voters a "blank cheque" to govern, and ask citizens to trust them to deal with pressing questions. They claim, in other words, to speak on behalf of a general will, with concrete social groups downplayed, dismissed, or even denounced as "special interests." (This parallels the shift from the essentially corporatist perspective of the UFA to the abstract and undifferentiated conception of the people trumpeted by Social Credit.) At the same time, governments have continually ceded authority to unelected domestic and international bodies, and the demands of international trade and investment agreements.[81]

In relation to this it is important to note that, in *Democracy in Alberta*, Macpherson did not develop just an account of the ideology and politics of the United Farmers of Alberta and Social Credit and the political theory of a quasi-party democratic order. He also provided a detailed treatment of the economic doctrine of Social Credit, including a lucid exposition of the notorious "A plus B" theorem, which Social Credit theorists and devotees offered as justification for monetary social "credits."[82] He showed how the movement responded, however inadequately and inappropriately, to the increasingly dominant role that commodity (i.e., monetized or market) relations had to come to play in a capitalist system that had left behind its liberal, competitive past and became "organized," with large monopolistic or oligopolistic corporations increasingly directing economic activity. For Social Creditors, money played a role in the economy roughly equivalent to that played by the party system in the polity: it was an instrument of those malign forces depriving them of political power, individual dignity, and economic independence. In both cases they saw something important: the evidence of conscious and purposeful human activity of organized interests in managing both the political and economic systems. Such evidence suggested that things need not remain as they had been – that conscious human will could be a force for change. However, by attempting to marginalize its significance, their response to the role of money was as misguided as their response to the party system. Just as they failed to recognize the essential functions of parties in a liberal democratic political system, so they likewise misunderstood the indispensability of money in a capitalist economy. Both are anchored in a system of property relations that went largely unchallenged. Or, to put it another way, populists tended to separate exchange from production and the power-laden economic relations within which productive activity was undertaken. They failed to see how money mediated both exchange and production – how it was necessarily political.[83]

For Macpherson, one expression of this fundamental acceptance of capitalist property relations was the extent to which Social Credit expressed the logic of advanced capitalism once it ascended to power. Particularly in the wake of the discovery in the late 1940s of massive petroleum reserves and their subsequent exploitation, the Social Credit government functioned with respect to its supporters and citizens rather like a corporation administering the province by proxy on behalf of dividend-receiving, primarily passive shareholders. There are contemporary echoes of this approach in the language of the citizen as a taxpayer/stakeholder.

Even more tellingly, the reconciliation with the dominant property institution can take the form, and arguably has taken the form, of an embrace of capitalist market relations *as these actually exist in the present* and not just as an ideal to be realized against monopolistic interests skewing them to their advantage. This likely would not have surprised Macpherson; indeed, he feared it as one possible consequence of the predicament confronting the independent producer class. As he appeared to see things, the direr the predicament of the class, the more ferociously its members would cling to their individualism, and the more necessary it would be under the circumstances to embrace the existing order. He argued that by the 1940s the increasingly corporate role of Social Credit was echoed in its doctrine. The party had come to view social ties on the model of those between buyers and sellers in the retail market. Expressing an essentially atomized conception of the social bond under which individual freedom was reduced to the right to accept or refuse choices on offer, consistent with the equal right of others to do the same, this position amounted to the claim that the "relations of the market were supposed to provide the ultimate in both individual freedom and popular sovereignty."[84] Needless to say, for Macpherson they did neither.

Macpherson thus anticipated the emergence of what has come to be called market populism: the claim that the popular good or will is realized by the fullest and freest operation of market forces – in other words, the interests of "the people" are identical with those of the dominant classes. This claim is often linked to the idea that the real threat to the popular will comes not from the wealthy and powerful but rather from equality-seeking groups that purportedly use the state to impose the values of feminism, environmentalism, multiculturalism, trade unionism, and what might loosely be called cultural modernism upon traditional communities and their commitments to productive work and personal responsibility.[85] What Macpherson might not have foreseen was that market populist views would spread beyond the ranks of the petite bourgeoisie and become influential throughout the society, although he was aware of the extent to which market values were deeply rooted. What I earlier noted about the spread of the *rentier* mentality, and, in light of Macpherson's analysis, what might be called a deepening monetary "obsession" that has taken the form of raging, global financial speculation and the overwhelming tendency to view economic activity and well-being almost exclusively in financial terms, speaks to this development. Of course this was a key reason why Macpherson made property so essential to his critical theory.

In light of all this, it is well to note that a core conclusion Macpherson intended his readers to draw from his analysis in *Democracy in Alberta*, one very much in the spirit of the early Frankfurt School, was that the contradiction between a vigorously asserted possessive individualism and the realities of a mature capitalist society that undermined such individualist claims was potentially explosive. This would be all the more so as possessive market values exerted a deep hold across the population, including among members of the working class upon whose actions, for Marxists, the fate of socialism rested. Macpherson's own conclusion to the book was sweeping and ominous. Where the relevant conditions prevailed, a quasi-party system "appears to be the most satisfactory answer that can be found … to the problem of maintaining the form and some of the substance of democracy." His final words are particularly sobering: "The quasi-party system may thus be considered either the final stage in the deterioration of the capitalist democratic tradition, or a way of saving what can be saved of liberal-democracy from the threatening encroachment of a one-party state."[86]

Further reflection suggests that a quasi-party system need not be restricted to the circumstances Macpherson examined, where one party was overwhelmingly dominant while others were subordinate, if not marginal. His interest lay in exploring the social basis of partisan composition, competition, and ideological outlook. Particularly where the contradiction between the claims of individualism and the realities of a mature capitalism was decisive, the narrowing of the acceptable range of policy options and the terms of political debate could occur even where there was serious two-party or even multi-party competition. This is surely at least part of what Macpherson had in mind when he referred to "maintaining the form and some of the substance of democracy." In a sense, his critical exploration of the "deceptive" task of political theory, and its diminished "economic penetration," offered a method of charting this development.[87]

And this in turn raises an issue that at the outset I suggested was a key implication of Macpherson's account of possessive individualism and that I briefly alluded to in the introduction to this chapter. This is what I take to be Macpherson's claim that a collectivist social order is the best that a bourgeois society can achieve. Recall that this was most likely to come about under conditions where people see themselves as equal in some fundamental and ultimately decisive respect that trumps other contexts in which they are evidently unequal and thus incapable of acknowledging a common interest. The greatness of Hobbes and indeed the thinkers in the dark tradition of the bourgeoisie down to Carl Schmitt lay in their recognition that the greatest equalizer was fear. So it might not be going too far to say that the social order they defended was a collectivism of fear, held together by a strong state able to impose order in the face of the centrifugal pressures generated by radical self-interest and justified on that basis. I think Macpherson, typically seen as a utopian idealist and optimist, understood this; hence his fascination with and appreciation of Hobbes.

Moreover, I also think he was aware of something else, and this explained at least in part his ultimate rejection of the Leninist party and the vanguard model of revolutionary transformation. Collectivist impulses rooted in the deeply entrenched values, practices, and institutions of capitalist society, based as they were on the evolving dynamics generated by the historically revolutionary emergence of liberalism and liberal society, were by no means absent from the revolutionary movements ideologically committed to supplanting liberalism and capitalism with something higher and finer. What took root instead under the Soviet model of socialism was the abolition of private property without its transcendence – what has been called bureaucratic collectivism. Collectivism, whether capitalist or (ostensibly) socialist, reflected the failure to appreciate and achieve a developmental individualism in and against the distorting pathologies of possessive or competitive individualism.[88] Hence Macpherson's claim that "if what I consider the basic liberal and the basic Marxist value of individual self-development is not made the mainstay of the whole attempt at transition to a good society, then there won't be any transition; it won't even get started."

Throughout this study I have argued that Macpherson's most important contributions to political thought emerged from his attempt to tease out the logic of possessive individualism – that analysis followed theory. But it may be as well that he developed his concepts, including possessive individualism itself, on the basis of not only earlier explicitly theoretical work but also the empirically and historically informed theoretical account offered in *Democracy in Alberta* – in other words, theory followed analysis.

And I would argue that it was not a coincidence that *Democracy in Alberta* was the work most explicitly indebted to Marx, while at the same time it did not dismiss liberal democracy, nor even view commitment to it as merely a strategic necessity, to be jettisoned by socialists after the revolutionary overthrow of capitalism. As with Horkheimer and Marcuse (the analysis of "Egoism and Freedom Movements" is germane here), so for Macpherson: the contradictions of liberalism generated the predicament of the agrarian petite bourgeoisie and thus the conditions for the quasi-party system with its potentially authoritarian possibilities. Yet what was authentic in the revolt of the prairie populists, namely the assertion of an individualism tied to demands for freedom, justice, dignity, and even community, meant that liberal institutions could not simply be cast aside. They had to be worked through. For this purpose, Marx and Marxian ideas were critical. But any Marxism worthy of the commitments to individual self-development Macpherson saw in Marx's own writings had to retrieve and not simply dismiss, suppress, or ignore what was authentic in the liberal inheritance that populism both expressed and denied. In other words, if a communal solidarity, and not an oppressive collectivism, were to be achieved, liberalism and socialism had to be brought together such that each defined the other.

This would be a society in which individuals as infinite developers of their human powers, as active doers and exerters of their distinctively human capacities, would come into their own as both the human basis of this society and this society's greatest accomplishment.

This complex of challenges and commitments would shape Macpherson's encounter with the demands of democracy and the contours of his democratic theory.

Chapter Four

C.B. Macpherson, Democracy, and Democratic Theory 1: Revisionist Liberalism and the Two Faces of Liberty

Alongside his path-breaking account of possessive individualism, which has secured him a lasting place in the ranks of political thinkers, C.B. Macpherson's treatment of democracy and democratic theory, most notably in his *Democratic Theory: Essays in Retrieval* and *The Life and Times of Liberal Democracy*, represents another key, and I believe underappreciated, dimension of his work and legacy. To be sure, this work has not gone unnoticed. Macpherson is praised by some for triggering the "democratic imagination" by providing a radical view of democracy as a political order that makes possible the fullest development and exercise by individuals of their distinctively human capacities (although, according to some Marxist critics, his vision was not radical enough). By contrast, he is criticized by others as offering an unrealistic and even dangerously utopian account of a radically egalitarian democratic society in a theory of democracy that is little more than a recycling of a long-discredited Marxism. But above all, he is seen by virtually everyone as defending a substantive, even statist, theory of democracy that, in the eyes of many, is no longer plausible in the face of social and value pluralism and the evidence of both the limits of and failures of the state in relation to civil society.

In this chapter, and the next one, I attempt to challenge the marginalization of Macpherson's account of democracy – that is, to retrieve his own efforts at retrieval. But at the core of what I wish to do lies a paradox. As with all analysts of Macpherson's work, I have referred in previous chapters to Macpherson's democratic theory and explored some of its key components. These include his accounts of human needs, powers, and capacities; his dissection of competing liberal-democratic ontologies; his examination of property; and his exploration of populism and democracy in Alberta.

Yet it seems to me that while analysts have referred to and written about Macpherson's democratic theory, a careful examination of his writings suggests that in fact he actually did *not* offer a fully worked out theoretical account. Nor did he claim that he did. In *Democratic Theory: Essays in Retrieval* he argued that, while the core essays were intended to address the need for a humanist theory of democracy that was liberal but not possessive individualist, nonetheless "I am aware that these essays do not amount to a new theory of democracy sufficient to the need I have propounded." He went on to say, "I publish them now as at least a contribution to identifying the problem."[1]

We know how Macpherson specifically defined the problem and his task: "to work out a revision of liberal democratic theory, a revision which clearly owes a good deal to Marx, in the hope of making that theory more democratic while rescuing that valuable part of the liberal tradition which is submerged when liberalism is identified with capitalist market relations." In pursuit of this purpose, Macpherson emphasized the idea of individual self-realization as the core of a democracy understood not merely as a mechanism for choosing and authorizing governments, but also as a kind of society that ensured as much as possible the equal, effective right of individuals to live as fully as they may wish. At the heart of his understanding of the requirements of democracy was, as we will see, the idea of positive or developmental liberty or freedom as the necessary condition of the exercise of this right to live as fully as one would wish, unconstrained by unnecessary internal and external barriers or impediments to exercising one's distinctively human capacities – where the source of such impediments was the institution of capitalist private property. In his view, this form of liberty complemented and enriched the classical liberal emphasis on negative or counter-extractive liberty, freedom from interference by others. These conditions ultimately required a participatory democratic system whose key elements Macpherson summarily laid out in *The Life and Times of Liberal Democracy*.

In the next two chapters, I examine this task and Macpherson's response to it in order to glean insights into how we might think about democratic possibilities in the present and what Macpherson has to offer for this purpose. It means taking seriously Macpherson's account of what a revised liberal democratic theory required and suggesting its continuing value, even as much current democratic theory has gone in a different direction. Such an approach, I believe, would not simply dismiss other alternatives but rather indicate what I hope would be a useful way of reading them to show what they might leave out, in spite of their intentions.

In other words, I want to argue that if Macpherson did not offer a theory of democracy, as he himself admitted, he did provide elements of a critique of democratic theory that pointed towards, without fully spelling out, what I would call a critical theory of democracy. My references to "critique" and to "critical theory" suggest once again what I have called Macpherson's suppressed philosophical dimension. And I attempt here what I have attempted in previous chapters: to provide an immanent reconstruction of Macpherson's key categories, in this case democracy, in order to highlight what I see as its rich possibilities for informing an analysis of the present.

What are the core elements of Macpherson's critique? My argument is that what is known as Macpherson's democratic theory emerges immanently from the critique of possessive individualism. A fully democratic society is one in which possessive individualism is de-emphasized, if not eliminated. Where this takes place, the conception of individuals as consumers and appropriators can give way to one under which they are active doers and exerters of their distinctively human capacities. This, in turn, becomes possible when and as the net transfer of powers is reduced or eliminated. Such a development requires, among other things, a new conception of, and institution of, property, which in turn further reinforces the move towards the entrenchment of the conception of humans as doers and exerters. The combination of institutional and conceptual change, each reinforcing the other, makes possible and requires a cooperative individualism in terms of which individuals enjoy what Macpherson calls counter-extractive and developmental liberty. Finally, a democratic theory incorporating these dimensions would be legitimately liberal democratic – liberal not in the sense of the stronger doing down the weaker using market rules, but rather the equal right of all to develop themselves; democratic not in the sense of a mechanism used by otherwise contentious individuals to choose and authorize governments, but rather a kind of society within which all can equally develop and exercise their distinctively human capacities.

In what follows I attempt to flesh out this model of critique. I begin in this chapter with some general observations about democracy as a concept that identifies what I believe are core elements of a critique of democratic theory that can pave the way for a critical theory of democracy. I then move on to explore Macpherson's own critical analyses of alternative attempts to reinvigorate liberal democratic theory, for it was primarily on the basis of these analyses that he worked up those elements he thought crucial for a normatively robust account. Particularly important here are his essays on John Chapman, John Rawls, and Isaiah Berlin. Macpherson saw Rawls and Berlin in particular as offering important arguments that he felt compelled to address, both because they at least implicitly (and in Chapman's case, explicitly) took issue with his own conception of what a theory of liberal democracy should be, and because he correctly foresaw that they would become hugely influential as political and social theorists cast about for ways to deal with the challenges confronting liberal democratic polities.

One of these challenges is now seen to be the identification and protection of human rights. In the next chapter, I briefly explore key issues raised by human rights discourses and Macpherson's response to them, a response that I believe was both called forth and shaped by his analysis of Berlin in particular. I then focus in detail on Macpherson's own treatment of democracy as he worked it out in various places and as it addressed the terms of what I have suggested is his critique. Especially important here is his account in *The Life and Times of Liberal Democracy* and the "models" of democracy he offered there. But I also discuss other writings, including his later essays on the state, workers' control, and pluralism. Finally, I briefly relate Macpherson's account to what I see as key themes defining much contemporary democratic theory. I attempt to indicate how and where Macpherson's analysis contributes to this contemporary work by raising issues that, in my view, have not been given sufficient attention in it. Here Macpherson's emphasis on the need to link political theory to political economy, and beyond this, what I have argued is his implicit critical theory approach, loom as particularly significant.

The Complex and Contested Meanings of Democracy

In a fascinating essay Josiah Ober, an American classical scholar of democracy and ancient politics, has sought to clarify the complex meanings associated with the concept of democracy on the basis of its hybrid Greek character as a combination of *demos* (the people) and *kratos* (power).[2] He claims that while democracy is typically understood as majority rule, where the majority is numerical and based on the aggregation of choices, it would be more accurate to view *kratos* or power as relating to the empowerment of the people, and not just as a measure of what individual members of a body politic might "want" as indicated by their choices through, for example, voting.

This issue emerges when we consider the classical way in which different regimes or forms of government are understood. Typically they involve the nature of the ruling body or unit, the question whether authority is held by the one, the few, or the many. In this respect, democracy is usually contrasted with monarchy and oligarchy, where *monos* indicates the solitary, the one, and *hoi oligoi*, the few. But *demos* does not refer to a number, specifically the number of those who have power, but rather to the collective body. The term for the many is *hoi polloi*; but there is no regime named *pollokratia* or *polloarchia*. Somehow, democracy is about more and other than the number who rule.

Ober raises another issue. The terms *monarchy* and *oligarchy* incorporate the *-arche* suffix, not the *-kratos* suffix. Ober notes that *arche* can mean "origin," or "empire." or "domination," or "office/magistracy." The idea is that terms for regimes that have the *-arche* suffix refer to those who have access to power in the existing offices that characterize some kind of constitutional order. Thus, in an oligarchy, access to offices was restricted to those of elite ancestry who met a property qualification and frequently engaged in certain occupations. By contrast, *kratos* refers not to offices but to power, with the meaning of power ranging widely from "domination" to "rule" to "capacity." While numbers and offices are clearly important, democracy seems to involve something more and even more significant.[3]

Democracy also had parallels with another *-kratos* term: *isokratia*, or equality. When connected with two other terms used to describe democracy, particularly by the fifth century BCE historian Herodotus – *isonomia* (equality before the law), and *isegoria* (roughly, equal citizenship where this involves access to public fora for deliberation and an equal right to speak and be heard there) – *isokratia* suggests equality of a kind of active power, namely, "public power that conduces to the common good through enabling good things to happen in the public realm."[4] The emphasis is on the generation and exercise of political capacities or capabilities – in other words, on empowerment. To this we could also add the term *isomoiria* (equal shares, which implies a kind of economic equality). The overall claim is that an equitable distribution of socially valued goods (legal equality, political equality, economic equality) would in turn lead to the achievement of the common good, the good for everyone as a member of the *demos*.

The connection between *isokratia* and *demokratia* suggests that democracy may best be understood as the capacity of the people as a body to enter and achieve good things in the public realm.

> If this is right, *demokratia* does not refer in the first instance to the *demos'* monopolistic control of pre-existing constitutional authority. *Demokratia* is not just "the power of the *demos*" in the sense of "the superior or monopolistic power of the *demos* relative to other potential power-holders in the state." Rather it means, more capaciously, "the empowered *demos*" – it is the regime in which the *demos* [a socially diverse body of individuals, the entire citizenry] gains a collective capacity to effect change in the public realm. And so it is not just a matter of *control* of a public realm but the collective *strength* and *ability* to act within that realm and, indeed, to reconstitute the public realm through action.[5]

Of course no political system and its explanatory and justificatory concepts operate in a social vacuum. Inequality and conflict characterized Greek societies, as they do our own. It may be no coincidence, then, that although we speak of democracy we do not speak about *monokratia* or *oligokratia*, but instead of monarchy or oligarchy. For the Greeks – and for us – there is little doubt of the capacity of those of wealth, power, high birth, and special education to exercise power. The question is about their control of the apparatus of government.

The implication is that because the people, the *demos*, had to be empowered as well as constitutionally charged with the exercise of power, democracy is a kind of ongoing project as well as, indeed more important than, a system for making social decisions. In other words, the reality of democracy is that it is both an ideal and an actuality – or rather, its actuality includes its ideal elements, which do not stand apart from its very meaning. And it is perhaps because of this that while Greek, and notably Athenian, democracy included voting and elections as ways of making decisions and determining policy, these were not the only methods of formulating and expressing a popular will, much less the definitive ones. Lotteries for offices and other deliberative bodies were also important and widely used. According to Ober, the equation of democracy with voting and control of the apparatus of government by the many (i.e., the poor) was the position taken by *critics* of democracy, not its supporters or practitioners. I would argue we might confront the same question now: whether our contemporary understanding of the theory and practice of democracy is more powerfully shaped by its defenders or critics, or perhaps even by its critics who define themselves as, and are understood as, its defenders. So it is an enduring question. It is worth noting here that, as Ober points out, in the second century BCE Polybius, to whom we owe one extremely influential variant of the idea that regimes rise and fall cyclically, came up with the term *ochlokratia*. This was derived from *ochlos* (mob) and was intended as a pejorative variant of *demokratia*. That democracy was or could be equivalent to mob rule has been a fear that has haunted debates about democracy and its viability down to our own time.

The idea that the meaning of democracy is both complex and contested stands at the centre of the democratic theory of C.B. Macpherson. When we consider what I have noted were the two distinctive ways in which Macpherson understood democracy, the issues raised by Ober come to the fore. They can be seen in the distinction Macpherson draws between democracy as a mechanism for choosing and authorizing governments (*arche*) and as a kind of society devoted to the full and equal development by all individuals of their distinctively human capacities (*kratos*). So understood, these distinctive conceptions of democracy in turn expressed at the level of both institutional structure and normative commitments what Macpherson had identified as liberal democracy's competing ontological perspectives.

But beyond this, I think that the move from ontology to democracy, considered in light of Ober's argument, suggests what is at stake in terms of the normative orientation of democratic practices. To distinguish between *arche* and *kratos* is to put into bold relief the reality that in the context of the historical development of liberal democracy the latter has been folded into the former: democracy is typically viewed in terms of ruling (and fitness to rule) rather than empowerment. In the measure that empowerment implies capabilities, a democracy (really what rather ironically is the closest approximation to the submergence of the latter into the former, namely Robert Dahl's and Charles Lindblom's characterization of existing liberal democracy as polyarchy[6]) that is about ruling or access to offices means that the capacity to do good things in the public realm by and through the reconstitution of that realm through action is significantly diminished, if not lost altogether. In a process particularly relevant to the emergence of actually existing liberal democracy, the people, once they become a ruling body, are an aggregation – the collectivism that I have argued Macpherson insightfully saw as the closest a possessive market society could come to a political community. (And Horkheimer's "Egoism and Freedom

Movements" can be understood as what happens when ruling trumps empowerment.) As was evident from the rather pessimistic conclusion of *Democracy in Alberta,* Macpherson saw in this the element of truth in claims about "totalitarian" democracy or the tyranny of the majority. And as Hannah Arendt argued, acquiring power (or, more accurately, rule) is not the same as being empowered.[7] Empowerment changes those engaged in it by generating a public life under the conditions of equality Ober identifies, and this alters the nature of political office and fitness to hold it. (This will turn out to be important for understanding and appraising different conceptions of the politics of human rights.) In Macpherson's terms, the change would coincide with the creation of a social setting in which individuals would be able to view themselves as doers and exerters of their capacities and have that view reinforced by real opportunities to do so.

The urgency Macpherson appeared to bring to his treatment of ontology becomes more understandable when ontology is related to democracy in the way suggested here. He demonstrated in a particularly instructive way the necessity to link assumptions about human nature to the requirements of democratic theory in his account of what he called revisionist liberalism.

C.B. Macpherson, John Chapman, and John Rawls: The Critique of Revisionist Liberalism

As Macpherson saw it, revisionist liberalism was late twentieth-century normative theory that was post-liberal democratic in the sense that it took as its basis the historically achieved reconciliation of democracy and capitalism, or possessive individualism, that culminated in the emergence of the managed capitalism of the welfare state. Macpherson distinguished this theory from so-called empirical theories of democracy, essentially positivist accounts of democracy taken up by mainstream social scientists that purported to be value-free and purely explanatory, with a focus on the supposedly actual workings of democratic institutions. Such theories claimed to be scientific and realist. They dismissed "classical" theories of democracy for their allegedly unrealistic views about active citizenship and participation. They viewed as unsupportable and even dangerous the humanist ideal of democracy as a form of life essential for fostering the development and exercise by individuals of their human capacities – that is, the idea that democracy could transform both individuals and social institutions. At best, democracy was a means by which individuals voting from time to time in elections exercised some measure of indirect control over political authorities by selecting one elite group over another for the right to govern the society.

From Macpherson's perspective, this separation of empirical from normative theory offered another manifestation of the erosion of a critical political science and political economy that he had addressed in "The Deceptive Task of Political Theory" and "The Economic Penetration of Political Theory." The specific context here was the post-1945 Cold War fear among elites that the eruption of mass popular movements, an inevitable result of "excessive" political engagement, would threaten political stability and undermine liberal values and political institutions.

Macpherson took seriously attempts by his key "revisionist" liberals, John Rawls, John Chapman, and, in a different sense, Isaiah Berlin, to restore the normative core of liberal democratic theory by revisiting and reviving the moral dimension of individualism, a dimension either slighted or occluded by empirical theories. He believed, though, that however well-intentioned, their efforts were doomed to fail. Their key flaw lay in their attempt to hold together both humanist liberal and capitalist market values. In the case of Rawls, Macpherson specifically linked what he saw as Rawls's conception of a just and well-ordered society to his ontological assumptions.

In the process of making his case, Macpherson reiterated in the context of democratic theory his criticisms of the late nineteenth-century ethical liberal approach to human needs by thinkers such as John Stuart Mill and T.H. Green. Recall that while ethical liberal thinkers rejected as normatively inadequate a purely market determination and justification of needs, whereby what mattered were the demands registered by the market, irrespective of quality, they nonetheless accepted and even defended possessive market society. In this respect, the utilitarian purveyors of the hedonistic calculus were more realistic, because they accepted fully the logic of possessive individualism and in particular the idea that the power of an individual depended upon the ability to command the services of others and so acquire the wealth needed to ensure a continuous flow of utilities. The same was true of the "new" ethical liberals like Rawls and Chapman.

And in this respect, too, the so-called empirical theorists of democracy, twentieth-century inheritors of the Hobbes-to-Bentham tradition of thought, had it over their ethical counterparts. Like its classical utilitarian forbearers, empirical theory – of which Macpherson singled out

Joseph Schumpeter and the (mid-career) Robert Dahl as key architects[8] – was "based on the implicit postulate that man is essentially a consumer of utilities, and it proceeds by assuming that any realistic and honest democratic theory will treat man so. The point is, of course, that where and when and in so far as men *do* behave as consumers rather than exerters, democracy *is* reduced to a means of letting people have some indirect say in who gets what, when, and how: in that case, the Schumpeter-Dahl model makes very good sense."[9] It made good sense because the system elicited the very qualities of behaviour it required for its stable functioning – and this stability itself commended the system. The spectre of Hobbes and his truth hovered over the theory. It was the theory of a hard-driving, competitive market social order. This meant in a nutshell that the claims of distributive justice so central to revisionist liberal thought would necessarily have to give way to the determinations of the market. In the case of Rawls, this accounted, as Macpherson saw it, for "the curious fact that a theory of justice which starts from egalitarian premises should be mainly concerned with enquiring what justifies an inequality of life prospects as between members of different social classes."[10]

Indeed the same might have been said as well of the other "revisionist" liberal-democratic theorist Macpherson addressed, John Chapman. In Macpherson's reading, Chapman offered a theory of liberal democracy based on three pillars: principles of justice, economic rationality, and equal individual moral freedom. Specifically rejecting Macpherson's argument that, because of its contentiousness and invasiveness, a possessive market society was inherently inconsistent with the values of a humanist and egalitarian liberal democracy, Chapman claimed that it was possible to combine the economic rationality of capitalism with both a robust theory of distributive justice and a conception of moral freedom understood as the right of all individuals to make the best of themselves. The key lay in taxing and redistributing returns from capital through a combination of productive reinvestments and the provision of free public services. Any income inequalities that remained would reflect differential contributions to productive effort in response to the demands of sovereign consumers and so would be optimizing and therefore economically rational. Moreover, as long as the role of "owner" of capital was open to anyone on the basis of full equality of opportunity, and income differentials reflected marginal contributions to a rational allocation of resources through fully competitive markets, there would be neither a transfer of powers nor structurally determined invasive behaviour. Thus Chapman's principles of justice – respectively, that inequalities were just only insofar as they worked to everyone's advantage, that is, were optimizing; and that no one ought to gain at the expense of another – were under these circumstances fulfilled. And because in a system of consumer sovereignty of the kind set out and defended, all benefited and were free to pursue their choices, individual moral freedom was respected and secured.

Macpherson responded to Chapman by offering a detailed critique of his conception of economic rationality, and in light of this, his proposals for taxing and distributing returns to capital within a capitalist market framework.[11] As usual, the essence of Macpherson's criticisms turned on Chapman's failure/unwillingness to see or acknowledge the net transfer of powers – in effect, the realities of class. Or, to put it another way, Chapman failed to distinguish income from wealth, which is to say capital as a monetary return on investment from capital as a structured social relation rooted in access or lack of access to the means of life and labour. Under the circumstances, (capitalist) economic rationality was the rationality of continuous accumulation based on the exploitation of labour power, i.e., an ongoing and pervasive net transfer of powers. Quite apart from whether or not capitalists would have an incentive to invest if their returns were taxed from them, the dynamic driving the system was the pursuit of profit, the monetary or value equivalent of the reproduction of an ongoing set of possessive market relations. These relations had not only powerful economic but also political, psychological, social, and cultural forces standing behind them. Consumer desires and consumer sovereignty were the products, not the basis, of the system. And even under the fullest equality of opportunity and of access to the top positions in an ongoing capitalist system, the net transfer of powers and the invasive behaviour that was its necessary concomitant – that is, the existence of classes – would remain. What there would be at best was greater inter-class mobility.

Chapman was not unaware of the existence of exploitation. But he assumed it to be a contingent and thus eliminable quality of an economy based on private property and market competition, a contingency that was the product of oligopolistic concentration of wealth. He believed his proposals for taxing capital, coupled with the fullest possible equality of opportunity, would ward off oligopoly. In effect, he appeared to envisage a society that under modern conditions of high productivity and social complexity would preserve something of a simple (i.e., non-exploitive) market society. However, the dynamic of accumulation that is the driving force of a full-fledged capitalist market economy would, by means of the very competition Chapman clearly favoured, foster the emergence of large agglomerations of capital: "Economic rationality in a system of private ownership of capital requires that owners be rewarded for using their resources, or allowing them to be used, in the production of goods wanted by the members of the society considered as consumers. The more rationally the owners are so rewarded, the more concentrated their control will become." This would be true, even if all profits were to be taxed away, for "some firms would, in the normal course of competition in efficiency at meeting (or creating and meeting) consumer demands, fail. They will either go out of business or will be taken over by their more successful competitors. In either case, the mass of capital becomes more concentrated."[12] Concentration of capital means concentration of economic power that offends against Chapman's principle of moral freedom. It permits those who control access to the means of life and labour to set the terms and conditions under which those without their own means can gain this access.

Moreover, restricting claims of justice to questions of distributive justice around the fullest equalization of income possible within the confines of a system of private property and market competition for accumulation, and thus the need for capitalist incentives to enter resources into market exchanges, fails to distinguish between income and wealth, with wealth tied to ownership of capital. From Macpherson's perspective this leaves a dilemma: either in the interests of the fullest realization of distributive justice all income inequalities to the greatest extent possible are eliminated, thus offending against the principle of economic rationality, or income inequalities are maintained in order to assure optimal production in response to the requirements of consumer sovereignty, thereby threatening to undermine or even violate the principles of justice. (Chapman conceded this could occur, although he thought welfare state transfers would go a considerable way to offset it.) And in either case, the principle of moral freedom would be impaired.

For Macpherson, the problem ultimately came down once again to ontology. Chapman's picture of human nature was that of individuals as consumers and not exerters and developers of their distinctively human capacities. This undermined his account of a normatively appropriate liberal democratic society, which he believed "must claim that it provides its members with an equal ability to make the best of themselves – this is his equal moral freedom." Such an account and the principle of moral freedom required a conception of humans as doers and exerters, not simply consumers. Yet Chapman's principle of justice was "concerned primarily with the distribution of *income*, that is to say, with the distribution of utilities between men as consumers. This is not the same as the distribution of men's ability to use and develop their human capacities ... [which] requires ... not only equal rights as consumers (or, which is all Chapman can allow, such an approach to equality of income as is consistent with economic rationality), but also something like *control* of the exercise of their capacities."[13]

It is worth noting the contemporary significance of the critique of distributive justice and its emphasis on income to the exclusion of wealth as power that Macpherson suggested here. In the wake of the 2008 global financial crisis and the ongoing larger economic turbulence it spawned, there has been much concern expressed, even in elite circles, about intensifying worldwide income inequalities and their destructive impact on individuals and societies.[14] Yet there is little effort by governments and other institutions to explore the roots of income inequality in the structures and operations of the capitalist market economy. Indeed the standard response seems to be to permit market forces, particularly the labour market, to operate even more freely, with deficit reduction and fiscal austerity, including reduced expenditures on social supports, trumpeted as the appropriate policy responses by governments everywhere. The image of individuals as consumers and appropriators is robust and virtually unchallenged.

Distributive justice has come to set the limits on the political imagination, the boundaries of the possible. At the level of political theory, this situation has reinforced and been reinforced by the impact in particular of the better-known "revisionist" liberal thinker Macpherson discussed: John Rawls. At least in the academic realm, Rawls has arguably been the most influential theorist of the past four decades, certainly in the United States, but elsewhere as well. And while this is always difficult to demonstrate with any precision, a case could be made that this influence has not been restricted exclusively to the academy but has infiltrated the larger political culture of liberalism and democracy.[15] Rawls viewed his account of justice as fairness as fitted specifically to the traditions, demands, and requirements of what he called a constitutional democracy. This was a democracy that was faithful to the deepest impulses of liberal individualism, while at the same time respectful of the democratic need for social cooperation and identification of, and concern for, the common good.

Like morality, with which it is closely associated, justice has occupied an ambiguous place in Marxism. It has often been viewed as tied to the requirements of capitalism and the condition of scarcity created by the need to preserve capitalist social relations. With the massive development of the productive forces unleashed by capitalism, the overcoming of such scarcity, and consequently the transcendence of justice and those conditions that require it, had become a historical possibility.

Although Macpherson at times flirted with this position – recall that he alluded to Hume's view that if scarcity were overcome, justice would be unnecessary – his analysis of Rawls demonstrated a more complex picture. Rawls's procedure for establishing the principles of justice, the "original position" and the Kantian-influenced agent-neutral deliberations to which it was designed to give rise under a revised form of a social contract, has generated extensive scholarly interest. For Macpherson, however, more important for his purposes were Rawls's specific core principles of justice, namely, the equal liberties principle and the difference principle. To be sure, these, too, have drawn considerable attention, in particular the difference principle.[16] As is well known, under it, inequalities of income and wealth are justifiable if they serve to the advantage of the least well-off and the offices and positions to which they attach are open to all on the basis of merit, i.e., there would be fair equality of opportunity. (This suggests something equivalent to Chapman's view that the position of "owner" would be, in principle, open to all.) The decisive element of the difference principle that attracted Macpherson's attention was Rawls's acceptance of the apparent unavoidability of class-based inequalities in income and wealth, that there would always be an initial inequality in life prospects. Hence the difference principle "is designed to show when class inequality in life-prospects is justified ... Rawls, if I understand him rightly, thinks [unequal classes] are consistent with a substantial equality in liberty and personal rights, in any society, including a capitalist market society." On the contrary, for Macpherson "these are inconsistent in a capitalist market society, where class-inequality of income or wealth is the result and the means of an inequality in power which reaches to the liberties, rights, and essential humanity of the individuals in those classes."[17]

In other words, Rawls failed to see the net transfer of powers, that is,

> he does not see that class division in any society, not least in his free market society, is based on such continuous transfer: the transfer is the means

> and the result of class division ... Having thus abstracted from exploitation, Rawls is able to conceive "the social injustices which now exist" as due to such present phenomena as monopolistic restrictions and absence of equality of opportunities (including educational opportunities), all of which are held to be remediable by the regulative welfare state. Their being remedied would indeed, as he says, leave natural differences of ability: it would also leave the transfer of powers, which permits, and in a market requires, the more able to extract some of the others' powers, and so reproduces class differences.[18]

Rawls's failure to see the net transfer of powers, which was, as we have seen, a failing he shared with others in the traditions of liberalism, including the humanist tradition, was, according to Macpherson, the result of an inadequate grasp of the structures of a capitalist market society. His model of a good society in which the two principles of justice are realized is one characterized by a fully free market system, "although the means of production may or may not be privately owned." According to Rawls, "there is no essential tie between the use of free markets and private ownership of the instruments of production."[19] In Rawls's view, both what he calls private-property and socialist economic systems rely on markets and market incentives. The difference is that a socialist regime deploys the market to allocate goods for consumption but uses planning or collective decision-making for basic choices about production: "Collective decisions made democratically under the constitution determine the general features of the economy, such as the rate of saving and the proportion of society's production devoted to essential public goods. Given the resulting economic environment, firms regulated by market forces conduct themselves much as before."[20]

However, according to Macpherson, Rawls failed to see that it was not markets in the abstract but the capitalist market that served as the core institution of the kind of regulated welfare state with permanent class divisions that Rawls assumed for his argument and saw as consistent with his principles of justice. He seemed to misunderstand what it would mean under socialism for firms to behave as they would under a regime of private property, that is, a regime in which individual behaviour would manifest a significant degree of "normal capitalist motivations ... What is omitted is any consideration of the absence, in any model of socialism, of *capitalist* market forces, the force of which derives from the desire of entrepreneurs and firms to increase their capital, and their ability to do so by virtue of the property institutions which facilitate and require exploitation," where exploitation "in the strict sense" involves "transferring to oneself for one's own benefit some of the powers of others."[21] Capitalist society was not simply a market society in the sense of pervasive relations of exchange, an expansive commercial society in which the imperative of "buying cheap and selling dear" predominated. Rather, it was a social order compulsively driven by "the inescapable imperatives of competition, profit-maximization, constant accumulation and the endless need to reduce the costs of labour by improving labour productivity" – a social order in which wealth is generated "by means of cost-effective production in integrated competitive markets."[22]

The institution of private property embodies capitalist incentives – it is the primary vehicle for the exercise of extractive power. The unavoidable presence of extractive power, on the one hand, necessarily limits the extent to which welfare state regulations can ensure equality of opportunity and prevent monopolistic restrictions, and transfers can offset inequalities of wealth and income that would jeopardize equality of opportunity and political liberties. On the other hand, it necessitates that in order to behave rationally individuals must operate according to incentives for material gain. This flies in the face of Rawls's key conception of rational behaviour as governed by the individual's desire to obtain "primary goods," not in order to acquire without limit but rather "as means to realize his plan of life or concepts of the good, to develop his capacities to the fullest."[23] Moreover, in Rawls's own words, individual life plans, at least in a well-ordered and harmonious society, need not conflict – they can be "both rational and complementary. Human beings have various talents and abilities the totality of which is unrealizable by any one person or group of persons. Thus we not only benefit from the complementary nature of our developed inclinations but we take pleasure in one another's activities ... Human beings have a desire to express their nature as free and equal moral persons."[24] As Macpherson noted, with its stress on harmonistic self-development, this seems far removed from the typical picture of the necessarily competitive bourgeois individual.

Yet, like the nineteenth-century ethical or humanist liberals such as T.H. Green, Rawls wanted both: "His rational moral man, the man with his own plan of life and concept of the good, who is apparently so unbourgeois ... bears the very hallmark of bourgeois man: he *both* puts a high value on individual liberty *and* accepts as inevitable a class-divided society in which class determines life prospects."[25] The failure to see that the extractive power upon which the class-divided bourgeois order rests and which enforces and is enforced by individual competitive striving after unlimited satisfactions stands in the way of achieving the moral individualism Rawls envisaged, and the harmonious social order this required and made possible. It undermines the ability to realize the principles of justice. In a society without extractive power, "Rawls's principles of justice ... would probably make very good sense."[26] The failure to recognize extractive power, that such power was unavoidable in a capitalist market system, and that a realistic theory in the circumstances required the recognition that the competitive model of human nature necessarily trumped that of individuals as potentially harmonious self-developers defined the limits of the revisionist liberal project. It pointed to those dimensions of democratic theory that a more humanist and radical account needed to address.

It should be noted that, in the course of developing his criticisms of Rawls, Macpherson alluded tantalizingly to elements of a post-capitalist democratic society he has not normally been seen as sufficiently stressing. With his evident Marxist sympathies, Macpherson has been criticized for upholding an unrealistic and potentially dangerous picture of a fully harmonious, classless society without significant social divisions. It is an important criticism to which arguably Macpherson did not devote proper attention, although it is certainly worth noting that liberal theorists such as Rawls, and even free market liberals such as Milton Friedman, were not without their own harmonistic assumptions or even illusions. Indeed in his recognition that a class-divided society with relations of extractive power will inevitably be conflictual, Macpherson was arguably more realistic about the prospects for social harmony. This could be seen as another aspect of his critique of Hobbes, political power, and the inherent collectivism of a possessive individualist social order.

Yet in his analysis of revisionist liberalism, and in particular, Rawls's theory of justice, Macpherson indicated that the elimination of extractive relations did not necessarily mean the absence of differences, even in income or wealth. Class relations based on the net transfer of powers do preclude the possibility of a fully humanist liberal-democratic society faithful to the most laudable aspirations of both liberalism and democracy. However, "non-capitalist models which utilize or permit differences of income or wealth are of course possible, and may result in classes by income or wealth. But these need not create unequal liberties and rights since they are not necessarily either the result of or the means of domination, of gaining at the expense of others."[27] Elsewhere he noted that, "granting that individual ends are very diverse, and even for the sake of argument granting that the myriad individual ends make *conflicting* demands on scarce resources, this does not in the nature of things necessarily set up *class* differences."[28] To be sure, these are only hints. But they do suggest the significance that individual flourishing and the need to secure in an ongoing way the conditions under which it could take place held for Macpherson's account of democracy and democratic possibilities.

That this was the case is also evident from the attention Macpherson gave to questions of freedom or liberty and human rights. Challenging the continuing central place occupied by capitalist economic rationality and thus extractive power in the work of Chapman and Rawls was vital, but not by itself sufficient to justify the argument for a more radical democracy that could still be called liberal. Doing away with extractive power turned out to be a necessary but not sufficient condition for promoting developmental power, the ability of all equally to enjoy and exercise their human capacities. Rights and liberties were crucial, and a liberalism that distinguished them from capitalist market compulsions posed both a challenge and an opportunity for the kind of democratic theory Macpherson attempted to promote. It was for this reason, I believe, that he turned his attention to the ideas of Isaiah Berlin.

Isaiah Berlin: From Negative and Positive Liberty to Counter-Extractive and Developmental Liberty

Isaiah Berlin is justly renowned for making the distinction between negative and positive liberty a key theme in contemporary political thought, in the process offering a powerful argument on behalf of the claim that only negative liberty, "the permitted range of individual potential choices," is genuinely in tune with the requirements of individual freedom. This by itself has commended his ideas to mainstream liberal theory. And since what Berlin identified as positive liberty was in effect what Macpherson had defined and defended as the maximization of powers, "if his case against positive liberty is sustained, a democratic theory built on the maximization of powers would have little claim to embody genuine liberal values."[29]

But just as importantly, Berlin's negative liberty was not restricted to market freedoms. Indeed, according to Macpherson, Berlin was not enamoured of market rationality in the same way as were Chapman and Rawls. He did not link political freedom exclusively to the capitalist market. He did not embrace the possessive individualism of rational choice and strategic action. Indeed there were clear elements of intersubjectivity central to positive or development liberty in his work, even as he identified negative liberty with liberty as such. All of these elements of Berlin's account represented key issues that provided Macpherson the opportunity, as well as the need, to clarify the meaning of liberty and individualism for his own thought.

Berlin intended the distinction between positive and negative liberty as a defence of liberal political freedom, or negative freedom, freedom from external coercion, in the face of what he saw as the implicitly totalitarian implications of what he termed positive freedom. This conception of freedom identifies it with rational self-mastery. This means that as an individual I am "moved by reasons, by conscious purposes which are my own, not by causes which affect me, as it were, from the outside ... I wish, above all, to be conscious of myself as a thinking, willing, active being, bearing responsibility for my choices and able to explain them by references to my own ideas and purposes. I feel free to the degree that I believe this to be true, and enslaved to the degree that I am made to realize it is not."[30] For Berlin, this last sentence carries the key to understanding the dangers of positive freedom: I may not realize that I am unfree and so must be "made" to do so by those who can see what I cannot. Charles Taylor believes it is possible to "second guess" an agent by pointing out what Macpherson called internalized impediments to the articulation and pursuit of one's freely and rationally chosen purposes.[31] Seconding-guessing the individual can thus foster self-development. For Berlin, however, this instead becomes a recipe for domination under which the allegedly more fully rational can coerce those not (yet) fully rational and thus not aware of what their "real" interests require. It is a formula for forcing people to be free – for Berlin an evident logical contradiction that has had monstrous historical consequences.

The problem in Berlin's eyes is that notions of positive freedom, which elicit the creation of "great, disciplined authoritarian structures [incorporating] the ideal of 'positive' self-mastery by classes, or peoples, or the whole of mankind," assume an ultimate harmony of human purposes and one "true" way of life, whereas in fact human goals are plural and often contentious. Since self-mastery, or self-government, and the ideal of harmonious human purposes can readily connect up with the idea of popular sovereignty or the general will, and thus radical democracy (as they are often seen to do in Rousseau), the key political point to be drawn from the critique of positive freedom is that "there is no necessary connexion between individual liberty and democratic rule ... The desire to be governed by myself, or at any rate to participate in the process by which my life is to be controlled, may be as deep a wish as that of a free area for action, and perhaps historically older. But it is not a desire for the same thing."[32]

On its own, Berlin's position has had significant influence. But the thrust of his argument has been even more important, for much current democratic theory operates under its shadow. On the one hand, there is unease about assuming the possibility of anything resembling a substantive general will in the face of the evident reality of social pluralism (this is particularly characteristic of the central place now assumed by questions of multiculturalism in political theory in general and democratic theory in particular). On the other hand, Berlin's distinction survives largely intact in the differences characterizing contemporary conceptions of liberal versus republican forms of democracy.[33] Both liberal and republican theories have raised important issues and concerns. But both seem to take for granted that indeed there is a gulf between negative and positive liberty. In other words, according to these theories there is an inherent and uneliminable tension between liberalism qua individual rights and freedoms, and democracy qua popular sovereignty. With the rise of discourses on human rights and multiculturalism, liberalism so understood has won out, even among theorists who put democracy first.[34]

Macpherson challenged Berlin's position and its implications for democratic theory in a powerfully argued attempt to recast the distinction between negative and positive liberty or freedom. For Macpherson, positive and negative liberty are closely linked, because freedom should not be restricted to deliberate coercion emerging from interference by the state, invasive behaviour by other individuals, or the pressures of social conformity in the area within which individuals should not be constrained or pushed around. It should also take into account those impediments to both free choice and the determination of pursuit of one's conscious, rational purposes that result from denial of access to the means of life and labour, that is, the institution of capitalist private property and the workings of the market mechanism. While cognizant of these, and as a supporter of the welfare state sympathetic to efforts to ameliorate the inequalities of capitalism, Berlin consigns such impediments to the category of conditions of liberty.

Macpherson thought this was a terrible mistake. It led to an impoverished and excessively mechanistic conception of freedom, a conception more appropriate to the world of Hobbes and Bentham than to contemporary political reality and its challenges. At the same time he acknowledged that some notion of positive freedom could serve and has served historically to justify authoritarian regimes that deny the reality of freedom under the guise of realizing it. But the problem lay not in anything necessarily intrinsic to the concept of positive freedom itself, but rather in two other areas. One was the unduly restricted understanding of its implications by both certain theorists of positive liberty and Berlin himself. The other was the political hurdles those committed to egalitarian and developmental goals have historically confronted, specifically the unwillingness of holders of political power in unequal, class-divided societies to concede ground to movements for fundamental democratic change except under the threat or reality of force. Both turn on the failure, inability, or unwillingness to consider impediments to liberty created by capitalist market relations, that is, in capitalist societies the denial to the majority of people of that access to the means of life and labour required for individual self-development. Most theorists have failed to recognize this; most power-holders have resisted it.

What is interesting about this account is that it draws together what I have suggested are the core elements of Macpherson's critique of democratic theory around an understanding of individual agency in terms of the intersubjective nature of human activity and thus social – that is to say, positive – freedom. The failure to grasp intersubjectivity represents, after all, the core of possessive individualism and the internal tension between individualism as self-ownership and as self-determination. It is also, as a result, central to the inability to see the net transfer of powers. Together these in turn ground a narrow conception of negative liberty that treats impediments to individual self-development as conditions of liberty, and not as elements of liberty itself.

Insofar as he failed to recognize the intersubjective nature of human activity as an element of liberty itself, Berlin erred in equating positive liberty with authoritarianism tout court. Because he did not embrace fully possessive individualist assumptions that stressed self-interested rational choice and strategic action, Berlin attempted to take intersubjectivity into account, while retaining the notion of negative liberty. Thus he defended welfare state measures that served as social preconditions for the exercise of (negative) liberty. But they could never form elements of liberty as such, which for Berlin could only mean freedom from conscious coercion.

In light of these issues, Macpherson developed a complex reading of positive liberty, and indeed freedom itself. His recasting of positive freedom to, as he saw it, more adequately address theoretical and practical questions can contribute to a critical diagnosis of the present able to illuminate the existing state of affairs from the vantage point of the majority of those required to make a fully democratic society possible and actual.

Macpherson saw Berlin as having fused together three different concepts of positive liberty into one, which he then contrasted with negative liberty and which he saw as the basis for authoritarianism in the name of freedom. One form "is individual self-direction or ... self-mastery. It is the ability to live in accordance with one's own self-conscious purposes, to act and decide for oneself rather than to be acted upon and decided for by others." A second, according to Macpherson, that is logically distinct from freedom as self-mastery, is participation in the exercise of popular sovereignty or self-government, "the democratic concept of liberty as a share in the controlling authority."[35]

It is a third conception that, as Macpherson saw it, posed the problem and made Berlin's position seem plausible. Although it appeared to follow naturally from the idea of freedom as self-mastery, and indeed in Berlin's eyes was virtually indistinguishable from it in practice, it is logically distinct historically and practically as well. This was the idea that "liberty is coercion, by the fully rational or by those who have attained self-mastery, of all the rest; coercion by those who say they know the truth, of all those who do not (yet) know it."[36]

That liberty as self-realization or self-mastery has been transformed, in theory and practice, into the debased form of allegedly rational coercion of the less by the more fully developed has, as noted above, been the product both in theory and practice of the failure to acknowledge or deal with non-intended but necessary impediments to self-realization thrust up by capitalist market relations. Idealist theories such as that of T.H. Green fell down because they attempted to reconcile individual self-development as the full, non-contentious development of human capacities with capitalist private property. Macpherson saw Stalinism as an example of a putatively radical political movement committed to the egalitarianism needed for self-development embracing supposedly rational coercion, with authoritarian or even totalitarian consequences. This outcome apparently ensued "only after long-continued and intensive refusal of the beneficiaries of unequal institutions, on a world scale, to permit any moves to alter institutions in the direction of more nearly equal powers."[37]

But not only radical political movements were in the circumstances prone to embrace a debased notion of positive liberty and to govern their actions accordingly. Macpherson also alluded to a conservative form of political movement committed to the goals of positive freedom as self-mastery and moral autonomy. By failing to recognize, even to the extent that idealist philosophers such as Green did, much less radical leftist movements, the impediments to self-realization that emerged from the denial of access to the means of life and the means of labour, conservative movements for positive liberty were apt to become disillusioned with the apparently intractable deficiencies of the people with whom they must achieve their goals. Believing that it nonetheless must be possible to realize the ends of positive freedom, such forces "are pushed into the position of holding that it can be done and should be done by an authoritarian elite using whatever coercive means are necessary."[38] Liberty as self-direction becomes liberty as rational coercion.

Macpherson offered no historical examples of conservative authoritarian movements or states committed to some notion of positive freedom that end up exercising coercion on a mass scale supposedly in the interests of realizing this freedom. But it is perhaps not too much of a leap to see certain contemporary fundamentalist religious or cultural movements as exhibiting at least some elements of what Macpherson had in mind. (And such movements are not necessarily so far from mainstream liberalism, or ostensibly liberal values, as is usually thought.)

Obviously, Macpherson's claims are contentious, particularly in his reading of history. But I think his key point was to demonstrate that negative and positive freedoms were not inherently at odds, as Berlin thought. Indeed he went further: if properly understood, and under the right circumstances, these two forms of freedom were compatible and even mutually reinforcing. The critical element here was the question of impediments. Where access to the means of life and labour is severely restricted, the range of negative liberty, that is, the area within which individuals cannot be interfered with, is likewise narrowed. In other words, inequality limits all freedom, and the greater the inequality, the greater the limits.

As noted above, there has emerged increasing concern about inequality in society. Much contemporary democratic theory has taken inequality seriously as well.[39] However, Macpherson went further. It is not just that inequality *limits* freedom. Rather, inequality *constitutes unfreedom*. For Macpherson, unequal distribution of goods and resources limited life chances. But inequality also involved normative questions of how social organization simultaneously expresses and denies human potentialities, because it is not just a fact about individuals. It is also an ongoing, continuously produced modality of individual and social experience. Inequality has emerged in the face of a specific, historical situation and predicament: the present and potential futures of human powers understood as capacities of a certain sort, namely, capacities for rational self-constitution.

And this gives us an important clue about what, for Macpherson, a critical, radical theory of democracy had to take on board – confronting Berlin's argument allowed Macpherson, indeed required him, to lay out more explicitly his normative assumptions. In discussing Macpherson's account of the economic penetration of political theory, I had suggested that undergirding his attempt to demonstrate the appropriate relation between political economy and political theory was a kind of wager about the future and fate of capitalist society and the possibilities for its transformation. This turned what appeared to be a set of hypotheses, a form of traditional theory, into a historically informed normative judgment that combined fact and value – that is, a form of critical theory. There is, I think, the same wager in play in Macpherson's critique of Berlin.

Specifically, the wager here is that what people have been driving at, and could under appropriate conditions more self-consciously and perspicuously articulate, is self-realization understood as the development and exertion of their distinctively human capacities. As we saw in my previous discussion of Macpherson's ontological assumptions, this distinctiveness rests on these capacities being, at least in principle, non-contentious. His conception of freedom is in effect linked to an emancipatory normative commitment to the reduction of destructive conflict. Once again the theory of possessive individualism as critique looms large: possessive individualist self-assertion is not identical with developmental autonomy.

Contrary to Berlin, Macpherson held that there was a difference between the idea of non-contentious human capacities and conscious purposes, and the claim that under positive liberty "the ends of all rational beings must of necessity fit into a single universal, harmonious pattern."[40] That is, "a proliferation of many ways and styles of life which could not be prescribed and would not conflict ... is a necessary stipulation if a society of positive liberty is to be worth striving for. But it is not the same as the postulate of preordained harmonious pattern."[41] This is not a dubious and dangerous utopian leap but an essential dimension of any truly democratic society that claims to maximize the prospects for the equal development by all of their distinctively human capacities. "For what would be the use of trying to provide that everyone should be able to make the most of himself, which is the idea of a democratic society, if that were bound to lead to more destructive contention?"[42]

This conception of human capacities as developmental carries with it a specific understanding of individual rights: the rights that are morally justifiable on egalitarian (i.e., democratic) grounds "are only those which allow all others to have equal effective rights; and ... *these are enough* to allow any man to be fully human."[43] The first part of this claim is familiar enough. It is the second that captures in a nutshell the core of Macpherson's critical account, his diagnosis of the present and his hopes for the future. His challenging claim is that not only would a developmental democracy maximize human powers, understood as those that facilitate the exercise of one's distinctively human capacities, but that only those capacities are fully human, that is, genuine and fulfilling, the exercise of which does not prevent others from exercising theirs. In other words, exercising one's developmental capabilities required institutions and practices of cooperative self-actualization.[44]

And for Macpherson this claim was not an outlandishly extreme product of a radical Marxism at odds with the values of liberalism. Rather, it expressed, or ought to express, the deepest commitments of humanist liberals. even if, like Berlin, they rejected positive liberty. That they implicitly held to the necessarily non-destructive character of morally justifiable individual rights was clear from their willingness to deploy state power against the exercise of destructive capacities. Generally failing, however, to consider the conditions under which human capacities are forged and thus the historical variability of these capacities, liberals have found themselves stuck in the Hobbesian dilemma whereby a potentially oppressive collectivism represents the most cohesive society possible, at least where possessive individualism prevails.

To be sure, the move to a society within which possessive individualism was diminished would take a considerable period of time, during which the necessary process of moral learning took root. And as Macpherson suggested, even where destructive capacities were dramatically reduced, if not altogether eliminated, individuals would still need protection from others and from political authorities. No human society, including one in which developmental individualism and positive liberty were entrenched and dominant, could exist without some contention and even moral failings. This meant that at least a certain degree of coercive state power would remain essential, even if the need for it could, in principle, be reduced over time. However, to be faithful to their commitments, humanist liberals had to, in effect, shift from Hobbes and Locke to Kant and the normatively transformative possibilities of securing through the exercise of political authority impediments to impediments to freedom, whereby the reconciliation of the freedom of each with the freedom of all under a universal law guaranteed individual autonomy.

It was, I think, in light of these considerations that Macpherson saw negative and positive liberty as complementary and even mutually determining, and not antagonistic. The area within which I cannot be interfered with, that is, have benefit from the use of my capacities extracted from me, both requires and facilitates my ability to develop my capacities under my conscious direction, and vice versa. In order to emphasize this connection, and thus ensure there is no theoretical space within which it would be possible to justify the debased authoritarian view of positive liberty (Berlin's great concern), Macpherson suggested we dispense altogether with the terms *negative* and *positive liberty*. We should instead conceive these dimensions of freedom as *counter-extractive* and *developmental* liberty.[45] What connects them is the role of those impediments thrown up by the denial of access to the means of life and labour.

Although Macpherson stressed positive or developmental liberty, which carries with it the idea of social rights and freedoms in terms of which our individuality is tied to shared, inter-subjective practices, it is important again to note that there are still in his work *two* notions of liberty. The "classical" liberal idea that people must be protected from invasion of other individuals and political authorities remained central to Macpherson's account. Whether he felt there would always be a need for both concepts – and those who have viewed him as a utopian proponent of total harmony thought he mistakenly believed we could dispense with negative liberty – is not totally clear. He certainly appeared to doubt the separation between the two was necessarily ontological and permanent rather than historical and, at least potentially, alterable. In other words, Macpherson's exploration of liberty as a decisive component of individual self-development manifested his ongoing concern with the competing ontological assumptions and commitments he detected in liberal democratic theory and practice.

To see this more clearly, and thus to grasp more completely Macpherson's ongoing commitment to negative liberty, but at the same time to see why he felt it essential to reformulate it as counter-extractive liberty, it is helpful here to note his critical analysis of the work of Milton Friedman, arguably the most influential libertarian, free market economist of our era, whose work has decisively shaped contemporary neoliberal ideas and models.[46]

What would likely stand out for most readers of this essay is Macpherson's spirited defence of a socialist economy over and against Friedman's vigorous justification of a fully capitalist economic order as the sole guarantee of political freedom – in effect, the claim that capitalism and democracy are equivalent, or at least only that form of democracy compatible with virtually unfettered private property and economic freedom is justifiable. So understood, Friedman's account has decisively informed individualist, rational choice accounts of a democratic political system, where this system serves as a means for aggregating individual choices and thus producing binding social decisions. Macpherson's analysis was very clearly based on a conception of positive liberty over and against Friedman's classical liberal emphasis on negative liberty, and thus spoke to the conception of democracy as a way of life and not merely a vehicle for choosing and authorizing governments.

C.B. Macpherson and Milton Friedman: Beyond Capitalism and (Negative) Freedom

In his classic study, *Capitalism and Freedom*, Friedman asserted that competitive capitalism provided the only firm guarantee of political freedom. Political freedom involved the ability to openly promote radical social change and required those civil liberties that secure individuals from state coercion. A socialist society (i.e., one in which positive or developmental freedom would be central) could not do so because, in Friedman's model of socialism, the government would be a monopoly employer and thus could deprive political opponents of their livelihood. Since it would be difficult if not impossible to promote transformation to capitalism, a socialist order could not meet the standard of political freedom.

Friedman defended a model of a simple market economy that assumed free and equal exchange among individuals and households who control the resources needed to produce goods and services. As a result, they had the choice of either exchanging goods and services or producing their means of subsistence themselves. Hence all exchanges were voluntary, because individuals and households enter into them only if they benefit. There would be social cooperation without coercion.

For Macpherson, the flaws in Friedman's position became clear when he moved to the real world, capitalist market economy. Friedman argued that, in a complex economy, cooperation remained voluntary as long as enterprises were private and parties to exchange were individuals, and as long as individuals were freely able to enter into or refuse any particular exchange. But as Macpherson saw it, voluntary cooperation required not simply that individuals had the ability to refuse any particular exchange – they also had to be free to refuse to engage in exchange at all. In a capitalist market economy, the conditions of the simple model do not and cannot hold, because the division between those who own productive resources and those whom they employ – between capital and labour – leads to unequal power between the two groups and hence coercion by the one over the other, because of "the existence of a labour force without its own sufficient capital and therefore without a choice as to whether to put its labour on the market or not."[47]

Friedman clearly assumed a statist model of socialism, which hardly exhausts the range of possible socialist options. However, Macpherson did not focus on Friedman's account of socialist economic relations. Instead he offered a subtle and complex response to Friedman's account of freedom. He took up Friedman's arguments on their own grounds. So understood, they failed in their own terms. Since Friedman understood freedom as negative liberty but did not recognize coercion where some would control the labour of others, the claim that capitalism secures this freedom and is in fact the only system that can do so, is questionable at the very least. In spite of the significant differences between them, both Friedman and Berlin missed such coercion because of their equally narrow conceptions of negative liberty as only the absence of conscious, deliberate constraint, whether by private individuals or political authorities.

But there was another element of Macpherson's position, one implied in his claim that the presence or absence of political freedom under socialism was a matter of political will and not an inescapable consequence of socialist economic and political structures, as Friedman argued.[48] As Macpherson saw it, while under capitalism the political and economic were intimately connected, they need not always be so in every conceivable circumstance. The problem with Friedman's position in this context – and by extension with the free market (neo) liberalism that he has been so influential in shaping – is not just that it emphasizes in theory the separation of the political from the economic, a realm of coercion from a realm of freedom, while contradicting it in practice. Rather, it unwittingly reveals that, in fact, the political and the economic should be separate but under capitalism cannot be.[49]

The issue of will suggests that politics should be, and ideally would be, autonomous. It also means, therefore, that individual civil and political rights would remain essential, even in a radically transformed and more fully democratic social order. On the one hand, in a complex and technically advanced productive system there would still be the need for structures of rational authority, even if such authority would no longer be subordinated to extractive, or class, power. This reflects again the Marxian dimension of Macpherson's work. But while accountable to the political will of the society, the productive apparatus could not be directly absorbed in it, nor could political authority dissolve into a free association of producers.

On the other hand, Macpherson assumed there would also remain the need for organized political authority to reconcile conflicting interests and to provide security for individuals in the face of possible threats from others. At the same time, this power would itself need to be held accountable, because there was no guarantee against holders of political authority abusing their positions. This highlights the liberal or individualist dimension of Macpherson's work. But it does not stand alone in opposition to the Marxian dimension, because, once again, Macpherson sought to synthesize both.

Thus Macpherson did not simply dismiss Friedman's conception of negative freedom. He sought instead to deepen and radicalize it by exploring those conditions under which it would be possible for individuals to escape all save necessary social coercion. Those conditions would make possible and be defined by the presence of counter-extractive and developmental liberty. Their achievement hinged on the elimination of extractive power, the abolition of those relations that permitted the net transfer of powers.

Clearly Macpherson believed the elimination of extractive power, tied to capitalist market institutions and property relations, was both desirable and possible. In any case, he thought this needed to be put on the agenda of a theory of democracy committed to the idea that each individual ought to have the fullest right of, as well as opportunity for, self-development. In the current historical context, what makes the need for two concepts of liberty important is not just the real existence or threat of invasion by other individuals and by political authorities, the actuality or threat of coercion from those clearly dedicated to quashing one's liberty. It is also needed because impediments to the development and exercise of one's distinctively human capacities have seemed to require, where those impediments have not been abolished (i.e., everywhere) the use of political authority to limit the extractive power of those in a position to deny to others access to the means of life and labour. What Macpherson had in mind here was the twentieth-century welfare state and its efforts to regulate the free play of capitalist market forces, although his theory envisioned a much more extensive challenge to capitalist institutions. But whether one is considering the welfare state or something more extensive, the issues involve the need and role for freedom-enhancing as opposed to freedom-denying coercion – that is, the use of democratic political authority to limit the extractive power of those in a position to deny to others access to the means of life and labour. Once again there are echoes here of Kant and lawfully guaranteed autonomy.

Macpherson was aware of the challenges this argument posed because, in the interests of a more robust democratic society, it required that the powers of some be limited in order to enhance the powers of others. But he suggested that the difficulty was not insuperable as long as one did not restrict oneself, as Berlin and classical liberals did, to that excessively mechanistic, Hobbesian view of freedom, where it is identified with the absence of *all* obstacles, all barriers to the fulfilment of one's desires. However, not all obstacles are equal. In Macpherson's view, establishing social ownership of capital may remove from the sphere of negative liberty those activities associated with "free" or "private" enterprise. But this might well enhance negative liberty overall "if the gain by those who had doors closed to them more than offsets the loss of liberty by those (relatively few) who had been in a position to take full advantage of market freedoms."[50] As already noted, liberals typically argue for freedom in principle from all obstructions, while at the same time they accept obstructions in practice. Departing from the mechanistic view of freedom allows for a richer, more consistent conception and a much more realistic grasp of negative liberty, while demonstrating why we still require such a concept and need to distinguish it from positive liberty. This was a need Macpherson accepted, even though he was obviously a staunch proponent of positive or developmental freedom. Redefining negative liberty as counter-extractive liberty clarifies what is at stake. According to him, Berlin seemed aware of what was at stake as well. But he could not successfully address the issues, because he defined freedom too narrowly by consigning to the category of conditions of liberty the removal of those impediments that Macpherson believed must be central to freedom itself.

I think the need to argue in terms of gains and losses of freedom, or in other words, obstructions to freedom that work to remove obstructions (a position that once again has clear if unacknowledged echoes of Kant), reflected for Macpherson this historically situated tension between the dominant market form of liberalism, or economic freedom, and democracy. This was not simply a question of class conflict under capitalism that a Marxian-influenced thinker such as Macpherson understandably enough emphasized. Aside from empirical political and sociological matters, profound normative philosophical issues are clearly at play here.

As Macpherson recognized, in the "real world" of actually existing liberal (capitalist) democracies, those who benefit from extractive power are at least in the position to exercise the very developmental power that democracy is supposed to promote. But because this capacity is beholden to the exercise of extractive power, it carries a cost for both those who hold it and those who are subject to it. However, if developmental democracy – that is, democracy as a kind of society within which potentially all are equally capable of developing and using their distinctively human capacities – hinges on the claim that not only can one imagine genuine human capacities as non-contentious, but that these just are those that are non-contentious, then the core issue "comes down to the postulate that a fully democratic society cannot permit the operation of any extractive power, and that a society without any extractive power is possible. The serious difficulty about a democratic society is not how to run it but how to reach it."[51]

The critique of negative liberty as insufficient for a radical and humanist democratic theory and society, the emphasis on positive liberty as crucial for both, and the reformulation of the two concepts of liberty as, respectively, counter-extractive and developmental in order to facilitate the task of laying out a non-market theory of democracy – all of these suggest two key overarching themes shaping Macpherson's account. One is the point just made: that much of what democracy is and can be depends upon the plausibility that there indeed are non-contentious human capacities and that such capacities are *the* most fully human or genuine ones. The other, and this is perhaps less obvious, is that democracy is at one level both a fact and a project that remains to be realized. Problems that today exercise many theorists of democracy, such as how to rationally aggregate individual preferences to produce logically coherent outcomes, are on this view second-order concerns, not primary ones.

Taking these themes as a basis, I want to break down Macpherson's approach to the core elements of a robust democracy into the two issues he identified: how to reach it and how to run it. I want to argue that, especially given the central role of his analysis and appraisal of Berlin's position, the first turns on the question of individual agency and thus, in light of current concerns, the issue of human rights. The second issue points to Macpherson's account of a possible participatory democratic system. But beyond the specifics of his participatory model, it also suggests how Macpherson's critique of existing democratic theory raises issues vital for a critical theory of democracy under contemporary conditions. In the next chapter, I turn my attention to these issues.

Chapter Five

C.B. Macpherson, Democracy, and Democratic Theory 2: Human Rights, Democratic Expressions, and Democratic Models

In light of the widespread contemporary interest in and professed commitment to international human rights as a core feature of democratic theory, a development that C.B. Macpherson recognized and felt compelled to address, James Ingram has recently offered a helpful picture of the different conceptions of rights that have played a role in current rights discourses. Drawing upon Hannah Arendt's formulation of "the right to have rights," Ingram explores the politics of human rights from the perspective of the "images" of politics each presupposes.[1] He identifies three such accounts of human rights and their respective images. Two of these have arguably dominated primarily liberal approaches to the definition of rights and what is required to protect and enhance them. The more prominent view, which Ingram associates with thinkers such as Michael Ignatieff and Michael Walzer, might be called the sovereign approach, in that it emphasizes the capacity and necessity of "finding an agency to implement and enforce rights, a surrogate for an absent, enfeebled, negligent, or malevolent state."[2] This view undergirds the current international commitment summarized as R2P: Responsibility to Protect. Since the "agency" most fully equipped to carry out this task is likely to be the dominant state or states, such an approach is often justifiably seen as a cover for old-fashioned imperialist power politics.

If this version of liberal human rights discourse might be said to derive its strength and significance from the classical English liberalism of Hobbes and Locke, the second strain owes its origins to the Continental tradition, especially the work of Kant. As exemplified in the writings notably of Jürgen Habermas and Seyla Benhabib, this approach reflects the dual meaning of *Recht* as "right" and "law." It does so by focusing on the prospects for the establishment of cosmopolitan institutional arrangements that would ideally bridge the gulf between the moral claims at the heart of human rights language and commitments, and legal norms in terms of which these claims are registered and legitimized. The idea is to break away from an exclusive emphasis upon state sovereignty that hampers the first conception. In so doing, the second version holds that "the best chance for human rights protection lies in the spread of regional and international legal regimes, which would limit state sovereignty by means of reciprocity enforced cosmopolitan law."[3] In the context of Habermas's argument about the necessary interrelation between private and public autonomy, the emphasis shifts from the vertical relations between state and citizen and the problem of implementation to the horizontal relation between citizens who are simultaneously authors and addressees of the law. This is intended to avoid excessive concern with control over the state's monopoly on violence, a key issue in the first model.

However, if the problem with the first version is that a professed commitment to human rights can, if implemented, provide an ideological cover for power politics, the problem with the second, which is more about justification than implementation, is the absence of a process for translating rights into law – that is, moving from sovereignty to cosmopolitanism. For Ingram, each suffers from the failure to lay out an appropriate conception of politics and political action. This he believes is evident from the distinctive images of politics, implicit assumptions about the nature of politics and political theory, that each takes on board. In turn such images shape specific understandings of the tasks involved in achieving human rights aims. Thus "those who take the first, liberal view tend to assume that their task is to identify justifiable uses of state power; those who take the second assume it is to outline how such power should be organized."[4]

The problem with both of these images of politics and the visions of human rights they support is that they conceive of rights as statuses that need to be secured and protected. In the process, those whose rights require support are treated as objects of rights-creating or preserving activity of others, be they holders of sovereign power or proponents of cosmopolitan law and institutions. In a way that suggests significant parallels with Macpherson's conception of individuals as active doers and exerters of their distinctively human capacities who must enjoy both counter-extractive and developmental liberty, Ingram argues that a meaningful and effective regime of human rights is possible only on the basis of the autonomous political action of associated individuals who, through such action, claim their rights in the course of creating and recreating their political bonds. In other words, rights should be an ongoing accomplishment of active agents who share a vibrant, democratic public life, not simply a formal status secured either through (sovereign) power or law.

The impetus for what Ingram calls human rights politics as democratic action, which suggests a third image of such a politics as the ongoing process of discovering moments or possibilities for autonomous political action, is Hannah Arendt's conception of politics *as* action. Highly critical of sovereignty but equally sceptical of cosmopolitanism, Arendt proposed an understanding of politics, and hence human rights, based upon power as a common capacity for acting together and principles that are realizable only through free action, rather than upon sovereignty or (moral) ends. What was critical for Arendt was the provision/creation of worldly "in-betweens," public spaces of appearance within which freedom could be made a reality, through the actions of individuals who enjoy an equal claim to political activity and who seek to insert themselves through word and deed into affairs going on around them. As Ingram correctly notes, with this conception of political activity – namely, "the practices of interaction and mutual recognition, conflict and cooperation, through which people construct a common public-political sphere," Arendt "seeks to reorient politics away from the use of power from above, away from individual or collective will, away from laws and institutions, and toward what she calls 'the world' or 'the in-between' – the intersubjective 'space of appearances' between people."[5]

So understood, for Arendt the loss of the right to have rights, which was for her the terrible situation confronted by the stateless, involved a fundamental deprivation. People were deprived, "not of the right to freedom, but of the right to action; not of the right to think whatever they please, but of the right to opinion."[6] For Arendt, freedom and opinion were specifically political and achievable only where possibilities for political action existed. In other words, infringements of human rights are not primarily about the loss of *status*, but rather the loss or restriction of *capacities* or *capabilities*. Thus a "democratic conception of rights suggests that we should regard rights as secure only when they are based on shared understandings and practices, people's readiness to act for and with one another, and their ability to do so ... Promoting human rights would then mean understanding the politics of human rights as an active, critical-democratic politics that rests first and foremost on the activity of rights bearers themselves, and human rights promotion as the practice of supporting and enabling such a politics."[7] Ingram views thinkers such as Claude Lefort, Étienne Balibar, and Jacques Rancière as significant contributors to this conception of human rights as politics.

Although he does not put it explicitly, I think that, for Ingram, conceiving human rights as critical-democratic practice could allow one to avoid or at least limit either cynicism about human rights discourses (where they are seen as merely pretexts for major power imperial ambitions), or despair and/or disdain (where rights claims are viewed as politically naive, unrealizable universal/utopian moral imperatives). I think that Ingram's analysis in general, and what I take to be this implied conclusion drawn from it, can provide a valuable context for examining C.B. Macpherson's own attempt to deal with questions of human rights. Certainly the idea that these rights involve capacities and not simply statuses fits well with Macpherson's own concerns. And although a Marxian-influenced critic of bourgeois ideology in general, and as we will see of human rights discourses in particular, he was neither cynical nor disdainful in his analysis.

Human Rights and Democratic Possibilities

Indeed it is well to recall that, for Macpherson, it was possible to claim that he made central to his thought a fundamental human right, namely, "an equal right, for everyone, to a certain quality of life, certain liberties to develop and enjoy the use of our capacities."[8] Indeed as we have seen, he felt this right was so important that he argued it might be more successfully pressed if it were seen as a property right, given the vital role property played in a liberal democratic culture. The actual right and institution of property had to be reworked from private property as the right to exclude to a new individual property right not to be excluded, a right tied to the notion of individuals as potentially active exerters and enjoyers of their distinctively human capacities. Moreover, "To do that requires no sleight of hand. To speak of human rights as individual property rights would indeed to be to restore the original liberal meaning of property, as when Locke and his contemporaries spoke of a property in one's person, one's life and liberty, as well as one's worldly goods."[9] I suggest that this echoes James Ingram's distinction between, on the one hand, the idea of a human right as a defined status and, on the other, the idea of right as realized in and through the development and exercise of one's capacities for free, that is to say, political, action. But beyond this, Macpherson indicated that the language of human rights and the impulses behind the emergence of human rights discourses opened up issues of what a fully democratic society required.

What Macpherson saw as the ambiguities and blind spots in our typical understanding of democracy were reflected in the different and even conflicting conceptions of human rights. One element was the failure to appreciate the realities of class and thus the net transfer of powers. Typically, he claimed, framers of individual rights, historically and still the most common form of human rights, "abstract the individual from history: they cut down the individual to the abstract pattern that was appropriate and most needed in the seventeenth and eighteenth centuries, when the big problem was to get the individual free from the many entrenched impediments to the flowering of the human personality."[10] This clearly reflected the Marxian dimension of his work. This is also evident in his claim that the degree of economic development and the type of economy may, depending upon the relations between them, account for differences in implementation of human rights in different countries.

But there was another dimension to Macpherson's analysis that points in the direction of a critical approach to characterizing and appraising rights claims. Responding to the reality that human rights are both proclaimed as a standard and at the same time unrecognized and even suppressed in practice, Macpherson suggested that perhaps

> the most general reason why the world is still so short of human rights ... is that people don't want human rights as much as they want other things which are, or which they believe are, incompatible with some human rights – colonial liberation, for instance (which may require revolutionary action and incur counter-revolutionary activities, not conducive to civil liberties, pro tem), or rapid economic growth, or what the sociologists call upward social and economic mobility, meaning a system where some people can expect to climb up some rungs on the socio-economic ladder, at the expense of others if necessary ... for national self-determination, for a place in the sun, for military security, for hegemony, for the maintenance of inequality between nations and (of which we are all guilty) inequality between rich and poor nations.

Certainly this claim, too, suggests the Marxian critique of ideology. But I think it suggests something more: the need to think about what it means to hold human rights, to be a rights-bearer. And this matters in this context, because while the first of those "other things" may appear strictly of its time, the rest most assuredly are not. So Macpherson's examination of "some of the reasons why human rights are limping"[11] calls to mind the kind of complexity around human rights that James Ingram identifies.

Macpherson began by offering a threefold characterization of human rights, one based on the United Nations Declaration of Human Rights of 1948. These are, respectively, the classical individual civil and political rights of freedom of speech, association, religion, etc.; the almost equally long-standing political right to a voice in government; and the comparatively more recent economic or social rights such as the right to work, the right to equal pay for work of equal value, and the right to social security. He noted that, while the first two sets of right have been generally accepted as core rights of the free individual that should be protected (even if they have frequently not been), the third set have proven extremely controversial, often especially by those who most vociferously defend the first two sets. For many – Macpherson specifically mentioned Maurice Cranston – only the first two sets count truly as human rights. Economic and social rights are not only logically incompatible but also likely to be threatening. Since in order to be implemented these rights require the power of the state, while civil and political liberties and rights are about securing individuals against all, except for warranted state intrusion, it was altogether too likely that the achievement of economic and social rights would come at the expense of civil and political rights.

Needless to say, Macpherson rejected this reading. At stake, then, were familiar concerns: the dilemmas of (possessive) individualism, competing conceptions of human nature and individual agency, and the relation of negative to positive, counter-extractive to developmental liberty. Perhaps the most straightforward way to capture what Macpherson was getting at in his treatment of human rights is something like this: We have seen that he believed human rights would be cast in a new light and made more secure if they could be seen as property rights. But I think his argument also suggests the opposite: that property rights should be seen as human rights. This is by no means as straightforward as it seems. Obviously the idea that the right to property is a human right has had a lengthy historical lineage. Indeed it has long counted as one of the traditional civil rights. But as earlier noted, Macpherson thought that the entrenchment of capitalist market relations, which was built upon and in turn reinforced the conception of humans as infinite appropriators, narrowed what had been a much broader conception of property as what was necessary for a genuinely free and human life to one focused exclusively on competitive acquisition. Inasmuch as economic and social rights were intended to facilitate a full life, one in which individuals would as much as possible be able to make the most of themselves, they were not necessarily logically or politically at odds with the classic liberties. That is, human rights, as they have come to include rights to the means of life and labour, challenge the human right to property only if and insofar as the property right is conceived as exclusively private. Restoring its broader meaning would open up other and richer possibilities for relating property to human rights.[12] In other words, were the broader meaning restored, "the logical disparity between the traditional and the newer concepts of human rights disappears. They are both then seen for what they are – claims for a right to life at a genuinely human level."[13] While these rights have traditionally been understood as purely individual rights, they are just as fully social and political rights as are the "newer" rights to an income, employment, or social security.

On the other hand, "while there is no logical disparity between the civil rights to property and the newly claimed economic and social rights, there is a real incompatibility between the capitalist property right and the new social and economic rights." The capitalist economic system requires the right of unlimited appropriation and thus accumulation. Hence, "the capitalist concept of property, treating it as a natural individual (and corporate) right rather than a social right, lends plausibility to the claim that the new social and economic rights are logically disparate from, and have less standing than, the older rights."[14] The status of the new rights, the extent to which they were recognized and respected, seemed to depend upon the extent to which the economic system was capitalist.

On this basis Macpherson returned to his comparison of First World capitalist, Second World socialist, and Third World (capitalist and non-capitalist) models and the prospects under each, for more traditional civil and more recent social rights. The comparisons per se need not concern us here; as before, there is much that is anachronistic in his account. But there are two elements of his analysis that are anything but anachronistic and irrelevant.

Human Rights and Possessive Individualism: Liberalism as Trade-offs

The first element involves the extent to which human rights, old and new, are sacrificed to the demands and requirements of economic growth by those in power. Macpherson identified this as a problem with post-colonial Third World countries seeking autonomous paths to development (they would now be called emerging or newly developing economies, or newly industrializing economies, or even fledgling democracies). While committed ostensibly to enhancing the lives of everyone in the society, rulers who saw growth as requiring capitalist market structures, policies, and incentives were likely to at least partially sacrifice social and economic rights to the demands of the capitalist property right. They might even sacrifice classic civil and political liberties insofar as these could facilitate the organization of social forces opposed to the strategy and its social and other costs. Ultimately, "the concept of economic growth – both its purpose and its practice – comes from the ideology and the experience of capitalist society … as an end in itself, to which everything else may appropriately be subordinated … an end which is then taken to justify otherwise unjustifiable means."[15]

I think this argument is still relevant today, and not merely for newly developing states. Under the impact of contemporary neoliberalism there has been a resurgence of the capitalist property right as the essential right. This has occurred to the point where social and human rights (call them solidaristic rights) have been redefined to conform to private property rights, as in the depiction of individual qualities as marketable human capital. This is evident in those contemporary social policies that are designed not to de-commodify labour but rather to facilitate its employment on the capitalist labour market. Policies tied to social rights that facilitate de-commodification are indeed often dismissed altogether as fundamentally at odds with the requirements of sound economic policy and even the demands of (market) justice. Added to this opposition to policies of decommodification is the current rage for austerity measures designed in the supposed interests of debt- and deficit-reduction, which limit the capacity of the state to respond to democratic electoral pressures. Such pressures were a key factor in the development and implementation of social and economic rights.[16] Arguably the emergence of austerity, often presented as respect for the rights of hard-pressed and overly burdened taxpayers, who in fact are identified primarily with the supposedly employment-creating wealthy, is linked to both claims. I would argue that these and related developments, which have gone along in many cases with diminishing civic engagement by large numbers of people, provide the largely underappreciated backdrop to what Ingram calls the sovereign and cosmopolitan conceptions of rights and their accompanying political imagery.

The second element has even greater currency. It involves the idea of trade-offs, in terms of which individuals and societies, "in so far as they act by rational calculation, are continually having to decide, as between two things they value, how much of one they are willing to do without in order to get some amount of the other."[17] In his discussion of human rights, Macpherson claimed that governments, particularly those confronted with a low level of material productivity and thus unable to meet the needs of all, justified the suppression of human rights on the grounds that some rights needed to be traded off for the benefits of economic growth. The claim, he argued, was that increases in productivity would eventually ensure that the needs and rights of all would be fully respected. Macpherson thought this a bad deal, since evidence suggested that the costs and benefits of the trade-off were not equitably distributed.

Currently, with the social and economic rights that Macpherson emphasized in retreat, the trade-off argument is most often, visibly – and notoriously – applied to classic civil liberties and their relation to "national security." In the face of the frequently claimed threat of global terrorism, it is now common to argue that people have to choose between, on the one hand, expansive civil liberties and rights and, on the other, the need for intensified state vigilance that would involve greater government intrusion into the personal as well as political affairs of citizens than would presumably be otherwise desirable or acceptable.

What characterizes and connects both "trade-offs" is a certain compulsiveness, a legacy of their common (Hobbesian) roots. For Macpherson, his specific concern was the capitalist obsession with unlimited accumulation and appropriation, the cornerstone of a worship of economic growth. This seemed to him irresistible, as long as we held to a virtually unlimited property right and the concomitant "faulty time-bound thinking" that "retains the early liberal notion of the individual as a being prior to and rightfully independent of society or community."[18] But he would have seen the parallel with the current understanding of the trade-off between rights and security: this, too, reflects a comparable fixation on the fear that society, whether at home or abroad, is a threat, a consequence of the compulsiveness of (possessive) individualist self-assertion, which is both the driving force behind unlimited appropriation and the basis for the unquenchable need for security. Indeed he might have seen more than a parallel. The trade-off and consequent suppression of human rights in favour of economic growth has, as Macpherson argued, exacerbated where it has not produced global inequalities that can serve as a breeding ground for terrorism and other sources of insecurity that supposedly justify the trade-off of rights versus protection in the first place.[19]

Macpherson viewed the concept of a trade-off as another expression of the contradiction woven through the fabric of liberalism, classical and modern, between its possessive and developmental individualist commitments – put otherwise, its commitments to negative and positive liberty. For Macpherson the idea of the trade-off had two historical dimensions. In what he saw as its nineteenth-century variant, the individual rights central to revolutionary liberals of the seventeenth and eighteenth were traded off for expanded economic growth, the maximizing of aggregate utilities. The twentieth-century variant, reflecting the emergence of the new social and economic rights under the impact of democratization, had two aspects that reflected the uneasy mix of democratic and liberal elements. On the one hand, with the rise of the welfare state, it involved the "marginal trade-off of the imperatives of capitalist expansion for a supportable level of human rights," a "marginal reversal which appeared to sacrifice growth to rights." On the other hand, it "asks us to forgo the democratic responsibility which was demanded by liberal-democratic theory in the nineteenth century … in the interests of individual freedoms which are thought to be endangered by any full measure of democracy … We are asked, then, to trade off democratic control for individual and corporate freedoms." What made the language of trade-offs central was that both held in common a conception of the individual as a rational, maximizing atomic agent: it treated the individual "as a maximizing consumer, not as an exerter and enjoyer of innate capacities. It has more of Milton Friedman than of John Milton."[20]

This conception of the atomic individual would seem to fit well with the idea of rights as statuses. And to recall Josiah Ober's account of Greek democracy, it would also seem to go along with the implications of *arche* versus *kratos*, power as a possession versus power as collective empowerment. In other words, what I have argued are key issues for a critical theory of democracy crystallize once again around the question of ontology – whether individuals are infinite consumers and appropriators of utilities or infinite developers and exerters of their human capacities. In fact, in "Liberalism as Trade-offs," Macpherson, perhaps surprisingly, offered a particularly lucid summary of the core components of his particular conception of a liberal democratic system that marries liberalism and socialism. This includes an allusion to the participatory model of democracy that, as we will see, he laid out in *The Life and Times of Liberal Democracy*. And in tandem with his treatment of human rights he also brought into his account his most specific reference to the idea of community as a vital element of a democratic society, which interestingly he connected less to the overcoming of material deprivation and more to the need for esteem, autonomy, and meaningful work – in short, what is now seen as recognition. The acknowledgment and fostering of communal bonds would represent the transcendence of the atomistic conception of the individual and the logic of trade-offs, and with it the potential to move beyond capitalism. Such a development would reflect "cumulative popular pressures" and a popular consciousness in terms of which the logic of trade-offs would give way insofar as the stronger and weaker parties to a trade-off bargain, i.e., the two parties to the net transfer of powers change places. In the measure to which this occurred, "the former stronger party loses its power to formulate the issues in trade-off terms, and the former weaker party, by the very activity which has brought it ahead, may gain the insight to transcend the trade-off choice."[21] At the level of political theory, this reversal would see developmental liberalism supplant possessive liberalism as the dominant cultural norm.

This analysis and the claims it supports are familiar and might be dismissed as further evidence of Macpherson's utopianism. However, he linked these claims to a cautious and by no means utopian conception of how democracy, individualism, and human rights are necessarily linked. He was very explicit. He acknowledged that "democracies have often been intolerant." They have sometimes threatened individual autonomy, and the "desire for such autonomy cannot be dismissed as simply a residue of bourgeois ideology, for that autonomy is also central to Marx's vision of a fully human being." And he further acknowledged that supposedly revolutionary regimes in the twentieth century became military/bureaucratic states that suppressed civil liberties – "freedom of speech, publication, and association, and freedom from arbitrary arrest or detention." Hence the "first thing at stake, then, for the liberal democrat, is the preservation of civil liberties ... Without them, democracy is a travesty."[22]

And the reverse was also true: civil liberties required democracy. Macpherson thought that democratic pressures would provide the "last safeguard of civil liberties," at least "in the measure that increasing tensions develop between popular demands and capitalism's ability to meet those demands."[23] Recent developments in the global economy, as well as changes in the role of the state that have both reflected and reinforced the erosion of democracy, give considerable credence to this claim. It is perhaps no accident in this light that the "trade-off" of privacy for security would take place as it has. As Macpherson argued, the alleged incompatibility of civil liberties and democracy was false – each required the other. But both in turn required a community in which rights would be accomplishments of those who, through their shared relations across a wide range of social practices, enjoyed not simply material utilities but also esteem and autonomy – a politics of redistribution *and* recognition. The contemporary reassertion of possessive individualist values has undermined both human rights and democracy.

So while he was critical of the ways in which human rights discourses took for granted atomistic individualism and unlimited appropriation – both at the heart of what he saw as the wrong-headed obsession with unlimited growth – Macpherson never rejected human rights as an idea or ideal. He felt the history of human rights claims demonstrated that, on the whole, these claims emerged as core elements of popular demands for democracy.

However, as we have seen, Macpherson believed that considerations about rights, be they the classical civil liberties or the newer package of social and economic rights, tended to be abstract, reflections of a conception of the individual as removed from social and historical ties. The socially and historically informed account of freedom that resulted in the reformulation of negative and positive liberty as counter-extractive and developmental, a reformulation that Macpherson believed could eliminate the gap traditionally seen between them, needed to be applied to human rights. Not only would this close the gulf between individual and social rights, and indeed show them to be complementary. It would also demonstrate the extent to which both were won through the growth of popular pressures in support of an ever more inclusive liberty and equality. The original meaning of rights, narrowed by the development of capitalism, could, in the face of contemporary social pathologies, be broadened once again, but now linked to a move from possessive to developmental individualism at the level of both culture and social institutions. Notions of human rights, in other words, ought to be treated as critical concepts whose unity "results less from the invariability of their elements than from the historical development of the circumstances under which their realization is necessary." If a civil right and democracy are held to be at odds and must be traded off, one against the other, then it is possible that either the right or democracy itself is misconceived. The trade-off would mask the real possibilities for developmental individualism and thus democracy as a kind of society within which all are equally capable of cultivating and exercising their distinctively human capacities in a potentially non-contentious setting.

Human Rights and Democracy: Individual Autonomy and Self-Development

So human rights, then, provided Macpherson with another vehicle for opening up the questions at the heart of democracy: power, ontology, and freedom. As with those, human rights can both reveal and obscure. With developmental individualism the heart of Macpherson's most fundamental concerns, human rights needed to be linked to the possibilities for establishing the conditions under which individual development and autonomy might be secured. And as his account of property made clear, such conditions included participation in a satisfying set of social relations. This necessarily entailed a significant element of joint political action by citizens enjoying equality, because "the individual can be fully human only as a member of a community." It was a manifestation of "the pre-capitalist idea that one's humanity was more a matter of one's membership in the community than one's freedom from the community, that the greatest human right was the right of belonging to the community, and the severest deprivation was to be cast out."[24]

Thus there is a communalist dimension to Macpherson's understanding of human rights, which are still nonetheless individual rights. I will return to the question of community in Macpherson later. For now, the point I wish to stress is that a community of individuals, each of whom enjoys developmental autonomy, provides both the essential context and accomplishment for human rights, in the form of both classical civil liberties and more recent social and economic rights. The community

Macpherson envisaged would not be an oppressive force, a macro-subject standing outside the individuals who make it up, because those individuals would, through their decisions and actions, continually constitute their bonds as free relations. The bonds would express their autonomy and not constrain it, because individuals would understand that their agency and the rights that enable it were made actual in and through their association with others. Their freedom was ultimately social.[25]

This is not to say that one is an agent only insofar as one is some sort of emanation of a community. It is to say that, as Habermas has it, our public and private autonomy are linked: both our contribution to common ends and our personal and private aims pursued and achieved apart from others are the products of common actions and, in a manner of speaking, "recognized" in public space. Something like this, I think, is what Ingram has in mind in writing of human rights *as* politics, and what Macpherson meant by the idea of a human right as an individual property right, namely, the right to participate in satisfying social relations. It points to the inner connection between human rights and democracy, where democracy is understood as a kind of society in which all are equally entitled to use and develop their distinctively human capacities.[26]

Carol Gould succinctly formulates what I take to be Macpherson's central concerns. In discussing the appropriate relation of democracy to human rights, she writes,

> Both democracy and human rights as conceptions emerge from our embedded social relations and are constructed out of our social practices ... Thus an appeal to a more substantive conception of democracy is required here ...; the exercise of democracy deserves to remain ineffective when its outcome is such that it violates the very rights and liberties for the sake of which democracy itself has been instituted. For if democracy is required by equal rights to self-development, the decisions made should not be allowed to undercut democracy's own ground. Here the conception of democracy is substantive in referring to an activity of self-development or self-transformation on the part of participants in which people reciprocally recognize each other's freedom and equality in the making of collective decisions. If the function and justification of democracy are that it serves freedom in this way, a democratic decision that violates these very conditions of recognition is inconsistent with democracy itself in this sense and undercuts it in practice.[27]

Gould's position, and its participatory and intersubjective dimensions, suggests that democracy should be understood along at least two dimensions: *sites* of democratic engagement, required by equal rights to self-*development* or self-*transformation*; and *institutions* and *practices* of democratic will-formation and decision, required by equal rights to *self*-development or *self*-transformation. I want to argue that Macpherson addressed both. His discussions here, in turn, involved the intersection of his two forms of liberty with the demands of human rights in the context of a democratic institution of property that represented the elimination of extractive power. They expressed, in other words, what needed to be taken on if possessive liberalism were to give way to its developmental challenger.

With respect to sites of democratic engagement, Macpherson wrote of the prospects for the achievement of economic and industrial democracy, democratization of the state, and the development and expression of a participatory pluralism. All of these requirements and possibilities in one form of another were keyed to the potential change of popular consciousness in the face of the crisis tendencies of advanced capitalism and the move from a possessive to a developmental understanding of individual freedom and fulfilment, i.e., from an emphasis on infinite appropriation and consumption to one of active, cooperative cultivation of capacities, where agents were viewed as doers, creators, and enjoyers of their human attributes. Applied to the prospects for economic democracy – "an arrangement of the economic system which will give a just distribution of work, income and wealth in a country" – and industrial democracy – "an organization of a productive unit whereby all those working in it have an effective voice in decisions affecting their work" – this move, which itself would reflect the unavoidable connection of political with economic questions, entailed workers "changing their priorities from consumer satisfaction to work gratification."[28]

Macpherson's explicit and systematic discussion of the state is, to be sure, more specifically directed at political theorists. Written in the context of the emergence in the 1970s of a robust neo-Marxian account of the state in capitalist society, which was seen as confronted with fundamentally conflicting demands for, on the one hand (capitalist) accumulation and, on the other (democratic) legitimation, Macpherson argued that this account properly reflected the need to return to what he called the "grand theory of the state." Unlike conventional accounts of the political process in existing liberal democratic societies, the stock-in-trade of empirical democratic political theorists and political scientists, the tradition of the grand theory of the state "tied the state back to supposed essentially human purposes and capacities, to a supposed essential nature of man." Macpherson saw the neo-Marxian account as much more able to take on board the normative demands associated with grand theory. It could do so because it was aware of the contradiction between capitalism and democracy, between possessive individualism and developmental liberalism. As a result, it did not pursue a timeless account of the political order, as empirical theorists were inclined to do, but instead focused on the historical determinants of the relation between state and economy. However, it appeared to Macpherson that the Marxian theory was better at the former, i.e., laying out the necessary relation between the state and capitalist society and the necessarily dominant role played by capital, than at the latter, i.e., "the limits of the possible relation of the capitalist society and state to essential human needs and capacities." This meant that the theory of the state "does have to come back from political economy to political philosophy, though it can only come back effectively in the measure that it has probed political economy. It also needs more empirical and theoretical work on human needs, wants and capacities." Of course this is a lucid summary of the essential nature of Macpherson's democratic project.[29]

And as was often the case with Macpherson, his primary intended audience was those ethical or humanist liberal theorists "who accept and would promote the normative values that were read into the liberal-democratic society and state by J.S. Mill and the nineteenth- and twentieth-century idealist theorists, but who reject the present liberal-democratic society as having failed to live up to those values, or as being incapable of realizing them."[30] They had to see that their normative commitments required that they abandon the possessive individualism in their outlook; this meant taking on board the critical analysis of the capitalist political economy central to the Marxian account. To do so meant that they required a new theory of the state, one that took off from the Marxian position. And although Macpherson did not explicitly say so, their willingness to recognize the need dictated by their humanist commitments to move to such a theory meant that, in turn, they could show Marxian theorists what *they* needed to do: take up the demands and requirements of developmental individualism.

And there was something else Macpherson did not explicitly indicate, but that could be adduced from his analysis. I think that as he saw it, most people in advanced liberal-democratic societies held roughly the same views as the humanist liberal theorists. That is, in varying degrees and with greater or lesser clarity and self-awareness, they embraced developmental aspirations and would therefore, in principle, prefer a society that allowed them greater scope for realizing them than seemed possible in the existing social order. But rather like the liberal theorists, they saw no realistic alternative to the possessive market society. In Macpherson's view, forged in the 1970s, most people at least accepted the system because it "delivered the goods" – material prosperity and order or stability, both highly valued. One could call this the Hobbes-Locke element of their outlook. At the same time, as we have already noted, there had also emerged demands for more meaningful work and at least some semblance of industrial democracy. In the measure that the system failed on both counts, mass pressures for a transformed society could conceivably begin to build.

However, as with the humanist liberals, so too for the masses of ordinary citizens: as theorists had to follow up on the logic of their commitment to a moral individualism, citizens had to come to see themselves explicitly as capable of and entitled to self-development, that is, as doers and exerters of their distinctively human capacities. In these circumstances, democratization of the state could involve, as Macpherson indicated in "Do We Need a Theory of the State?," a reinvigorated and responsive party and electoral system not subordinated to the demands of capital (there are clear echoes of *Democracy in Alberta* in this). And there is no reason to think that Macpherson would have objected to opening up bureaucratic administrative and planning functions and institutions to popular input (he was impressed with the then-current upsurge in civic activism around urban political and social questions). But given his emphasis not just on the descriptive but also the normative dimensions of the state, Macpherson, I believe, assumed that these institutional changes would not simply represent a supposedly new and improved way of registering and aggregating voter preferences. They would instead form vehicles for civic engagement that would be buttressed by other participatory institutions and practices. And indeed Macpherson's model of participatory democracy would represent an attempt to address comprehensively precisely the question of civic engagement based upon and in turn reinforcing demands for individual self-development.

The transcendence or abandonment of possessive individualism and what is associated with it, including the competitive maximization of utilities and the fundamental task of liberal democratic institutions as the aggregation of preferences, in favour of developmental individualism, is carried over into Macpherson's treatment of pluralism. That liberal democracy both requires and supports a plurality of choices in values, opinions, political options, and ways of life has long formed a key justification of liberal democratic systems. As Macpherson put it, "Pluralism, as practice and as theory, is clearly most at home in liberal-democratic states and is antithetical to one-party states."[31] Furthermore, while pluralism was normally associated with the formation and role of social groups, as indeed it was in the dominant forms of theory and social science, "the justificatory theory of pluralism can readily be shown to have its roots in some form of liberal individualism; indeed ... pluralism *is* individualism writ large."[32]

Hence the history of different forms of pluralism in theory and practice reflected "a concept of the individual as a morally self-sufficient being who seeks, and is justified in seeking, his or her own satisfactions whether as a consumer of utilities or as an exerter and developer of potentialities."[33] In turn Macpherson divided pluralism into forms that express developmental individualism and those that are extensions of possessive individualism. The former have included religious (perhaps the original liberal form), humanist or neo-idealist, anarcho-syndicalist, communitarian, and pragmatic forms. The latter, which were the dominant forms in existing liberal-democracies that are also capitalist, included mainstream, empirical, and conservative libertarian ones. Once again Macpherson's purpose was critical and not simply classificatory. His goal was to identify and assess the prospects for moving towards a participatory pluralist society. This meant a pluralism in terms of which plural groups would be internally democratic and participatory, and committed to developmental individualism in their purposes and actions. Each was necessary for the other.

Thus the meaning of pluralism and its place in a democratic society depended upon the form of individualism it represented, the social and political structures within which it operated, and the possibilities for social change. In Macpherson's view, given the prevailing structures of power and dominant ideological and cultural currents, possessive pressure groups, especially those representing organized capital and, to a more limited extent, labour, were well positioned to press their claims on the state and to have them addressed. This was because such groups could threaten to withhold services vital for the economy. In a market-driven social order in which the state was expected to maintain economic growth and stability on pain of losing legitimacy, threats of this type had to be taken seriously.

On the other hand, developmental groups – "associations of the unemployed, of students, of women, of ethnic minorities; movements for the protection of the environment against pollution and ecological damage; all those who want some structural changes in existing society which would open the way to more fully human development for this and future generations"[34] – lacked this sort of muscle. They were both relatively powerless and linked to demands not so readily accommodated by the utilitarian calculus of material compensations based on market calculations of costs and benefits. What success Macpherson envisaged them enjoying would have to occur in the electoral process. But as we have already seen, Macpherson viewed that process as itself in need of fundamental reform, in order to cut it loose from its own role in fostering possessive market values and practices. Moreover, in the measure that actually existing pluralism, whether possessive or developmental, tended to cover over the class question and thus the net transfer of powers – a process abetted by the propensity for developmental pluralist theory to uneasily combine developmental individualism with a continuing acceptance of capitalism – it was at best capable of realizing the gains historically associated with ethical liberalism. Macpherson believed that such liberalism had run its course, with the achievement of a welfare state now likely to come under siege, with the real prospect that the overwhelming body of citizens would embrace system-stability as the most important political goal.

Yet just as Macpherson did not dismiss human rights, but sought instead to suggest the role they might play in pushing forward the developmental ethos, so, too, with pluralism. A pluralism founded upon a commitment to developmental goals would necessarily be democratic because, to once again recall Ober's position, it would work in the service of empowerment. Such empowerment would, in this instance, revolve around developmental plural groups structured so as to require active participation by its members in a larger society itself given over to developmental and participatory purposes. Current possessive pressure groups could not become developmental. Not only did their commitment to possessive market values carry with it a conception of individuals as atomistic, rational, utility-maximizing agents standing apart, save in purely strategic terms from society – existing forms of pluralism, including the more developmentally inclined ones, "do not commonly see the individual as the product of relations, nor as being fully human only as a member of the community" – but the very role such groups played in society, where they necessarily mediated the conflicting demands of capitalism and democracy, precluded it. The managers of such groups "who must be in unending negotiation with the state's bureaucrats and executives and legislators, must have more room for manoeuvre than they could have if they were bound by decisions made by the rank-and-file members of the association through a genuinely participatory process."[35] It was the same problem that bedevilled political parties, as radical Social Creditors in Alberta discovered.

We might say, then, that, for Macpherson, the question of pluralism provided insight into both prospective sites and practices of democracy. Macpherson's own critique of, as well as commitment to, pluralism very much resembles his approach to property. As with property, the values of pluralism were deeply embedded in liberal-democratic political culture. And like property, existing forms of pluralism denied or at least failed to adequately fulfil their claims to facilitate a full and free life for individuals conceived as morally self-sufficient beings. The sobering reality laid out over three decades earlier in *Democracy in Alberta* remained: the liberal-democratic capitalist state cannot become a participatory one, or, for that matter, a genuinely democratic pluralist one, "as long as the bulk of the electorate accepts system-stability as the overriding value. For to accept that as the highest value is to license the state – a very unparticipatory state – to continue its role as supporter of the capitalist economy, and this will require increasing state manipulation and either no change in the present level of citizen participation or a delusive change by way of a plebiscitarian state."[36] This was another way of highlighting the strength, but also the contradictions, of the possessive individualist model of the individual. The immanent critique of possessive individualism gives rise to the critique of actually existing liberal democracy and thus the critical requirements for a fully democratic society.

The Historical Constituents of Democratic Development: C.B. Macpherson's Models of Liberal Democracy

This critique and these requirements provided the theoretical context, and the essential content, of Macpherson's account of the historical constituents of liberal democracy. In *The Life and Times of Liberal Democracy*, he developed these constituents by a series of analytic models. His account here most explicitly brought together the normative and descriptive/explanatory dimensions of his approach to democracy and democratic theory.

Macpherson's models of liberal democracy were indeed designed specifically to combine the normative and the descriptive/explanatory dimensions that he believed unavoidable in any democratic theory. He argued that, as with any political system, a liberal democratic polity "has two necessary ingredients that may not appear on the surface: (a) to be workable, it must not be out of line with the wants and capabilities of the human beings who are to work it; hence, the model of democracy must contain (or take for granted) a model of man; and (b), since it needs general assent and support in order to be workable, the model must contain, explicitly or implicitly, an ethically justificatory theory."[37] To reflect the historically evolving character of liberal democracy, and to demonstrate how its history is also its present, Macpherson laid out his models as palimpsests, or what he called an amalgam. This approach reflected the extent to which past models lived on in present ones. In turn he argued that, while the idea of democracy obviously had a lengthy history, as a distinctive political order *liberal* democracy emerged only in the nineteenth century. This was because, unlike earlier conceptions of democracy, which assumed the necessity of a one-class or classless society, the architects of liberal democracy sought to fit democratic institutions and practices to a class-divided social order, one they acknowledged, accepted, or even justified. Thus figures such as Jean-Jacques Rousseau or Thomas Jefferson, for whom democracy required a society dominated by independent proprietors who, in Rousseau's words, were neither rich enough to buy the services of others nor poor enough to have to sell themselves, should be seen as outside the liberal-democratic tradition. In Macpherson's wry depiction, their models "were, so to speak, handicraft models of democracy, and as such are best considered as precursors of liberal democracy."[38]

One might say that the "truth" of these precursor models, again very similar to the position staked out in *Democracy in Alberta*, was that democracy as a way of life or kind of society required economic equality. But the sort of equality envisaged by Rousseau in particular was in a world shaped by capitalist social relations both unachievable and undesirable, because it would require the kind of levelling that would undo the gains of the bourgeois era. (For his part, Jefferson hoped to avoid European class divisions in the new American republic; whether his own model was viable in the long run was another matter.) As we have seen, for Macpherson these gains were both material and moral. The material gains resulted from the unleashing of productive powers under the impact of the capitalist drive for accumulation. The moral gains revolved around the ideal and genuine if contradictory and incomplete realization of individual developmental autonomy. This dynamic was expressed most acutely in the tension between possessive and developmental individualism. The transcendence of the former by the latter represented, for Macpherson, the historical/normative trajectory he saw in the empirical/conceptual development at the core of the 150-year tradition of liberal democracy.

What was required was the need to move from liberalism as the equal freedom of all legal commodity owners to compete in the market – which meant in practice the freedom of the stronger to do down the weaker, using market rules – to liberalism as the equal and effective freedom of all to use and develop their capacities. It is the move from negative to positive liberty, or rather, the preservation of the essential core of negative liberty in the form of counter-extractive liberty as an uneliminable aspect of the achievement of developmental liberty, which itself preserves the essential core of positive liberty as both communal (or solidaristic) and individualist. This is why Macpherson was so adamant that, even though liberal democracy has historically been linked to capitalist society and its class divisions, a radical, non-capitalist democracy could and should be seen as liberal: the fullest realization of both liberalism and democracy demanded it. (And as Macpherson made clear often, the consequences of failure to bring this about could be dire: either a corporatist, pseudo-democratic plebiscitarian or an outright authoritarian/totalitarian state.) Just as the developmental ontology involved the retrieval of the pre-modern, Aristotelian conception of humans fit for the good life, but at a higher level, so a fully developmental liberal democracy – which, as we have seen, was, for Macpherson, both participatory and pluralist – would involve a similar mediated restoration, in this case of the egalitarian assumptions of Rousseau and Jefferson.

As is well known, Macpherson viewed the history of liberal democracy as we have come to know it in terms of three specific models whose ties with Macpherson's account of the different faces of liberalism were explicit and obvious. The protective democratic model of Jeremy Bentham and James Mill represented the high point of possessive individualist thinking about democracy and took for granted the hard-driving, competitive capitalist social and economic order. In this world of individuals seen as unlimited maximizers of utilities, and in which everyone sought power over others, the case for democratic government rested on the claim that only the democratic franchise could protect the governed from oppression by the government. Government was a double-edged sword. Its laws were needed to protect individuals and their property from others. But as an instrument of power in the hands of individuals themselves driven to seek power over others, it posed a real and pressing threat to the very people who relied on it for protection. So the challenge was to determine the kind of government that could, on the one hand, enact appropriate laws (i.e., those required to nurture the capitalist market society), but on the other hand, would also be prevented from invading the lives and properties of its citizens, who were themselves inherently invasive. The solution lay in establishing an appropriate franchise along with frequent elections, the secret ballot and freedom of the press. Out of this evolved the institutions and values of representative and responsible government.

The most noteworthy feature of the protective model was the absence of any sense that democracy represented a qualitative departure from the existing society, a manifestation of social progress. Macpherson ironically claimed that "in this founding model of democracy for a modern industrial society" there was "no enthusiasm for democracy, no idea that it could be a morally transformative force; it is nothing but a logical requirement for the governance of inherently self-interested conflicting individuals who are assumed to be infinite desirers of their own private benefits ... Responsible government, even to the extent of responsibility to a democratic electorate, was needed for the protection of individuals and the promotion of the Gross National Product, and for nothing more."[39] So understood, the continuing salience of this model for a capitalist society is obvious. Current accounts of democracy from a rational or public choice perspective that view the democratic political process as a forum for "rent-seeking" individual behaviour are descendants of the protective model. Their primarily libertarian, free market proponents hold the same conception of individuals as competitive, self-interested maximizers in quest of power over others, acquired by any means necessary and available; hence their scepticism about the state and the need to ensure it is insulated as much as possible from majoritarian or "populist" pressures that threaten property and good government.

The developmental democratic model took its bearings from the work of thinkers such as John Stuart Mill and T.H. Green; it was later supplemented by neo-idealist and pragmatist accounts offered by thinkers such as Ernest Barker, John Dewey, and especially, A.D.

Lindsay. (Interestingly, Macpherson did not specifically include here the revisionist liberalism of Rawls and Chapman, which, as I argued in the previous chapter, seems also to have been a direct descendant of Mill's developmental account. Perhaps this was because their ethical liberalism issued in a theory of justice rather than a theory of democracy as such.) Emerging in the latter decades of the nineteenth century, the architects of this model took issue with the harshly aggressive and competitive picture offered by the unalloyed possessive individualism of Bentham and James Mill. In a reaction both to this picture of human nature and its possibilities and the grim realities of early capitalist industrialization, including intensifying working-class restiveness, the developmental democrats sought to introduce a moral dimension to individualism. This was the ethical liberal outlook Macpherson examined in his treatment of ontology. Individuals were more than simply maximizers of utilities. In this light, democracy had to be seen as primarily a vehicle for the promotion and facilitation of individual self-development. Taking democracy as not just a means of choosing and authorizing governments but as a form of life dedicated to self-realization, the developmental model "is not satisfied with individuals as they are, with man as infinite consumer and appropriator. It wants to move towards a society of individuals more humanly developed and more equally so. It wants not to impose a utopia on the people but to have the people reach the goal themselves, improving themselves by participating actively in the political process, every instalment of participation leading to an improvement in their political capacity, as well as their all-round development, and making them capable of more participation and more self-development."[40]

J.S. Mill provided the most influential statement of this position. In Macpherson's view, Mill set the dominant tone for liberal democratic theory down to the middle of the twentieth century. His primary legacy was to combine elements of the protective model and its underlying presuppositions (the liberal, possessive individualist side) with a defence of equal, individual participation, including that of women (the democratic, developmental side). His key interests were the preservation of individual liberty, the provision of mechanisms to make government accountable, and the securing of effective and efficient governmental administration. In turn, these were linked to questions about the extent of democracy in social and economic life (and the accompanying question of who should be a full democratic citizen), the demands of reconciling democratic participation with effective administration, and the reach and range of state activities. In short, his theory combined representative government with a "free" (capitalist) market economy – the formula for actually existing liberal democracy itself.

Yet Mill's position, and the developmental model, was fraught with contradictions and ambiguities, a product of his effort to combine developmental ideals with a continuing commitment to private property. This was obviously no problem for the protective model and its proponents who fully accepted possessive individualism and its consequences. Mill was certainly a critic of the existing market society and its deleterious impact upon human character, made evident in the struggle between capital and labour and the deplorable condition of the working class. He hoped that eventually the hard-driving capitalist society of his time would give way to a "steady-state" economy dominated by producer cooperatives. However, although he was "deeply troubled by the incompatibility he saw between the claims of equal human development and the existing class inequalities of power and wealth," Mill nonetheless "accepted and supported a system which required individuals to act as maximizing consumers and appropriators, seeking to accumulate the means to ensure their future flow of consumer satisfactions, which meant seeking to acquire property. A system which requires men to see themselves, and to act, as consumers and appropriators, gives little scope for most of them to see themselves and act as exerters and developers of their capacities."[41] This contradiction was to plague the developmental model throughout its history, whether in its original form with Mill or in its later neo-idealist or pragmatist incarnations.

The contradiction – in effect, between possessive and developmental liberalism – was most clearly evident in the intellectual gymnastics Mill undertook to avoid the logical consequences of his democratic commitments: the necessity for a universal and equal franchise. Until the twentieth century, democracy was understood to mean rule by the (property-less) majority, which was held to threaten the property rights of the minority and indeed ultimately civilized society itself. This was the notorious "tyranny of the majority" that critics of democracy have always emphasized (and still do, if more subtly now than then).[42] In Mill's case, this fear was linked to another one: the growth of unaccountable state power that could stifle freedom and innovation under a suffocating bureaucratic domination.

The antidote to this threat, as it was for the theorists of the protective model, was representative democracy. Thus Mill's case for representative democracy stressed not only its ability to develop the moral capacities of individuals but also its role in guarding freedom. Perhaps he is best seen as a protective-developmental democrat, or maybe a developmental-protective democrat. It is a good question which of these elements predominated, for Mill's developmental ethos did not lead him to support direct democracy, which he rejected not only on practical but also principled grounds. Especially in the era of expanding state power, the fear that a popular majority left to its own devices would threaten the (property) rights of the minority was, for Mill, real and acute. A legislative body composed of the people's elected deputies would provide a vehicle both to secure individual freedom by controlling state power and to ensure as fully as possible that the most qualified individuals would, through the challenges of electoral competition, occupy positions in the legislature. Informed opinion, as opposed to the ignorance of a majority working class "that in their present condition ... were incapable of using political power wisely,"[43] would have a better chance than in a direct, purely majoritarian system.

But even this did not fully preclude the danger of popular demagoguery. To avoid this possibility, Mill proposed plural voting: while every qualified adult should be guaranteed at least one vote, the more able, as measured by occupation, should have multiple votes; and intellectuals capable of public spiritedness should have the most. Mill saw this as critical for protecting against an ignorant majority using state power for self-interested purposes, or what Mill and other liberals called "class" legislation.

As Macpherson acutely noted, Mill could never square his commitment to the full and equal participation of all, necessary for self-development, with the unequal participation he countenanced in the face of continuing class conflict and the consequent danger of majority class government that would act in its own and against the public interest. This set up a vicious circle, whereby unequal participation in fact reinforced the need for unequal participation in principle. Mill's developmental goals were the victim. And his inability to handle class opposition, which he hoped might be overcome through growing social and economic cooperation, itself fostered by individual and social improvement, reflected an even more fundamental contradiction between capitalist market relations and the democratic developmental ideal. As with the earlier noted contradiction between the ontology of possessive individualism and that of developmental individualism, this, too, would characterize the developmental model in all its forms.

However, Macpherson saw a significant difference between Mill's conception of developmental democracy and its twentieth-century successors; indeed it was sufficiently important and consequential that Macpherson presented the earlier and later versions of developmental democracy as separate models. He understood this difference in terms of a trajectory whereby the move from the protective model to the early and then later developmental models represented a decline in realism and hence penetrative power. Echoing the arguments advanced in "The Deceptive Task of Political Theory" and "The Economic Penetration of Political Theory," Macpherson linked this loss of realism to the decreasing ability to handle the realities of a possessive market society and the values it secreted in the face of increasing pressures and possibilities for a more humanist individualist and radical democratic form of life. Expressed philosophically, it was the increasing splitting off of the normative from the descriptive/explanatory dimensions of theory. This rupture carried an enormous cost for both.

To be sure, the realism of the protective model was, as Macpherson had argued in "The Deceptive Task," the scientific apogee of the tradition of possessive individualism, the reflection of a triumphant capitalist society prior to the organized working-class challenge to its institutions and values. As laid out there, normative and descriptive/explanatory dimensions "secreted" each other. The demands and requirements of realism that faced the architects of the developmental model(s) called for a confrontation with structurally determined social conflict that potentially left open the future direction of a social form that had appeared permanent. Neither Mill nor his successors were fully up to those demands and requirements.

This did not become so obvious until well into the twentieth century. This was because the severed normative and descriptive dimensions were supposedly reattached as a result of a historical development not earlier foreseen: the apparent solution of the class problem through the emergence of formally mass democratic systems in capitalist societies. The main vehicles were political parties, whose task was to blur the opposition of class interests and effect compromises between contending classes. Parties both provided candidates for office in representative democratic systems and created (and disciplined) electorates. While other social, cultural, and economic mechanisms did their part to reconcile democratic pressures with capitalist social institutions, party systems were decisive for ensuring that the class rule and subsequent class legislation Mill and others feared did not come to pass.[44] The key was the increasing insulation of parties themselves from democratic pressures – that is, from party members and from electorates at large. The price of compromise was the lack of responsiveness. Mass citizenship came at the cost of meaningful participation beyond the periodic exercise of the franchise.

From all appearances, though, this seemed to represent the triumph of community against selfish interests, the realization of the developmental ideal – or so the inheritors of Mill assumed. The blurring of class lines (and class consciousness, which is always largely a political accomplishment) was taken as the elimination of classes themselves, with individuals and plural groups now increasingly seen as the main social and political actors. The growth of social knowledge and education, moral awareness (including, as we have seen, consciousness of human rights), and social communication seemed to represent the triumph of citizen rationality and humanistic values. The market had come to appear (and to some extent, actually had been) tamed and made compatible with democratic values. What tended to escape notice, however, was the extent to which the political system had, in turn, been increasingly remade in the image of the economic system – that is, in "the image of the democratic political process as a market, a free market in which everything would work out to the best advantage of everybody (or to the least disadvantage of anybody)."[45]

The complex consequences and implications of ethical liberalism were paralleled by the historical experience of the developmental model, particularly in its mid-twentieth-century form. The contradictory impact of holding both developmental ideals and capitalist market, that is, possessive individualist, commitments became evident in what Macpherson saw as the failure of the developmental model and its replacement by one more explicitly and obviously attuned to market values.

In the face of the apparent stilling of class conflict, particularly at the level of the democratic political process, developmental theorists assumed the triumph of democratic justice and thus the entrenchment of democracy as the good society – or at least the ability of an engaged citizenry to use the democratic process to ameliorate social and economic problems and imperfections. What they *saw* were engaged, active, rational citizens, doers and exerters of their capacities, who, acting together, moved the society forward. What was actually *there* were citizens as (political) consumers, as vulnerable to the ministrations of political entrepreneurs, who functioned as engineers of consent, as were consumers in the markets for other products and the entrepreneurs who offered them for sale. This confusion was understandable. It reflected the attempt to hold possessive and developmental individualist assumptions together, which the theorists did by, in effect, submerging the latter in the former, while continuing to celebrate citizen rationality and developmental values. In the circumstances – where "the system had survived by reducing the responsiveness of governments to electorates"[46] and not by transcending class inequalities and so achieving developmental aims – the attempt was bound to fail.

The measure of this failure was the displacement of the developmental model by what for Macpherson became, and remained, the dominant paradigm of democracy in both political theory and political science from roughly the mid-twentieth century onward. This was equilibrium democracy, or more specifically, the pluralist-elitist-equilibrium model. Its key architects were the Austrian-American political economist Joseph Schumpeter and American political scientists and voting behaviour specialists, particularly Robert Dahl, Bernard Berelson, Paul Lazarsfeld, and William McPhee.[47]

This model and the system it purported to explain was *pluralist*, because it viewed society as essentially plural, composed of individuals pulled in many different directions by a multiplicity of interests. As a result, individuals came together in an immense variety of interest groups, which pursued their specific goals through social and political action. The system was *elitist*, because the leading role in the political process was played by self-chosen groups of leaders, whether interest associations or political parties. And it was an *equilibrium* model, because it saw the democratic process as a political marketplace, in which leaders functioned as political entrepreneurs who ensured there was a balance, or equilibrium, between the supply of and the demand for political or public goods.

Like the protective model, the pluralist-elitist-equilibrium model stripped democracy of its moral content. Democracy was a mechanism for choosing and authorizing governments. Its purpose was simply to register the desires of people as they were now, not to contribute to the development of people as they might become. It was a market model of the political process and was thus widely accepted in advanced capitalist democratic societies permeated with market values and market behaviour. Not only did this market model explain behaviour, it also seemed to justify this behaviour and hence the whole system. It emphasized consumer sovereignty, both economic and political (and these elements of the model have, of course, become even more paramount in recent years). Human beings were seen as utility maximizers. Political entrepreneurs, like their economic counterparts, were considered free competitors. The political market allocated political goods in an optimal manner, just as the economic market efficiently allocated economic goods. The model assumed that the demands for political goods shifted with such frequency that the entrepreneur who aggregated such demands in order to form a workable majority performed the key role in the political system.

Proponents of the model saw citizens as political consumers, assumed that competition for the votes of citizens was the motor of the system, and claimed that political equilibrium was the outcome of the political process. They did, however, differ in the extent to which they detected political consumer sovereignty, i.e., the autonomy of demand. Joseph Schumpeter, a central European pessimist perhaps best known for his fear that liberal capitalism was doomed to self-destruct over time, assumed that political consumers exercised very little control over the political process (nor should they). Their role was not to decide political questions themselves but to select representatives who would. By contrast, the most influential proponents of the model, typically and understandably American, were somewhat more optimistic (e.g., Dahl, Berelson, and others). While they held little regard for the so-called classical ideal of the rational citizen – that is, the core assumption of the developmental model – they tended, nonetheless, to claim that somehow the whole system worked – and sometimes with distinction. Its market-like nature was its saving grace. Put otherwise, if individuals were not particularly rational as *citizens*, they were as self-aware holders of political preferences rational as *consumers*.

So taking as a given "that political man, like economic man, is essentially a consumer and appropriator," it

> was easy for the political theorists to make the same assumptions as the economic theorists. In the economic model, entrepreneurs and consumers were assumed to be rational maximizers of their own good, and to be operating in conditions of free competition in which all energies and resources were brought to the market, with the result that the market produced the optimum distribution of labour and capital and consumer goods. So in the political model, politicians and voters were assumed to be rational maximizers, and to be operating in conditions of free political competition, with the result that the market-like political system produced

> the optimum distribution of political energies and political goods. The democratic political market produced an optimum equilibrium of inputs and outputs – of the energies and resources people would put into it and the rewards they would get out of it.[48]

It is worth noting that both the equilibrium and developmental models took for granted and built upon the apparent success of twentieth-century liberal democratic states in solving the main problem of democratic government: how to reconcile economic freedom and private property with mass democracy, the "free market" and democratic suffrage. The difference between the two reflected the competing ontological assumptions that undergirded each. Taking individuals as active doers and exerters of their capacities, proponents of the developmental model saw the apparent reconciliation of democracy and capitalism as the triumph of democracy over the market. By contrast, the equilibrium theorists, who understood individuals as unlimited utility maximizers, infinite consumers and appropriators, saw, if not the triumph of the market over democracy, nonetheless proof that the democratic political system was necessarily a kind of market. Their criticisms of so-called classical democratic theory and its supposed naivety about the "rational" public-spirited citizen testified to this hard-nosed commitment to market assumptions.

Neither the developmental nor the equilibrium model grasped the role of a party system in an unequal society in blunting class opposition and blurring issues. Parties were neither vehicles for realizing a transparent popular will nor pure aggregators of autonomous preferences. Yet each represented something important about the kind of liberal democracy found in mid- to late-twentieth-century Western capitalist societies. The equilibrium model was right against the developmental model: individuals behaved as "market men" – or, as Macpherson put it, continued "to prefer affluence to community (and to believe that the market society can provide affluence indefinitely)"[49] – and the political system was relevantly like a market. But the developmental model had it over the equilibrium model ironically where the developmental model was at its weakest: in upholding active participation by rational citizens as a core feature of a fully democratic society. If the equilibrium model was empirically more accurate, the developmental model was normatively both more appealing and in principle more attuned to the requirements of democracy as a kind of society.

Yet it was not a simple matter of abstract "ought" versus concrete "is." I earlier suggested that, in laying out his models of democracy, Macpherson brought together the normative and descriptive/explanatory dimensions central to any theory of democracy in an explicit way. This was especially the case with his treatment of equilibrium democracy, because he saw the stakes as high. The weight of the facts, namely the extent to which the equilibrium model highlighted the market basis of liberal democratic societies and the market behaviour of individuals, gave the equilibrium model a powerful claim to realism. For Macpherson, it held considerable descriptive accuracy.

But what he labelled its explanatory and justificatory claims were more problematic. With varying degrees of theoretical self-awareness, proponents of the equilibrium model tended to hold that the existing political system, with its imperfections, was the only workable democratic model, given the realities of human nature and social behaviour, and that the system met the normative requirements of democratic theory. That is, the system not only produced equilibrium outcomes but these outcomes were optimal. Consumer sovereignty was a real force. Since consumer sovereignty was an unalloyed good, a system facilitating it must also be good.

For Macpherson, while at least in principle the system might be a good market, it did not necessarily mean it was a good democracy. In any event, the political systems of existing liberal democratic societies were hardly competitive in the sense typically understood by liberal economic or political theory. Oligopoly, not free competition, ruled in both the economy and the polity. And in the measure that the system did respond to consumer demand, the consumers themselves were hardly equal. Effective demand was, to a large extent, a function of money and the direct expenditure of energy through participation in the political process. In other words, it reflected and reinforced social and economic inequalities. For Macpherson, the main consequence of unequal consumer sovereignty was political apathy among large numbers of citizens. Apathy appeared to support both the ontological assumptions behind the equilibrium model – people were essentially private consumers and appropriators who constantly sought to maximize their returns – and the picture of stability that seemed to justify the pluralist-elitist-equilibrium system as the best possible one.

For a number of reasons, the issue of apathy was vital for Macpherson – and for a clear understanding of how he viewed the relation of explanation to justification, the normative to the descriptive. Recall that, for him, the equilibrium model was in the tradition of the protective model. Indeed it could plausibly be seen as an attempt to reassert the centrality of that model in the present, where possessive market and democratic values had to be reconciled. Recall, too, that Macpherson argued in "The Deceptive Task of Political Theory" that in its classic Hobbes-to-Bentham form, possessive individualism combined explanation and justification, whereby in the absence of an alternative, to explain the system was automatically to justify it. Macpherson held that this was the case with the equilibrium model. Yet the attempt to do so was more ideological – that is, more deceptive – than was the case with the protective model, which was in the classic possessive individualist tradition. At one level, to be sure, proponents of the equilibrium model were right. Where the stability of the system as a value trumped the desire or demand for enhanced prospects for developmental individualism and the exertion of one's distinctively human capacities – where people preferred affluence to community and believed the system would continue to provide it indefinitely – the explanation of how the system functioned seemed, in the circumstances, a justification. The facts appeared to speak for themselves.

Yet in the historical context in which the equilibrium model took root, that is, after the emergence over a century or so of pressures for (social) democracy, the "facts" were no longer straightforward. They spoke against themselves. This contradiction embedded within the facts themselves defined the content of, and the use of, the term *apathy*. As a descriptor it carries a definite normative "slope." Partly, as Macpherson argued, the problem here was that equilibrium theorists misunderstood its meaning. They saw it as an independent datum, a rational choice by the apathetic, who calculated that their resources of money, time, and effort were better deployed elsewhere. They saw it, in other words, as a revealed preference for the system as it existed, a commitment to its stability.

But the other side of the argument about apathy showed the contradiction. Proponents of the equilibrium model often argued that not only did apathy reflect free, rational, individual choice. They also argued that apathy was beneficial for stability itself. "Too much" participation in the context of mass democratic demands and institutions would potentially undermine individual liberties and so threaten the system. (In a revised form, this argument would resurface in the 1970s and 1980s in the form of the "demand overload" analysis, and some version of it is at least implicit in contemporary fears about "populist" insurgency.) Macpherson confronted this tension by arguing that apathy was a dependent variable, not an independent one. It reflected, among other things, the blurring of accountability by party systems, whose task and role were to contain and occlude the opposition of class interests. With no meaningful ability to influence public policy, that is, to enjoy political efficacy, large numbers of individuals opted out. This was, in a manner of speaking, "rational." But it was the limited rationality of restricted options, a kind of functional rationality that made sense only where utilitarian motives were seen as, and existed as, the only meaningful possibilities.

The question of apathy was also hugely significant for Macpherson because the idea that democracy and apathy were compatible and indeed the former required the latter flew in the face of democracy's meaning and its historically developed claims. In Macpherson's view, apathy by its nature was necessarily at odds with democracy's humanistic aspirations, particularly as it drew its content from the class-based inequalities of a possessive market social order – that is, from a system characterized by a pervasive net transfer of powers. The presence of apathy *as a hallmark of democracy* represented a social pathology, however "real" its impact.

There are two points I want to emphasize here. The first one is that if apathy is real but false – that is, false to democratic possibilities for self-development – then there is a living tension built into the fabric of political experience. There could be stability, as the equilibrium theorists argued. But it was a destructive stability, destructive from the point of view of the very possibilities that have been submerged but continue to generate tensions in the present. A democratic system that needed apathy had little claim to the title of democracy, however consistent it might be with the values and practices of a market. For Macpherson, the lesson here was that democracy as a way of life dedicated to individual self-development was necessary but not inevitable, historically demanded but not historically guaranteed. As such it was more than merely a regulative idea but less than a substantial concept to be realized through the logic of history. It might be called a telos without teleology.

The second point calls to mind what I have argued is the intersubjective potential of Macpherson's position. It seems to me clear that, for Macpherson, individuals reflecting on their biographies and lived situations would have to conclude that the existing system based on mass apathy exacted a serious toll on their human possibilities. Other than through individuals coming to reject the preference for affluence over community, which Macpherson postulated and hoped would result from increasing recognition of the incompetence of state-managed capitalism (a recognition he thought at the time was becoming more widespread), he really saw no specific mechanism, such as a vanguard party or movement, that would advance a project of radical democracy built on developmental premises.

But what he did see, or thought he saw, were increasing demands for some form of participatory democracy. His final model, which laid out his version of participatory democracy, should be seen in this light. But we need to be very clear about his approach here. It was no accident that he linked his discussion of apathy to the question of participatory democracy. Participatory democracy, and not some collectivist/authoritarian/totalitarian nightmare, was the "other" of apathy. But this would be so only if the net transfer of powers was eliminated. Participatory democracy was in this sense both a way of moving beyond a system requiring class inequalities *and* the consequence of that move. And once again it involved the simultaneous realization of individualism and democracy, the entrenchment of both counter-extractive and developmental liberty. Any other move to abolish class structures would bring about an authoritarian collectivism, indeed would not really abolish class domination at all.

So Macpherson's model of participatory democracy was qualitatively different from the previous models. By contrast with the other models, not only was participatory democracy as yet historically unrealized. It also achieved in principle what the others could not: the synthesis of the key commitments of those other models that had shaped what was most valuable in the liberal democratic tradition. So while its specific institutional recommendations should be taken seriously, its function as a critical standard should also not be forgotten. It is, I would argue, a continuation of critique, not a definitive resolution of the historical tensions that Macpherson saw as its basis.

It is especially important to stress this function of participatory democracy as a standard of critique rather than a full blown institutional model, for another reason. Some contemporary proponents of deliberative democracy, which, to be sure, has parallels with participatory democracy, appear to view participatory democracy as at least potentially prone to authoritarianism, with a mobilized and activist majority, inflamed by collective passions, acting irrationally and running roughshod over minorities and dissenters; this clearly links up with the contemporary critique of populism. Political theorist Iris Marion Young noted this tendency and criticized it for its elitist implications.[50] For Macpherson, participatory democracy as a critical standard was designed to highlight the economic, social, and political conditions essential to a democratic society, conditions that models of deliberative democracy often ignore in their normative claims.

As noted earlier, Macpherson developed his account of models of liberal democracy against the backdrop of political ferment. Student, civil rights, women's, anti-war, and (nascent) environmental movements had emerged internationally as real political, social, and cultural forces. In addition there had been a resurgence of industrial action among some elements of the working class, which pressed for at least greater respect and control in the workplace, if not outright industrial democracy. In one way or another, these movements made participatory democracy – roughly direct popular engagement in identifying the key issues and making decisions about public affairs critical to the life of a community – a key goal or demand. For some this involved the outright replacement of representative institutions, which were seen as sclerotic, unresponsive, and beholden to the wealthy and powerful, with institutions of direct democracy where people made political decisions themselves. For others, representative institutions had to remain and play a key role, particularly given the impracticality in large, populous states of a direct democracy patterned after that identified with the classical Greek city state. To be sure, these institutions, particularly political parties and electoral systems, required substantial reform to ensure that their democratic potentials were realized. But whatever the commitments of different movements and activists, they all represented a challenge to both the elite party systems and limited participation that were the hallmarks of the equilibrium model.

Macpherson argued that any realistic model of participatory democracy would have to include both direct and indirect, that is electoral representative, components. His conception of direct democracy was pyramidal. It was constructed on the commonly held ideal of base-level participation at the community and enterprise level, which would address the need for both political and economic democracy.

> Thus one would start with direct democracy at the neighbourhood or factory level – actual face-to-face discussion and decision by consensus or majority, and election of delegates who would make up a council at the next more inclusive level, say a city borough or ward or township.

> The delegate would have to be sufficiently instructed by and accountable to those who elected them to make decisions at the council level reasonably democratic. So it would go on up to the top level, which would be a national council for matters of national concern, and local and regional councils for matters of less than national concern ... What is needed, at every stage, to make the system democratic, is that the decision-makers and issue-formulators elected from below be held responsible to those below by being subject to re-election and recall.[51]

But although only a pyramidal structure could plausibly bring elements of direct and thus participatory democracy into the political system, there would still be the need for representative institutions and thus competitive political parties. Macpherson made clear that a radical democracy that could still claim to be liberal required political parties. Moreover a competitive party system would be not only unavoidable but also desirable. Even in a society in which fundamental class divisions, that is, the net transfer of powers, had been either sharply reduced or eliminated, there "would still be issues around which parties might form, or even might be needed to allow issues to be effectively proposed and debated: issues such as the over-all allocation of resources, environmental and urban planning, population and immigration policies, foreign policy, military policy." To be sure, in what could be seen as a residue of classical or orthodox Marxism, Macpherson suggested that a participatory system *without* parties that could still nonetheless be called liberal was conceivable "in conditions of greater plenty and widespread opportunity for citizen participation other than through political parties."[52] This suggests the possibility of eliminating, if not any and all oppositional interests, certainly those that have typically required political parties to express them in a form that would facilitate their identification and, where possible, reconciliation. This might be thought both unrealistic and undesirable.[53]

Yet I think this was intended as a limiting condition designed to highlight Macpherson's real point about what makes for a fully humanistic liberal democracy. He sought to challenge the typical view that the existence of parties defined democracy tout court. Parties consistent with the kind of radical participatory and liberal democracy he envisaged would themselves have to be thoroughly democratized internally, a condition not possible, as we have seen, where there were opposed class interests that simultaneously required expression and occlusion.

What a competitive party system might look like in the absence of opposed class interests is an interesting question; certainly there would, on Macpherson's own account, likely always be the need for something like currently recognizable parties to ensure protection against arbitrary government. This was central to his conception of counter-extractive liberty, which was not simply about eliminating capitalist exploitation.

In other words, competitive party systems as they have emerged historically have crystallized the core features and commitments of the protective and equilibrium models of democracy. In the measure that key features highlighted by both models continued to exist and shape a liberal democratic social order – that is, the extent to which, in Macpherson's terms, the values of possessive individualism remained decisive for individual and social experience – then parties would continue to have a place. But ultimately what would guarantee the liberalism of participatory democracy, and the democratic character of liberalism, was "a strong and widespread sense of the value of that liberal-democratic ethical principle" that defined the developmental model of J.S. Mill and his successors: "the equal right of every man and woman to the full development and use of his or her capabilities."[54]

This was why the challenge of participatory democracy was not how to run it but how to reach it. To reach it required "a downgrading or abandonment of market assumptions about the nature of man and society, a departure from the image of man as a maximizing consumer, and a great reduction of the present economic and social inequality."[55] Once again, this is to move from possessive to developmental individualism, beyond capitalism to socialism. A radical participatory democracy that is also liberal is the (non-inevitable) telos of a transcended possessive individualism that preserves its historical accomplishments while moving beyond its unavoidable limitations.

There is one final point worth noting about Macpherson's participatory model. He developed it just as the possibility of widespread use of computers for mass communication was beginning to take shape. Pointing to an emerging enthusiasm among social theorists and political philosophers for a direct democracy where potentially millions of citizens would be electronically linked, Macpherson argued that, while the idea of individuals registering their votes in technologically mediated referenda might be intrinsically appealing, there would always be the matter of who would set the questions to be decided, as well as what sorts of questions could realistically be posed. While, in principle, certain moral questions might be relatively straightforward, complex issues of social and economic policy would not be. There would need to be government bodies that would both set appropriate questions and interpret the results. Unless such bodies were themselves responsible to mass electorates, there would be the likelihood of a pseudo-democratic plebiscitarian state: "the system would conceal the real location of power and would thus enable 'democratic' governments to be more autocratic than they are now."[56]

But there is another aspect, one only hinted at by Macpherson here but that I believe is central to grasping the full significance of his position. The idea that direct democracy consists of continuous referenda decided by voters with, as Macpherson saw it, an electronic console beside every bed,[57] is based on the view that citizens are atomistic individual consumers. Democracy, in this view, is achieved by the aggregation of revealed preferences. If the possibility of a non-market participatory democracy that would avoid the dangers of a pseudo-democratic plebiscitarian system depended upon people coming to see themselves not as consumers and appropriators but rather as developers, exerters, and enjoyers of their capacities, this was in no small measure because the development and exercise of capacities would, in the nature of the case, "be done for the most part in conjunction with others, in some relation of community."[58] A liberal democracy that would see participation beyond the voting booth as only a matter of the provision of alternative vehicles for the expression of current and supposedly autonomous individual preferences forged in self-contained isolation would simply be an extended version of the equilibrium model. This would reinforce the image of individuals as consumers and not developers of their capacities. It would fail to provide the interactive, communicative context that is both the basis and outcome of the articulation and manifestation of one's capabilities as both personal and social qualities. It would fail, in other words, to facilitate the development of a participatory democratic system as more and other than merely a mechanism for choosing and authorizing governments.

I earlier suggested that Macpherson's models of democracy were palimpsests, a set of transparencies that were designed to highlight features of liberal democracy and its history. Elements from all four models – and indeed what Macpherson called their non-liberal democratic precursors as well – have played and continue to play a role in shaping the democratic imagination, the sense people at different times have come to acquire about democracy's meaning and its possibilities. One could say that the models were intended to highlight the political/institutional significance of both possessive individualism – protective and equilibrium democracy – and its other – developmental and participatory democracy. And while there is no guaranteed historical teleology at work, these models suggest a historical development that can be grasped in terms of both the development of material possibilities in the form of enhanced human productive capabilities, and an increasingly enriched normative insight into the conditions and requirements of free individual human agency. The culmination of this essentially dialectical process was, for Macpherson, the emergence of the twin challenges confronting citizens of liberal democratic states if the historical possibilities for (developmental) liberty and democracy were to be realized: the need for a change in consciousness from a self-understanding as infinite consumers and appropriators to that of developers, exerters, and enjoyers of their human capacities; and the need to dramatically reduce if not eliminate class-based economic and political inequalities and transform the capitalist relations that necessarily bred them.

The normative and structural challenges are not and must not be reducible one to the other. To collapse the structural question of inequality into the question of consciousness would be to repeat the error of developmental liberal democratic theory, especially in its twentieth-century idealist, pragmatist, or modified utilitarian forms. On the other hand, to collapse the normative into the structural, that is, to assume that formally abolishing classes would generate the requisite normative shift, would be to repeat the fatal error of Soviet-style socialism. In each case – and this must be stressed once again – the humanistic potential and demands of both liberalism and democracy would be denied or sacrificed.

Yet the two dimensions are linked and need to be considered and pursued together. Political theory and political economy, as we have seen, had to be joined. Structural change in the direction of greater equality could emerge only on the basis of political action shaped by popular consciousness of the costs, human and material, of capitalist development. This consciousness, in turn, had to take on board the demands and possibilities of developmental individualism. The demand for, and realization of, democracy that respects both the ethical principle of equal self-development and the need for communal relations of solidarity that undergird political action in pursuit of social goals would represent the critical measuring rod for the achievement of the synthesis of liberalism, as the right of each to equal self-development, and democracy, as a kind of society within which all are able to exercise their distinctive human capacities. For Macpherson there was no liberalism faithful to its historical possibilities without democracy. But there could be no democracy that realized *its* historical possibilities without (developmental) liberalism. This was why Macpherson concluded *The Life and Times of Liberal Democracy* with the claim that a participatory democracy in which "there remained a strong sense of the high value of the equal right to self-development ... would be in the best tradition of liberal democracy."[59]

C.B. Macpherson and Contemporary Democratic Theory

How should we view Macpherson's effort to undertake a revision of liberal democracy, "which clearly owes a good deal to Marx," in the context of contemporary democratic theory? There has been an enormous outpouring in recent years of both normative and empirical work on democracy. A full treatment of this work is beyond the scope of this chapter. But in the universe of democratic theory, there are recurring broad themes or approaches that can provide us with a reasonably comprehensive picture of its important concerns and commitments. These undergird accounts of what democracy can and should mean in the contemporary world.

As examples that give a sense of what might be called the texture of current democratic theory, I want to focus here on two recently published pieces by Seyla Benhabib and Nadia Urbinati, important and influential contemporary thinkers who have written extensively on democracy. I believe their work offers a useful way of both identifying key themes and limitations of contemporary democratic theory that Macpherson's work illuminates. Again, I must stress that my focusing on these pieces is intended to show how they exemplify trends in democratic theory, not to provide a full-scale overview of the field.

Seyla Benhabib has assumed prominence as both a democratic theorist and a critical theorist in the tradition of the Frankfurt School, in particular the work of Jürgen Habermas. Since I believe that there are significant affinities between Macpherson and the Frankfurt School, democratic and critical theory – indeed that the two entail each other – Benhabib's work is particularly apt. She has suggested that, in the ranks of critical theorists, there is a pronounced division over what critical theory can mean in the contemporary setting. Specifically, "the current generation of critical theorists is ... deeply divided among those who believe in continuing the crisis model of critiquing late capitalism (Axel Honneth and Nancy Fraser) on the one hand, and those who continue critique in the mode of normative reconstructions of liberal constitutional and democratic theory, on the other (Hauke Brunkhorst, Rainer Forst, William Scheuerman, and myself)."[60]

This separation of the critique of capitalism from the normative requirements of liberalism and democracy, which owes its origin to the distinctions Habermas drew between work and interaction, and later system and lifeworld, would have been rejected by both the first-generation critical theorists such as Horkheimer and Marcuse, and even to a significant if often ambiguous extent by Habermas himself, and by Macpherson. From the perspective of Macpherson's analysis, the separation would repeat the contradiction built within Mill's ethical liberalism and the developmental model, and in particular its later manifestation in the revisionist liberalism of John Rawls (to whose work the "reconstructive" branch of critical theory is clearly indebted). Of course critical theorists of democracy who undertake the reconstructive normative approach are not inclined to simply accept the hegemony of capitalist social relations. They often stress the importance of social rights, which entails some measure of economic regulation in the interests of distributive justice. But echoing certain themes also found in the work of Habermas, they tend to assume that the imperatives of the economic system in complex societies rule out anything more substantial in normatively informed conscious social direction of the processes of material reproduction. Certainly the classical socialist model whereby capitalist market forces were to be subjected to rational control by a social macro-subject is understandably ruled out (as it was, at least implicitly, by Macpherson). Yet it might be assumed that putting out of play a thoroughgoing critique of what Macpherson called the net transfer of powers and the property relations within which the transfer is embedded might well limit the critique both normatively and empirically. In other words, the kinds of democratic possibilities that a normative reconstruction must assume cannot be divorced, at least under contemporary conditions, from empirical constraints established by capitalist social relations.

To put matters in terms of Macpherson's analysis, the sort of critically informed normative reconstruction that Benhabib and others have in mind, which typically stresses deliberative and discursive relations among rights-bearing agents who enjoy equal (communicative) liberties, presumes some form of developmental individualism or developmental liberalism. Yet the conditions and possibilities of developmental individualism assume the working through of the immanent logic of possessive individualism – and this cannot be done without taking on board the nature and impact of possessive market relations. Separating the critique of capitalism and its crisis tendencies – especially in the current era, when global neoliberal capitalism most assuredly *is* in crisis – is another way of dividing Macpherson's work into possessive individualism and democracy. As I have tried to show throughout this study, I do not believe this distinction can stand up.

Moreover, if critical theory as the normative reconstruction of liberal constitutionalism and democracy is a descendant of the developmental model and ethical liberalism, it is vulnerable to the same charge of the lack of realism and even utopianism that afflicted its predecessor and resulted in the triumph of the equilibrium model. A current parallel might be the strength in both the academic and political and social worlds of rational choice liberal democracy, and in this particular context the rational choice critical theory of thinkers such as Joseph Heath, James Johnson, and Jack Knight.[61] This approach is clear about its assumption of self-interested maximization as the fundamental property of strategically rational individuals. In the face of the hegemony of capitalist market values, theorists of rational choice critical theory have staked a claim to realism that is difficult to refute without combining normative reconstruction with capitalist critique.[62] In this, they share something in common with proponents of the equilibrium model. And as with the "realism" of that model, the realism of rational choice comes at the cost of the occlusion of the normative and empirical issues of a humanist democratic order.

From a somewhat different perspective – she does not link her treatment of democracy to the tradition of critical theory – Nadia Urbinati has also sought to provide a normative reconstruction of a robust democracy adequate to contemporary conditions and challenges. In a recent essay authored by Urbinati and Maria Paula Saffon, they argue that what they call proceduralist democracy, whereby "proceduralism defines democracy as the very political process that puts it in motion," offers the best normative defence of democracy and its possibilities and promises. This is because of its "unbeatable capacity to protect and promote equal political liberty." Saffon and Urbinati contrast procedural democracy with epistemic democracy, which "is dissatisfied with procedural democracy because it neglects the quest for truth," thereby "merging consent and truth," and populism, which disclaims proceduralism "in the name of a more spontaneous and direct consensus than that achieved by the rules of the game" and thus seeks to establish "a deeper unification of the masses, preferably under a charismatic leader." They also distinguish their model from the "minimalist" proceduralism of Joseph Schumpeter, who, they argue, "explicitly renounced the normative value of the democratic method" and "portrayed democracy as an instrument devoid of intrinsic worth."[63]

Avowedly dedicated to representative institutions and the vigorous partisan competition they (ideally) facilitate and require, proceduralist democratic theory

> insists that equal political liberty is the most important good for which democracy should strive. And it posits that the modern democratic procedure – based on every individual's equal participation in fair and competitive elections for selecting political representatives and thereby contributing to the production of decisions by majority – is the best way of respecting equal liberty in a context of pluralism and dissent. Equal liberty implies not only the right to participate in politics via voting and freely expressing one's mind but doing so under equal conditions of opportunity, which entails protecting civil, political, and basic social rights with the aim of ensuring a meaningful equal participation.

Suspicious of any claims that there is or can be a substantial and unified popular will to which democracy must give full expression, proceduralist democracy, with its assumption of pluralism of both values and groups, accepts and even legitimizes robust conflict: "The robustness of political conflict is good for democracy, since it illustrates that no group has sufficient power to excessively influence decision making." This conflict ideally finds expression in electoral competition in principle open to all, where majorities and minorities can form and reform under conditions of equal liberty and equal participation, and where parties bring competing interests and ideologies into the political arena. Partisan political leaders strive for legal authorization to represent citizens who are the final judges of their work. Citizens do so as bearers of equal liberty, which "consists not only in political competition between factions but also in the effective participation of all individuals in defining the results of that competition. Liberty is made possible through equality in political rights, which entails the right to participate through voicing opinions and organizing to make them effective, and a basic equality of opportunities that can make participation matter evenly."[64]

As the guarantee of equal liberty, procedural democracy – with its parliamentary institutions, principles of majority rule and protection of minority rights, and multiparty competition – is self-legitimating. It cannot and ought not to be judged by external criteria, epistemic or populist. Opinion, not truth; decision-making by contestable majority rule, not consensus – these qualities define proceduralist democracy in the context of equal liberty. As "an open game of uncertainty," democracy "makes of fallibility a good, by making all decisions open to change, and hence preventing mistakes from becoming permanent … people should participate in democracy not because they are capable of making correct decisions, but because their participation minimizes the rise of power abuse."[65]

There is undoubtedly much that is salutary in this position. Saffon and Urbinati acknowledge that their notion of equal liberty is akin to Habermas's notion of autonomy, with both linked to self-rule through participation.[66] Habermas's conception of the equal status and mutual determination of private and public autonomy has, in turn, clear parallels with Macpherson's conceptions of counter-extractive and developmental liberty. Equal liberty or autonomy is a worthy aspiration that must find a place in all democratic theory and democratic societies.

Also valuable is Saffon and Urbinati's argument about the unavoidability of conflict and the danger of suppressing it, and potentially oppressing those who engage in it, in the supposed interests of achieving a common will. Recalling Bachrach and Baratz, the two faces of power and decisions and non-decisions, they claim that the positive features of procedural democracy "only make sense if democracy channels and decides most of the significant conflicts existing in society … If, despite the formal operation of democracy, the most relevant decisions of society are taken outside of it, democracy becomes trivial. This can induce citizens to think that participating in democracy is irrelevant for their interests or their liberty, making them apathetic and docile, and hence a potential instrument of the stronger. Democracy can thus become a facade of clientelism or technocracy, and the representative system a theater for an audience that has no control, only visual attendance."[67]

But this very point suggests the problem with the analysis offered by Saffon and Urbinati. As was the case with Benhabib, their exercise in normative reconstruction misses the mark in a way that highlights what

I see as the continuing relevance of Macpherson's position. Consider the following claims they make:

- "Democracy is better than any other form of government not because it produces good decisions, but because it allows us to feel directly responsible for the decisions we make. We are autonomous under democracy because we obey our own laws, and because 'we set the agenda' concerning the types of problems that we want to decide upon."[68]
- "Democracy's capacity to internalize threats of rebellion and to induce incumbents' moderation implies an implicit capacity to limit power. True, elections allow a temporal majority to rule over minorities and to impose their particular preference. However, under the democratic equilibrium, this dominant stance is restricted by the existence of an opposition that may, someday, become the majority. This can lead the numerical majority to be aware, while in power, of the possibility of becoming a minority in the future, and therefore to respect the rights of the current minority with the expectation that it may be similarly treated when it becomes the minority. Hence, democracy as a self-enforcing equilibrium does not only impede violence, it also constrains power."[69]
- "Historically, the establishment or widening of democracy has typically involved the exclusion of some – the property-less, women, or currently immigrants. But such exclusion has been difficult to maintain and has often ended up being transitory. Once granted, democratic concessions signal to the excluded that they, too, could be their beneficiaries. This can lead them to feel wrongly excluded and motivate them to struggle for inclusion. Democracy is thus expansive by nature. As such, although democratic procedures provide stability to the competitive political system, they do not foster the status quo. To the contrary, they are safe and predictable tools for changing the established majority, which gives citizens the sense of having the capacity to be in control of their society."[70]

As normative commitments, these claims are hard to criticize, and Saffon and Urbinati's purpose is to explicitly justify procedural democracy on normative grounds. Yet even acknowledging this, these claims require at least some sense of the conditions of their own possibility. This means that the socio-historical context has to be brought directly and explicitly into the formulation of the normative standards. To cite

Max Horkheimer once again, "The unity of such concepts results less from the invariability of their elements than from the historical development of the circumstances under which their realization is necessary." Macpherson's attempt to (re)connect political theory and political economy speaks directly to this issue. And claiming that the criteria for procedural democracy rooted in equal liberty "allow us to evaluate existing political systems in terms of the extent to which they fulfill or approach the standard of equal liberty, and hence of their 'degree of democracy,'"[71] does not accomplish the task. Viewing the critical role of concepts as comparing existing political systems to the normative demands of (procedural) democracy fails to address the historically situated hermeneutic or interpretive dimension in terms of which those who must carry the democratic project come to acquire the self-understandings and accompanying commitments essential to make democracy a living reality.

This is the matter that Macpherson's treatment of ontology helps illuminate. Saffon and Urbinati eschew this issue, no doubt because, for them, a theory of democracy is, in a manner of speaking, political and not metaphysical, and because such considerations suggest that democracy ought to be evaluated by external criteria. In this case ontology would likely represent an illicit epistemic standard. However, ontology cannot easily be avoided, if at all. Indeed Saffon and Urbinati's frequent references to individual preferences imply something like self-interested rational maximization as a driving force in individual behaviour. However, this is never made explicit, much less highlighted; nor is there any suggestion, either, that democracy might require and facilitate developmental possibilities of the sort Macpherson explored.

This, I think, gives to Saffon and Urbinati's account some of the characteristics of protective democracy along with elements of a protective republicanism, notably the idea of participation, rooted in equal liberty, as a bulwark against the abuse of power. But there is something else, no doubt unintended and likely unnoticed in this account. If the "rules of the game" by which everyone must abide in order to ensure equal liberty, potential rotation in office, and thus changeable majorities and minorities, the limitation of violence, if not its outright elimination, the control of power, and so forth, are the essence of procedural democracy and give it its normative weight, then the question arises of who makes the rules and who interprets and enforces them. It will not do to claim they are self-enforcing and re-enforcing. Some agency, formal or informal, necessarily takes on this role. If we assume that in the "real world" of liberal democratic states, in which there are socially weighted differences in the capacity and willingness to participate – and evidence suggests this is currently a major and increasingly serious problem – then the "rules" as structured must play a role in maintaining and legitimizing this state of affairs. A theory of procedural democracy giving normative pride of place to them becomes, in effect, a version of elite theory – to be sure, a more subtle version, in that the elite is less in the open.[72] This is, I believe, a strong implication of Saffon and Urbinati's analysis, in spite of their distancing their views from those of Schumpeter and "minimalist" democratic theory.

Moreover, and this further highlights their own minimalism, as well as the implicit elitism of their model, while Saffon and Urbinati dismiss truth and the idea of a unified popular will as incompatible with procedural democracy, and indeed threatening to it, people do think of political issues, at least to some degree, in terms of both. No doubt, from the proceduralist perspective, commitments to truth and a common will are "preferences" to be aggregated, reconciled, and tamed in the give-and-take of vigorous partisan competition (another element of the elite theory). But by, in effect, identifying such commitments as "preferences," this analysis slights the motives that arguably shape the willingness to participate and give it meaning. It diminishes the communicative dimensions of intact relations to self and other that potentially render politics capable of facilitating the articulation of developmental aspirations and the pursuit of developmental possibilities. Without some (pre)conception of them, it is hard to see why the common bonds essential for any coherent and workable democratic order would be possible or matter. Here Macpherson's attempt to at least consider the idea of potentially non-contentious human capacities as the central element of his developmental ontology, and thus of democracy as a kind of society, is very much to the point.

And if truth and a unified popular will – epistemic and populist versions of democracy – are illegitimate from the point of view of a normatively superior proceduralist democracy,[73] then we are back at the implicit if not hidden elitism of the model. There have to be "gatekeepers" ready and able to detect the presence of these destructive elements and to ensure they are suitably purged of their threatening qualities, if not eliminated altogether. Again, powerful interests would in all likelihood carry out this task via the mechanisms of social power within and outside of the democratic system.

I am not saying the problems or threats Saffon and Urbinati identify are not real; nor would have Macpherson said so. Indeed, as earlier noted, he was no dewy-eyed optimist about democracy – there were forces at work that threatened it, including authoritarian and plebiscitarian possibilities that would make a mockery of claims to democratic legitimacy. But we need a far richer account than offered here of what these threats are and where and how they might emerge. Such an account, I suggest, cannot take shape where the normative and descriptive, the justificatory and explanatory, are separated.

I think that ultimately much contemporary democratic theory is really a defence of liberalism. There is a real fear that liberalism is supposedly always at risk in the face of popular, democratic forces that can get out of hand. There remains in such thinking something of a residue of Cold War ideology. To be sure, Saffon and Urbinati follow Norberto Bobbio in arguing against the thesis that liberalism and democracy stand at odds, that democracy is a form of "brute power that only liberalism can tame." Yet their democracy is such only as "a constitutionalized form of politics" where power is limited by the rules of the procedural game. They go on to argue that, although historically "democratic movements had to fight – even violently – to make liberalism accept democracy, the latter is a 'natural extension' of liberalism."[74] But this raises the question: which liberalism? As Domenico Losurdo has compellingly argued, the history of liberalism is more complex. Liberalism has been associated with rights and the dignity of the individual; it has also comported with slavery, racism, and imperialism.[75] Here, too, Macpherson, with his analysis of the twin and frequently intertwined dimensions of liberalism as possessive and developmental, and his efforts to link liberalism's fate with that of capitalism, has something valuable to add to the discussion.

Democracy is everywhere threatened, not, or not only, by populist insurgencies fuelled by demagogic and charismatic leaders, or by supposedly truth-determining, technocratic "experts" or truth-driven leaders and movements promoting a democratic perfectionism, in the process trumping decisions reached by popular engagement in the democratic process. It is threatened overwhelmingly by unaccountable centres of social power rooted in the dynamics of global capitalism and the states that sustain and legitimize it. Indeed, the first two threats or challenges may plausibly be seen as consequences of the dynamics of global capitalism, rather than autonomous forces.[76] In the face of this challenge, normative theories of democracy such as those of Benhabib and Saffon and Urbinati, whatever their strengths, seem disappointingly incapable of offering guidance. They go hand-in-hand with the sovereigntist and cosmopolitan images of the politics of human rights that James Ingram explores; indeed they may be thought the bases of these. And they are vulnerable to the same criticisms. In this light, Macpherson's critique of democratic theory, his account of the themes that such a theory should address, continues to merit a hearing.

Chapter Six

Political Theory, Social Science, and Social Critique: C.B. Macpherson, Philosophy, and Methodology

Throughout this study I have argued that the political thought of C.B. Macpherson displays what I have called a suppressed philosophical dimension. In other words, I have sought to demonstrate that there is an essentially systematic, meta-conceptual basis and framework for his specific concepts and ideas, and that this dimension gives these concepts richness and meaning. Borrowing from Erica Sherover-Marcuse, I have suggested that it is possible and worthwhile to identify and distinguish a theory from a body of thought, and to disengage the former from the latter. The idea is to highlight aspects of a thinker's overall orientation to the phenomena with which he or she is engaged that could further our understanding of key categories or concepts and suggest actual and possible contexts for their articulation.

As a result of this approach, I have argued that Macpherson's work had much in common with that of the Frankfurt School and in particular its first generation, notably Max Horkheimer and Herbert Marcuse. Without, for the most part, an explicitly articulated meta-theoretical or methodological framework, Macpherson nonetheless provided his own distinct version of critical (versus traditional) theory. This was, I argued, particularly evident in his treatment of possessive individualism. This signal concept should not or not only be understood as a description of the assumptions held by theorists in the English liberal tradition. Rather, it should be seen as a normatively enriched category of articulation that allows us to appreciate the dilemmas, social pathologies and historical possibilities, and necessities that have emerged from the development and entrenchment of capitalist market relations. Unpacking the concept of possessive individualism leads immanently via the generation of ontological postulates to the nature and possibility of a democratic society within which all are equally able to develop and exercise their distinctively human capacities. In other words, the requirements of democracy can come into view only via the critical appraisal that possessive individualism subtended.

I argued in chapter 2 that this theoretical commitment, implied or embedded, suggested a strong affinity with Max Horkheimer's conception of critical theory as laid out in his landmark essay, "Traditional and Critical Theory." To recall, traditional theory sought to establish the sum total of universally applicable propositions about a subject that took the form of a unified set of logical deductions whose truth was guaranteed by the impartial objective vantage point of an external observer. By contrast, critical theory saw theory and theorist as intertwined with the historically conditioned social process, with both formed and transformed by a changing historical reality. This reality possessed a normative thrust or slope because it is inextricably linked to the practical activity of humans, who are themselves shaped by normatively charged aspirations for a fulfilled and fulfilling life. Critical theory both identified with, and offered an immanent critique of, the commitments and practices of historically situated agents with a view to clarifying from the participants' perspective the historical effort to establish a rational social order adequate to human powers and needs. Its concepts, then, possessed changing historical content, even as they retained common features that rendered them communicatively accessible across time and space.[1]

Far from undermining the scientific basis of social analysis, from the point of view of the architects of critical theory their approach secured it. The problem with the concepts of traditional theory – often labelled positivism – is that, absent an appreciation of their social and historical content, the attributes of these concepts become arbitrary. The failure to embed one's categories in the social context within which they have been generated and function prevents the fullest analysis and account of phenomena that are the hallmarks of science. Moreover, the lack of self-reflexivity by the theorist or social scientist who fails to see one's connection to the agents and circumstances that one engaged means that one's own social role is obscured. And both aspects of the inability to address and account for social conditioning, namely, of concepts and of the role of the analyst, are themselves socially conditioned. They manifest the presence and power of reification.

For the theorist, breaking through the appearances thrust up by the process of reification and getting hold of the forces that drive it entails, as I argued in chapter 2, not a value-free external account that, while presenting itself as objective, would in reality be narrowly subjective, thereby avoiding the demands of both objectivity and subjectivity. Rather, it would be an elucidation of the social process in its interconnections and its developmental tendencies. Proceeding in this way facilitates capturing or recapturing the constellation of elements that define concepts, and why these elements might do so. In the measure that such elements, now put into motion, demonstrate tensions, they broaden the range of socially relevant material that the analyst or theorist might take on board in order to provide the fullest account of social life, its predicaments and possibilities. In other words, conceptual tensions express and reinforce social tensions.

Thus there remains considerable value in the "existential judgment" Max Horkheimer attributed to critical theory: that the current commodity form of the economy generates and regenerates the tensions and contradictions of the modern era, to the point that the development of the system, which holds the promise of liberation from the demands of compulsive labour and domination, instead reinforces both at ever higher levels and so undermines the very gains in freedom and reason it has brought about. Critical theory sets out, then, to diagnose the social pathologies of the contemporary era, typically by laying out potentially stark alternatives: either democratic advance or social decline.

As we have seen, Macpherson largely shared this position. It is evident in the ways he pointed out the historically rooted challenges, threats, and contradictions he thought confronted social actors. Hence he wrote in *Democracy in Alberta* that the "quasi-party system may thus be considered either the final stage of the deterioration of the capitalist democratic tradition, or a way of saving what can be saved of liberal-democracy from the threatening encroachment of a one-party state."[2] And in one of his last published writings he offered this claim about the likely fate of the concept of economic justice: "It will struggle along for some decades yet in the capitalist countries (and longer in the Third World) until in the advanced countries it is either brought down entirely by a totalitarian or corporatist state, or transcended in a new society by a concept of human fulfilment which will surpass the concept of economic justice."[3] There are other examples. These were intended as social diagnoses and points of orientation in the present for social actors, theorists, and scientists, and not as causal predictions. They were interpretive rather than apodictic. As interpretive guides they hold considerable merit.[4]

Yet even given what I believe is significant if not always explicit evidence of Macpherson's "Continental" proclivities, Macpherson betrayed little specific interest in developing this line of thought. He was content to work within what he took to be the boundaries of Anglo-American liberalism from a critical vantage point shaped by certain Marxian assumptions. This gave his work its distinctive tincture and served his stated purposes well.

However, if I am right about his suppressed philosophical dimension, Macpherson's concepts "overshot" their targets – and this is what makes him valuable as a source of critical insight in the present. He may have worked within the liberal tradition, but he was not bound to it. His approach, though, tended to mask this relationship. In chapter 2 I noted Alkis Kontos's criticism that by framing his ontological postulates – humans understood as either infinite consumers and appropriators or as developers and exerters of their distinctive capacities – exclusively in relation to the liberal tradition and what he took to be its fundamental alternatives, Macpherson limited the role ontology could and should play in fostering critical insight into contemporary social pathologies and challenges.

In a comparable analysis, Ian Angus has argued that there is a key ambiguity in Macpherson's contrast between the utilitarian, possessive conception of individualism and the developmental alternative.[5] Angus attributes it to Macpherson having overlooked the distinctive epistemological bases of his two ontological postulates. The utilitarian perspective is grounded in an empiricist epistemology that sustains a consumerist ethic, while developmental individualism draws upon an idealist epistemology that supports autonomy. While Macpherson saw the conflict between the two ontologies, his failure to systematically engage the epistemological issues prevented him from seeing something equally important: that both utilitarian and developmental ethics support within liberalism a commitment to private property. The former justifies it as the basis of expanding productivity in the service of ever-growing human desires. The latter does so on the grounds that private property supports autonomy by permitting individuals to embody their wills in the external world. The idealist/autonomist defence is unconditional and thus stronger than the empiricist/utilitarian view. By failing to take on the epistemological issues involved, Macpherson could not do full justice to his own insights. Given his own autonomist commitments, he needed to deal with both the utilitarian and autonomist justifications of private property.

> So Macpherson's two principles rely on different epistemologies and involve two different justifications of private property (and hence market society). In particular, the principle of self-development is also tied to market assumptions and cannot be counter-posed to the utilitarian ethic as the foundation of a critique of market society. Indeed, in order to develop one's capacities, one must have an exclusive right to them. At the very least, a critique based on autonomy and self-development would have to show how this ethic could be disentangled from its historical justification of private property – a task Macpherson does not address ... One can argue that liberalism must rediscover the self-development principle that was originally present in natural law. But it cannot be simply opposed to consumerism, since in this case they have a common basis ... And, as noted earlier, the market assumptions must be traced and criticized also in the "autonomy" tradition.[6]

This argument is telling (William Leiss made a somewhat comparable point in his debate with Macpherson on the question of ontology and false needs). I do think Macpherson went some way to at least implicitly address both the utilitarian and autonomist defence of private property in his treatment of property as a cornerstone of a democratic society. Angus notes that Marx sought to supersede both the consumerist and autonomist positions via his account of labour. Macpherson would no doubt have agreed.

But while I certainly concur that Macpherson bequeathed us important ambiguities in his work, I have a somewhat different take on what it could mean to explore and clarify them. Angus seeks to identify and illuminate what he views as Macpherson's *missing* philosophical dimension, as opposed to what I have called his *suppressed* dimension. Certainly there is overlap between our approaches and conceptions of the task; both of us believe that the idealist or Continental dimensions of Macpherson's work were important and needed more systematic treatment. However, Angus wishes to strengthen Macpherson's project by finding a better way to incorporate the principle of self-development, currently muted in both liberal theory and practice, into a revamped and renewed liberalism more adequate to the requirements of a post-market society. This means that empiricism and idealism, and the consumerism and autonomism they subtend, must be analysed and transcended in a critique of contemporary society that takes leave of market assumptions. This is where Macpherson's missing philosophical critique should be filled in.

Yet, even given Angus's insights, I would still hold that the idea of a suppressed philosophical dimension, rather than a missing one, more successfully captures both Macpherson's intent and his contemporary relevance. As I earlier noted, many liberal critics of Macpherson see him as "one of us" – a liberal, if one in a bit of a hurry. This is certainly not the view of Ian Angus, who wants to move Macpherson beyond liberalism to a non-market theory of democracy still faithful to individualist values, as indeed Macpherson himself desired. However, perhaps ironically, his position ends up sharing something in common with that of the liberals. He seems to hold the view that Macpherson's commitment to liberalism, even in the improved and enriched form he gave it, was, in a manner of speaking, self-contained. Put otherwise, Angus appears to accept that the concept of possessive individualism is a description of the commitments held by important thinkers in the liberal tradition, rather than an internally contradictory articulation that always and already points beyond itself as a normatively charged core of the self-understanding of individual agents embedded in a specific historical form of social life. Therefore, for Angus, to move towards a non-market society required something like an external critical vantage point.

By contrast I have attempted to argue throughout this book that in fact Macpherson's critique of liberalism was immanent: given its historically embedded commitments, the very logic of liberalism necessarily required that it transcend itself, so to speak, in a radical democracy, while retaining its historical achievements. *And the roots of these achievements themselves can already be detected in Hobbes and Locke, however much they covered them over with their commitments to the possessive side of individualism.* (I think Angus implicitly acknowledges this.) I do not think that Macpherson's analyses of property and human rights, for example, can be fully grasped or appreciated otherwise. Marx, of course, represented that transcendence. But his meaning and significance for Macpherson cannot be understood apart from his project of developing a theory of a radical participatory democracy that could still be called liberal. To repeat: Macpherson was neither a pure liberal nor a pure Marxist but a synthesis of both. His synthesis of liberalism and socialism was such that each required the other.

Once again I want to be clear that I see great value in Angus's approach. Macpherson did need to more explicitly address the Continental elements embedded in his work, and that would include the autonomist defence of private property. However – and I acknowledge that this is clearly challengeable – I continue to claim that the

Continental perspective is in important ways already there. It does not need to be provided from the outside.

The arguments of Kontos, Angus, and others clearly suggest that Macpherson's work poses important issues of methodology. So what indeed can we say about Macpherson's relation to methodology? Does it make sense to pursue this line of inquiry, especially given that Macpherson himself devoted relatively little explicit attention to it? In what follows I attempt to offer tentative answers to these questions.

C.B. Macpherson and the Critique of Social Science

I should begin by immediately offering a qualification. When I suggest that Macpherson devoted relatively little attention to questions of methodology or meta-methodology, I do not mean to imply that he was utterly indifferent to such questions. In fact a canvass of his body of work reveals an ongoing, if less than extensive, concern with the social sciences, and in particular political science.[7] And while he did not give much attention to specific techniques of research and evaluation, he did demonstrate considerable interest in the theoretical assumptions he thought shaped the objects of research and the questions posed by organized political inquiry. He saw, in other words, a social function beyond the disinterested quest for knowledge. In terms of analytic approach, he was deeply concerned about the tendency for political scientists to adopt the assumptions of mainstream, neo-classical economics, supposedly in the interests of greater scientific exactitude and validity. In terms of the practice of political science, and indeed other social sciences, he was interested in the historical roots and vicissitudes of the identities and purposes taken on by these forms of inquiry. In his concern with both dimensions, which he saw as linked, he once again demonstrated, I believe, his affinities with critical theory and the social content of social science, including its role in either sustaining or challenging existing relations of power.

Macpherson offered his most explicit account of the analytic approach in "Market Concepts in Political Theory." Although originally published in 1961, the essay demonstrates considerable contemporary relevance. Its task was to identify and assess the impact of the discipline of economics on a political science in search of scientific credibility. What commended – and indeed still commends – mainstream, neoclassical economics to political scientists was its elegance and supposed rigour, which was associated with the idea (and ideal) of equilibrium and the possibility of a general theory of the economic process. Equilibrium emerged from the workings of a determinate system whereby calculations made by rational maximizing individual agents generated prices that in turn constituted an objective system of values. This system guided those same individuals in making choices about how best to maximize returns from the deployment of their resources. "Large numbers of independent decisions issued in prices, while the prices determined the decisions in the sense that every decision had to be that which, given the prevailing prices, was calculated to maximize the gain of the person deciding ... The whole thing was a determinate system which tended to equilibrium, in that prices tended to be just what would induce buyers to buy what was produced and producers to produce what would be bought."[8]

With such a conceptual framework it was possible to infer causal connections, a unified set of propositions taking the form of a unified set of deductions – the essence of traditional theory. The appeal of economics to political scientists already inclined to view the democratic political system as an analogue of the market and its price system – that is, to those themselves committed to traditional theory – was in the circumstances understandable. It offered the prospect of a general theory of the political process as also a determinate system, while at the same time respecting liberal values inasmuch as the individual wills that drove the system were not themselves determined. The refinement and increasing precision of equilibrium theory bearing the impact of marginal utility analysis, which itself reinforced the atomistic assumptions of both neoclassical economics and political science, only strengthened its appeal.

As we have already seen, the equilibrium assumptions taken on by political scientists formed the core of the equilibrium, or pluralist-elitist-equilibrium, model of democracy. The democratic political system was seen to be relevantly like the market and its price system, where the supply of political goods was equated with the political demands of individual consumers: "Because of the competition between parties for votes and between voters for governmental action favourable to themselves, the system tends to produce just that set of decisions (or, that allocation of political goods) which the citizens are willing to pay for in expenditure of political energy and other resources."[9]

Much of the essay is subsequently devoted to exploring the implications of the equilibrium model and is familiar: the occlusion of class by the assumption of individual maximizing agents holding undifferentiated demand schedules whose plural preferences could be aggregated by parties and interest groups; the role of party systems in moderating and containing the opposition of class interests; and the overall relevance of the theory to expanding and prosperous capitalist democracies in which plural interests could trump class concerns. In the context of the discussion here, the key point was that theoretical generality was purchased at the cost of realism: the equilibrium model could not account for either the communist systems of the time or the non-capitalist, non-communist developing nations in Africa and Asia. And its occlusion of class, even in expanding and prosperous capitalist democracies where class consciousness was muted and to which the theory was primarily directed, meant that it was unhistorical and hence misleading. "The trouble with the equilibrium theory of democracy, we may conclude, is that, like the economists' marginal utility theory, it leaves out of account the historical determinants of effective demand. It treats class interests in advanced countries, and national aspirations in advancing countries, as just one among many kinds of political pressure. In doing so it averts its thoughts from the most serious problems of democracy."[10] One could call this the cost of elegance.

So the analogy with the market as an explanatory model for the political system was at best superficial. For that matter, as Macpherson saw it at the time, even some economists had taken issue with pure price theory and equilibrium analysis and recognized the role of organized power blocs in determining economic outcomes. Political science, however, was going the other way: "As economics adopts power concepts in a search for realism, political science adopts market concepts in a search for theoretical elegance."[11] It is an open question whether what Macpherson viewed then as economists' reinvigorated quest for realism is evident now, although there are, to be sure, a significant number of dissenting economists. But the search by many political scientists for a theoretical elegance modelled on neoclassical economic thought very much continues today.

And it was not just the loss of realism, in the sense that the otherwise evident existence of power blocs in both the economy and the polity was covered over by general abstract claims about human behaviour. The misleading attribution of (free) market characteristics to the political system was the other side of the failure to recognize the extent to which the market *had* penetrated liberal democratic thought in its most avowedly normative, non-market domain: its ethical dimension. This is, of course, the basic formula for possessive individualism, "namely, that the individual personality (which is the supreme value in the liberal tradition) consists of capacities which the individual *owns*, and for which he owes nothing to society." And the implications for liberal democracy are clear: "The justification of liberal democracy still rests, and must rest, on the ultimate value of the free self-developing individual. But in so far as freedom is still seen as possession, as freedom from any but market relations with others, it can scarcely serve as the ultimate value of modern democracy."[12]

So "political theorists have paid too much attention to the superficial analogy between the market and the political process at the operative level, and not enough attention to the market concept at the deeper level of the postulates about the nature of society and the nature of human freedom."[13] In light of his overall analysis of possessive individualism and its relation to liberal democracy and theory, this claim is understandable. Yet, in a way that suggests what I earlier argued was the case in his account in "The Economic Penetration of Political Theory," I do not think he quite got it right here, and this is another indication of Macpherson's suppressed philosophical dimension. It is clear what he meant by a superficial and therefore misleading analogy. The analogy is with a free market theory that takes as both theoretically elegant and practically realistic the idea that the economy is driven by the decisions of free, equal, and rational individuals. There are no permanent (class) concentrations of power, emerging from the economic process itself, that tilt market outcomes. These outcomes are inherently just, or, in any event, necessary. Such a model obscures or denies the socio-historical determinants of capitalist market relations.

Yet at another level, the analogy is anything but superficial. Without perhaps realizing it, or in any event without explicitly addressing it, Macpherson demonstrated the strength of this analogy in a brief but fascinating discussion of marginal utility analysis based on Anthony Downs's classic *Economic Theory of Democracy*. Specifically, he identified two propositions emerging from Downs's work. One was the tendency of political parties to discourage rational voter behaviour by offering ambiguous platforms that rendered judgments of their merit difficult, if not opaque. It was rational for parties to do so in the interest of broadening their potential bases of support. But in limiting the capacity of voters to distinguish policy options in a rational way, the system brought other non-rational or even irrational factors into play that in the extreme could threaten democracy itself. (And one could assume that, with the development of increasingly sophisticated and expensive contemporary polling and advertising methods – the rise of what has been called the money-and-media election complex – this tendency has only been exacerbated.[14])

The other proposition was that, although a liberal democratic political system was designed to distribute political power equally, in fact if voters behaved rationally, power would be unequal, because of the differential costs of obtaining the information necessary for the rational appraisal of political options. This meant that for some voters, the overwhelming probability that any one individual's vote would have little impact on overall political outcomes made the cost of acquiring this information greater than its benefits. It was therefore rational for such individuals to avoid paying these costs and to rely instead on the biased information of some interested agency – again a process likely exacerbated by contemporary political technologies. One could call this the "truth" of apathy as a consumer "preference," a truth Macpherson had attempted to critically dissect in his account of apathy and democracy.

From these two propositions, Macpherson drew a pointed and incisive conclusion: "To the extent that politicians are rational, voters cannot be so; to the extent that voters are rational they cannot have the equal effective demand that democratic theory asserts; if all men are rational there cannot be a rational democracy."[15] He argued that this made the market concept of democracy self-contradictory. But if the market *concept* was self-contradictory, this was because a capitalist democratic *society* was also self-contradictory. Citizens were caught up in the tension between possessive and developmental individualism.

Moreover, in a manner that prefigured current theoretical issues about the ways in which not just political decisions are made but political subjects are formed through political action, Macpherson noted that, aside from equilibrating the supply of and demand for political goods, the political system "has to produce and sustain a government. That is, it has recurrently to confer on identifiable persons the power to make (and the responsibility for making) the laws and orders by which political goods are distributed."[16] In the measure that the market concept of democracy fails to capture this dimension of the democratic system, it cannot deal with structures as well as processes, and the ways in which these are complexly related. It cannot deal with the inherently normative slope or dimension of practices that, grasped externally, appear to be objectively given by the nature of things. It can only view political institutions as impersonal, market-like mechanisms without any formative capacity of their own – in other words, strictly as vehicles for possessive self-assertion on the part of individuals. As we have seen, from Macpherson's point of view it could not accomplish what the classical theory of the state did. It failed to deal with the historical conditions under which market behaviour was possible and the alternatives denied in light of the potential for individual self-development; that is, it could not show how contexts of action were formed and recreated. For this, a theory of the state was indispensable. This necessarily meant that one had to confront ontological issues as elements of social scientific analysis. The denial of reality in pursuit of theoretical elegance by both economists and political scientists was itself a product of that reality.

Macpherson further addressed the analytic commitments of a political science enthralled by neoclassical economics in "After Strange Gods: Canadian Political Science 1973."[17] This essay surveyed the discipline of political science in the wake of its massive growth during the previous two decades, both in numbers of academics and in the expansion of fields and sub-fields of study, which brought with them substantial increases in research output and graduate education. Macpherson's starting point was consideration of a survey of Canadian political scientists and what he saw as gaps or lacunae in both its content and implications. One element involved what he took to be a serious underestimation of the work being done by political theorists in Canada that had achieved international recognition. He also noted that the survey was virtually a direct copy of one administered in the United States by the American Political Science Association. This led him to wonder whether Canadian political science had been undergoing a process of Americanization that could significantly affect how Canadian political scientists studied and understood their own society.

But the most significant focus of the essay involved once again a comparison with the current state of economics. Macpherson cited one comprehensive review of Canadian political science that appraised the discipline on the basis of its contributions to an understanding of Canadian politics, without addressing Canadian contributions to non-Canadian fields of scholarship. By contrast he noted that an equivalent contemporary assessment, by the distinguished Canadian-born neoclassical economist Harry Johnson, sought to evaluate Canadian contributions to economics, which was seen as, and accepted as, a universal science.

Echoing his argument in "Market Concepts in Political Theory," Macpherson explained this difference as a reflection of the fact that economics had evolved a general theory, neoclassical, microeconomic, in relation to which new work had to be assessed, wherever it appeared. In spite of efforts to move in this direction, notably in the area of systems theory, political science had been unable to develop a comparable general theory.

Macpherson's response to the question of why political science had been unable to develop such a theory reached back to the heart of his account of the task of political theory/science that had its origins in his landmark treatment of Hobbes and the problem of deducing value from fact – in other words, the relation of traditional to critical theory. As he had argued in "Market Concepts in Political Theory," the problem was not so much the quest for a general theory as such but rather one that was elegant, rigorous, universal, and deductive. The inherent normativity of any realistic political science made this task impossible. The fate of what passed for a general, if largely unarticulated, theory of politics at the time, namely, the pluralist-elitist-equilibrium model, was instructive in this respect. So any plausible general theory would have to incorporate not simply explanation but evaluation in its very structure.

However, developments within both the discipline of political science and the larger society of which it formed an element, and to which many of its practitioners contributed by virtue of "the unconcerned willingness of members of the political science establishment to sell themselves to the highest bidders – in the wealthiest countries often the government itself"[18] reinforced the separation of explanation and evaluation or justification. Hence it was no surprise that political science had, to that point, failed to come up with a general theory. To some considerable extent, this reflected a developing post–Second World War focus on political behaviour and thus an increasing concern with parties, movements, pressure groups, elections, and voting. There were so many empirical data in these areas of research to be acquired and organized that the task of developing a general theory could safely be deferred, if not set aside.

But for Macpherson the more fundamental explanation was to be found in the social context of political and social science, "the aggressive, bourgeois, individualist culture, which has been at its strongest in North America, especially in the United States, during the whole period when the tone of current political science was set." He went on to argue that such a society "neither demands nor welcomes serious discussions of the extent to which the going political system serves defensible social purposes and values. Nor does it want fundamental explications of the way its governing mechanisms actually work as functioning parts of the whole society. The first activity might call too much into question; the second might reveal too much. Such a society does not want the political system to be *understood*. It is, however, happy to have the system's superficial performance *measured*." To be sure, as Macpherson had argued in his account of equilibrium democracy, the prevailing analytic paradigm into which the empirical data were fitted – "the pluralist model of society and the brokerage model of the political system" – that was widely accepted in both the United States and Canada was not completely wrong. Such models "do fit quite well any society – like the American and Canadian up till now – which is affluent, market-oriented, materially individualist, and careless of the consequences."[19] But as we have seen when Macpherson offered this analysis, there was considerable evidence of increasing, and increasingly widespread, dissatisfaction with this society, its values, practices, and institutions. Supposedly pluralist harmony was giving way, at least to some significant degree, to social polarization. Even prominent mainstream political scientists such as David Easton, who served as president of the American Political Science Association, noted this and argued the need for the discipline to more fully and effectively address social and political issues. The prevailing paradigm would become increasingly unable to accommodate this development and would thus become ever more unreal – both empirically and normatively.

Macpherson's solution to what he saw as the increasing unreality of political science and the dilemmas it confronted was to restore "the willing interpenetration of the disciplines of politics and economics, a plea for the renewal, on what could now be a higher plane, of the tradition of political economy."[20] We have already seen that Macpherson consistently argued the need for political theory to take up political economy. He now proposed that the discipline of political science as a whole follow suit. The abandonment of political economy, with its focus on the state and economic life, had harmed political science everywhere. But its impact was especially acute in Canada, because an indigenous tradition of political economy that had been forged in the context of the specific path of political, social, and economic development that somewhat distinguished Canadian from American experience had been essentially set aside by the 1970s.[21] This, in effect, made the already evident lack of realism in mainstream political science doubly so, in a manner of speaking: both the more general dynamics of capitalist development everywhere and their specific Canadian manifestation were the victims. Greater realism and the reintroduction of political economy went together.

Of course the question involved who wanted and needed greater realism. What Macpherson saw as social pressures for a society less driven by market imperatives had a parallel in reform movements within the world of political science that were promoting a discipline more attuned to the humanist task of identifying and rectifying the deep structural flaws in society. It was in these developments that Macpherson placed his hopes for a restoration of political economy in terms of which the study of political institutions would once more be linked to a historically informed, dynamic analysis of economy and society. As we have seen, this stood at the heart of Macpherson's own efforts to return the state to a central role in social and political theory.

The direction in which political science should *not* proceed was precisely what would emulate economics. That discipline had in the form of neoclassical theory developed "a body of theory which had so effectively shut out any social dimension of economic life that it easily met the requirement of unreality." (Macpherson seemed here to have abandoned the cautious optimism he had expressed in "Market Concepts in Political Theory" that economics was becoming more realistic.) Moreover, "however shortsighted and culture-bound" it might be, the theory "has both theoretical elegance and considerable usefulness, to governments (which continually regulate the economic mechanism) and to business (which can sometimes profit from employing it)."[22] The core idea that economics had refined and political science had taken up – that what made a social phenomenon distinctively political as opposed to economic was that it involved power or control over others – was the basis of the unreality of both (however greater this unreality was in economics). Of course this was another way of urging a return to political economy, which left no doubt that both political and economic activity were about control.

Once again, although he did not explicitly or systematically lay it out, I think Macpherson's suppressed philosophical dimension, that is, his own take on a critical theory of politics and society, emerges here. The fate of a robustly critical and humanist political science (and economics) depended upon the strength and commitment of those forces, inside and outside of the academy, pressing for fundamental social change in the direction of a non-market, but still liberal, democratic society in which possessive individualism and the net transfer of powers were diminished, if not eliminated. The task and social context at play shaped the structure of social scientific thought at empirical and justificatory, explanatory and normative, levels. As Macpherson saw it, both political science and economics shared an aversion to reality in both of their dominant paradigms, however much the pluralist-elitist-equilibrium model of liberal democracy fell short of the kind of general theory that characterized neoclassical economics. And the cost of this lack of realism, which was defended as the essence of realism itself, was enormous. Both pluralism and self-interested rational maximization were increasingly seen as normatively lacking, however much they comported with the supposed facts. And even here the deficiencies were telling. However congruent with the surface appearance of things these theories might have been, that is, with the facts as they manifested themselves to and within the analytic frameworks in which they were fitted, their normative failings ultimately entailed empirical failings as well. The facts themselves harboured an internal tension that reflected the realities of continuing domination in the face of the possibilities for freer and fuller individual lives.

As I noted with respect to Macpherson's argument in "Market Concepts in Political Theory," it would be interesting to consider the trajectory of political science from then until now, and how Macpherson might have appraised it. Whatever its considerable deficiencies, the equilibrium model, with its pluralist and partisan brokerage dimensions, in its own way reflected a commitment to both inclusive political competition and a growing economy that generated sufficient, and widely distributed, resources. Both were seen as essential for democratic progress. This is why the model assumed and more or less defended the postwar welfare state. With welfare states withering virtually everywhere, it has essentially been supplanted, although elements of it remain. These remaining elements are primarily the market assumptions we examined earlier.

However, in spite of efforts to take political science in a more critical direction, notably through "bringing the state back in"[23] and attempts, many Marxian inspired, to restore political economy along the lines Macpherson had recommended (a particularly noteworthy phenomenon in Canada[24]), the pluralist-elitist-equilibrium paradigm has not been replaced by a general theory more attuned to power and history. In the measure that such a theory, or more accurately an orientation, has developed, it has taken the form of rational choice. In this context, there has indeed emerged, rather ironically, a "new" political economy. But instead of economics being recast in the image of politics, as Macpherson had hoped, whereby both political and economic spheres and activities are seen as profoundly shaped by relations of power and control, something like the reverse has taken place. This new political economy has instead represented the recasting of politics in the image of (neoclassical) economics. That is, both political and economic activities and institutions have come to be understood as fora for self-interested, individual, rational, maximizing behaviour – in other words, a reinvigorated and robust possessive individualism. Micro-economics has become micro-politics.

To be sure, the idea that politics was about coercion and economics was about (market) freedom has remained central. This is why politicians and bureaucrats, self-interested "rent-seekers," have to be carefully watched and checked, less by popular democratic forces than by entrenched constitutional limits on state power, or by international trade and investment agreements that possess quasi-constitutional status. In effect, a new and muscular version of protective democracy, rather than a radical, participatory democracy, has supplanted the equilibrium model. As neoliberalism has taken hold, this shift has become more visible and consequential.[25] And it manifests its own dialectic of realism and unreality. The realism expresses the presence in the society and its culture of possessive individualist values and behaviour. The unreality consists in the denial of, or at least failure to consider, alternative developmental possibilities and necessities. It involves the failure/unwillingness to consider structurally determined social tensions and pathologies.

These developments demonstrate once again the need to link the content and role of political and social theory, and social sciences, to socio-historical forces and developments. As Macpherson put it with specific reference to this issue, "Social and historical thought is to a peculiar degree formed by the very forces it seeks to interpret."[26]

Once again, Macpherson's account pointed to his suppressed philosophical dimension, his own contribution to a critical theory of society. The embrace of marginal utility equilibrium analysis (and more recently rational choice) by political theory and science manifests and points towards social pathologies. One methodologically attuned way of dealing with the issues here, which I think would be consistent with Macpherson's suppressed philosophical dimension, is what Ray Morrow has called interpretive or hermeneutic structuralism. As Morrow defines it, interpretive structuralism involves the following claims:

> that social relations and social analysis always have an interpretive (hermeneutic) dimension; that meaning and language (hence discourses) are the basis of forms of reality construction that both reveal and conceal the experiences of subjects; that structures may be species-specific or historically constituted and sometimes consciously transformed even if they have a kind of objective facticity that appears independent of immediate actors; that social and cultural structures constrain human action as does a grammar language, hence not in the way implied by variables of probalistic [*sic*] determinants; and that meaning and structures constantly are reproduced (statically) and produced (dynamically) across space and time.[27]

Each of the qualities Morrow here identifies can reasonably be seen at work, or at least inferred, in Macpherson's approach to critical social and political analysis. Specifically, the category of possessive individualism itself might be thought to incorporate all of them when its immanent implications are pursued. So understood, it opens up key issues in the production and reproduction of social structures and individual agents.

In light of this reading of Macpherson's methodological and meta-methodological commitments, I want now to put these matters into a broader context, one shaped by what I believe are key considerations that any critical social and political theory or science must address. I hope this will further demonstrate the nature and impact of Macpherson's suppressed philosophical dimension on the task of critical social theory, particularly in light of the interpretive or hermeneutic structuralist assumptions that Ray Morrow has laid out. As I noted in the introduction to this study, my observations here are tentative and provisional, but I hope they suggest theoretical possibilities for coming to terms with contemporary dilemmas and challenges. I will then conclude this chapter by returning to the point at which I began this study: Macpherson's response to the criticisms of Kenneth Minogue.

Macpherson and the Frankfurt School Revisited: The Challenges of Critical Theory

In light of my claim throughout this study that his position shares much in common with the critical theory of the Frankfurt School, I want now to argue that Macpherson's work can be understood as a form of post-Marxism dedicated to the development of a critical theory of democracy.[28] Post-Marxism is obviously an extremely loose category that can encompass many possible meanings. It has emerged in the wake of both the collapse of nominally socialist regimes that claimed to base their core principles and practices on Marxism, primarily the ideas of Marx, Engels, and Lenin, and new theoretical initiatives that have sought to repair the evident deficiencies in what might be called classical Marxism, in both theory and practice. However else it might be understood, my own use of the term is intended to suggest a revisiting of, or fresh examination of, key ideas of Marx and others – including those of the Frankfurt School – in a way no longer constrained by the frequently sectarian demands of classical or orthodox Marxist thought or analysis. Put otherwise, post-*Marxism* does not necessarily mean post-*Marx*.

From this vantage point I suggest that post-Marxism involves certain assumptions about society, theory, and the relation between the two that continue to hold significant value for understanding the present. I think Macpherson would have thought so as well and that his own ideas, and in particular his attempts to put liberal democracy on a more strongly humanist basis, can be understood in the context of these assumptions, which can be summarized in the following way:

- *Society is dynamic and historical, and its structures of power and authority possess historical roots and exhibit a broad historical trajectory.* At one level, this is simply a restatement of the core idea of classical Marxism. Yet much of the reaction against Marxian-influenced social and political thought, particularly from recent democratic theory, denies or at least challenges this assumption. It does so on grounds of both analytic realism and moral sensitivity, given that the view that society was historical and history had a direction led in the hands of ostensibly Marxist revolutionaries to the ruthless sacrifice of real human beings to history's putatively ultimate purpose: the realization of socialism as a fully transparent, radically free, and egalitarian form of life. Current democratic theory professes greater awareness of the limits of human possibilities, particularly in overcoming those elements of the human make-up, such as greed and power, that sustain the quest for domination. In many respects, this has been important and valuable. Yet it can lead, and I would argue it has led, to an inability to clarify which current forms of power and authority are potentially alterable or even eliminable, and thus how distinguishing the changeable from the unchangeable might affect the democratic prospects the theory defends. The irony here is that contemporary theory itself claims that the current era of globalization represents a distinctive historical epoch or even turning point. But given its own commitments, it seems to lack the tools to assess what this might entail from the vantage point of its own normative commitment to viable democratic institutions (it obviously would not need such tools if it were not so committed). By contrast, a post-Marxist account remains attuned to the idea of historically emergent and potentially alterable structures of power and authority, while jettisoning the eschatological dimensions of its traditional predecessor.

- *A radical social and democratic theory committed to the pursuit of enhanced freedom and equality above all offers a critical diagnosis of the present.* A post-Marxist theory of democracy and society is sustained by a value judgment: that in their social and personal lives, people struggle to realize integrally certain aspirations to a fulfilled life revolving around the satisfaction of needs for material well-being, emotional gratification, and connectedness with others, and that the social relations within which they are embedded in complex ways facilitate and block the achievement of their purposes. The idea here is that the lives of individuals, as well as the structures within which they conduct those lives, can and must be seen in relation to the historical context of their emergence and the direction in which they might be tending: the present is history and must be grasped and appraised in light of aspirations realized and/or denied. This suggests that a meaningful and insightful democratic and social theory must connect up with those who would have to be called upon to make it effective, and to do so it must clarify their existing situation from the perspective of the claim that the current state of affairs requires alteration if the real possibilities it provides for the realization of their purposes are to be identified and pursued.

In other words, the theory requires addressees, not only or even primarily for advocacy purposes but for philosophical/theoretical validation – as a theory that does not purport to stand outside its object but to engage it in a living way and so satisfy the claim to be both descriptively and analytically accurate and normatively appropriate.

- *The status of the theory's concepts is dependent upon its success in illuminating for its audience the realities and possibilities of their situation.* A theory with historical intent must itself be historical. The concepts it advances should be able to account for themselves in their very structure and meaning as manifestations of the conditions that have made them coherent, if obviously challengeable. For those whom the theory addresses, they should be able to illuminate the historical circumstances within which they live and act, and the challenges and opportunities these circumstances provide. In other words, the theory must "prove" itself in practice. This claim obviously resembles, as well, the demand posed by classical Marxism – except that this can no longer plausibly be linked to the purported requirements of proletarian revolutionary activity – or even, in the current situation, the practice of any specifically identifiable group or prospective social agent of transformation. Hence the conditions of validation have changed from the theory's own perspective. But the standards of validation have not: even with only a tentative and even ambiguous sense of who the addressees might be, a post-Marxist theory must seek to establish the distinctive value of its concepts by referring to the capacity to more comprehensively make sense of the existing situation, its constraints and possibilities, and at least potentially for more people, than can other theoretical positions.

In my judgment, the critical theory of the Frankfurt School has at its best made these propositions central to its work, from its earliest days down to the present. Two key dimensions of its approach to political and social questions are particularly valuable here: self-reflexivity in the relation of theorist to object of inquiry; and commitment to a form of theory that incorporates in its structure both a critical diagnosis of the present and a practical intent to promote domination-free social relations.[29] Here, too, Macpherson both implicitly articulated what is required for such a theory and significantly contributed to its ongoing development.

When Max Horkheimer developed the project of "critical theory," he had in mind a new version of Marx's linkage theory and practice. Theory was not intended to provide simply an accurate description of the world as such from the perspective of an objective observer. Rather the theorist was a member of the social world and of the social life that was studied. Of course theory was not merely strategic: it was not to be put simply in the service of power while tested by its own standards of validity. To the contrary, Horkheimer was interested in incorporating the methods of social science into critical theory. However, knowing, like acting, was a feature of our involvement in the world. We have seen how, in his critical accounts of political theory and political science, Macpherson expressed comparable views.

This practical understanding of the theoretical enterprise requires *self-reflexivity*: the ability of participants to grasp the relation of their own activity, theoretical or practical, to their own involvements. For the researcher, this means their comparable ability to grasp the relation to what was being investigated and analysed, and hence to understand and articulate the ways in which theoretical formulations and empirical methods were themselves conditioned by the very object – society itself – being explored and examined.

Such self-reflexivity is not simply a methodological commitment or heuristic device adopted by a researcher independently of the object of inquiry, Cartesianism by another name. Rather it is made possible and rendered coherent and meaningful by its being intertwined with the self-understandings and motives for action by social actors themselves. As noted in chapter 2, the object – society – is not a compendium of facts to be catalogued and subsumed under covering empirical laws but a range of meaningful interactions mutually constituted by social agents who are capable of giving reasons for their actions and responding to reasons given by others. In short, agents are capable of and exercise self-reflexivity in the forging and renewal of their social bonds. The perspectives of the participants are central to social analysis and social practice; indeed, neither makes sense or is possible without the other. Self-reflexivity is a substantive link between analyst and social agent: making coherent the tie between analyst and agent provides the medium of verification for the concepts of a theory.[30]

Self-reflexivity connects up with the second key quality of critical theory. Throughout its history, critical theory and its theorists have been committed to the idea of a social theory with a practical intent. For them, the key motive for understanding society has been to change it. Thus the theory can also be understood as an attempt to offer a *critical diagnosis of the present social situation* with a view to unearthing real potential for social change. Since domination and injustice continue to exist, and in some respects have even intensified in recent times, such a diagnosis will inevitably take the form of the identification and critique of key individual and social pathologies. Emphasis on the participants' perspective for the purposes of self-reflexivity is crucial for the ability of the theory to provide this sort of diagnosis of the present: it demonstrates the relation between social and self-transformation.

What links these qualities of critical theory together is the idea that an empirical or scientific analysis of society is inherently and necessarily normative at the same time – and as an idea, democracy itself clearly expresses both dimensions. Critical theory, then, ultimately stands or falls on its ability to both theoretically and practically grasp existing society in all its complexity from the perspective of the possibility of, but equally necessity for, human flourishing. Human flourishing is understood here as involving an emancipated form of life. And the theory is cast in such a way that values like "human flourishing" or "emancipation" are not mere ideals but real dimensions of social experience, already implicitly present in existing patterns of individual identities and social practices and thus cognitively accessible. They are pieces of what might be called "living reason": elements of a lived social context that is not to be understood merely as a complex of behavioural regularities whose explanation ultimately requires an objectifying stance and subsumption under atemporal laws. Rather, it is a shared situation incorporating historical tendencies and options – one, in the words of Hannah Arendt, wedged "between past and future." For critical theorists – and for Macpherson – the present is history.

On one level, critical theory speaks to social scientists and social theorists about the requirements and demands of theory itself, including democratic theory. In its stress on the interconnection of method and object and the malleability of both in the context of history as a real and active presence and force, it expresses key elements of what has come to be known as the Continental (versus analytic) approach to social science.[31]

But there is another issue here as well. As argued above, critical theory has always included attention to the participants' perspective in its very structure. This involves the idea that how social agents understand, respond to, and act within the personal and social conditions within which they inevitably find themselves is indispensable, and in any event in one way or another, inescapable, for any comprehensive social and political theory. Socially situated agents are the "carriers" of the categorically accessible "material" that is the stuff and substance of the critical theory (and indeed any theorizing, insofar as it holds explanatory "resonance") and they confirm or disconfirm its propositions by their intentionally driven actions.

What is important to note about the participants' perspective is that it is neither replaceable nor incorrigible; it is neither strictly empirical nor purely normative. As Ray Morrow suggests, social agents are not probabilistically determined instances of covering social laws. Rather, they are participants always and already actively engaged in forms of life within which they take up positions towards the world in and through their practical engagements and come to understandings about their commitments and projects. The "facts" of their situation relate to a learning experience acquired in relation to constraints on their actions. Possibilities for action and the character and perception of constraints change, each in relation to the other.

Critical theorists have always stressed this engaged quality of the role of theorists and their relation to society – it is central to the argument Max Horkheimer famously advanced in 1937 in "Traditional and Critical Theory"; and Jürgen Habermas touches upon similar themes in his "Relationship between Theory and Practice Revisited," published in German in his 1999 work, *Warheit und Rechtfertigung* and included in the 2003 English translation, *Truth and Justification*.[32] With respect to this relationship, the first generation of critical theorists, strongly influenced, at least initially, by classical Marxism, and in particular the work of Georg Lukács, focused on class consciousness, its actual and prospective rational content, and its future-oriented, projective qualities. More distant from the commitments of classical Marxism, Jürgen Habermas (and to some extent, Axel Honneth) have tended instead to focus on the implicit structures of communicative interaction and mutual recognition whose rational content consists in claims to intelligibility, truth, truthfulness, and normative appropriateness that make possible and give life to mutual accountability.

But what they have all held in common is a strongly Hegelian element, an emphatic conception of reason, where reason is a productive force made actual in life situations, commitments, orientations, and projects of human agents who are understood as possessing historically developed and developing capacities of a certain kind. Recently, Kenneth Baynes has claimed that Hegel, and Habermas to a considerable extent, actually share a commitment to an intersubjective reading of Kant's view that to act autonomously is to act on the basis of certain kinds of reasons. Both relate the rational basis for autonomous action to the achievement of relations of mutual recognition that provide for the capacity for subjects to hold each other accountable, such that in doing so, these subjects exercise, embody, and instantiate reason.[33] Hegel's rich account of freedom as he developed it in his *Philosophy of Right* – where it emerges as personal, moral, and social – clearly provides the backdrop and context for this position, although shorn of the metaphysical pretensions of (objective and absolute) spirit within which all contradictions are taken up and resolved in a thoroughly transparent unity. I have suggested that, in his treatment of populist movements in *Democracy in Alberta,* Macpherson provided something like a nonmetaphysical account of objective spirit and a (potentially) rich conception of freedom, also without the pretensions to absolute unity and transparency.

Horkheimer and Adorno were of a more orthodox Hegelian temper in this respect. They tended to hold to something like spirit as rational essence, while remaining fearful of its totalizing implications, of the domination of the concept over (lived) life. Nevertheless, active subjects constituting a world adequate to their purposes, a world of mutuality and solidarity, were also central to their theoretical reflections. The historical materialist elements of Marx's work more adequately in their view captured this necessity for and commitment to mutuality and solidarity; hence the continuing presence of Marxian themes, even as Horkheimer and Adorno moved away from classical Marxian positions. (And there remains some resonance of Marx in Habermas and certainly in Honneth.)

By stressing the power of reason in this way, critical theorists have reasserted the claims of classical philosophy that theory – rational insight – is ultimately the standard by which practice is to be understood and judged. But – and here the relevance of Hegel and Marx (but also Nietzsche and Heidegger) is particularly crucial – they see reason as having a history, as indeed embedded in history and taking the form of recognizable patterns over time of human interactions with external nature and other humans. In other words, philosophy becomes "practical." On this view – again shared by all critical theorists – practice takes priority over theory. The goal of theory is not the triumph of reason but a rational society – which was Macpherson's project, too. Hence democracy is to be defended on the grounds that, under modern conditions, it is the most rational form of social order, in light of a reason still bearing its normative content.

In this sense, democracy as such is not the absolute standard. Reason is. There are elements of this position in Macpherson as well – this is why I argued that he offered a critique of democratic theory rather than a fully fleshed out theory of his own. But the emphasis on reason and a rational society does not herald the return of the philosopher-ruler (Marcuse is somewhat of an exception here), because this rationality is now seen as "impure." It is embedded in ongoing forms of life, immanent in social practices understood as forms of mutual recognition and accountability. This makes the challenges and possibilities of democracy both more and less manageable. They are more manageable precisely because they are and must be immanent in forms of experience that are potentially always and already available to people living in them. But they are less manageable for the same reason: the barriers to realizing the demands of reason are themselves immanent as a kind of second nature in the ongoing practices in which individuals are engaged. This is why possessive individualism is a "living" concept. Not merely an external descriptive attribute, it articulates and thereby opens up for reflection the second nature of those who are embedded within and reproduce a certain set of social relations.

So Macpherson's work stands at the intersection of post-Marxism and critical theory. One could say that he not only synthesized Marx and Mill, but also Marx and Mill on the one hand, and Horkheimer on the other. And he did so by addressing key limitations in all three, limitations made evident precisely in the context of how Horkheimer laid out the tasks of a critical theory of society.

Although they offered powerful insights crucial to a critical theory of democracy, the first generation of critical theorists did not always explicitly put democratic theory at the centre of their concerns. Beginning from Marxist premises, Horkheimer tended to look at law and politics as features of capitalist and pre- capitalist societies. These would disappear when capitalism was superseded. In capitalism, law provided the basis for an atomistic conception of social relations based on exchange that separated individuals from communal solidarities – as I argued in chapter 2, Horkheimer laid this out in terms strikingly comparable to Macpherson's account of possessive individualism. Horkheimer provided an alternative notion of the bases of solidarity in the concern for suffering nature (human and non-human), which still could be found in the family. In a post-capitalist society, political conflict would be unnecessary. Individuals would be able to pursue their own self-chosen purposes. Politics would be replaced by administration. Even where democracy was a concern, as in the works of critical theorists such as Franz Neumann and Otto Kirchheimer, the idea of democracy was contained within the idea of a common will.

Critical theorists were more concerned with the pathological role of liberalism in contemporary society. For the most part, they associated liberalism with capitalism and its irrational rationality. Establishing democracy meant overcoming the limits of capitalist rationality and, later, instrumental rationality.

Yet although, as earlier noted, critical theorists retained a tie to Hegel, in the end they could not employ his conception of a rational social totality, and Marx's understanding of politics became less persuasive as critical theory became a critique of instrumental reason, a critique that also targeted some of Marx's own ideas. It became less clear how to incorporate reason as a productive force made actual in the life situations, commitments, orientations, and projects of human agents, who are understood as possessing historically developed and developing capacities of a certain kind. Yet they were not able to critically incorporate some of the achievements of liberalism into a critical theory of democracy.

This is a defect Macpherson's ideas helps repair. There has been a tendency among political and social theorists to counter the evident limitations of classical Marxism and socialism by vigorously reasserting the virtues of liberalism and/or a scaled-down democracy that avoids the perils of the "totalitarian temptation." American theorists typically represent the former in the context of a focus on distributive justice; French thinkers the latter.[34] Throughout this study I have tried to show that Macpherson's account represents an important attempt to challenge the either/or logic that has seemed to characterize much current post-Marxist, and post-welfare state, theory. A robust liberalism need not be fearful of communal, democratic bonds of solidarity, at least not exclusively. Democracy, even and especially a non–market dominated form of democracy, need not be, indeed to be fully faithful to its historical promise cannot be, illiberal. But this requires that we revisit concepts whose meanings have been taken for granted and even obscured, and to do so not in order to deny historical reality but to heighten it.

This is what the kind of critical theory I have attributed to Macpherson does. The challenge posed to such thinking, as Horkheimer pointed out, was that in the given circumstances it would unavoidably appear as arbitrary and unjust. This is why conceptual self-awareness and socio-political analysis were necessarily joined – for Macpherson, why political theory needed political economy (and vice versa). It represented what Ray Morrow had argued was the necessity for theorists to make central the claims that "meaning and language (hence discourses) are the basis of forms of reality construction that both reveal and conceal the experiences of subjects," and "that structures may be species-specific or historically constituted and sometimes consciously transformed even if they have a kind of objective facticity that appears independent of immediate actors."

That the challenge confronting Macpherson's theoretical analysis was to demonstrate not only its plausibility but also its normative defensibility – to show that it was not merely partisan or arbitrary – was made evident by the exchange between Macpherson and Kenneth Minogue that I noted at the very beginning of this study. Minogue made both plausibility and defensibility central to his critique. Macpherson responded to both issues in a way that I believe uniquely highlighted his own theoretical and thus methodological self-awareness.

Macpherson versus Minogue: The Limits of Traditional Theory

In his critical appraisal of Macpherson's "humanist" democracy, Minogue echoed liberal, individualist criticisms that have always confronted Macpherson's work. In a manner reminiscent of Isaiah Berlin's account of positive liberty, Minogue argued that Macpherson was a monistic thinker who believed he possessed the ultimate truth about politics and human nature, and as a result sought "to derive all the features of politics from a single principle ... The Macphersonite principle from which everything else derives is most commonly called 'democracy.'" Macpherson was able to do so because he had created a narrowly circumscribed philosophical vision of ultimate harmony that was essentially impervious to the messy realities of human pluralism and individual foibles, of unavoidable personal, moral, and political conflicts and differences. Macpherson offered instead a picture of human homogeneity, whereby our "full humanity is conceived entirely in social terms, and men would live in the closest possible association with each other. To be independent of one's fellow men has always been a cherished aspiration of many people, because human beings are at best unpredictable and at worst have behaved pretty unpleasantly towards each other." In the end, "Macpherson's universalisation of democracy means that *everything* will depend upon political decision."[35]

But beyond these widely shared criticisms of Macpherson's position, Minogue also took specific aim at what he viewed as Macpherson's approach. He advanced two claims about Macpherson's theoretical and methodological commitments that, in his view, permitted Macpherson to subsume all issues under a single principle. First, he claimed that Macpherson adopted "the rhetorical device of switching many practical questions over into the more manageable territory of conceptual coherence" This was abetted by a second gambit, "the removal of a term from its ordinary contextual moorings." That is, he took a concept such as democracy and essentially manipulated its meaning by turning it from a "perfectly useful political term" into "a single basic moral criterion of a much vaguer entity called 'society' ... Severing democracy from its ordinary moorings thus allows Macpherson to move from the limited point of majority rule (which may or may not be desirable, according to circumstances) to something assumed to be impregnably desirable." According to Minogue, the desideratum was the achievement of a society in which the individual has the capacity "to make the most of oneself."[36] This technique of wrenching concepts from their accepted contexts extended to virtually the whole range of Macpherson's key ideas, from the notion of powers (and their net transfer) to the idea of property.

Moreover, because Macpherson resorted to "the rhetorical device of switching many practical questions over into the more manageable territory of conceptual coherence," he freed himself from the need to specify the real empirical circumstances under which his envisaged model of democracy would actually work. As a result, "the level of argument is virtually without exemplification." Despite the fact that it exhibited "a very evident strain of genuine feeling for individuality," Macpherson's position had to be rejected as incompatible with the demands and possibilities of genuine individual human freedom.[37]

Minogue's emphasis on "ordinary conceptual moorings" for political and social ideas suggests a positivist emphasis on concepts as empirical descriptors with fixed meanings. Such a view ignores the question of what those moorings actually are, and whether they could shift as individuals engaged in practical (normative/empirical) activities in pursuit of their aims and aspirations establish new realities and come to new understandings. Thus Minogue assumed that individualism meant independence from living in the closest possible proximity with others who potentially posed a threat to them. This was certainly how Hobbes understood the matter. But the historical and conceptual transformation of the meaning of individualism after Hobbes would seem to call this claim into question. In other words, it is not self-evident that atomism equals independence, nor that to own (private) property necessarily insulates one from immediate dependence on others, as Minogue also claimed.

That there was a positivist blind spot to Minogue's analysis is apparent from his concluding remarks. He alluded to "the curious mixture of individualism and communal sentiment" in Macpherson's thought and noted, correctly, that he was "likely to be assailed by liberals for his communal bias, yet attacked by socialists for the individualist undertones of his work." He summed things up with the puzzled, if not puzzling, observation that Macpherson "has provided for us a kind of individualist utopia built upon communal foundations."[38]

What is truly curious is that these observations appear to have had little impact on Minogue's analysis. It is striking, if hardly unique, that the liberal Minogue, with his staunch defence of individualism against the supposedly freedom-stifling collectivist impulses of socialism, did not consider or even apparently notice the richer notion of individuality that Macpherson sought to develop and defend. This notion was designed precisely to enhance the prospects for individual freedom, not limit them in the supposed interest of defending what would amount to the forced harmony of a totalitarian society – which was, according to Macpherson, "a prospect which revolts me as much as it revolts him."[39]

This again poses the issue of conceptual moorings, or historical meanings. Minogue did not elaborate on his notion of society, other than to suggest an apparent meaning, namely, collectivist impositions on individuals that are unfortunately unavoidable and frequently undesirable. The idea that I have argued is crucial for Macpherson's account of possessive individualism – that the more radically aggressive the individualist strivings of atomistic competitors, the more oppressively collectivist the response was likely to be – nowhere finds a place in

Minogue's account. This suggests that Minogue failed to explore the issue of conceptual moorings in a sufficiently self-reflexive way that ironically undermined the strength of his own arguments. The blind spot(s) in his own account precluded him from recognizing the depth and possibilities of Macpherson's.

As I suggested in the introduction, the nature of Minogue's critique drew out of Macpherson an unusually explicit articulation of his own assumptions, one that challenged the claim, implicit in Minogue's account, that his position was "biased and unjust." Partly, for Macpherson, this was a matter of taking issue with Minogue's view that he had remained purely at the level of abstraction and thus avoided the messily concrete realities of political life. He argued that, in order to highlight key features of a social order, all scientific or philosophical analysis required conceptual abstractions. The question was "whether, when they are applied to the concrete phenomena, they enable us to explain it better than before." Macpherson claimed that he had in fact done so: "I have repeatedly offered historical and analytical accounts of actual social, economic, and political relations, accounts which seem to me more revealing because they are applications to reality of newly formulated concepts, for example, the net transfer of powers, extractive power, developmental power."[40] The selection of these categories was no accident. With respect to these specific concepts, Minogue had accused Macpherson of adopting a mechanistic picture of human relations where powers, access, energies, transfers, and the like held sway. For Minogue, such mechanical thinking allowed Macpherson both to remain at the level of abstract conceptual coherence and to offer a kind of pseudo-scientific or naturalistic gloss to categories of dubious explanatory and normative value.

Macpherson disputed this characterization, especially when applied to his efforts to quantify the net transfer of powers in light of his accounts of extractive and developmental power. Indeed Macpherson took strong issue with what he saw as Minogue wanting it both ways: reproaching him both "for staying too much at an abstract conceptual level" and at the same time "for trying to make a concept like developmental power concrete, by treating it as a quantity and showing that it can be measured in terms of access and transfers."[41] In a related vein, Minogue had criticized Macpherson for collapsing the distinction between democratic politics and a market economy by presenting wealth as fundamentally political and not simply economic. The charge here was that Macpherson had relied strictly on historical evidence and thus had not "philosophically ... explained either economic exchange or political rule."[42]

This I think points to the fundamental differences between Minogue and Macpherson, which are not merely political or ideological. They are rooted in alternative understandings of what constitutes the nature of political thought and its tasks. Simply put, for Minogue, within the framework of traditional theory, the justification and value of concepts lie in their expressing the attributes of an existing reality whose truth is guaranteed by their ostensibly accepted "usual" conceptual moorings. Reality is what is and can be so captured. By contrast, for Macpherson, taking on the demands of critical theory, reality is not so straightforward and capable of being captured exclusively by empirical concepts. It is, at least potentially, tension-laden, contradictory. To be fully faithful to the phenomena with which they are concerned, concepts must have the capacity to reveal possibilities, not simply to characterize attributes. We saw Macpherson explicitly do this with his deployment of ontological categories. He argued they were neither pure fact nor pure value, but a combination of the two. They needed to manifest or point towards both visible appearances and the social relations that these appearances constituted and expressed. Minogue's apparently inconsistent simultaneous criticisms that Macpherson was guilty of both excessive abstraction and overreliance on historical data reflected this profound difference in underlying presuppositions about how to undertake theoretical or philosophical reflection. He assumed a seamless fit between data and concept that, from his perspective, Macpherson could not and did not assume. The differences between Minogue and Macpherson, and how Macpherson saw them, came most tellingly to the fore in the context of two key issues: the nature of moral conflict, and the meaning of extractive power.

The first issue goes to the core of Minogue's criticisms of Macpherson and more generally the theoretical commitments he and others in the tradition of Marxism and critical theory have upheld. In making his case that Macpherson assumed away the possibility of genuine, permanent, and ultimately irreconcilable moral conflict, and indeed sought to prevent even the appearance of such conflict, Minogue echoed Isaiah Berlin. That is, he took issue with the idea that it was possible to conceive essential human capacities as non-contentious once scarcity, real and contrived, had come to an end and individuals no longer viewed themselves as infinite consumers and appropriators engaged in an endless struggle to overcome it. "Clearly Minogue (like Berlin) either is not persuaded that those conditions can ever be realized or does not believe that there are *any* conditions in which there would be no opposition between the exercise of essentially human capacities."[43]

For Macpherson, while this position was defensible, it was not self-evidently true. It therefore did not follow that he denied, assumed away, or even sought to suppress moral conflicts. What he did argue was that we had to at least consider whether or not some conflicts viewed as permanent and intractable were in reality the products of a competitive society of scarcity and in principle might be eliminated in a different kind of social order (in this, Macpherson echoed the claims of both Max Horkheimer and Herbert Marcuse). While he admitted that the move to a non-contentious society that was also non-totalitarian would be difficult, and attempts so far to realize it had failed, "it is far from certain that the causes of past failures lie in the very nature of things, and that they can never be transcended."[44] In other words, Macpherson's position was linked to an enriched notion of individual flourishing and not collective suppression. For Minogue the idea of potentially eliminating some moral conflicts could meaningfully involve only the latter and never the former.

On the second point, Macpherson challenged Minogue's view that extractive power on Macpherson's definition applied to any situation in which one gained benefit from the work of another. Thus in Minogue's examples someone buying a chocolate bar would have exercised extractive power over the factory workers who produced it; and the consumer who called in a television repair specialist would have likewise done so by taking away the technician's ability to engage in alternative pursuits, such as mowing the lawn or learning Swahili. Minogue clearly intended with such examples to deny the value or theoretical utility of the concept of extractive power, to paint it as sweepingly imprecise and even ridiculous.

Macpherson's initial response was to remind Minogue that extractive power was about control over the use of capacities of others and thus extracting benefit from their exercise. Minogue's examples were intended to show that everyone exercised extractive power, but in fact they showed the opposite: they were most assuredly not about control over others. He had confused exchange with exploitation, a surface appearance with a social relation that was not immediately accessible. Minogue demanded that categories adumbrate the immediate without mediation. But neither his concepts nor anyone else's could really do so. Ironically, in his evident distaste for what he saw as Macpherson's escape from reality into abstraction, he had fallen prey to precisely that malady. In his case he professed to see extractive power – which indeed is visible only via abstraction – in what was, as Macpherson saw it, a specific empirical phenomenon. With respect specifically to Minogue's claim that I exercise extractive power over a television service technician because, by retaining his services, I deny him other, perhaps more desirable opportunities, Macpherson wrote, "It is not the customer who takes the repairman away from learning Swahili, it is his need to earn a living ... But it is not anybody's exercise of extractive power over him that does this: it is simply the fact that we do not yet live in such a world of plenty (partly because we do not use the present productive capacity of the system at all fully) that an acceptable material standard of life can be maintained without society requiring that sort of amount of work."[45] A further irony: Minogue charged Macpherson with promoting a freedom-denying, rigidly constraining model of a harmonious society. Yet is that any more Procrustean than the unquestioned assumption that we are doomed to permanent scarcity under a compulsive and apparently unalterable economic order?

So Macpherson concluded with the comment with which I began this work: Minogue

> wants to stay closer to the observable world of affairs than he believes I have done. He complains repeatedly ... that I never give down-to-earth examples to support my general propositions. But see what happens when he gives such examples for his propositions. The trouble is that down-to-earth examples are likely to illustrate not real underlying relations between people, or between things, or between people and things, but only apparent relations. This is so in the nature of the case: if the example is down-to-earth enough it is bound to deal with appearances, not realities. It is indeed evident that the sun sets in the west: this is the level of appearance beyond which down-to-earth examples generally do not get.[46]

Throughout this study I have attempted to show that the commitment expressed in this passage informed the whole body of Macpherson's work. It undergirds what he believed to be the (non-deceptive) task of political theory and political science. It is at the heart of what I have called his suppressed philosophical dimension. It is a commitment that is still worth taking seriously.

Would Macpherson have recognized himself in the account I have laid out in this chapter? Likely not, or at least not fully. Would he have sympathized with the commitment to critical theory and method I have sought to defend here? And would he have welcomed a reading of his ideas that attempted to demonstrate their capacity to encourage critical reflection on the social pathologies of the present and the need for a radical response? I think the answer to these questions is an emphatic yes. Whatever else might be said about him, I do not think there is any doubt that, in Macpherson's view, if it was to be non-deceptive, the task of political theory and political science involved the need for committed humanist intellectuals and thinkers to capture in their concepts the potential in the present for a different kind of society that was faithful to long-standing humanist goals. And intellectual responsibility required that thinkers and scholars at least reflect on their *own* role in either sustaining or challenging the status quo. In his preface to *Powers, Possessions and Freedom,* the collection he edited in honour of Macpherson's work and contributions, Alkis Kontos wrote of Macpherson, "He proposes to extricate individualism from the dehumanizing and negating effects of capitalism, the possessive passions of market society. Macpherson has been performing this task over the years in his solitary, dignified fashion. His scholarship is impeccable, his challenge constant."[47] I have tried to show that this commitment subtends a critical theory and method in Macpherson's work, however "suppressed" this philosophical dimension might have been.

I would like to conclude this book with two apparently unrelated statements that crystallize the meaning and significance of C.B. Macpherson's work, and explain why this work remains valuable. They might be considered my own modest attempt to define a small constellation of concepts that express what we might take away from an encounter with his ideas.

The first is by Max Horkheimer, with whose work I have attempted to link that of Macpherson. It is an aphorism in a collection of aphorisms: "Tolerance – since everything has to be the way it is. Protest – against everything being the way it has to be."[48] This aphorism captures the essence of critical theory. But it also expresses the core impulse behind Macpherson's concepts and categories. And just as importantly, with its hint of respectful, even understated, but at the same time steely, commitment to clear-eyed analysis and fundamental social and political change, it says something important about Macpherson, the thinker, and what he viewed as the task of political theory.

The second comes from a reviewer of the manuscript upon which this book is based. This reviewer noted that, after reading his work, a student had commented that "Macpherson makes me feel good about being a human!"

C.B. Macpherson would not have wished a better epitaph.

Notes

Introduction

1 C.B. Macpherson, "Humanist Democracy and Elusive Marxism: A Response to Minogue and Svacek," *Canadian Journal of Political Science* 11, no. 3 (September 1976): 423.

2 In this respect the "memorial" conference dedicated to identifying and evaluating Macpherson's key contributions that was held at the University of Toronto in 1989, two years after his death, and the subsequent published volume based on the conference papers, is exemplary: both the normative and historical adequacy of Macpherson's work provide the unifying theme for the presentations. See Joseph H. Carens, ed., *Democracy and Possessive Individualism: The Intellectual Legacy of C.B. Macpherson* (Albany: State University of New York Press, 1993). For a critical analysis of the limits of this approach, see Brian Caterino, "Review of Joseph H. Carens (ed.), *Democracy and Possessive Individualism: The Intellectual Legacy of C.B. Macpherson*," *Prairie Forum* 20, no. 1 (Spring 1995): 141–5. For Caterino the title itself reflects the fundamental problem, namely, that the very separation of democracy and possessive individualism distorts Macpherson's approach, in terms of which the critique of possessive individualism and his distinctive theory of democracy entail each other. Interestingly for Caterino the one essay that seems to avoid the problems he identifies with the approach in the book is by William Leiss, whose own work has been powerfully shaped by the Hegelian-Marxian critical theory of the Frankfurt School. From a broadly Marxian perspective the separation between normative and historical political theory is untenable.

3 Kenneth Minogue, "Humanist Democracy: The Political Thought of C.B. Macpherson," *Canadian Journal of Political Science* 11, no. 3 (September 1976): 393.

4 Macpherson, "Humanist Democracy and Elusive Marxism," 430,

5 Macpherson himself was apt to see his work in this way. In the preface to his final published book he wryly noted that on the basis of the book's content "the critic who remarked that I never write about anything except possessive individualism will here find no need to retract." C.B. Macpherson, *The Rise and Fall of Economic Justice and Other Essays* (Oxford: Oxford University Press, 1985).

6 In this respect Macpherson's response to a critic of his treatment of liberal ontology is telling: "He is looking for an intellectually satisfying abstract principle: I am looking for a practical principle on which one can base a move to a more human society." C.B. Macpherson, "Commentary: The Politics of Self-Development," *Canadian Journal of Political and Social Theory* 8, no. 3 (Fall 1984): 99, Macpherson was responding to Alfonso J. Damico, "Liberal Still: Notes on the Political Theory of C.B. Macpherson," *Canadian Journal of Political and Social Theory* 8, no. 3 (Fall 1984): 86–97.

7 C.B. Macpherson, "The Deceptive Task of Political Theory" (1954), in Macpherson, *Democratic Theory: Essays in Retrieval*, 194–203 (1973; Don Mills, ON: Oxford University Press, 2012). I believe this essay to be an important but overlooked part of Macpherson's work and I discuss it more fully later on in this study. And I also want to offer a caveat: at different times in his career Macpherson took an interest in and wrote about the character and role of the social sciences in Canada, especially political science. Of necessity this drew him into more general questions of method with significant philosophical implications. Perhaps because of its primarily Canadian focus, this work has not been taken up by scholars to any significant extent. I will attempt to discuss this work as well later in this study.

8 To be sure Macpherson's response to Minogue has not gone totally unnoticed. See, e.g., Jules Townshend, *C.B. Macpherson and the Problem of Liberal Democracy* (Edinburgh: Edinburgh University Press, 2000), 107–8. However, Townshend implicitly links Macpherson's response to the Marxian critique of ideology and does not pursue what I see as its larger metaphysical and meta-methodological potential.

9 Erica Sherover-Marcuse, *Emancipation and Consciousness: Dogmatic and Dialectical Perspectives in the Early Marx* (Oxford: Basil Blackwell, 1986), 2, 3. She notes further, "To disengage a theory is to interrogate a text or group of texts from a perspective which reveals that the body of work

so interrogated contains answers to questions which hitherto could not be posed. As a result of the interrogation, previously unnoticed facets of an intellectual system may appear; sometimes points of tension may become apparent. To disengage a theory is to examine a thought structure through a more powerful critical lens as it were, a lens which illuminates the theoretical significance of what were previously taken to be either merely anomalous remarks or unimportant comments" (2–3). I am not certain I will be saying much about anomalous remarks or unimportant comments, but I do hope to bring to light some previously unnoticed, or perhaps under-recognized and under-appreciated, facets of Macpherson's thought.

10 I realize this proposition is controversial. I hope to at least suggest throughout the body of this study that it is plausible. To draw again from Sherover-Marcuse's position, one possible way of conceiving this distinction might be to argue that political *theory* in this context relates to the ideas to be "disengaged" in the process of critical reflection and reconstruction, while political *philosophy* refers to the body of thought to be probed for as yet unnoticed or under-theorized dimensions.

11 For a comparable attempt to link Macpherson's views to explicitly philosophical concerns – in this case what he sees as "the tradition of Canadian Idealism … that offers an original formulation of the question of freedom, community, and history, one that combines the common purpose of the community with individual self-realization," see Robert Meynell, *Canadian Idealism and the Philosophy of Freedom: C.B. Macpherson, George Grant, and Charles Taylor* (Montreal and Kingston, ON: McGill-Queen's University Press, 2011). I believe there is much of value in Meynell's work, especially in its attempt to link Macpherson to Canadian philosophical themes, and will comment on it later in this book. I do think that Meynell somewhat overstates the Hegelian elements in Macpherson's work, or at least the impact of the specific reading he brings to Hegel's work.

12 William Leiss, *C.B. Macpherson: Dilemmas of Liberalism and Socialism*, 2nd ed. (Montreal and Kingston: McGill-Queen's University Press, 2009).

13 This suggests that for Macpherson, as well as the first-generation members of the Frankfurt School, political theory must be integrated with political economy. As Frank Cunningham puts it in his excellent introduction to the newly reissued *Political Theory of Possessive Individualism*, "The overall approach of this justly acclaimed work … is that of political economy. Macpherson's entire academic career was pursued on a terrain where political and economic matters were seen

as intimately related. This was the domain in which Adam Smith, David Ricardo, and Karl Marx developed their views." I fully agree with this claim. My approach in this study is intended to deepen our appreciation of this connection, not to deny or diminish it. It's interesting that Cunningham goes on to note that Harold Innis, an important architect of a distinctive tradition in Canadian political economy, and also a noteworthy theorist of the role of communication in the history of civilizations, which gave his political economy a cultural dimension, was a senior colleague of Macpherson's at the University of Toronto. Thus, it "is within this specific framework – that of political/economic/cultural studies – that Macpherson must be placed." Frank Cunningham, "Introduction," in C.B. Macpherson, *The Political Theory of Possessive Individualism: Hobbes to Locke* (1962) (1962; Don Mills, ON: Oxford University Press, 2011), iii. I would argue that locating Macpherson in this way suggests the value of viewing his work from the vantage point of a philosophically informed critical theory of society.

14 See the classic essay by Max Horkheimer, "Traditional and Critical Theory," in Horkheimer, *Critical Theory: Selected Essays*, trans. Matthew J. O'Connell and others (New York: Seabury, 1972), 188–243. I hope to demonstrate throughout this study that Macpherson's work is informed by this distinction, even though he nowhere made it explicit or systematically developed it.

15 See Hannah Arendt, *The Human Condition* (Chicago: University of Chicago Press, 1958). Although it is doubtful that either would have been thrilled by the comparison, I think there is also common ground shared by both thinkers on a variety of issues.

16 Macpherson, "Humanist Democracy and Elusive Marxism," 425.

17 The idea of a constellation as a vehicle for bringing different concepts or dimensions of phenomena into a relation that seeks to avoid rigidity and closure is generally attributed to Walter Benjamin, for whom ideas were related to phenomena as constellations were related to the stars. It was subsequently taken up by Theodor Adorno. Martin Jay offers a good description of a constellation as "a juxtaposed rather than integrated cluster of changing elements that resist reduction to a common denominator, essential core, or generative first principle ... The result was not a relativistic chaos of unrelated factors, but a dialectical model of negations that simultaneously constructed and deconstructed patterns of a fluid reality." Martin Jay, *Adorno* (Cambridge, MA: Harvard University Press, 1984), 14–15. The idea of a constellation is often linked, as noted above, to the notion of a force field; it is also frequently associated with

the idea of an elective affinity. All of these concepts carry the sense of relations that are not rigidly or causally fixed and determined, but are also not arbitrary. See also Susan Buck-Morss, *The Origin of Negative Dialectics: Theodor W. Adorno, Walter Benjamin, and the Frankfurt Institute* (New York: Free Press, 1977), esp. 90–5.

18 C.B. Macpherson, "The Economic Penetration of Political Theory: Some Hypotheses," *Journal of the History of Ideas* 39, no. 1 (January–March 1978): 101–18.

19 In the face of this claim that Macpherson was Anglo-American-analytic in approach but Continental in substance, it might be suggested that with respect to Macpherson's conception of political theory in general, and Marx and Marxism in particular, the philosopher to whom he was actually closest in spirit was the Canadian Marxist thinker G.A. Cohen. Indeed, on the face of it, Macpherson could be seen as – and might well have seen himself as – closer to Cohen than to thinkers of the Frankfurt School with whom I attempt to associate him. They both wrote in a decidedly Anglo-American argot, although to be sure, as a philosopher, Cohen was obviously more committed to a methodological reconstruction of Marxism based on the dominant scientific paradigm as permanent and transcendental. This led to what I take to be a rather standard, almost classical, version of Marxism, at the cost of Marxism as critique.

On the surface at least, although Macpherson was neither interested in nor viewed himself as particularly competent to undertake the kind of methodological reconstruction that Cohen offered up, it certainly seems that Macpherson would have held a comparable position on the nature of science. This could well have undergirded what was in many instances his own rather orthodox reading of Marx. And as far as explicit political commitments went, Macpherson would no doubt have sympathized with Cohen's late work, *Why Socialism?*

Yet on the other hand, and this gets to the depth or suppressed philosophical dimension of Macpherson's work, things are not so straightforward. As I try to show throughout this study, Macpherson's political analysis is richer than might be thought, and this manifests the implicit presence of an alternative (social) science, a presence I will particularly attempt to demonstrate and explore in the concluding chapter of this book. There is a dimension to Macpherson's theory that offers sharp critical insight and is, I think, missing from "analytic" Marxism, however suggestive it might be about the realities of life in capitalist society. An important key here involves what I intend to demonstrate in chapter 1: that *The Political Theory of Possessive Individualism* has a methodological structure comparable to volume 1 of *Capital* and that as a result the concept of possessive individualism is more a mediation and less an empirical descriptor.

20 For two extensive and valuable summaries and discussions of contemporary currents in democratic theory, see Frank Cunningham, *Theories of Democracy: A Critical Introduction* (London: Routledge, 2002); and David Held, *Models of Democracy*, 3rd ed. (Stanford, CA: Stanford University Press, 2006).

21 C.B. Macpherson, "Democratic Theory: Ontology and Technology" (1967), in Macpherson, *Democratic Theory: Essays in Retrieval*, 24–38.

1. Possessive Individualism as Critique

1 In making this claim I most assuredly do not intend a "Whiggish" reading of history whereby the achievement of liberal democracy is seen as an inevitable triumph of human reason and goodwill, the product of the irresistible march of progress. What in any case has been a multifaceted, contradictory, and contested development has been very much the product of conflict and struggle, particularly of social forces committed to a radical restructuring of society. Alan Wolfe has argued perceptively that the achievement of liberal, individual rights was very much the result of struggles undertaken by social forces that were not themselves animated by liberal values; in particular he has in mind the organized working class. See Wolfe, "Waiting for Righty: A Critique of the Fascism Hypothesis," *Review of Radical Political Economics* 5, no. 3 (October 1973): 46–66. I should also note that a triumphalist reading of the history of liberal democracy overlooks the extent to which actually existing liberal democratic institutions have often comported with oppressive practices, such as slavery. On this point, see Domenico Losurdo, *Liberalism: A Counter-History* (London: Verso, 2011).

2 C.B. Macpherson, *The Political Theory of Possessive Individualism: Hobbes to Locke* (1962) with a new introduction by Frank Cunningham (1962; Don Mills, ON: Oxford University Press, 2011), xiii.

3 Martin Hartmann and Axel Honneth, "Paradoxes of Capitalism," trans. James Ingram, *Constellations* 13, no. 1 (March 2006): 45.

4 It should be noted here that Macpherson does not *reduce* Hobbes's ideas to mere reflections of the social relations of a possessive market society. Right at the beginning of *The Political Theory of Possessive Individualism* he writes, "It cannot be said that the seventeenth-century concepts of

freedom, rights, obligation, and justice are all entirely derived from this concept of possession [i.e., 'the individual as essentially the proprietor of his own person or capacities, owing nothing to society for them'], but it can be shown that they were powerfully shaped by it" (Macpherson, *Political Theory of Possessive Individualism*, 3). I think this is an important qualification to any purely historicist reading of Macpherson's position and opens up a number of key questions about what I have called his suppressed philosophical dimension.

However, Macpherson is not always his own best advocate in this regard. With respect to critics of Hobbes who claim he was wrong to present his theory of human nature as universally true (and thus, in spite of his own claims to the contrary that he had deduced his robust account of political obligation from that theory, wrong to have so presented this account), Macpherson argues that "when Hobbes's universal claims are *reduced to an historical measure* [my emphasis] there is no need to divorce his theory of human nature from his political theory in order to rescue the latter; both theories are seen to have a specific historical validity, and to be consistent with each other" (ibid., 13). For some readers this clearly establishes Macpherson as a "historicist" through and through. As I see it, however, it rather represents a defence, admittedly implied, of a situated or immanent universality, as opposed to a purely transcendental (i.e., Idealist) one. But this needs to be more fully drawn out, which I hope to accomplish in my treatment of the matter.

5 To be sure, Macpherson does not in *The Political Theory of Possessive Individualism* explicitly compare or associate his approach with that of Marx. However, he does so in an important essay published prior to the book, "The Deceptive Task of Political Theory," where he draws a parallel between the development of political economy, and what Marx saw as its ultimately ideological and apologetic turn, and the trajectory of classical liberal political theory. What David Ricardo represented for political economy, Thomas Hobbes did for political theory: each was scientific within the limits of the bourgeois vision both accepted. I discuss this essay more fully in chapter 3.

6 Macpherson, *Political Theory of Possessive Individualism*, 15.

7 The hermeneutic point that social facts never stand alone but necessarily and unavoidably relate to a totality, and are always and already normatively tinged because they involve situations and conditions about which as humans we are not indifferent because they necessarily impinge upon our wants, needs and purposes, is I believe a key but underdeveloped theme in Macpherson's work, a core element of his

suppressed philosophical dimension. On the basis of my experience as a student in his graduate seminar in political theory held at the University of Toronto during the 1971–2 academic year, at which the papers later included in *Democratic Theory: Essays in Retrieval* were presented and discussed, I can attest that in the face of prodding from students he acknowledged the significance of this issue.

8 Macpherson, *Political Theory of Possessive Individualism*, 15.

9 I owe the distinction between historical events and the historical constitution of a social structure to the fine study by Michael Heinrich, *An Introduction to the Three Volumes of Karl Marx's Capital*, trans. Alexander Locascio (2004; New York: Monthly Review, 2012), 31.

10 Macpherson, *Political Theory of Possessive Individualism*, 1, 2.

11 Hobbes subjects to his typical withering criticism Aristotle's conception of a natural hierarchy among humans, which had heretofore provided an influential basis for political obligation. His claim here is particularly telling: "I know that *Aristotle* in the first booke of his Politiques, for a foundation of his doctrine maketh men by Nature, some more worthy to Command, meaning the wiser sort (such as he thought himselfe to be for his Philosophy;) others to Serve, (meaning those that had strong bodies, but were not Philosophers as he;) as if Master and Servant were not introduced by consent of men, but by difference of Wit … For there are very few so foolish, that had not rather governe themselves, than be governed by others." Thomas Hobbes, *Leviathan* (1651) ed., intro. C.B. Macpherson (London: Penguin Books, 1988), chap. 15, p. 211. By in effect claiming that Aristotle's arguments were driven by self-interest, even as they purported to represent transcendent truths beyond anyone's interests, Hobbes anticipated one form of what would later emerge as ideology critique. No doubt this aspect of Hobbes's work very much attracted Macpherson to him.

12 The idea of "real abstraction" figures centrally in the landmark study by Alfred Sohn-Rethel on Marxism and epistemology. See Sohn-Rethel, *Intellectual and Manual Labour: A Critique of Epistemology* (Atlantic Highlands, NJ: Humanities, 1978).

13 Karl Marx, *Capital: A Critique of Political Economy*, trans. Ben Fowkes (Toronto: Penguin Books, 1976), 1:102.

14 For an extensive examination of what he calls "critical interpretation," see Hans Herbert Kogler, *The Power of Dialogue: Critical Hermeneutics after Gadamer and Foucault*, trans. Paul Hendrickson (Cambridge, MA: MIT Press, 1999).

15 Macpherson, *Political Theory of Possessive Individualism*, 16.

16 Ibid, 14.

17 Macpherson himself seems to note this without, I think, emphasizing it as much as he might have. In discussing his key point that Hobbes's state of nature is not a description of the individual stripped of all socially acquired attributes but rather a deduction from the appetites and other faculties of "civilized man," he asks, "Where did civilization get into the argument" about the necessity for a sovereign given that Hobbes apparently intended through his account of the necessary nature or motion of man to provide a picture of human nature as such? Macpherson's response: "The question might be thought unnecessary, *since in a sense civilization was always there*" (ibid., 29–30; emphasis added). Macpherson has in mind here Hobbes's famous injunction that to confirm his propositions about our nature we ought to look into ourselves.

18 Macpherson, *Political Theory of Possessive Individualism*, 3, 4.

19 Ibid., 34.

20 Thomas Hobbes, *Leviathan*, ed., intro. C.B. Macpherson (London: Penguin Books, 1988), 134; my emphasis.

21 Ibid., 151–2.

22 Ibid., 160–1.

23 Macpherson, *Political Theory of Possessive Individualism*, 37.

24 Ibid.

25 Ibid., 55, 57.

26 Ibid., 59.

27 The parallel between Marx's account of surplus value and Macpherson's conception of a net transfer of powers has been noted by scholars of both thinkers. Macpherson's notion no doubt represents and was intended to represent this parallel. But in my view it does more than this and in fact entails a distinctive normative enrichment of the core critique of capitalist social relations that both share, an enrichment that has considerable potential for adding significantly to a normatively informed contemporary critical theory of society. I attempt to develop this position more fully in subsequent chapters of this study. For a treatment of the net transfer of powers along these lines, see Brian Caterino and Phillip Hansen, "Macpherson, Habermas, and the Demands of Democratic Theory," *Studies in Political Economy* 83 (Spring 2009): 105–8.

28 Macpherson, *Political Theory of Possessive Individualism*, 51.

29 Karl Marx and Friedrich Engels, *The Communist Manifesto*, ed., intro., and notes David McLellan (1848; New York: Oxford University Press, 1998), 6.

30 Macpherson, *Political Theory of Possessive Individualism*, 79.

31 Ibid., 85–6, 87.

32 Macpherson will, in the 1970s and 1980s, explicitly address the question of legitimacy in the context of the then-significant theoretical interest from a wide variety of perspectives of the prospects for legitimation crises in advanced liberal democratic capitalist states. See, for example, his "Do We Need a Theory of the State?," in C.B. Macpherson, *The Rise and Fall of Economic Justice and Other Essays* (Oxford: Oxford University Press, 1985), chap. 5. I will discuss this issue below in chapter 4.

33 In a paper that discusses Macpherson's later work, *Democratic Theory: Essays in Retrieval*, Alasdair MacIntyre would contrast the notion of possessive individualism with what he calls "cooperative and creative individualism," a distinction Macpherson accepted. Alasdair MacIntyre, "On *Democratic Theory: Essays in Retrieval* by C.B Macpherson," *Canadian Journal of Philosophy* 6, no. 2 (June 1976): 177. I will more fully discuss the question of competing ontologies that MacIntyre's distinction implies in chapter 2.

34 Macpherson, *Political Theory of Possessive Individualism*, 106.

35 In his contribution to a recent collection that explores what the authors view as the overlapping political and philosophical concerns of Hannah Arendt and Theodor Adorno, Robert Fine refers to "the vast contradictions of the modern age that at once elevate the freedom of the individual as its supreme value and subordinate individuality to forces of instrumental rationality and economic determination." Robert Fine, "Debating Human Rights, Law, and Subjectivity: Arendt, Adorno, and Critical Theory," in *Arendt and Adorno: Political and Philosophical Investigations*, ed. Lars Rensmann and Samir Gandesha (Stanford, CA: Stanford University Press, 2012), 154. I think the title itself is instructive: it indicates the ongoing significance of Macpherson's account for themes and concerns that stand at the forefront of much current political theory and philosophy.

36 Macpherson, *Political Theory of Possessive Individualism*, 106.

37 Ibid.

38 Macpherson, "Introduction," in Hobbes, *Leviathan*, 62.

39 Macpherson, "Deceptive Task of Political Theory," 199; emphasis added.

40 Macpherson, *Political Theory of Possessive Individualism*, 93.

41 Ibid., 194.

42 Ibid., 220; emphasis added.

43 Ibid., 221.

44 Robert Nozick, *Anarchy, State, and Utopia* (New York: Basic Books, 1974). A good, brief account of Nozick's position as it relates to Locke's theory

of property is provided by Andrew Levine, *Engaging Political Philosophy: From Hobbes to Rawls* (Malden, MA: Blackwell, 2002), chap. 4.

45 John Locke, *Second Treatise of Government*, ed. C.B. Macpherson (1690; Indianapolis: Hackett, 1980), ss 5, 6.

46 Ibid., s. 4. Locke follow this with the claim that there can be no subordination or subjection "unless the lord and master of them all should, by any manifest declaration of his will, set one above another, and confer on him, by an evident and clear appointment, an undoubted right to dominion and sovereignty." While interestingly and perhaps surprisingly he does not specifically refer to this passage, Macpherson does argue that Locke's view of Christianity underwrote his claim that labourers and the indigent could not be granted the full rights of citizenship and were thus under political authority, without having a say in who exercised this authority or how it ought to be exercised. In other words, it is as if Locke did in effect claim that that there had been a "manifest declaration of his [i.e., God's] will." This "declaration" was evident from the class structure of society, which in turn reflected a class differential in rationality. Macpherson suggests that the "Puritan doctrine of the poor," which was hugely influential in Locke's time, "treating poverty as a mark of moral shortcoming, added moral obloquy to the political disregard in which the poor had always been held." He points to "a suggestive similarity between this view of the poor and the Calvinist view of the position of the non-elect. The Calvinist church, while claiming to include the whole population, held that full membership could be had only by the elect ... The non-elect ... were thus at once members and not members of the church; not full members sharing in the government of the church, but sufficiently members to be subject, rightfully, to its discipline" (Macpherson, *Political Theory of Possessive Individualism*, 226–7).

47 Macpherson, *Political Theory of Possessive Individualism*, 250.

48 Ibid., 251.

49 Locke, *Second Treatise*, s. 25.

50 Ibid., ss 27, 28.

51 Ibid., ss 27, 31.

52 Ibid., ss 32, 34.

53 Ibid., s. 36.

54 Ibid., ss 50, 46, 47.

55 Macpherson, "Editor's Introduction," Locke, *Second Treatise*, xvii. Compare Macpherson, *Political Theory of Possessive Individualism*, 211–14.

56 Locke, *Second Treatise*, s. 32.

57 Ibid., s. 31.

58 Ibid., ss 50, 48.

59 John Locke, *Works* (1759), ii. 19, cited in Macpherson, *Political Theory of Possessive Individualism*, 206.

60 Macpherson, *Political Theory of Possessive Individualism*, 208.

61 Locke, *Second Treatise*, s. 48.

62 Ibid., ss 48, 37.

63 Macpherson, *Political Theory of Possessive Individualism*, 212–13. One might say that private virtue is thus transformed into a distinctively bourgeois social virtue where the appropriate institutions and incentives are in place, as Locke assumed they were empirically and thus normatively. Since this all ostensibly takes place in the state of nature prior to the establishment of civil and political society, this might in turn be thought the core of Locke's conception of natural human sociability.

64 Locke, *Second Treatise*, s. 28. Compare s. 85.

65 Macpherson, *Political Theory of Possessive Individualism*, 214–20.

66 Macpherson's extensive discussion of the Levellers and James Harrington in *The Political Theory of Possessive Individualism*, both of whom he sees as having recognized the existence of market relations and wage labour and thus establishing their political theories on the basis of this, is designed to set the stage for Locke's better-known account. It is central to Macpherson's core argument that the possessive individualist character of post-seventeenth-century English liberalism involved importing into its treatment of human nature assumptions derived from a developing bourgeois society.

67 Locke, *Second Treatise*, s. 14.

68 Ibid., s. 19.

69 Ibid., ss 16, 17, 19.

70 Ibid., s. 21.

71 Ibid., s. 123.

72 Macpherson, *Political Theory of Possessive Individualism*, 234.

73 Ibid., 217.

74 The complexity of Locke's conception of property served as a trigger for Macpherson's later efforts to develop his own account of property as a central component of a more radical theory of liberal democracy. See C.B. Macpherson, "A Political Theory of Property," in *Democratic Theory: Essays in Retrieval*, 120–40. I discuss this in more detail in chapter 3.

75 Macpherson, *Political Theory of Possessive Individualism*, 245.

76 Ibid., 245–6.

77 One of the strongest and most provocative statements of this position is Willmoore Kendall, *John Locke and the Doctrine of Majority-Rule* (1941, Urbana, IL: University of Illinois Press, 1959). The term *totalitarian democracy* is most commonly associated with J.L. Talmon, *The Rise of Totalitarian Democracy* (Boston: Beacon, 1952).

78 A milder version of the individualist versus collectivist split was the individualism versus communitarianism debate that gained considerable attention, primarily in the 1980s and 1990s.

79 Macpherson, *Political Theory of Possessive Individualism*, 255.

80 "It is true, governments cannot be supported without great charge, and it is fit every one who enjoys his share of protection should pay out of his estate his proportion for the maintenance of it. But it still must be with his own consent *i.e.* the consent of the majority, giving it either by themselves, or their representatives chosen by them." Locke, *Second Treatise*, s. 140.

81 Macpherson, *Political Theory of Possessive Individualism*, 256.

82 If I am right about this, then it provides more evidence of links between Macpherson and the Frankfurt School, notably the work of Herbert Marcuse. Marcuse offered a comparable critique of liberalism as a whole and in particular read Hegel's explicitly political theory in the *Philosophy of Right* as offering (reluctantly) a collectivist solution to the problem of order in civil society and in so doing representing the culmination of classically rationalist liberal political philosophy. See Herbert Marcuse, *Reason and Revolution: Hegel and the Rise of Social Theory* (1941; Boston: Beacon, 1960). Compare Marcuse, "The Struggle against Liberalism in the Totalitarian View of the State," in Marcuse, *Negations: Essays in Critical Theory*, trans. Jeremy J. Shapiro, 3–42 (Boston: Beacon, 1968).

It is also possible to detect here an intrinsic connection between individualism as self-proprietorship, the compulsions of the market, and the historical formation of human needs and powers, the focus of Macpherson's account of ontology and the subject of my next chapter. An individual whose freedom consists in the natural proprietorship of one's own person is compelled to act according to the requirements of property as an institution, however much he or she has internalized the demands of acquisitiveness as Hobbesian "desirers." In other words – and this is decisive, I think, for grasping the core challenges of possessive individualism as a historically conditioned and complex concept – owing nothing to society is not the same as enjoying free, rational, and autonomous self-determination. I believe Macpherson understood this.

And of course this is yet another way of demonstrating a link with the Frankfurt School and critical theory.

Aside from the association with the Frankfurt School, Macpherson's position also suggests something of what Hannah Arendt had in mind when she wrote of the triumph of the social over the public and private as a distinguishing hallmark of the modern world. On this see Arendt, *The Human Condition* (Chicago: University of Chicago Press, 1959), 38–58. For a detailed critical account of this aspect of Arendt's thought, see Hanna Fenichel Pitkin, *The Attack of the Blob: Hannah Arendt's Concept of the Social* (Chicago: University of Chicago Press, 1998).

83 I see this as an important, if mostly implicit, element of Macpherson's critique of Isaiah Berlin's two concepts of liberty and his defence of positive or what he will call developmental liberty. See Macpherson, "Berlin's Division of Liberty," in Macpherson, *Democratic Theory: Essays in Retrieval*, 95–119. I will discuss this essay in chapter 4.

84 Ibid., 253–4.

85 See Macpherson, *Life and Times of Liberal Democracy*, 16–17.

86 This is essentially the argument Macpherson makes in his *Democracy in Alberta: The Theory and Practice of a Quasi Party System* (Toronto: University of Toronto Press, 1953). The book was reissued with a new preface and an altered subtitle in 1962, the same year *The Political Theory of Possessive Individualism* was published. While the timing of the reissue was coincidental in that it reflected certain developments in the Canadian political system that year, it is nonetheless instructive to note the parallels. I discuss this work in chapter 3.

At the same time it should be noted that Macpherson's appraisal of populism was rather mixed. He later argued that alongside Western liberal and Soviet-style communist democracy, what he saw as Third World populist democracy represented an understandable response on the part of postcolonial political elites to the failures and limitations of the other two models. See Macpherson, *The Real World of Democracy* (Toronto: CBC Publications, 1965).

87 Jürgen Habermas, "Three Normative Models of Democracy," in Habermas, *The Inclusion of the Other: Studies in Political Theory*, ed. Ciaran Cronin and Pablo De Greiff, 239–52 (Cambridge, MA: MIT Press, 1998) Compare Caterino and Hansen, "Macpherson, Habermas, and the Demands of Democratic Theory."

88 Macpherson, *Political Theory of Possessive Individualism*, 262.

89 Ibid., 275.

90 Arendt, *The Life of the Mind* (New York: Harcourt Brace Jovanovich, 1978), 1:5.

2. Human Nature and Democratic Possibilities

1 Macpherson, "Do We Need a Theory of the State?," 55–75.

2 Macpherson, *Political Theory of Possessive Individualism*, 276–7. It is interesting to note that the new justification of political obligation could no longer apply effectively at the level of the nation state but only to "a wider authority," a kind of cosmopolitan order. I do not believe Macpherson ever really followed up this intriguing possibility in his subsequent work.

3 Ibid., 276.

4 This is one reason why, unlike many Marxists, Macpherson never completely rejected the idea of negative liberty, essentially Hobbes's view that liberty was the absence of impediments to motion, that is, of restrictions on what one had a desire to do. Indeed, as what he called "counter-extractive" liberty, in terms of which Macpherson linked the individualist and class dimensions of the market-based struggle and transfer of powers, it would come to assume a key place in Macpherson's democratic theory.

5 Macpherson, *Political Theory of Possessive Individualism*, 55, 56.

6 Ibid., 56.

7 With respect to this issue, see Frank Cunningham, *The Real World of Democracy Revisited and Other Essays on Democracy and Socialism* (Atlantic Highlands, NJ: Humanities, 1994), 1–24.

8 I use this expression to note what I see as similarities between Macpherson's critique of liberal democracy and the contemporary parallel account by Peter Bachrach and Morton Baratz of what they called the two faces of power. For them, this involved both the capacity to visibly enforce one's will on others through the political system in the context of contentious questions that come to occupy a place on the formal political agenda, and, perhaps even more significantly, the ability to *prevent* the emergence of issues requiring democratic deliberation and decision that powerful groups believe would be damaging to their interests. There is in effect a political (because power-based) decision *not* to decide with respect to such questions. Hence the idea of the two faces of power: a full empirically and normatively informed treatment of power in a liberal democratic society required attention to both decisions and what Bachrach and Baratz called non-decisions. See Peter Bachrach and Morton S. Baratz, "Two Faces of Power," *American Political Science Review* 56 (December 1962): 947–52; Bachrach and Baratz, "Decisions and Non-Decisions: An Analytical Framework," *American Political Science*

Review 57 (September 1963): 632–42; Bachrach and Baratz, *Power and Poverty: Theory and Practice* (New York: Oxford University Press, 1970). A lucid summary of the analysis in response to criticism of the model is Bachrach and Baratz, "Power and Its Two Faces Revisited: A Reply to Geoffrey Debnam," *American Political Science Review* 69 (September 1975): 900–4. A decade later, Jürgen Habermas would, from a more systematically explicit and detailed social-theoretical and philosophical perspective, make a comparable argument: "A social theory critical of ideology can, therefore, identify the normative power built into the institutional system of a society if it starts from the *model of the suppression of generalizable interests* and compares normative structures existing at a given time with the hypothetical state of a system of norms formed, *ceteris paribus*, discursively ... Of course, the model of the suppression of generalizable interests – which explains at one and the same time the *functional necessity* of the apparent legitimation of domination and the *logical possibility* of undermining normative-validity claims by a critique of ideology – can be made fruitful for social theory only by making empirical assumptions." Jürgen Habermas, *Legitimation Crisis*, trans. Thomas McCarthy (Boston: Beacon, 1975), 113. The marriage of social theory and empirical research is at the heart of the Frankfurt School approach; in their subsequent efforts to develop a model of decisions versus non-decisions, Bachrach and Baratz attempted something comparable (and in a fashion that would later be reflected in the critical social science of Claus Offe, himself influenced by Habermas and the Frankfurt School approach. While further treatment of the issues raised here must be deferred until my more extensive discussion of Macpherson's democratic theory, I would claim that this analysis is still valuable for an account of contemporary liberal democratic systems, indeed perhaps more so today than in the recent past.

Macpherson was very much aware of this analysis as an important contribution to the then-current critical accounts of what he would later call the pluralist-elitist-equilibrium model of liberal democracy, to which he was highly sympathetic. On this topic particularly, see Peter Bachrach, *The Theory of Democratic Elitism: A Critique* (Boston: Little, Brown, 1967).

9 C.B. Macpherson, *The Real World of Democracy* (Toronto: CBC Publications, 1965), 40.

10 Ibid., 41.

11 Ibid., 41, 42.

12 Ibid., 43.

13 Ibid., 44. It should be noted that Macpherson offered these claims at a

time in Western liberal democratic capitalist states during which there was both strong economic growth and an expanding welfare state, both of which contributed to lessening the material impact, if not the presence, of the net transfer of powers.

14 Ibid., 45.
15 Ibid., 48.
16 Ibid., 53.
17 Ibid., 50.
18 Macpherson, "The Maximization of Democracy," in Macpherson, *Democratic Theory: Essays in Retrieval*, 3–23.
19 Ibid., 9.
20 Charles Taylor, "Neutrality in Political Science," in *Philosophy, Politics and Society*, ed. Peter Laslett and W.G. Runciman, 3rd ser. (Oxford: Basil Blackwell, 1967), 56. Coincidentally, "The Maximization of Democracy" was initially published in this collection as well.
21 Ibid., 9, 10.
22 Ibid., 19.
23 Macpherson, "Democratic Theory: Ontology and Technology," 38.
24 Macpherson, "The Maximization of Democracy," 19.
25 Ibid.
26 The following discussion draws in part upon Brian Caterino and Phillip Hansen, "Towards a Critical Theory of Democracy" (unpublished, 2010).
27 Horkheimer, "Traditional and Critical Theory," 188, 189, 190. The last citation is provided in the text of the article by Horkheimer and is taken directly from his contemporary, Edmond Husserl. Horkheimer also explicitly cites Descartes from his *Discourse on Method*: "Those long chains of deductive reasoning, simple and easy as they are, of which geometricians make use in order to arrive at the most difficult demonstrations, has caused me to imagine that all those things which fall under the cognizance of men might very likely be mutually related in the same fashion."
28 Max Horkheimer, "Postscript," in Horkheimer, *Critical Theory: Selected Essays*, 246.
29 Horkheimer, "Traditional and Critical Theory," 218.
30 Ibid., 227.
31 Max Horkheimer, "Materialism and Morality," in Horkheimer, *Critical Theory: Selected Essays*, 15–16. For two lucid and suggestive, if somewhat conflicting, accounts of Marx, Marxism, and morality, see Allen W. Wood, *Karl Marx*, 2nd ed. (New York: Routledge, 2004), 127–61; and Willis H. Truitt, *Marxist Ethics: A Short Exposition* (New York: International Publishers, 2005).

32 Horkheimer, "Materialism and Morality," 20.
33 Ibid., 19.
34 Ibid., 20.
35 Ibid., 25, 33.
36 Ibid., 30.
37 Ibid., 28.
38 Ibid., 36. There are echoes of Rousseau in this and, especially, Schopenhauer who exerted a lifelong influence on Horkheimer. On this, see Max Horkheimer, "Schopenhauer Today," in *The Critical Spirit: Essays in Honor of Herbert Marcuse*, ed. Kurt H. Wolff and Barrington Moore Jr, 55–71 (Boston: Beacon, 1967).
39 The redefinition of bourgeois ideals arises for Horkheimer from the reality that materialist theory, in which these concepts must find a place, "is not a metaphysics of history but rather a changing image of the world, evolving in relation to the practical efforts toward its improvement … The blind worship of success determines people even in the most private expressions of life. For the materialist, the presence of a historical magnitude alone, or the prospects which it has, by no means constitutes a recommendation. The materialist asks how this dimension at a given point in time relates to the values he affirms, and acts according to the concrete situation." Horkheimer, "Materialism and Morality," 44.
40 Ibid., 44, 45.
41 Ibid., 34–5. There is a theological motif here in that the solidaristic conception of love implied calls to mind the idea behind agape: the Christian notion, derived from the Greeks, of love of humanity as caritas, as a necessary outcome of the reciprocal relation of love with God; and especially the idea that one should promote well-being even and especially when confronting a situation of ill-being. On this, see Herbert Marcuse, *Eros and Civilization: A Philosophical Inquiry into Freud* (New York: Vintage Books, 1962), chap. 5; and Hannah Arendt, *Love and Saint Augustine*, ed., with an interpretive essay by Joanna Vecchiarelli Scott and Judith Chelius Stark (1929; Chicago: University of Chicago Press, 1996). In Marcuse's case, the relation of agape to eros, the Christian and romantic notions of love, is vital.
42 For appraisals of Horkheimer's argument here and the question of normative justification, see Herbert Schnadelbach, "Max Horkheimer and the Moral Philosophy of German Idealism," *Telos* 19, no. 1 (Winter 1985–6): 81–101; and Peter M.R. Stirk, *Critical Theory, Politics and Society: An Introduction* (London: Continuum, 2000), chapter 10. See also John Abromeit, *Max Horkheimer and the Foundations of the Frankfurt School*

(Cambridge: Cambridge University Press, 2011), 238–45. This is a very thorough and comprehensive study of Horkheimer's work, particularly in the 1930s before his better-known collaboration with T.W. Adorno. In this book, which is likely to become the definitive source on the subject, Abromeit makes a compelling case for the contemporary relevance of this earlier work.

43 Max Horkheimer, "Egoism and Freedom Movements: On the Anthropology of the Bourgeois Era," in Horkheimer, *Between Philosophy and Social Science*, 60, 72–3, 99.

44 Ibid., 97, 95, 97.

45 Ibid., 97, 61, 108.

46 C.B. Macpherson, "Problems of a Non-Market Theory of Democracy," in Macpherson, *Democratic Theory: Essays in Retrieval*, 58–9.

47 Horkheimer, "Egoism and Freedom Movements," 95, 108.

48 It should be noted here that while Macpherson offered nothing really comparable to Horkheimer's psychoanalytic perspective, he was not completely indifferent to the role played by psychic forces in shaping individual and social behaviour. In his treatment of liberty and its relation to democracy, Macpherson will take off from the perspective of another member of the Frankfurt School, Herbert Marcuse, in raising the issue of what he called internal impediments to the exercise of liberty as autonomous self-direction. I will discuss this more fully in chapter 4.

49 Horkheimer, "Egoism and Freedom Movements," 110. Of course Horkheimer later abandoned this position without, however, completely shedding the meta-theoretical framework out of which in his case it emerged. This issue is obviously beyond the scope of this study, but I would suggest it reflects Horkheimer's life-long ambivalence about liberalism, an ambivalence Macpherson did not share.

50 Seyla Benhabib, *Critique, Norm, and Utopia: A Study of the Foundations of Critical Theory* (New York: Columbia University Press, 1986).

51 Horkheimer, "Egoism and Freedom Movements," 110.

52 Macpherson, "Problems of a Non-Market Theory of Democracy," 40; italics in original.

53 Ibid., 41; italics in original.

54 In the context of his analysis, Macpherson distinguished *capacities* (various capabilities and potentialities of a physical, mental, or psychic kind) from *power* (the ability to exercise one's capacities). See ibid., 52–3, for his justification for this shift.

55 It might be argued that Macpherson's analysis here assumed too great a concentration of capital, an assumption belied by the relatively wide

distribution of wealth, much in the form of housing and pension income, at least in advanced capitalist countries. However, the economist Anthony Atkinson has persuasively argued that we should distinguish "wealth" from "capital." Whereas wealth involves income-bearing or generating assets, capital entails something else: control over economic decision-making. Thus, "much of the wealth that people own conveys little or no control over the productive activities of the economy beyond their own front door ... The application of capital in productive activities is different from the beneficial ownership of wealth." Anthony B. Atkinson, *Inequality: What Can Be Done?* (Cambridge, MA: Harvard University Press, 2015), 95. Atkinson's suggestion I think fits well with Macpherson's intention here, for it alludes to questions of power(s) and not just possession.

56 Macpherson, "Problems of a Non-Market Theory of Democracy, 44, 45.

57 Ibid., 41.

58 Ibid.

59 The following account draws upon Phillip Hansen, "Macpherson, Habermas and the Demands of Democratic Theory" (Paper prepared for the Annual Meeting, Atlantic Provinces Political Science Association, University of Moncton, Moncton, New Brunswick, 24–6 September 2004). A revised version was later published as Caterino and Hansen, "Macpherson, Habermas, and the Demands of Democratic Theory."

60 Macpherson, "Problems of a Non-market Theory of Democracy," 65–6.

61 Ibid., 66.

62 Macpherson does spell out what he considers distinctively human attributes; these include (but are not necessarily restricted to) "the capacity for rational understanding, for moral judgement and action, for aesthetic creation or contemplation, for emotional activities of friendship and love, and, sometimes, for religious experience." Macpherson, "The Maximization of Democracy," 4. So stated, it would be difficult to disagree with any of these. Indeed they find their way into the recent work of Axel Honneth for whom intact and fulfilling relations of recognition require maximum opportunities for recognition in terms of respect as a bearer of legal and political rights, inclusion as a contributor to collective processes of social production, and acknowledgment of one's distinctive personal qualities in relations of love and intimacy.

63 Macpherson, "Problems of a Non-Market Theory of Democracy," 50.

64 This suggests that there are elements of what David Held has identified as two models of republicanism, namely developmental and protective republicanism, in Macpherson's position. This is, of course, another

way of identifying Macpherson's attempt to combine democracy and liberalism in a new synthesis. The relation of Macpherson's thought to republican models will be treated in chapter 4.

In a related vein there are also here intimations of Kant's account of right, whereby under a regime that secures the principles of right, public and private, laws act as hindrances to hindrances to freedom. For a comprehensive and fascinating account of Kant's work in this respect, see Arthur Ripstein, *Force and Freedom: Kant's Legal and Political Philosophy* (Cambridge, MA: Harvard University Press, 2009). In a little-noted passage in which he elaborated upon his claim that the exercise of our distinctively human capacities "to be fully human, must be under one's own conscious control rather than at the dictate of another," Macpherson argues that, for an individual, "the rules by which he is bound should be only those that can be rationally demonstrated to be necessary to society, and so to his humanity. Or it may be put that the rules society imposes should not infringe the principle that he should be treated not as a means to other's ends but as an end in himself. With all its difficulties, this is at bottom simply the assertion of the dignity of man." Macpherson, "Problems of a Non-Market Theory of Democracy," 56. There are clearly resonances of Kant here as well.

On the other hand, in an early book review essay, Macpherson explicitly took issue with one author who favourably contrasted Kant's theory of historical progress with that of Marx, suggesting that it represented an inadequate eighteenth-century response to twentieth-century problems. C.B. Macpherson, "A Disturbing Tendency in Political Science," *Canadian Journal of Economics and Political Science* 16, no. 1 (February 1950): 98–106.

65 I should note that in response to the specific criticism of Alasdair MacIntyre that he had insufficiently stressed the social basis and nature of human capacities, Macpherson admitted that there was the question "whether I have given enough attention to the need for community as a *sine qua non* of a humanist individualism. I should have perhaps been more insistent about this. But I have said explicitly … that society is a positive agent in the development of human capacities, that those capacities are socially derived, that their development must also be social, and that society is the medium through which human capacities are developed." He went on to connect this with "the optimistic assumption that a post-scarcity society, in which there will be zero extractive power, is possible." C.B. Macpherson, "Individualist Socialism? A Reply to Levine and MacIntyre," *Canadian Journal of Philosophy* 6, no. 2 (June 1976): 199.

I continue, however, to stand by my criticism of the insufficiently social dimension of Macpherson's account on the basis that he did not fully take up or work out the intersubjective potential of his analysis. In this respect, at least, more recent developments in political and social theory and philosophy provide valuable insights that can enrich our understanding of what Macpherson was trying to do, while pointing beyond the limitations of his treatment of power and capacities.

66 C.B. Macpherson, "Needs and Wants: An Ontological or Historical Problem?," in *Human Needs and Politics*, ed. Ross Fitzgerald (Rushcutters Bay, NSW: Pergamon, 1977), 26.

67 Perhaps the most subtle and interesting of works that explored this shift and advanced this argument is Daniel Bell, *The Cultural Contradictions of Capitalism* (New York: Basic Books, 1976). What came to be called neo-conservatism built upon many of the issues and themes Bell treated, although his relation to neo-conservatism was complex.

68 Macpherson, "Problems of a Non-Market Theory of Democracy," 50. Andrew Feenberg and William Leiss offer a comparable appraisal: "Taken at its best, the counterculture celebrated a rejection of endless consumerism, of rigid nuclear-family suburban lifestyles, of sexual repression – especially for women, of the fear of intoxication (except for alcoholic excess, still today the one officially approved recreational drug in American culture), of hypocritical churchgoing, and of the social ideologies that affirmed war, racism, and inequality." Balancing the ledger, they do note that "the counterculture had its own darker side, in drug excess, in persistent male domination, in 'communes' where the old games of leaders and followers were reproduced, in the failure to bridge the racial divide in America or take up the cause of the poorest and most exploited social strata." Andrew Feenberg and William Leiss, "Introduction: The Critical Theory of Herbert Marcuse," in *The Essential Marcuse: Selected Writings of Philosopher and Social Critic Herbert Marcuse*, ed. Feenberg and Leiss , xxix–xxx (Boston: Beacon, 2007).

The literature on what is typically characterized as "the sixties" is vast. Two still very useful and comprehensive surveys are Todd Gitlin, *The Sixties: Years of Hope, Days of Rage* (Toronto: Bantam Books, 1987); and James Miller, *"Democracy Is in the Streets: From Port Huron to the Siege of Chicago* (New York: Simon and Schuster, 1987). A more recent collection that offers new perspectives on the era is John McMillan and Paul Buhle, eds, *The New Left Revisited* (Philadelphia: Temple University Press, 2003).

69 William Leiss, "Review of Stewart Ewen, *Captains of Consciousness* and Tibor Scitovsky, *The Joyless Economy*," *Telos* 9, no. 3 (Fall 1976): 207. The

cited passage is from a review of two studies that deal critically with issues of consumption, consumerism, and advertising. Leiss, himself, who was a student of Marcuse, has over several decades contributed significantly to a consideration of the issues raised here. See especially William Leiss, *The Limits to Satisfaction: An Essay on the Problem of Needs and Commodities* (Toronto: University of Toronto Press, 1976); Stephen Kline and William Leiss, "Advertising, Needs, and 'Commodity Fetishism,'" *Canadian Journal of Political and Social Theory* 2, no. 1 (Winter 1978): 5–30; William Leiss, Stephen Kline, and Sut Jhally, *Social Communication in Advertising: Persons, Products, and Images of Well-Being*, 2nd ed. (Scarborough, ON: Nelson Canada, 1990); and William Leiss, *Under Technology's Thumb* (Montreal and Kingston: McGill-Queen's University Press, 1990).

70 A lucid statement of this argument is Frankfurt Institute for Social Research, "Ideology," in Frankfurt Institute for Social Research, *Aspects of Sociology*, trans. John Viertel, 182–205 (Boston: Beacon, 1972).

71 Herbert Marcuse, *One-Dimensional Man: Studies in the Ideology of Advanced Industrial Society* (Boston: Beacon, 1964), 1. Compare Marcuse, *Eros and Civilization*, 91.

72 Max Horkheimer, "Materialism and Metaphysics," in Horkheimer, *Critical Theory: Selected Essays*, 45.

73 Herbert Marcuse, "On Hedonism," in Marcuse, *Negations: Essays in Critical Theory*, trans. Jeremy J. Shapiro (Boston: Beacon, 1968), 183, 182, 198–9.

74 Breaking with the asceticism of classical bourgeois and socialist revolutionary movements would ideally, from Marcuse's point of view, shatter the continuum whereby mass movements for social change had through the internalization of the morality of self-denial become repressive and oppressive – subject to what Marcuse called a "psychic Thermidor." See Marcuse, "Progress and Freud's Theory of Instincts," in Marcuse, *Five Lectures: Psychoanalysis, Politics, and Utopia*, trans. Jeremy J. Shapiro and Shierry M. Weber (Boston: Beacon, 1970), 38–9. The impact of Horkheimer's "Egoism and Freedom Movements" was clearly decisive here.

75 Herbert Marcuse, "The Foundation of Historical Materialism," in Marcuse, *Studies in Critical Philosophy*, trans. Joris de Bres, 3–48 (Boston: Beacon, 1973).

76 For an analysis along these lines, see Ross Fitzgerald, "Human Needs and Politics: The Ideas of Christian Bay and Herbert Marcuse," *Political Psychology* 6, no. 1 (1985): 87–108. For a defence of the distinction

between true and false needs, see Alkis Kontos, "Through a Glass Darkly: Ontology and False Needs," *Canadian Journal of Political and Social Theory* 3, no. 1 (Winter 1979): 25–45. Marcuse stated the case (with some tentativeness, if not irony, it should be pointed out) in *One-Dimensional Man*. On occasion he also expressed support for the Leninist vanguard party, largely for the same reasons. See Marcuse, "33 Theses," trans. John Abromeit, in *Collected Papers of Herbert Marcuse*, vol. 1, *Technology, War and Fascism*, ed. Douglas Kellner (London: Routledge, 1998), 227. Marcuse submitted this document to Horkheimer in the late 1940s as a research plan for a newly reconstituted Institute for Social Research.

Coincidentally, in 1972 Christian Bay joined the Department of Political Economy at the University of Toronto and thus became a colleague of Macpherson.

77 Macpherson, "Needs and Wants," 26–35.

78 For an excellent account and appraisal of Macpherson's treatment of needs in this essay, see Kontos, "Through a Glass Darkly."

79 "History without the enlightenment of a philosophy of history is nothing but a babel of contradictions, the fusion of appearances and reality, the thoughtless interplay of light and darkness ... To render history coherent and meaningful, it is imperative that we distinguish appearance from reality, the true from the false, the human from the inhuman." Ibid., 27.

80 Macpherson, "Needs and Wants," 27.

81 Ibid., 30.

82 Ibid., 31.

83 With Macpherson's account of classical liberalism clearly in mind, Alkis Kontos criticizes Macpherson for continuing to maintain the distinction between needs and wants, even as he had, correctly in Kontos's view, challenged it. I would suggest instead that although he was not in a short piece particularly clear about it, Macpherson used the distinction, even as he otherwise criticized it, to indicate in the language of liberalism itself how the Utilitarian conception of human nature as infinite desire prevents a critical evaluation of desires, so "there is no place in the liberal theory for a distinction between 'needs' as more essential and 'wants' as less essential." Macpherson, "Needs and Wants," 30. Ironically, in making this claim, Macpherson implicitly suggested that although on the one hand liberalism maintains the distinction between needs and wants, on the other it collapses it. Both the distinction and its occlusion are one-sided; both are the product of the distorted relation between ontology and history. Kontos, "Through a Glass Darkly," 28.

There is another possible dimension to Macpherson's position here, although he did not explicitly raise it. The distinction between needs and wants expresses the view of Horkheimer and Marcuse that in a class-divided society the masses must be restricted in asserting their egoistic desires, even as the dominant elites are encouraged to pursue theirs. The effacement of the distinction reflects, on the other hand, the economic requirements of capitalism, as well as the frequent attempts to mobilize subordinate classes in support of the system by promising gratification, even as this gratification must be continuously deferred. The development of consumer capitalism along with the emergence of the consumerist ethic – that is, a regime of "false" needs – was from Marcuse's point of view a continuation of this deferral in the guise of the realization of genuinely fulfilling gratification.

84 Macpherson, "Needs and Wants," 31.

85 Ibid., 32.

86 Ibid., 30.

87 Ibid., 31.

88 Of course Rousseau himself could also be read as offering a critique of the very idea of "natural man." The point of departure is his claim from *A Discourse on the Origin of Inequality* that philosophers who have purported to reach the state of nature have never gotten there. The strategy then is to imagine what it would be like to strip humans of all socially acquired attributes. Such a human would be rather a proto-human who, as such, provides no direct basis for the critical appraisal of social and political forms. Rousseau's strategy of argument deliberately undermines his own explicit claims. Those claims themselves are derived from the socially and historically dominant discourse around the state of nature; in other words, Rousseau offered an immanent critique. For an analysis along these lines, see Asher Horowitz, *Rousseau, Nature and History* (Toronto: University of Toronto Press, 1987).

89 Macpherson, "Needs and Wants," 33. Hegel had earlier advanced the same claim in the *Philosophy of Right*. His influence on the "young" Marx was considerable.

90 Ibid., 34. For an excellent sympathetic yet critical account of the question of needs in Marx and Macpherson, see William Leiss, "Marx and Macpherson: Needs, Utilities, and Self-development," in *Powers, Possessions, and Freedom*, ed. Alkis Kontos, 119–38 (Toronto: University of Toronto Press, 1979).

91 Kontos, "Through a Glass Darkly," 32–4.

92 Ibid., 31–2.

93 Kontos's criticism of Macpherson calls to mind Hegel's distinction in his *Philosophy of Right* between the history of law or right and the philosophy of law: the latter attends to the concept (or the truth or the Idea of law); the former deals only with its empirical existence. Historical existence as such is not yet truth. History can only provide the material for philosophy, not replace it. Hegel puts it this way: "When a historical justification confuses an origin in external factors with an origin in the concept, it unconsciously achieves the opposite of what it intends. If it can be shown that the origin of an institution was entirely expedient and necessary under the specific circumstances of the time, the requirements of the historical viewpoint are fulfilled. But if this is supposed to amount to a general justification of the thing itself, the result is precisely the opposite; for since the original circumstances are no longer present, the institution has thereby lost its meaning and its right [to exist]." G.W.F. Hegel, *Elements of the Philosophy of Right*, ed. Allen W. Wood, trans. H.B. Nisbet (Cambridge: Cambridge University Press, 1991), 3:30.

94 Macpherson, "Second and Third Thoughts on Needs and Wants," *Canadian Journal of Political and Social Theory* 3, no. 1 (Winter 1979): 46.

95 Ibid., 47.

96 Ibid., 47–8, 49.

97 Still, in my view the fullest and best critical appraisal of Macpherson's treatment of needs and their relation to ontology that is sensitive to these issues is Leiss, "Marx and Macpherson: Needs, Utilities, and Self-development."

98 See, for example, "The Maximization of Democracy," 44–6; "Problems of a Non-Market Theory of Democracy," 63; *Life and Times of Liberal Democracy*, 33, 43, 48; "Liberalism as Trade-offs," in *The Rise and Fall of Economic Justice and Other Essays*, 46–51.

99 See William Leiss, "The End of History and Its Beginning Again; or, the Not-Quite-Yet-Human Stage of Human History," in Carens, *Democracy and Possessive Individualism*, 263–74.

100 There is an interesting conclusion that emerges from this approach. While Macpherson would not have put it quite this way, no doubt because of his aversion to explicitly Hegelian themes, as he presents it liberalism occupies a privileged world-historical position precisely because it incorporates within its very make-up the full range of plausible, contemporary, historically rooted ontological possibilities. In effect the dialectic of liberalism is the driver of historical development, whether progressive or regressive.

Macpherson himself did offer some implicit support for this reading of his understanding of liberalism. In his response to Kontos's claim that only within liberal democratic thought does the idea of the two competing ontologies hold up, Macpherson argued: "I do not ... see any *present* contexts where my two ontological postulates are not exhaustive. They are, surely, in Marx: is it not essentially those two postulates that he had in mind in his distinction between the wealth and poverty of political economy and the rich human need of a totality of human life-activities ... Would anarchists or Maoists see it any differently, or conservative libertarians such as Nozick and Milton Friedman, or non-liberal idealists such as Leo Strauss and his followers? I do not think so, nor do I see any other significant schools of political theory in our time which would dissent more than marginally from the exhaustiveness of the opposed postulates I have heard." Macpherson, "Second and Third Thoughts on Needs and Wants," 48.

101 Macpherson "Democratic Theory: Ontology and Technology," 24.

102 Ibid., 28. It is evident from this passage why some Marxists have criticized Macpherson for offering at its core a moral, and thus essentially liberal, critique of capitalism, a form of philosophical Idealism; the paradigm for this is Ellen Meiksins Wood, "C.B. Macpherson: Liberalism, and the Task of Socialist Political Theory," in *The Socialist Register 1978*, ed. Ralph Miliband and John Saville, 215–240 (London: Merlin, 1978). Aside from the fact that Macpherson allegedly failed to provide a "materialist" account of these ideas and institutions, he seemed to have made an illicit separation between ownership for the purpose of maximization of returns or utilities and unlimited appropriation. He failed to recognize that the two are connected via the mechanism of exploitation and the extraction of surplus value.

With respect to such Marxist criticisms of Macpherson, I would only note here that they seem to misunderstand what Macpherson was doing, namely, establishing the normative conditions for the spread of capitalist market relations. Such conditions cannot be reduced to the status of the merely "superstructural": human agents are such that, as a core element of their engagement with others in the course of reproducing their existence as social beings, normative considerations play a decisive role in their judgments and choices.

103 Ibid., 30.

104 The relation I'm suggesting here between maximization of utilities and unlimited appropriation relates to the issue posed by John Seaman

and Thomas Lewis in their interesting and thoughtful critique of Macpherson's ontological assumptions. They argue that Macpherson held both a liberal ontology of self-governance and a humanist ontology of self-development that ultimately conflicted. Claiming that the humanist assumptions had authoritarian implications at odds with his central commitments to a non-market democratic society, Lewis and Seaman argue that Macpherson had in his liberal ontology all he needed for his critical account of the barriers to freedom erected by capitalism, an account that could be both liberal and non-market. See John W. Seaman and Thomas J. Lewis, "On Retrieving Macpherson's Liberalism," *Canadian Journal of Political Science* 17, no. 4 (December 1984): 707–29.

With respect to the position of Seaman and Lewis, in a sense my earlier claim (see note 100) that Macpherson implicitly appeared to understand his competing ontological views as emerging from the historical dialectic of liberalism shares some common ground with their stance. However, Seaman and Lewis fall into the camp of those who tend to see Macpherson at his best as a critical or radical (renegade?) liberal out to make liberalism and liberal society live up to their own claims. As should be obvious, my own view is that Macpherson offered instead an immanent critique of liberalism, one that points to a society beyond liberalism, a society that nonetheless incorporates, and is needed to incorporate, liberalism's most fully humanist values. This is what Macpherson meant by a fully democratic society that might legitimately be called liberal or even liberal-democratic socialist. It is more than, but not at odds with, reform liberalism – it is Mill transcended, and transformed, by Marx. It is based on what I have argued is Macpherson's position that the dialectic of liberalism qua possessive individualism cannot, within liberalism and liberal capitalist society itself, resolve the tension/contradiction between individualism as self-ownership and individualism as self-development, or what Seaman and Lewis call self-governance. It is for this reason that I suggest that it might be worth following up on the distinction Macpherson seemed to draw between the maximization of utilities and the pursuit of unlimited appropriation.

105 Macpherson, "Democratic Theory: Ontology and Technology," 32.

106 Ibid.

107 Ibid., 34.

108 Macpherson, "Maximization of Democracy," 18–19.

109 Macpherson, "Democratic Theory: Ontology and Technology," 31.

110 Hwa Yol Jung, "Democratic Ontology and Technology: A Critique of C.B. Macpherson," *Polity* 11, no. 2 (Winter 1978): 247–69.

111 Macpherson, "Democratic Theory: Ontology and Technology," 38.

112 Ibid., 37.

113 Horkheimer, "Materialism and Morality," 37.

114 Macpherson, "Democratic Theory: Ontology and Technology," 35.

115 Macpherson, *The Life and Times of Liberal Democracy*, 91–2.

116 Macpherson, "Democratic Theory: Ontology and Technology," 38. As I write this I have before me an interesting article on the rapidly developing technology of wireless, mobile communication, specifically so-called tablets and smartphones, which offer a wide range of options allowing us to connect with others and the world. The author views these devices as an attempt to create "a seamless integration of work and play," allowing the user to simultaneously submit a work report and play online computer games or pursue other so-called play or leisure activities. But he offers a telling observation about this development: "At one time, it was thought that such technologies would free us from work and give us more time for leisure. But, as is obvious to anyone who owns a tablet or a smartphone, work ends up following us to the golf course and to the sidelines of our kid's soccer game. Bosses and managers know play also follows us to work … cutting U.S. productivity by 9.4 per cent, resulting in $1.4 trillion in lost profits." However, something quite insidious seems to be taking place in this fusion of work and play, which one media theorist has labelled "playbour." Many popular online games themselves have come to take on the characteristics of work, evident in such games as *Farmville*, where participants "play" by simulating the operation of a farm business. Thus, "we may be at a technological tipping point where the critical balance between labour and leisure is lost. Rather than freeing us from work, technology turns everything into work."

The author notes that the idea that leisure or play has a critical humanizing role in human existence goes back to Aristotle, for whom leisure was supposed to provide an alternative to work and so facilitate contemplative reflection on the meaning of life. Work was to serve leisure. But now things have been reversed. And the consequences are potentially ominous. "More and more, time with our friends, families and even by ourselves is mediated by devices initially designed for work." If we "end up recreating work environments in our games … [if] play is being eclipsed by technology, all we may be left with is the strange drudgery of playbour." David Edward Tabachnick, "The Strange

Drudgery of 'Playbour,'" *Globe and Mail* (Toronto), 11 February 2013. The critique of technology, upon which Macpherson drew for his discussion of the human essence, clearly resonates with these contemporary concerns.

3. Capitalism, Socialism, and Self-Development

1 This has certainly been the position of the Frankfurt School. It is also at the heart of the approach that Erica Sherover-Marcuse called the disengaging of a theory from a body of thought that I indicated in the Introduction reflected what I hoped to accomplish with my own efforts to explore and bring to the surface what I have called Macpherson's suppressed philosophical dimension.

The self-reflexive quality of Marx's writings, in contrast to the rigid dogmatism that friends and foes alike have typically identified with him, has been recently and vigorously re-emphasized and defended in Terry Eagleton, *Why Marx Was Right* (New Haven, CT: Yale University Press, 2011), esp. chap. 6.

2 Hartmann and Honneth, "Paradoxes of Capitalism," 45. For Habermas, see the still-valuable collections from earlier in his career: *Theory and Practice*, trans. John Viertel (Boston: Beacon, 1973); *Legitimation Crisis*; and *Communication and the Evolution of Society*, trans., intro. Thomas McCarthy (Boston: Beacon, 1979). For Honneth's most recent work, see his *The I in We: Studies in the Theory of Recognition*, trans. Joseph Ganahl (Cambridge: Polity, 2012).

3 Harry Braverman, *Labour and Monopoly Capital: The Degradation of Work in the Twentieth Century* (New York: Monthly Review, 1974). Braverman's insights have parallels with Marcuse's analysis of technology as incorporating the demands of social control in its very structures and processes.

A comparable analysis of the relation between the organization of production and social control in the interests of capital accumulation is Stephen A. Marglin, "What Do Bosses Do?," parts 1 and 2, *Review of Radical Political Economics* 6, no. 2 (July 1974): 60–112; 7, no. 1 (April 1975): 20–37. This detailed, historically informed work may be even more relevant to understanding Macpherson in that it dealt specifically and systematically with authority relations in a way that addresses questions of individual autonomy and democracy as a way of life – key issues for him.

As an aside, I would note here that the work of Braverman, Marglin, and others has, I think, been unfortunately and unjustly forgotten under the impact of a neoliberal capitalism that has attempted to "naturalize" existing social and economic relations, and seems to a considerable extent to have succeeded. For one recent attempt to retrieve Braverman's position and relate it to contemporary concerns, see Jonna and Foster, who authors argue that the "continuing relevance of Braverman's analysis has to do with the fact that his overall vision of the transformations taking place in modern work relations was much wider than has usually been recognized. Viewed from a wide camera angle, his work sought to capture the complex relation between the labor process on the one hand, and the changing structure and composition of the working class and its reserve armies on the other. This broad view allowed him to perceive how the changes in the labor process were integrally connected to the emergence of whole new spheres of production, the decomposition and recomposition of the working class in various sectors, and the development of new structural contradictions." R. Jamil Jonna and John Bellamy Foster, "Beyond the Degradation of Labor: Braverman and the Structure of the U.S. Working Class," *Monthly Review* 66, no. 5 (October 2014): 1.

Another important, and, in my view, underappreciated, attempt to demonstrate that the organization of production under capitalism reflects not simply technical but also political imperatives is Samuel Bowles and Herbert Gintis, "Contested Exchange: New Microfoundations for the Political Economy of Capitalism," *Politics and Society* 18, no. 2 (June 1990): 165–222. Writing from the perspective of micro-economic analysis, Bowles and Gintis argue that class-weighted power relations define the "free" contractual relations between employers and employees in a capitalist economy. On this basis they claim that what distinguishes the employment contract is that it is not self-enforcing. The employer pays an employee a wage in return for a work effort over a certain period of time, but the extent of this effort and the willingness of the employee to provide it cannot be written into the wage contract itself. The employer must enforce fulfilment of the terms of the contract. Thus the structure of the firm or enterprise reflects not just the efficient mobilization of resources, but also the requirements of labour contract enforcement. The employer must be able both to monitor the work effort and to impose costly sanctions upon non-complying employees. The authority structure of the firm accomplishes the former aim; the threat of unemployment the latter.

I examine the argument of Bowles and Gintis in relation to issues in Marxian political theory in Phillip Hansen, "The *Communist Manifesto* and the Power of Capital," in *The Social Question and the Democratic Revolution*, ed. Douglas Moggach and Paul Leduc Browne, 167–85 (Ottawa: University of Ottawa Press, 2000).

4 Frank Cunningham, "C.B. Macpherson on Marx," in Cunningham, *The Real World of Democracy Revisited*, 15, 21.

5 Ibid., 16. On the impact such developments have had and continue to have on expanding the range of individual choices with respect to social roles and options, even as these have been used to reinforce capitalist social relations, see Axel Honneth, "Organized Self-Realization: Paradoxes of Individualization," in Honneth, *The I in We*, 153–68.

6 Ibid., 17.

7 Ibid., 18.

8 Ibid., 20.

9 Macpherson, *Life and Times of Liberal Democracy*, 1.

10 Horkheimer, "Traditional and Critical Theory," 227.

11 Honneth, *The I in We*.

12 Macpherson, "The Economic Penetration of Political Theory: Some Hypotheses," in Macpherson, *The Rise and Fall of Economic Justice*, 102.

13 Ibid., 101, 104.

14 Ibid., 104.

15 Ibid., 109; italics in original.

16 Ibid., 108; italics in original. The issue of alternative explanations for the origin of profit in a capitalist economy is hardly anachronistic. It could plausibly be argued that in the current era of "free market" liberalism, variations of the first three accounts continue to dominate both popular and intellectual/academic discourse.

17 Ibid.; italics in original.

18 Ibid., 116–17.

19 Macpherson specifically exempted orthodox Marxist and Communist theory from this charge, an indication perhaps of lingering identification with the Communist movement. This represents a political and, even more importantly for our purposes here, a theoretical blind spot. As Macpherson would have well understood, given the overall content and trajectory of his political thought, much orthodox Marxism and official Soviet theory in their own fashion demonstrated an insufficient degree of economic penetration in that they failed or refused to acknowledge the class question in actually existing socialist societies. See Macpherson's intriguing little-noticed review of Herbert Marcuse's *Soviet Marxism: A Critical Analysis* in *Political Science Quarterly* 74, no. 1 (March 1959): 152–4.

20 Ibid., 117.

21 Ibid., 118.

22 Ibid., 119.

23 Ibid. Macpherson here cites Hume to this effect. Of course for liberalism there can be no end to scarcity. As we have seen in discussing his ontology, Macpherson believed liberalism had naturalized what was in fact a socialized form of scarcity as a goad to unlimitedly appropriative behaviour.

24 Ibid.

25 Aside from "The Economic Penetration of Political Theory," Macpherson explored along these lines what he saw as the deterioration of economic and political thought in several places in his work, notably the essays "Post-Liberal Democracy?" and "Market Concepts in Political Theory," both included in *Democratic Theory: Essays in Retrieval*, 170–94. See as well his "After Strange Gods: Canadian Political Science 1973," in *Perspectives on the Social Sciences in Canada*, ed. T.N. Guinsburg and G.L. Reuber, 52–76 (Toronto: University of Toronto Press, 1974). I discuss these essays in more detail in chapter 6. Macpherson's most systematic examination of the basis of this transformation at the level of theory, and the one most explicitly indebted to Marx, is "The Deceptive Task of Political Theory," discussed below.

The separation of political economy from political theory that so concerned Macpherson remains an important issue, given ongoing worldwide economic instability and the apparent inability of mainstream political and economic thought to successfully address it and to inform appropriate political action in response to it. For Axel Honneth, as for Macpherson, the capacity of political thinking to inform political praxis is decisive. But according to Honneth, contemporary theories of justice fail to secure the link between theory and praxis largely because of their core assumptions, which Honneth describes, respectively, as their proceduralist mode of justification, their virtually exclusive concern with distributive justice, and a fixation on the state as the primary vehicle for achieving "just" outcomes. The result is that justice and thus a fulfilling way of life is seen as a divisible "good" rather than a network of social relations. That is, justice is seen as a matter for individuals, and not a question of communal ties. From Honneth's recognition-theoretic perspective, justice should be more appropriately understood, to use Macpherson's language, as involving a kind of society and not simply an allocative mechanism: it should, in other words, be seen as akin to a "fabric." See Honneth, "The Fabric of Justice: On the Limits of Contemporary Proceduralism," in Honneth, *The I in We*, 35–55. In his account Honneth very much appears to assume something like the severing of the descriptive/explanatory from the normative that Macpherson addressed.

26 That Macpherson ultimately intended that the economic penetration of political theory be transcended by the political penetration of the economy is, I think, evident in his political theory of property. This theory culminates in the claim that in order to realize a society in which all would be equally able to use and develop their distinctively human capacities, property would have to be transformed from the individual right to exclude others from the use or benefit of something to the equally individual right to participate in the exercise of political power over society's resources and ultimately to the right to participate in a satisfying set of social relations. See my discussion of property, below.

27 Georg Lukács, "What Is Orthodox Marxism?," in Lukács, *History and Class Consciousness: Studies in Marxist Dialectics*, trans. Rodney Livingstone (Cambridge, MA: MIT Press, 1971), 1–26.

28 Macpherson, "Deceptive Task of Political Theory," 195.

29 Ibid., 196–7.

30 Ibid., 198, 199.

31 Ibid., 198, 200, 202.

32 Ibid., 197.

33 Ibid., 200.

34 Horkheimer, "Egoism and Freedom Movements," 110.

35 And while, as I have argued, late in his life Macpherson explicitly repudiated the vanguard model of revolutionary change, as Peter Lindsay has noted Macpherson, echoing Marcuse, had in earlier times written more positively, or at least understandingly, of the idea of a vanguard state, its potential unavoidability if not necessity, and even its claim to be democratic. In this respect, see Macpherson, *The Real World of Democracy*, 19, 22. For Lindsay's analysis, see Peter Lindsay, *Creative Individualism: The Democratic Vision of C.B. Macpherson* (Albany: State University of New York Press, 1996), 84–7.

36 C.B. Macpherson, "Property as Means or End," in *Rise and Fall of Economic Justice*, 86. To be sure, Macpherson presented each of these approaches as distinct alternatives (and in turn contrasted them with another approach, which involved exploring the Western tradition in quest of a pattern in terms of which property was seen either as a means to an ethical end or as an end in itself). However, in another indication of his suppressed philosophical dimension that owed a debt to critical theory, Macpherson

in effect synthesized the historical with the logical approaches, which in turn I would argue undergirds a dialectic of means and ends.

37 C.B. Macpherson, ed., *Property: Mainstream and Critical Positions* (Toronto: University of Toronto Press, 1978), 61–74.

38 Macpherson, "Political Theory of Property," 121.

39 "Political economy proceeds from the fact of private property … Private property has made us so stupid and one-sided that an object is *our* only if we have it, if it exists for us as a capital or is immediately possessed by us, eaten, drunk, worn, lived in, etc., in short, *used* … Hence, *all* the physical and spiritual senses have been replaced by the simple alienation of them *all*, the sense of *having*. Human nature had to be reduced to this absolute poverty so that it could give birth to its inner wealth." Karl Marx, "Economic and Philosophic Manuscripts," in Marx, *Selected Writings*, ed., intro. Lawrence H. Simon (Indianapolis and Cambridge: Hackett, 1994), 58, 74; italics in the original. These claims offer a powerful statement of what Macpherson saw as the pathologies of possessive individualism, even if the development of a possessive market society at the same time provided the basis for further human development.

40 In at least one instance in his treatment of property and different property regimes, Macpherson specifically used the Marxian account of history as the dynamic succession of modes of production: "From Aristotle to say Bentham, the successive prevalent theories were those which supported the structure of property that was required by successive modes of production – slave, feudal, nascent and expanding capitalist." Macpherson, "Property as Means or End," 91.

41 C.B. Macpherson, "Human Rights as Property Rights," in Macpherson, *Rise and Fall of Economic Justice*, 76–85.

42 Macpherson, "Political Theory of Property," 124.

43 C.B. Macpherson, "The Meaning of Property," in Macpherson, *Property: Mainstream and Critical Positions*, 4 (emphasis in original).

44 The distinction I have in mind here between the institution of property and its effects is, I believe, crucial to current concerns about intensifying economic inequality both within individual states and on a global basis. While it is seen as a serious matter requiring some sort of significant policy responses, the problem is curiously detached from any attempt to relate this to the institution of (private) property itself. The problem is acknowledged at the same time as the key institutions of global capitalism are continuously and vigorously defended as unquestioned facts of nature, and even as the source of any solutions to the problem of inequality. I imagine that were Macpherson alive today, he would see

in this, at least on the part of more sensitive contemporary humanist liberals, a replay of John Stuart Mill's attempt to wed a concern with the condition of the working class to a continuing commitment to possessive market institutions – with likely the same results.

45 Macpherson, "Political Theory of Property," 124; emphasis in original. Macpherson in turn distinguishes common property from state property, where the latter is the property of that corporate body legitimately authorized to command the citizenry, and thus as any other corporate body or individual has the right to exclude.

46 Ibid., 127–8, 133.

47 Ibid., 129.

48 Ibid., 130.

49 Macpherson, "Meaning of Property," 11.

50 Macpherson, "Political Theory of Property," 129.

51 Ibid., 133.

52 Ibid., 136.

53 Ibid., 138.

54 Ibid., 139. Such an expanded conception of property suggests what contemporary theorists have in mind with the idea of recognition.

55 Ibid., 140.

56 In addition to "Political Theory of Property," see C.B. Macpherson, "Liberal Democracy and Property," in Macpherson, *Property: Mainstream and Critical Positions*, 199–207. This essay offers a more detailed account of a transformed conception of property based on the right not to be excluded and its compatibility with the core values of liberal democracy.

Macpherson's view that there could be a partial breakdown of the political order in the context of perceived deficiencies of state-managed capitalism also drew on the then-current neo-Marxian efforts to develop a theory of the contemporary capitalist state. This theory sought to demonstrate that the changes wrought in twentieth-century capitalism had resulted in the displacement of the economic contradictions and crises tendencies endemic to capitalism onto the state, which was now seen as prone to legitimation deficits or even legitimation crises. For Macpherson's appraisal and contribution to this analysis, see his "Do We Need a Theory of the State?" in Macpherson, *Rise and Fall of Economic Justice*, 55–75.

57 C.B. Macpherson, "Problems of Human Rights in the Late Twentieth Century," in Macpherson, *Rise and Fall of Economic Justice*, 32.

58 C.B. Macpherson, "Human Rights as Property Rights," in Macpherson, *Rise and Fall of Economic Justice*, 78.

59 Ibid., 80.

60 Ibid., 84.

61 Hartmann and Honneth, "Paradoxes of Capitalism," 49.

62 This process has been examined in detail by Leo Panitch and Sam Gindin, who have described it as the "democratization of finance" and relate it to the development of the post–Second World War global economy and American hegemony. See their sweeping and comprehensive work, *The Making of Global Capitalism: The Political Economy of American Empire* (London: Verso, 2012).

63 On the role of financialization in contemporary capitalism, see John Bellamy Foster and Robert W. McChesney, *The Endless Crisis: How Monopoly-Finance Capital Produces Stagnation and Upheaval from the USA to China* (New York: Monthly Review, 2012). For an account of the process of financialization that emphasizes state policies and their impact on the establishment of conditions that facilitated this process, with a focus on the United States, see Greta R. Krippner, *Capitalizing on Crisis: The Political Origins of the Rise of Finance* (Cambridge, MA: Harvard University Press, 2011).

64 There is another intriguing side to this as well. I would call it the emergence of a popular Idealism wonderfully expressed by the zealous free market enthusiast George Gilder, whose *Microcosm* celebrated the overthrow of matter. He wrote, "The powers of mind are everywhere ascendant over the brute force of things." This celebration of the immaterial as a reflection of the supposed emergence of the knowledge-based economy in which intellectual capital had become the most important kind was echoed by Alan Greenspan during his heyday as chair of the United States Federal Reserve. On this development, see Doug Henwood, "Marxing up the Millennium" (paper prepared for the Marx at the Millennium conference, University of Florida, 19 March 1999). The citation from Gilder is on page 10 of the essay.

65 The following draws upon Murray Knuttila and Phillip Hansen, "The Rise and Fall of the Agrarian Petite Bourgeoisie and the Dilemmas of Populist Democracy: C.B. Macpherson Revisited" (unpublished); and Phillip Hansen, "*Democracy in Alberta*: (Over) Fifty Years Later," in *The Prairie Agrarian Movement Revisited: Centenary Symposium on the Foundation of the Territorial Grain Growers Association*, ed. Murray Knuttila and Bob Stirling, 273–80 (Regina, SK: Canadian Plains Research Center, 2007).

66 C.B. Macpherson, *Democracy in Alberta: Social Credit and the Party System* (Toronto: University of Toronto Press, 1962), xi, 3.

67 Ibid., 225.
68 Ibid.
69 Ibid., 219.
70 Ibid., 222–4.
71 Ibid., 243–4. Compare Macpherson, *Life and Times of Liberal Democracy*, 64–9.
72 However, recent legislative efforts in both Canada and the United States that, ostensibly in the interests of guarding against voter fraud, have made it more difficult both to register to vote and to exercise the franchise suggest that, at least among political elites, there is the fear that the class question might resurface as a dominant point of contention in the electoral arena. The impact of restrictive measures would likely be felt most acutely among the poor, racial minorities, and the working classes more generally.
73 Ibid., 238.
74 Ibid., 239.
75 Ibid., 240.
76 Robert Meynell correctly suggests that there is a strong if largely implicit and unacknowledged Hegelian element to Macpherson's work and traces in detail what he believes to be its origins and character. I agree with much of Meynell's account, especially insofar as it brings to the fore what I have called Macpherson's suppressed philosophical dimension. Thus Meynell notes that "Macpherson shares Hegel's project of synthesizing individual autonomy and political unity through a notion of freedom involving intersubjectivity … Macpherson's freedom, like Hegel's is neither the atomistic individualism of classical liberalism that emerged from the mechanistic ontology of the Enlightenment, nor an oppressive collectivism wherein the individual is subordinated to rules dictated by an external authority, be it tradition or the tyrant. Freedom is inherently intersubjective and reason plays a vital role" (66).

The difference between Meynell's and my accounts is that Meynell develops his analysis on the basis of what might be called an orthodox Hegelian perspective, while I emphasize instead a Hegelian-Marxian reading of Macpherson more in line with that of Lukács and the Frankfurt School. Meynell is not indifferent to the Marxian dimension of Macpherson's work but reads Marx himself as Hegelian. By contrast, Hegelian-Marxian analysis stresses the extent to which Marx sought to move beyond Hegel by critically appropriating important Hegelian themes, while at the same time remaining indebted to his work. See Meynell, *Canadian Idealism and the Philosophy of Freedom*, chaps. 3–4.

See also the perceptive review of Meynell's book by Colin Campbell in *Philosophy in Review* 33, no. 1 (2013): 54–6. A rather more critical, indeed hostile, review that illuminates the politics of political theory is offered by Barry Cooper in *Review of Politics* 74, no. 3 (Summer 2012): 535–8.

77 Macpherson, "Human Rights as Property Rights," 83.

78 Macpherson, *Democracy in Alberta*, 239–40.

79 Ibid., 240.

80 In this respect it is worth noting that the current Canadian federal Conservative government has abolished the Canadian Wheat Board in the interests of market "freedom." The Wheat Board, which was a single-desk marketing agency to which under permit grain farmers in western Canada were required by law to deliver their product, with returns from sales distributed on a pooled basis to the producers, was a legacy of the very populist pressures Macpherson analysed. The board was created as a counterweight to the corporate interests that dominated the grain trade and ensured some measure of economic security for independent producers. The neoliberal federal government abolished the board ostensibly on behalf of "popular," pro–free market pressures from farmers, although there remained a considerable number who fought the move, perhaps even a majority. Nonetheless, in the name of the same individualism that the UFA and especially Social Credit celebrated and promoted, a significant number of agrarian producers have come to believe that the common property the Wheat Board represented stood as a barrier to their freedom and well-being. It will be interesting to see the impact of the shift to the "free" market on producer returns, and indeed their financial and economic viability, including of course the viability of the most vociferous supporters of the government's decision.

81 For one thorough and comprehensive account of the development of these new "economic constitutions," see Stephen Clarkson, *Uncle Sam and Us: Globalization, Neoconservatism, and the Canadian State* (Toronto and Washington: University of Toronto Press and the Woodrow Wilson Center Press, 2002).

82 Macpherson, *Democracy in Alberta*, 107–12.

83 The recent emergence of Bitcoin, a virtual currency, suggests the continuing presence of the monetary concerns that drove Social Creditors. Supporters of this new, ostensibly non-political alternative to conventional, state-sanctioned currencies tend to view it as an antidote to what they see as a hopelessly corrupt, decadent, and ultimately doomed international monetary system. That Bitcoin has also been yet another attempt to restore the gold standard, and thus diametrically opposed

it would seem to the inflationist tendencies of Social Credit, testifies to the contradictory character of the movement and its doctrines: the simultaneous defence of private property coupled with a rejection of the consequences of a regime of private property.

84 Macpherson, *Democracy in Alberta*, 233–4.

85 For an examination of market populism and its social roots, in this case with regard to the Reform Party of Canada, which was formed in Alberta in 1987 and represented a contemporary expression of many of the same ideas that Social Credit had espoused, see Richard Sigurdson, "Preston Manning and the Politics of Postmodernism in Canada," *Canadian Journal of Political Science* 27, no. 2 (June 1994): 249–76; and David Laycock, *The New Right and Democracy in Canada: Understanding Reform and the Canadian Alliance* (Toronto: Oxford University Press, 2002). In addition to an examination of the Reform Party (and its successor, the Canadian Alliance, which was established in order to enhance its role as a national political force), Laycock offers a comparative account of similar developments in other countries, notably the rise of the right in Europe. Preston Manning, a driving force behind the creation of the Reform Party and its first leader, is the son of Ernest Manning, long-time Social Credit premier of Alberta.

86 Macpherson, *Democracy in Alberta*, 249, 250.

87 For a contemporary analysis of the transformation of party systems in liberal democratic states that bears considerable affinity to Macpherson's, see Peter Mair, *Ruling the Void: The Hollowing Out of Western Democracy* (London: Verso, 2013). Mair argues that party systems have undergone a process of cartelization. He claims that parties have historically fulfilled two important functions that have formed the core of what he calls party government: the representative function of organizing and expressing the interests of concrete social groups; and the governance function of fulfilling leadership roles in the state. Increasingly the latter has overtaken the former; in the process the links between parties and electorates have atrophied. Increasingly tied to the state apparatus, and in a context in which both policy options have dwindled and political decisions are increasingly made by "experts" clustered in non-majoritarian (i.e., non-elected) bodies, partisan differences, while acute, are decreasingly shaped by ideological or policy conflicts. Parties have increasingly converged on an "acceptable" range of policy choices; this is the essence of cartelization. This may be thought a version of a "quasi-party" system and its basis is similar: the power of a now globalizing capitalism to limit democratic options.

Mair summarizes it this way: "In many different respects – including their patterns of incumbency, their policy commitments, and their electoral profiles – parties within the mainstream have become less easily distinguished from one another than they were in the polities of the 1970s. Despite the growing evidence of bipolar competition …, the parties now share government with one another more easily and more readily, with any lingering differences in policy-seeking goals appearing to matter less than the shared cross-party ambition for office. Policy discretion has become increasingly constrained by the imperatives of globalization … Even when parties are in government, in other words, the freedom for partisan manoeuvre is severely limited, and this too makes the task of differentiating between parties or between governments more difficult. Finally, a combination of increasing social homogenization – the blurring of traditional identity boundaries – and individualization has cut across differences in partisan electoral profiles, leaving most of the mainstream protagonists chasing more or less the same bodies of voters with more or less the same suasive techniques. Through the sharing of office, programmes and voters, even as competing coalitions, the parties have become markedly less distinct from one another" (59). While Mair focuses his analysis on the European Union, he argues that similar forces have been at work in all democratic political systems.

88 For a critique of orthodox Marxism-Leninism from the perspective of critical theory that addresses the issues noted here, see Robert J. Antonio, "Immanent Critique as the Core of Critical Theory: Its Origins and Developments in Hegel, Marx and Contemporary Thought," *British Journal of Sociology* 32, no. 3 (September 1981): 330–45.

4. C.B. Macpherson, Democracy, and Democratic Theory 1

1 Macpherson, *Democratic Theory,* vii.

2 Josiah Ober, "The Original Meaning of 'Democracy': Capacity to Do Things, Not Majority Rule," *Constellations* 15, no. 1 (March 2008): 3–9. For a comparable attempt to revisit the Greek legacy and its impact on the theory and practice of contemporary democracy, see Philip Resnick, "Twenty-First Century Democracy, or Cleisthenes Revisited"; and Resnick, "*Isonomia, Isegoria, Isomoiria,* and Democracy at the Global Level," in Resnick, *Twentieth-First Century Democracy* (Montreal and Kingston: McGill-Queen's University Press, 1997), 13–28, 29–44. It should be noted that there is archeological evidence of at least proto-democratic

practices in the form of popular pressures to hold monarchs accountable 2000 years before ancient Athens in Syria-Mesopotamia – what is now widely known as the Middle East. See John Keane, *The Life and Death of Democracy* (New York: W.W. Norton, 2009). Of course this does not alter the impact of the classical Greek experience on Western democracy, to which Keane devotes significant attention.

3 As an aside, the same goes for aristocracy, usually understood as rule of the best or the most excellent. This suggests an interesting issue that is very much central to the political thought of Jean-Jacques Rousseau: although democracy and aristocracy are seen to be at odds, it is possible that under certain circumstances they might have more in common than would appear at first glance.

4 Ober, "Original Meaning of 'Democracy,'" 6.

5 Ibid., 7.

6 For the classic account of polyarchy, see Robert Alan Dahl and Charles Edward Lindblom, *Politics, Economics, and Welfare: Planning and Politico-Economic Systems Resolved into Basic Social Processes* (New York: Harper, 1953). See also Charles E. Lindblom, *Politics and Markets: The World's Political-Economic Systems* (New York: Basic Books, 1977).

7 See Arendt, "What Is Freedom?," in Arendt, *Between Past and Future: Eight Exercises in Political Thought*, enl. ed. (New York: Penguin Books, 1968); and Arendt, "On Violence," in Arendt, *Crises of the Republic* (New York: Harcourt Brace Jovanovich, 1972), 103–33.

8 It should be noted that late in life Robert Dahl became a much more vigorous proponent of greater equality and a more robust democracy. See, for example, Robert A. Dahl, *On Political Equality* (New Haven, CT: Yale University Press, 2006). This book was published when Dahl was ninety!

9 C.B. Macpherson, "Revisionist Liberalism," in Macpherson, *Democratic Theory*, 79–80.

10 C.B. Macpherson, "Rawls's Models of Man and Society," *Philosophy of the Social Sciences* 3, no. 4 (December 1973), 341.

11 Macpherson, "Revisionist Liberalism," 82–6.

12 Ibid., 84, 85.

13 Ibid., 87.

14 For a extensive analysis of contemporary global economic inequalities and their consequences, see Joseph E. Stiglitz, *The Price of Inequality: How Today's Divided Society Endangers Our Future* (New York: W.W. Norton, 2013). See also Pauline Jelinek, "Richest 7 Per Cent in U.S. Got Richer during Recovery," *Globe and Mail* (Toronto), 23 April 2013. Jelinek cites a

2011 report from the U.S. Congressional Budget Office, which indicated that between 1979 and 2007, the richest 1 per cent of income-earners in the United States saw their incomes increase by 275 per cent while the middle 60 per cent saw increases totalling just under 40 per cent. A similar development occurred with respect to wealth. The larger global picture is comparable.

15 It should, of course, be noted that the rise of neoliberalism and the consequent move away from support for the welfare state, and even the dismantling of many of its achievements, has brought thinkers such as Hayek to greater prominence and, at least in the political and economic realm, diminished the influence of Rawls and his commitment to a vigorous welfare state.

16 For a particularly brief and lucid treatment of Rawls's theory of justice and especially the difference principle, see David Miller, *Political Philosophy: A Very Short Introduction* (Oxford: Oxford University Press, 2003), 89–91.

17 Macpherson, "Revisionist Liberalism," 89, 90.

18 C.B. Macpherson, "Review Symposium III – Rawls's Models of Man and Society," *Philosophy of the Social Sciences* 3 (1973): 341–2.

19 John Rawls, *A Theory of Justice* (Cambridge, MA: Harvard University Press, 1971), 66, 271.

20 Ibid., 280.

21 Macpherson, "Rawls's Models of Man and Society," 345, 341.

22 Ellen Meiksins Wood, *Liberty and Property: A Social History of Western Political Thought from Renaissance to Enlightenment* (London: Verso, 2012), 81.

23 Macpherson, "Rawls's Models of Man and Society," 345.

24 Rawls, *Theory of Justice*, 448, 528.

25 Macpherson, "Rawls's Models of Man and Society," 346. Compare Macpherson, "Revisionist Liberalism," 94.

26 Macpherson, "Revisionist Liberalism," 90.

27 Ibid.

28 Macpherson, "Rawls's Models of Man and Society," 343.

29 C.B. Macpherson, "Berlin's Division of Liberty," in Macpherson, *Democratic Theory*, 95.

30 Isaiah Berlin, "Two Concepts of Liberty," in Berlin, *Four Essays on Liberty* (Oxford: Oxford University Press, 1969), 131.

31 Charles Taylor, "What's Wrong with Negative Liberty," in Taylor, *Philosophy and the Human Sciences* (Cambridge: Cambridge University Press, 1985), 211–29.

32 Berlin, "Four Essays on Liberty," 130, 131.

33 Compare Jürgen Habermas, "Three Normative Models of Democracy," 239–52.

34 For an interesting take in this context on the issues posed by the contemporary significance of human rights, see James D. Ingram, "What Is a 'Right to Have Rights'? Three Images of the Politics of Human Rights," *American Political Science Review* 102, no. 4 (November 2008): 401–16. I discuss Ingram's essay in greater detail in the next chapter.

35 Macpherson, "Berlin's Division of Liberty," 109.

36 Ibid.

37 Ibid., 115.

38 Ibid., 114.

39 See, for example, Ian Shapiro, *The State of Democratic Theory* (Princeton: Princeton University Press, 2003), chap. 5; and John S. Dryzek, *Democracy in Capitalist Times: Ideals, Limits, and Struggles* (Oxford: Oxford University Press, 1996).

40 Berlin, "Two Concepts of Liberty," 154.

41 Macpherson, "Berlin's Division of Liberty," 113–14.

42 Macpherson, "Problems of a Non-Market Theory of Democracy," 55.

43 Ibid.; emphasis in the original.

44 On the central role of cooperative self-actualization for all generations of critical theory, see Axel Honneth, "A Social Pathology of Reason: On the Intellectual Legacy of Critical Theory," in Honneth, *Pathologies of Reason: On the Legacy of Critical Theory*, trans. James Ingram and others, 19–42 (New York: Columbia University Press, 2009).

45 Macpherson, "Berlin's Division of Liberty," 117–19.

46 C.B. Macpherson, "Elegant Tombstones: A Note on Friedman's Freedom," in Macpherson, *Democratic Theory*, 143–56. The following discussion is drawn from Caterino and Hansen, "Macpherson, Habermas, and the Demands of Democratic Theory."

47 Macpherson, "Elegant Tombstones, 146.

48 Ibid., 144–5.

49 I would argue that this problem is not restricted exclusively to neoliberal or free market theories. It has also emerged in mainstream theories generally in that they tend as well to separate the political from the economic and build their normative accounts on that basis. There is a pronounced tendency to conflate the desirable with the actual.

50 Macpherson, "Berlin's Division of Liberty," 103.

51 Macpherson, "Problems of a Non-Market Theory of Democracy," 74.

5. C.B. Macpherson, Democracy, and Democratic Theory 2

1 James D. Ingram, "What Is a 'Right to Have Rights'?," 401–16. A study that offers a comparable treatment of the politics of human rights is Carol C. Gould, *Globalizing Democracy and Human Rights* (Cambridge: Cambridge University Press, 2004). Gould explicitly identifies the work of Macpherson as an important influence on her own.

2 Ibid., 403.

3 Ibid., 406.

4 Ibid., 402.

5 Ibid., 410. Ingram also offers an insightful claim about Arendt's opposition to world government and defence of delimited territorial political units that would make possible the concrete practices of citizenship that would give substance to the right to have rights. In response to criticisms that this contradicts Arendt's disavowal of sovereignty because in the words of Seyla Benhabib it involves the claim that "exclusionary territorial control is an unchecked sovereign privilege which cannot be limited or trumped by other norms and institutions," Ingram argues, correctly I think, that "what Arendt objects to is not the *scope* of such a politics ('exclusionary territorial control') but its *mode* or *form* ('unchecked sovereign privilege'). Arendt does not oppose a national-statist paradigm to 'other norms and institutions' (a matter of scope), but to what she calls 'authentic politics' (a matter of mode)." Ibid., 409. I think one could offer a similar response to critics of Macpherson's supposed "statism," which I believe misses the meaning and significance of Macpherson's own version of a appropriate mode of politics, namely, his twin conceptions of liberty as counter-extractive and developmental.

6 Hannah Arendt, *The Origins of Totalitarianism* (New York: Harcourt Brace Jovanovich, 1973), 296; cited in Ingram, "What Is a 'Right to Have Rights'?," 410.

7 Ingram, "What Is a 'Right to Have Rights'?," 414.

8 Macpherson, "Human Rights as Property Rights," 84.

9 C.B. Macpherson, "Problems of Human Rights in the Late Twentieth Century," 32–3.

10 Ibid., 23.

11 Ibid., 22, 31.

12 It is worth recalling that capitalist (or indeed any) private property is inherently social. Not only does it require political enforcement but it is inherently relational. This is why critical analysts of property, including

Macpherson, believe it essential to move beyond the idea of property as "things" or property ownership as simply an individual status.

13 Macpherson, "Problems of Human Rights in the Late Twentieth Century," pp. 25–6

14 Ibid., 26–7.

15 Ibid., 29.

16 Compare C.B. Macpherson, "The Rise and Fall of Economic Justice," in Macpherson, *Rise and Fall of Economic Justice*, 1–20. With regard to the political and social implications of the commitment to policies of austerity, and in particular its impact on democracy, see Armin Schafer and Wolfgang Streeck, eds, *Politics in the Age of Austerity* (Cambridge: Polity, 2013). An outstanding exploration of the logic and history of austerity as a policy is Mark Blyth, *Austerity: The History of a Dangerous Idea* (Oxford: Oxford University Press, 2013).

17 Macpherson, "Problems of Human Rights in the Late Twentieth Century," 27. Compare C.B. Macpherson, "Liberalism as Trade-offs," in Macpherson, *Rise and Fall of Economic Justice*, 45.

18 Ibid., 33.

19 It is instructive in this respect that there is currently interest among some theorists supposedly committed to leftist and left-liberal conceptions of radical democracy in what is being called militant democracy. The idea behind militant, or "defensive democracy or fighting democracy," is that of a regime "willing to adopt pre-emptive, prima facie illiberal measures to prevent those aiming at subverting democracy with democratic means from destroying democracy." Jan-Werner Muller, "A 'Practical Dilemma Which Philosophy Alone Cannot Resolve'? Rethinking Militant Democracy: An Introduction," *Constellations* 19, no. 4 (December 2012): 538. This implies the sort of "trade-off" of rights for some other supposed value that concerned Macpherson. In the case of militant democracy, there seems to be some lack of clarity in two key respects. First of all, it is not clear exactly what (or whose) democracy is being subverted by what means. Second, those who would "subvert" democracy seem to be primarily populists, terrorists, and religious extremists. There appears to be here little interest in or exploration of whether the wealthy constitute a threat to democracy, although it is at least arguable that contemporary neoliberal capitalism has seriously subverted democratic values and practices, with massive numbers of citizens alienated from institutions they rightly believe have little to offer them.

Muller does note that it is necessary to "develop an account of how to recognize what might be legitimate targets for militant democracy and to distinguish these from cases where the instruments of militant democracy might be deployed to suppress party-political competition or even silence voters' legitimate concerns" (538). However, it is never really made clear how this would occur. That democracy, itself, might be a contested and contestable concept does not seem to register for this sort of thinking. From Macpherson's perspective, militant democracy would appear to have little place for either counter-extractive or developmental liberty.

20 Macpherson, "Liberalism as Trade-offs," 48, 50, 52.

21 Ibid., 51, 54.

22 Ibid., 52, 53.

23 Ibid., 53.

24 Macpherson, "Problems of Human Right in the Late Twentieth Century," 33.

25 It is Axel Honneth who, building upon his recognition-theoretic reworking of Hegel's *Philosophy of Right*, has made social freedom an essential element of justice and democracy. See his *Freedom's Right: The Social Foundations of Democratic Life*, trans. Joseph Ganahl (Cambridge: Polity, 2014).

26 It should be noted that Habermas has recently argued the need to move beyond the conventional conception of cosmopolitanism, which he views as rather loose, so long as it fails to adequately confront the question of how to advance the achievements of the constitutional state beyond the confines of the nation state. He relates this problem to a contradiction between the expansion of mechanisms for international cooperation, on the one hand, and the weakness, if not absence, of democratic legitimation, on the other. There is thus the need for movement toward transnational democratic institutions and practices. The key here is political solidarity, which, significantly, Habermas distinguishes from moral and legal duties and obligations, i.e., justice. (Equally significantly he suggests that in the past he had connected solidarity too closely to moral justice, thereby moralizing and de-politicizing it.) Obviously drawing upon his theory of communicative action, Habermas links solidarity to expectations of reciprocal conduct over time. So understood, solidarity involves the integrity of a shared form of life that includes individual well-being, i.e., a post-metaphysical *Sittlichkeit*. See Jürgen Habermas, "Plea for a Constitutionalization of International Law," *Philosophy and Social Criticism* 40, no. 1 (January 2014): 5–12. (Accompanying this piece are commentaries by David Rasmussen and Arne Johan Vetlesen.)

I cannot here pursue more fully Habermas's position and its implications. I believe, however, that it represents a response to the concerns laid out by James Ingram and has significant resonance with Macpherson's position, including his attempt to connect political theory with critical political economy.

27 Gould, *Globalizing Democracy and Human Rights,* 198, 197. Gould acknowledges an explicit debt to Macpherson's work, although she parts company with him somewhat on the question of how to conceptually articulate human capacities, and what she sees as his tendency to conflate human rights and democracy, a conflation that would strip the concept of human rights of its ability to serve as a critical standard for appraising democratic decisions (48). As should be evident from my own discussion, I would be inclined to take issue with Gould on this latter point in particular. I rather see Macpherson as having argued that democracy and human rights are mutually determining; this is different from conflation. In short they are best appreciated as elements of Macpherson's constellation of concepts. Nonetheless, the common ground they share is considerable. Gould bases her analysis on what she calls a social ontology. This is a "quasi-foundationalist although nonessentialistic approach to the grounding of rights, liberties, and entitlements" that "makes no appeal to a transempirical or transcendent moral reality but rather is based on what I believe to be experientially or phenomenologically well-evidenced features of the action and interaction of human beings. Moreover, this is a regional ontology, which does not make claims about the nature of being or reality as such but rather addresses itself to the domain of individuals in their social relations. Furthermore … every social and political theory has an ontological commitment of this sort, whether recognized or not" (32). Clearly this position is very close to Macpherson's. And both based their views substantially upon the ideas of Marx.

28 C.B. Macpherson, "The Prospects for Economic and Industrial Democracy," in Macpherson, *Rise and Fall of Economic Justice,* 35, 36, 43. In the context of the post-2008 global financial and accompanying economic crisis that has seen the interests of wage- and salary-earners suffer as governments have shored up financial institutions while cutting back on social spending, the question of the need and prospects for industrial democracy has once again arisen among progressive theorists. One model of industrial democracy that has received attention is the workers' self-directed enterprise (WSDE). "The idea is simple. Basic enterprise decisions are no longer to be monopolized by the major

shareholders and the boards of directors those shareholders select, the norm in capitalist corporations. Instead they are to be democratized. Workers are to become, collectively, their own board of directors in fully cooperative enterprises. As such, they would democratically decide what to produce, and how and where, and they would distribute the surpluses (or profits) generated in and by their enterprise." In this light, "WSDEs represent the goal of a transition beyond capitalism at the micro-level, inside the enterprises that produce the goods and services upon which modern civilization depends." Richard D. Wolff, *Capitalism Hits the Fan: The Global Economic Meltdown and What to Do About It* (Northampton, MA: Olive Branch, 2013), xviii, xix. As was the case with Macpherson, the assumption is that the incompetence of state-managed capitalism would potentially trigger a political response in the form of working-class political and social action. Obviously, the possibility for this to occur is a matter of speculation and judgment about the likelihood of fundamental changes in consciousness and behaviour, as indeed Macpherson had claimed.

While I cannot pursue this here, there are also in Macpherson's account of economic and industrial democracy elements of a broader, more comprehensive social theory. These relate to his Weber-like observations about the convergence he detected between capitalist and then-existing socialist societies on the commitment to unlimited economic growth. As we have seen, Macpherson saw this commitment as manifesting the powerful impact of capitalist market values. He never, of course, pursued this line of analysis to any significant degree. But subsequent developments in the socialist world would suggest that he might well have contributed to our appreciation of the momentous changes on the global scene after 1989.

29 Macpherson, "Do We Need a Theory of the State?" 61, 56, 72. An interesting feature of Macpherson's argument here, one no doubt dictated by the demands of the material he confronted, was the way he framed the argument as emerging from the relation between the descriptive and normative dimensions of political theory. One hallmark for him of the classical or grand tradition of the state was that it more or less self-consciously saw itself as laying out both in their necessary relation. This connection, he argued, was severed by twentieth-century empirical theorists and philosophical liberals such as Rawls and Nozick. (This was why, ironically, both groups did *not* require a theory of the state in the grand tradition: their position could not accommodate one. The best Rawls and Nozick in particular could achieve was a theory of distributive

justice.) The neo-Marxian theory, by contrast, was able and indeed needed to address both the descriptive and the normative together – it was in the tradition of the grand theory of the state.

In other words, this line of analysis in Macpherson suggested once again his version of the distinction between traditional and critical theory. I will return to this question in my discussion of Macpherson's contribution to methodology in the next chapter.

30 Ibid., 56.

31 C.B. Macpherson, "Pluralism, Individualism, and Participation," in Macpherson, *Rise and Fall of Economic Justice*, 92.

32 Ibid.

33 Ibid., 95.

34 Ibid., 98.

35 Ibid., 95, 99.

36 Ibid., 100.

37 Macpherson, *Life and Times of Liberal Democracy*, 6.

38 Ibid., 21.

39 Ibid., 43.

40 Ibid., 60.

41 Ibid., 48, 61. For a lucid and perceptive treatment of the contradictions in Mill's political theory, one demonstrating the impact of Macpherson's analysis, see Patricia Hughes, "The Reality versus the Ideal: J.S. Mill's Treatment of Women, Workers, and Private Property," *Canadian Journal of Political Science* 12, no. 3 (September 1979): 523–42. For critical appraisals of Hughes's position, see George Feaver, "Comment: Overcoming History? Ms Hughes's Treatment of Mr Mill," *Canadian Journal of Political Science* 12, no. 3 (September 1979), 543–54; and Barbara Cameron, "Mill's Treatment of Women, Workers, and Private Property," *Canadian Journal of Political Science* 13, no. 4 (December 1980): 775–83.

42 For contemporary examples of what might be called saving democracy from itself, in this instance with respect to the politics of the European Union, see Peter Mair, *Ruling the Void: The Hollowing of Western Democracy*, chap. 4. And sometimes the expression of fear of majority tyranny is anything but subtle. See Perry Anderson, "The Intransigent Right: Michael Oakeshott, Leo Strauss, Carl Schmitt, Friedrich von Hayek," in Anderson, *Spectrum: From Right to Left in the World of Ideas* (London: Verso, 2007), 3–28.

43 Macpherson, *Life and Times of Liberal Democracy*, 56.

44 For a comprehensive treatment of the role of culture and communications in facilitating this process, a key concern of the Frankfurt School, see "The

Cultural Apparatus of Monopoly Capital," special issue, *Monthly Review* 65, no. 3 (July/August 2013).

45 Macpherson, *Life and Times of Liberal Democracy*, 76. For an account of the "marketization of politics and the politicization of the private economy" that defined the development of liberal democracy and the rise of the welfare state in the twentieth century, especially in advanced capitalist societies, see Claus Offe, "Competitive Party Democracy and the Keynesian Welfare State," in Offe, *Contradictions of the Welfare State*, ed. John Keane (Cambridge, MA: MIT Press, 1984), 179–206.

46 Ibid.

47 These are the individuals Macpherson identified as the key contributors to the formulation of the equilibrium model. I would also add the scholars associated with the University of Michigan Survey Research Center, particularly Angus Campbell, Philip Converse, Warren Miller, and Donald Stokes, the authors of the influential *American Voter*, in many ways a comprehensive and definitive statement of the assumptions about voting behaviour that informed the equilibrium model.

Macpherson believed, correctly I think, that the empiricist bent of such studies masked fundamental theoretical and normative issues around democratic theory and practices that needed an airing. A powerful and I believe unfortunately under-appreciated exchange that raises many of the issues that Macpherson's critique of models of democracy sought to highlight was published in the *American Political Science Review* 68, no. 3 (September 1974): 1002–57. The exchange, which at times was extremely pointed, an indication of the stakes involved, was conducted by Walter Dean Burnham, Philip Converse, and Jerrod Rusk.

48 Macpherson, *Life and Times of Liberal Democracy*, 80, 79.

49 Ibid., 91–2.

50 Iris Marion Young, "Activist Challenges to Deliberative Democracy," *Political Theory* 29, no. 5 (October 2001): 670–90.

51 Ibid., 108–9.

52 Ibid., 112–13, 114.

53 Macpherson himself seemed at various points to acknowledge the unavoidability of parties under any conceivable circumstances. "It may be doubted whether any political structure is really non-party. Parties, at least of a tenuous sort, are apt to be formed in any body which needs continuous government and in which the government is formally chosen by the governed." Macpherson, *Democracy in Alberta*, 238.

54 Macpherson, *Life and Times of Liberal Democracy*, 114.

55 Ibid., 115.

56 Ibid., 97.

57 Ibid., 95.

58 Ibid., 99. As Peter Lindsay has insightfully argued, this did not make Macpherson a "communitarian," for whom a concrete living community trumped the abstract individual. While Macpherson shared the communitarian critique of the "unencumbered self," like Marx he provided an account of the social relations that gave rise to this picture of the individual, a picture that was simultaneously true and false. The relations were those of a possessive market society. See Peter Lindsay, "The 'Disembodied Self' in Political Theory: The Communitarians, Macpherson and Marx," *Philosophy and Social Criticism* 28, no. 2 (March 2002): 191–211.

59 Macpherson, *Life and Times of Liberal Democracy*, 115.

60 Seyla Benhabib, "Book Review: *Habermas: An Intellectual Biography* by Matthew G. Specter," *Constellations* 18, no. 4 (December 2011): 592. An excellent overview of the various dimensions of Benhabib's position is her collection *Dignity in Adversity: Human Rights in Troubled Times* (Cambridge: Polity, 2011).

61 See, for example, Joseph Heath, "Ideology, Irrationality, and Collective Self-defeating Behavior," *Constellations* 7, no. 3 (September 2000): 363–71; and James Johnson and Jack Knight, *The Priority of Democracy: The Political Consequences of Pragmatism* (Princeton: Princeton University Press, 2011). I am grateful to Brian Caterino for drawing this work to my attention.

62 In response to Matthew Specter's claim that Habermas's "universal pragmatics" culminates in a theory of justice as fairness in communication, Benhabib argues that "this conflates the norms of a just social order that would *result* from practical discourses with the normative *preconditions* of a discourse situation, which indeed, must themselves be governed by some lifeworld understanding of fairness in the distribution of speech-acts, chances for questioning the agenda of discourses and the rules governing them, etc." I do not see how the proposed separation can be sustained. To be sure, Benhabib does go on to write that some theorists "describe this structure of practical discourses as a vicious circle … I see this as an expression of the inevitable hermeneutic circle of practical reason, and … I distinguish norms that inform discourses from norms of social justice that *recursively* are agreed upon in practical discourses." Benhabib, "Book Review," 591; italics in original. I certainly agree that there is an essential and unavoidable hermeneutic dimension to the generation and articulation of norms. However, as Habermas argued in his debate with Hans-Georg Gadamer,

the conditions of hermeneutic understanding are not fixed but are historically variable and are shaped by changing constellations of power and power relations. Especially in the current era, one could plausibly argue that capitalism disproportionally "conditions" the normative preconditions of discourses; perhaps it could be called the "meta-hermeneutic" of the hermeneutic circle of practical reason.

63 Maria Paula Saffon and Nadia Urbinati, "Procedural Democracy, the Bulwark of Equal Liberty," *Political Theory* 41, no. 3 (June 2013): 441–2, 450, 455. Urbinati further develops the arguments of this paper in *Democracy Disfigured. Opinion, Truth, and the People* (Cambridge, MA: Harvard University Press, 2014). This book came to my attention too late to consider here, but it undoubtedly represents the most complete statement of her position.

64 Ibid., 442, 461, 460.

65 Ibid., 461.

66 Ibid., 444. This said, as I noted earlier, Urbinati would not identify with critical theory, which, given her perspective, would likely strike her as "metaphysical" and so in effect a form of epistemic democracy, to which she and Saffon indeed link the deliberative democracy they associate with Habermas. For that matter, they also take John Rawls to task for slighting group bargaining in the political arena as inadequately narrow for a democracy, because it supposedly enshrines a limited or group-interest standpoint in the minds of citizens, instead of a more expansive concern for the common good (443).

67 Ibid., 462. For a somewhat different, yet related, take on the question of the suppression of conflict and its baleful effects on democracy, see John P. McCormick, *Machiavellian Democracy* (Cambridge: Cambridge University Press, 2011). McCormick criticizes certain currents in contemporary republican political theory with their emphasis on the necessity for normative standards that would supposedly render democratic systems more just. This analysis shares common ground with that of Saffon and Urbinati and their critique of epistemic democratic thinking. However, unlike them, McCormick argues that, for democracy to be truly effective, there is the need for class-specific institutions beyond conventional representative bodies. These are required to ensure greater popular engagement in the political process than is possible under elite-dominated legislatures elected by a universal suffrage that abstracts from real social relations. This is the lesson McCormick draws from his close and detailed reading of Machiavelli's work.

68 Ibid., 450.

69 Ibid., 456.
70 Ibid., 458.
71 Ibid., 463.
72 I want to thank Brian Caterino for identifying and raising this point with me.
73 In fact while Saffon and Urbinati view populism in its various forms as a (dangerous) species of democracy, their treatment of specific populist views and leaders actually calls to mind Horkheimer's historical account of bourgeois mass social movements in "Egoism and Freedom Movements." In other words, whatever their intentions. their analysis suggests the contradictions of liberalism rather than the evils of "totalitarian" democracy.
74 Saffon and Urbinati, "Procedural Democracy, the Bulwark of Equal Liberty," 456.
75 Losurdo, *Liberalism: A Counter-History.* For a brilliant account of slavery in the late eighteenth and early nineteenth centuries – an age of liberalism, revolution, and globalizing capitalism – see Greg Grandin, *The Empire of Necessity: Slavery, Freedom, and Deception in the New World* (New York: Metropolitan Books, 2014).
76 For a suggestive analysis along these lines, see Claus Offe, "Participatory Inequality in the Austerity State: A Supply-Side Approach," in Schafer and Streeck, *Politics in the Age of Austerity*, 196–218.

6. Political Theory, Social Science, and Social Critique

1 As a contemporary example of the historically specific and changing content of concepts nonetheless recognizable across different historical settings, Axel Honneth notes that, although "the concept of the 'group' is highly plastic and applicable to very different social phenomena, each historical epoch picks out, from this variety of appearances, individual and especially striking features in order to construct its own image of what constitutes a group. These constructions reflect the fears and hopes, concerns and expectations that motivate individuals, through contemporary experiences of coming together, to form relatively stable and continuous associations. Even a cursory glance at the turbulent history of the twentieth century reveals the diversity of the associations linked, under the pressure of certain quickly generalized experiences, to the emergence and dissemination of social groups." Axel Honneth, "The I in We: Recognition as a Driving Force of Group Formation," in Honneth, *The I in We*, 201.

2 Macpherson, *Democracy in Alberta*, 250.
3 Macpherson, "Rise and Fall of Economic Justice," 20.
4 Compare George Packer, *The Unwinding: An Inner History of the New America* (New York: Farrar, Straus and Giroux, 2013). What is being "unwound" – "the coil that held Americans together in its secure and sometimes stifling grip" – could plausibly be summarized as the idea and reality of economic justice (3).
5 Ian Angus, "On Macpherson's Developmental Liberalism," *Canadian Journal of Political Science* 15, no. 1 (March 1982): 145–50.
6 Ibid., 148–9, 150.
7 See, for example, C.B. Macpherson, "On the Study of Politics in Canada," in *Essays in Political Economy in Honour of E.J. Urwick*, ed. H.A. Innis, 147–65 (Toronto: University of Toronto Press, 1938); Macpherson, "The Position of Political Science," *Culture* 3 (1942): 452–9; Macpherson, *Report for the International Political Science Association, June 1951*; Macpherson, "The Social Sciences," in *The Culture of Contemporary Canada*, ed. Julian Park, 181–221 (Ithaca, NY: Cornell University Press, 1957); and Macpherson, "After Strange Gods: Canadian Political Science 1973," in *Perspectives on the Social Sciences in Canada*, ed. T.N. Guinsburg and G.L. Reuber, 52–76 (Toronto: University of Toronto Press, 1974). I discuss the last essay in greater detail below.
8 C.B. Macpherson, "Market Concepts in Political Theory," in Macpherson, *Democratic Theory: Essays in Retrieval*, 186.
9 Ibid., 187.
10 Ibid., 192.
11 Ibid., 185.
12 Ibid., 192, 194.
13 Ibid., 194.
14 John Nichols and Robert W. McChesney, *Dollarocracy: How the Money and Media Election Complex Is Destroying America* (New York: Nation Books, 2013).
15 Ibid., 189.
16 Ibid., 188.
17 See note 7, above.
18 Macpherson, "After Strange Gods," 63.
19 Ibid., 63, 71.
20 Ibid., 71.
21 Macpherson himself had painstakingly documented the emergence and central place of the indigenous tradition of political economy in Canada in a generally overlooked essay from the 1950s. See "The Social Sciences,"

esp. 198–208. His own *Democracy in Alberta* of course represented one attempt to keep this tradition alive. Indeed, in an endnote to "After Strange Gods," he wryly noted that, "in the opinion of some critics at the time," he "overdid it" (75).

22 Macpherson, "After Strange Gods," 68, 70.

23 Peter B. Evans, Dietrich Rueschemeyer, and Theda Skocpol, eds, *Bringing the State Back In* (Cambridge: Cambridge University Press, 1985). For a more explicitly Marxist perspective on the need to bring the state back in, see Stanley Aronowitz and Peter Bratsis, eds, *Paradigm Lost: State Theory Reconsidered* (Minneapolis: University of Minnesota Press, 2002).

24 A key development in this respect was the publication of Leo Panitch, ed., *The Canadian State: Political Economy and Political Power* (Toronto: University of Toronto Press, 1977); and the journal it inspired, *Studies in Political Economy*, which first appeared in 1979. The dates here were no coincidence: they reflected what Macpherson had seen at the time as the emergence of new possibilities for both intellectual/cultural and social change.

25 This I think is evident in the tendency among free market defenders to blame the financial crisis of 2008 and subsequent economic decline on "excessive" government intervention – even though state policies of financial deregulation facilitated and legitimized the reckless speculative behaviour at the heart of the crisis.

26 Macpherson, "Social Sciences," 181.

27 Raymond A. Morrow, with David D. Brown, *Critical Theory and Methodology* (Thousand Oaks, CA: Sage Publications, 1994), 24.

28 The following discussion draws upon two unpublished papers of mine: "Macpherson, Habermas and the Demands of Democratic Theory" (the published article of the same title, co-authored with Brian Caterino, was a revised version of this paper); and "Towards a Critical Theory of Democracy." Both papers were presented at annual meetings of the Atlantic Provinces Political Science Association in 2004 and 2007, respectively.

29 I am grateful to Brian Caterino for helping me clarify both these assumptions and the arguments that follow.

30 In light of the Marxian roots of the Frankfurt School, this perspective illuminates the question of praxis, or the unity of revolutionary theory and practice, and its basis in proletarian class consciousness. The failure of revolutionary consciousness to emerge during social and economic crisis, where from the vantage point of traditional Marxism it ought to

have done so, provided a key motive for the work of the first generation of critical theorists. An important element of the critique of traditional Marxism – and one carried forward under changing historical conditions and theoretical commitments by the Frankfurt School throughout its history – has been the tendency of the traditional account to view such class consciousness as a material fact grounded in the dynamics of capitalist production. The inherent positivism of this view, which overlooked or failed to recognize the importance of and possibilities for, as well as constraints on, the self-reflexive activity of the workers (and hence failed adequately to take into account the participants' perspective) has long been a target of critical theory down to the current era; indeed this critique is central to the very lifeblood of the theory itself.

31 On this issue, see, e.g., Morrow with Brown, *Critical Theory and Methodology*; and Yvonne Sherratt, *Continental Philosophy of Social Science: Hermeneutics, Genealogy, and Critical Theory from Greece to the Twenty-First Century* (Cambridge: Cambridge University Press, 2006).

32 Jürgen Habermas, *Truth and Justification*, ed., trans. Barbara Fultner (Cambridge, MA: MIT Press, 2003).

33 Kenneth Baynes, "Freedom and Recognition in Hegel and Habermas," *Philosophy and Social Criticism* 28, no. 1 (January 2002): 1–17. See, e.g., Frederick Neuhouser, *Foundations of Hegel's Social Theory: Actualizing Freedom* (Cambridge, MA: Harvard University Press, 2000); Axel Honneth, *Suffering from Indeterminacy: An Attempt at a Reactualization of Hegel's Philosophy of Right* (Amsterdam: Van Gorcum, 2000); and Honneth, *The Pathologies of Individual Freedom: Hegel's Social Theory*, trans. Ladislaus Loos (Princeton: Princeton University Press, 2010).

34 See, for example, Claude Lefort, *Complications: Communism and the Dilemmas of Democracy*, trans, intro. Julian Bourg (New York: Columbia University Press, 2007); and Pierre Rosanvallon, *Democracy Past and Future*, ed. Samuel Moyn (New York: Columbia University Press, 2006).

35 Minogue, "Humanist Democracy," 378, 393, 394.

36 Ibid., 380–1.

37 Ibid., 393, 394.

38 Ibid., 394.

39 Macpherson, "Humanist Democracy," 429.

40 Ibid., 426.

41 Ibid., 428.

42 Minogue, "Humanist Democracy," 392.

43 Macpherson, "Humanist Democracy," 428.

44 Ibid., 429.

45 Ibid., 430.

46 Ibid.

47 Kontos, *Powers, Possessions and Freedom.*

48 Max Horkheimer, "Two Aspects of Materialism," in Horkheimer, *Dawn and Decline: Notes 1926–1931 & 1950–1969*, trans. Michael Shaw, with an afterword by Eike Gebhardt (New York: Seabury, 1978), 139.

Index

www.ingramcontent.com/pod-product-compliance
Lightning Source LLC
LaVergne TN
LVHW090147080826
844660LV00013B/706/J

* 9 7 8 1 4 4 2 6 3 0 5 9 8 *